THE PARK

OSCAR ZARATE

THE PARK

SELF MADE HERO

First published 2013
by SelfMadeHero
5 Upper Wimpole Street
London W1G 6BP
www.selfmadehero.com

© 2013 Oscar Zarate

Written and Illustrated by: Oscar Zarate
Cover Design by: Oscar Zarate & Txabi Jones
Textual Consultant: Richard Appignanesi

Editorial & Production Manager: Lizzie Kaye
Sales & Marketing Manager: Sam Humphrey
Publishing Director: Emma Hayley
With thanks to: Nick de Somogyi and Jane Laporte

A CIP record for this book is available from the British Library

ISBN: 978-1-906838-47-8

10 9 8 7 6 5 4 3 2 1

Printed and bound in China

FOR AVA

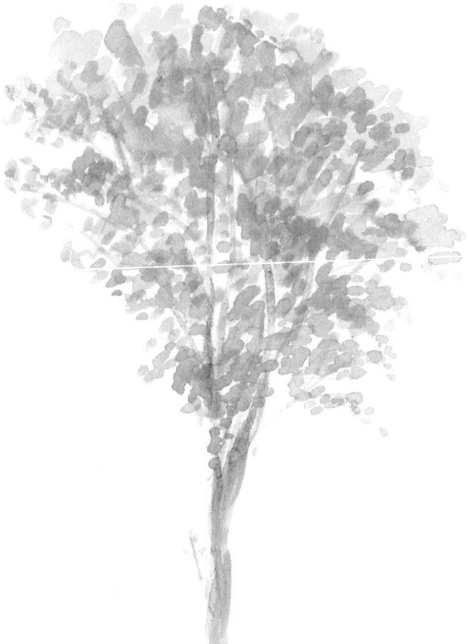

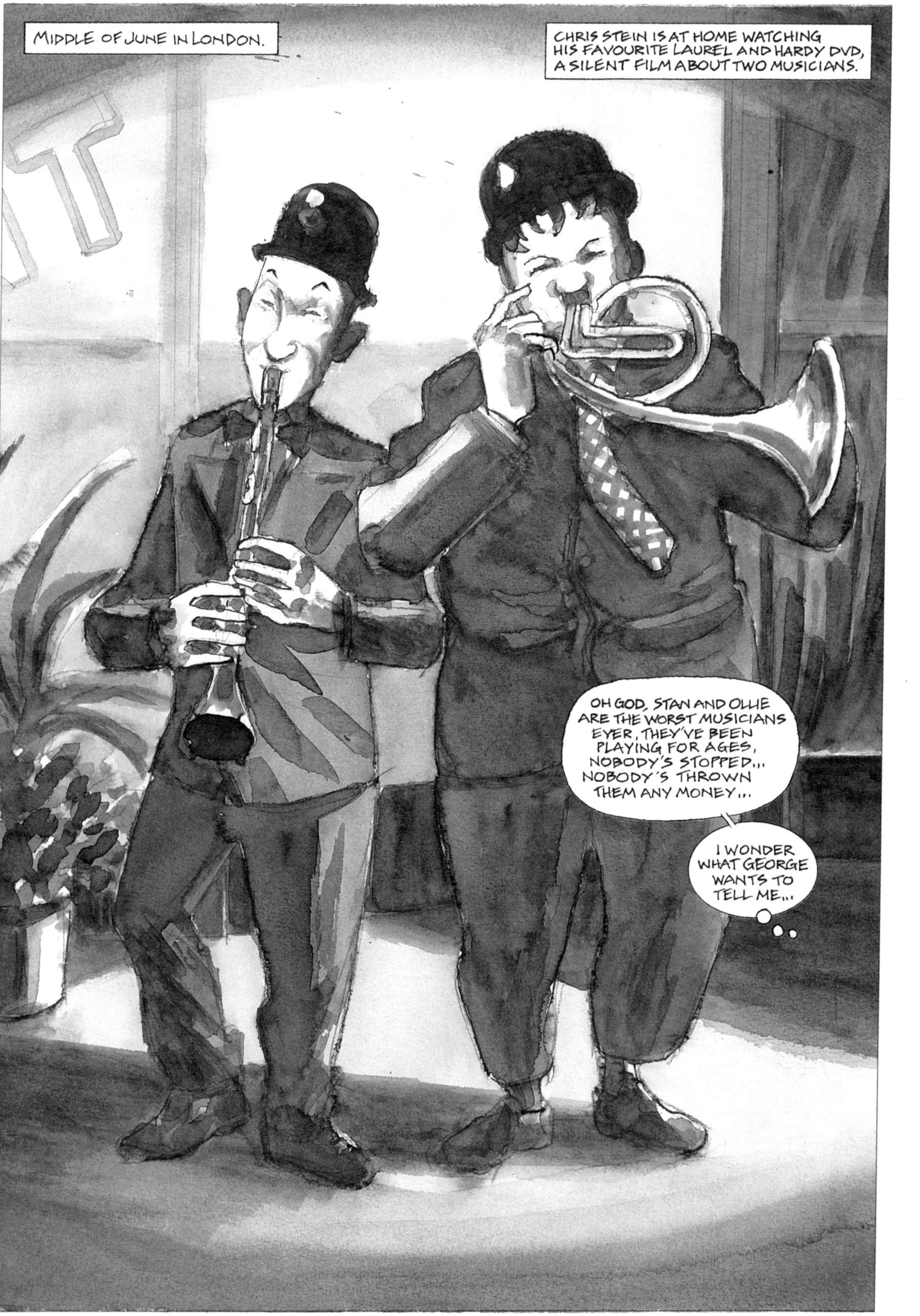
MIDDLE OF JUNE IN LONDON.
CHRIS STEIN IS AT HOME WATCHING HIS FAVOURITE LAUREL AND HARDY DVD, A SILENT FILM ABOUT TWO MUSICIANS.
OH GOD, STAN AND OLLIE ARE THE WORST MUSICIANS EVER, THEY'VE BEEN PLAYING FOR AGES, NOBODY'S STOPPED... NOBODY'S THROWN THEM ANY MONEY...
I WONDER WHAT GEORGE WANTS TO TELL ME...

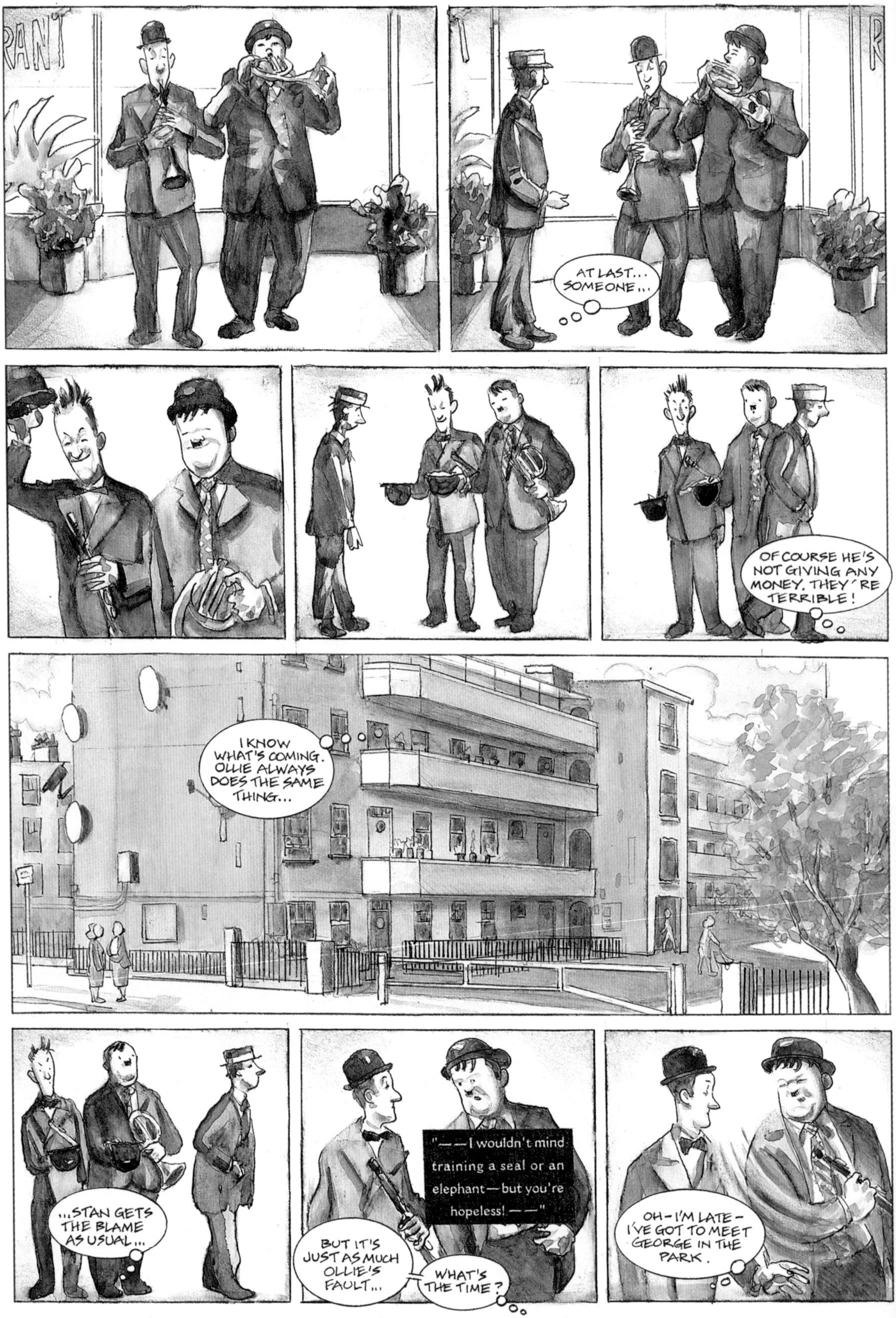
AT LAST... SOMEONE...
OF COURSE HE'S NOT GIVING ANY MONEY. THEY'RE TERRIBLE!
I KNOW WHAT'S COMING. OLLIE ALWAYS DOES THE SAME THING...
...STAN GETS THE BLAME AS USUAL...
"— —I wouldn't mind training a seal or an elephant—but you're hopeless! — —"
BUT IT'S JUST AS MUCH OLLIE'S FAULT...
WHAT'S THE TIME?
OH-I'M LATE-I'VE GOT TO MEET GEORGE IN THE PARK.

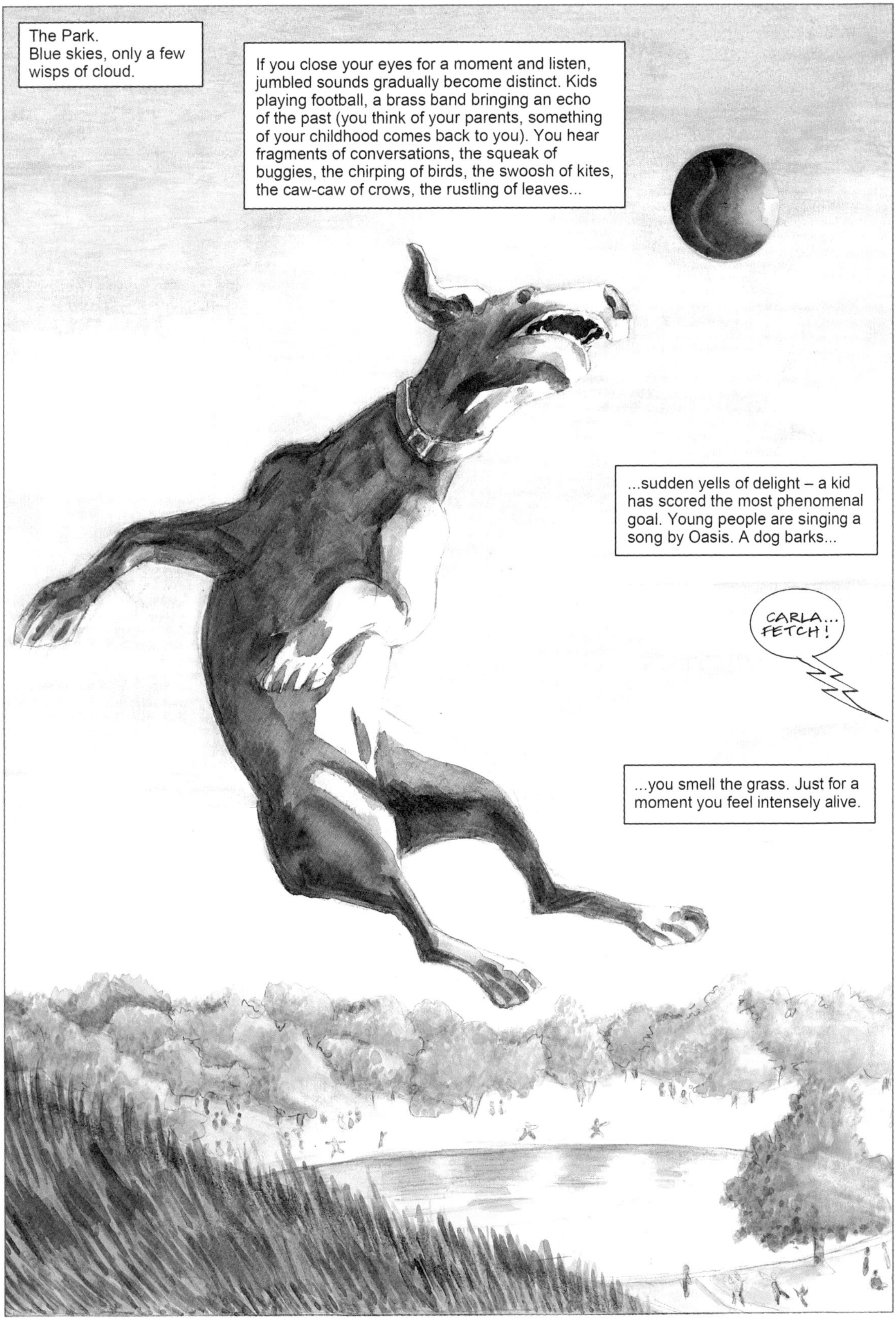

The Park.
Blue skies, only a few wisps of cloud.
If you close your eyes for a moment and listen, jumbled sounds gradually become distinct. Kids playing football, a brass band bringing an echo of the past (you think of your parents, something of your childhood comes back to you). You hear fragments of conversations, the squeak of buggies, the chirping of birds, the swoosh of kites, the caw-caw of crows, the rustling of leaves...
...sudden yells of delight – a kid has scored the most phenomenal goal. Young people are singing a song by Oasis. A dog barks...
CARLA... FETCH!
...you smell the grass. Just for a moment you feel intensely alive.

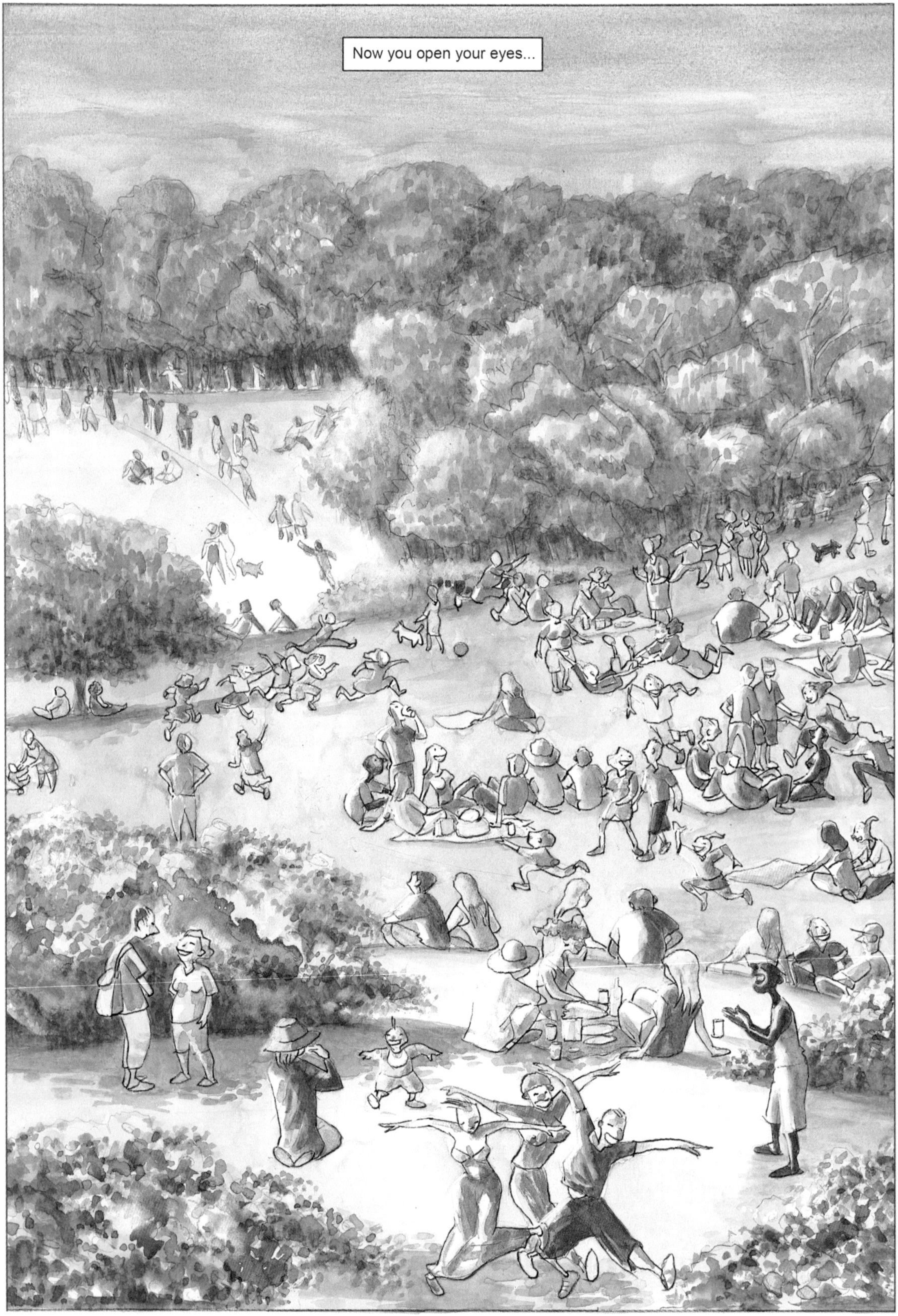
Now you open your eyes...

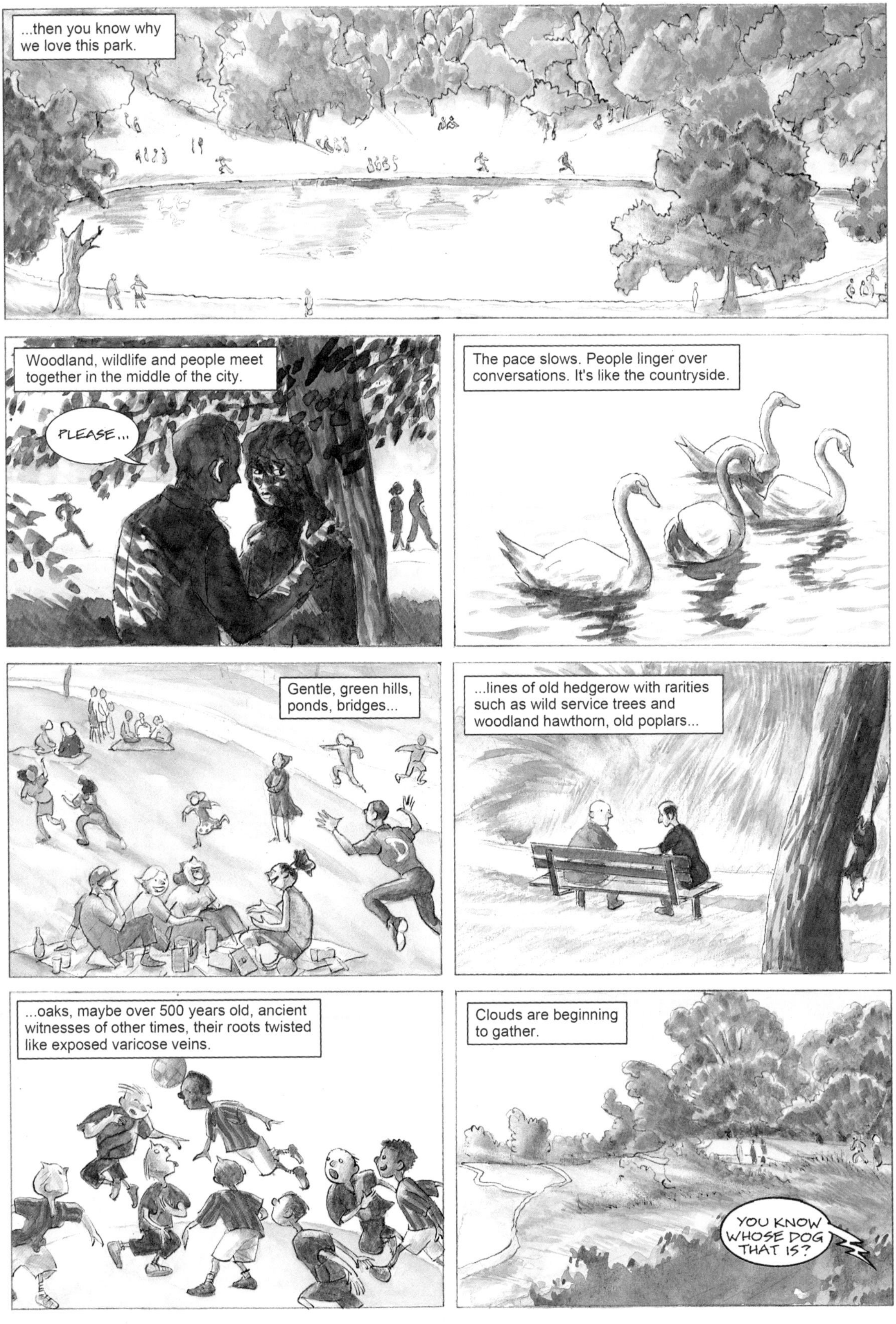
...then you know why we love this park.
Woodland, wildlife and people meet together in the middle of the city.
PLEASE...
The pace slows. People linger over conversations. It's like the countryside.
Gentle, green hills, ponds, bridges...
...lines of old hedgerow with rarities such as wild service trees and woodland hawthorn, old poplars...
...oaks, maybe over 500 years old, ancient witnesses of other times, their roots twisted like exposed varicose veins.
Clouds are beginning to gather.
YOU KNOW WHOSE DOG THAT IS?

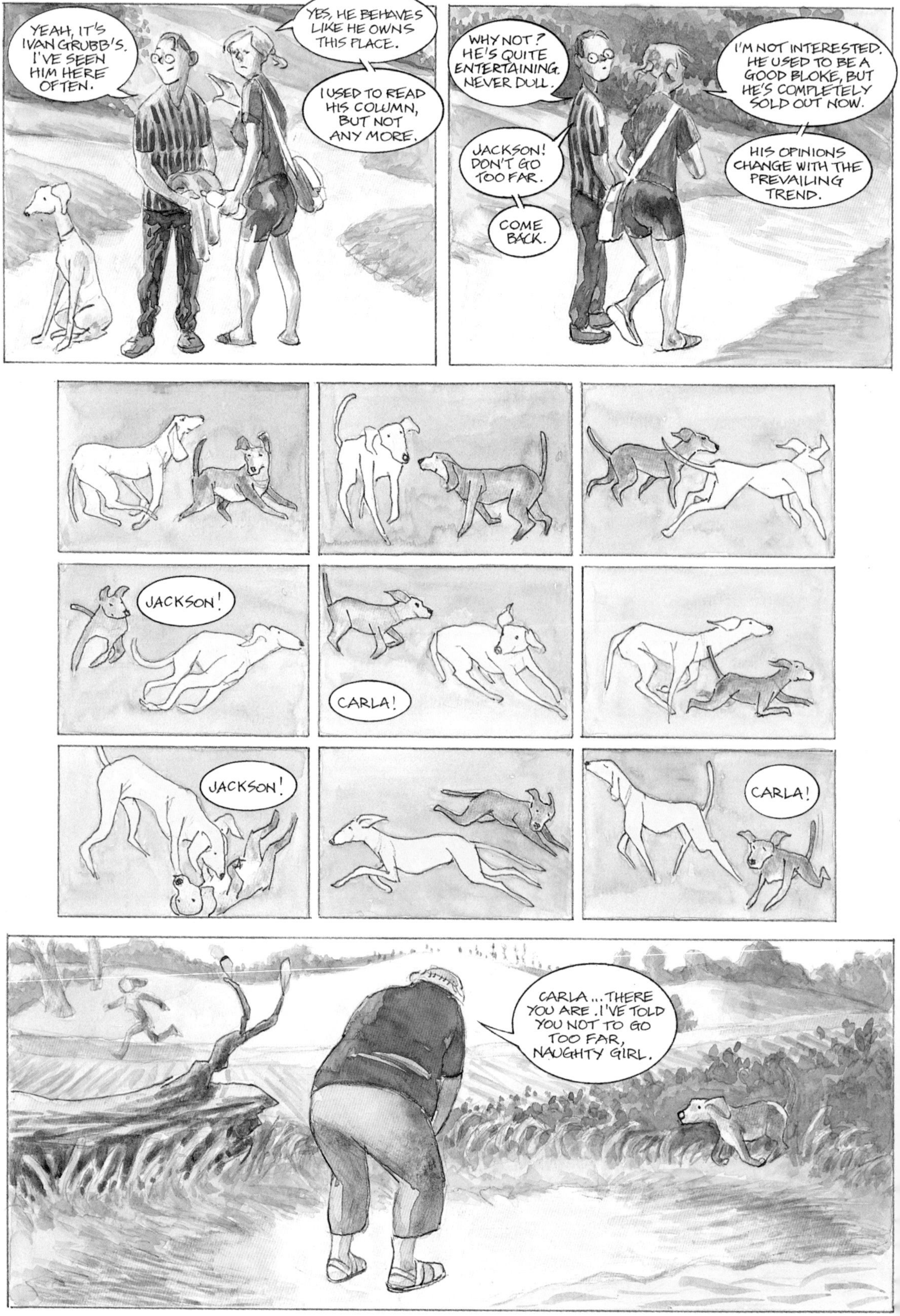
YEAH, IT'S IVAN GRUBB'S. I'VE SEEN HIM HERE OFTEN.
YES, HE BEHAVES LIKE HE OWNS THIS PLACE.
I USED TO READ HIS COLUMN, BUT NOT ANY MORE.
WHY NOT? HE'S QUITE ENTERTAINING. NEVER DULL.
I'M NOT INTERESTED. HE USED TO BE A GOOD BLOKE, BUT HE'S COMPLETELY SOLD OUT NOW.
HIS OPINIONS CHANGE WITH THE PREVAILING TREND.
JACKSON! DON'T GO TOO FAR.
COME BACK.
JACKSON!
CARLA!
JACKSON!
CARLA!
CARLA... THERE YOU ARE. I'VE TOLD YOU NOT TO GO TOO FAR, NAUGHTY GIRL.

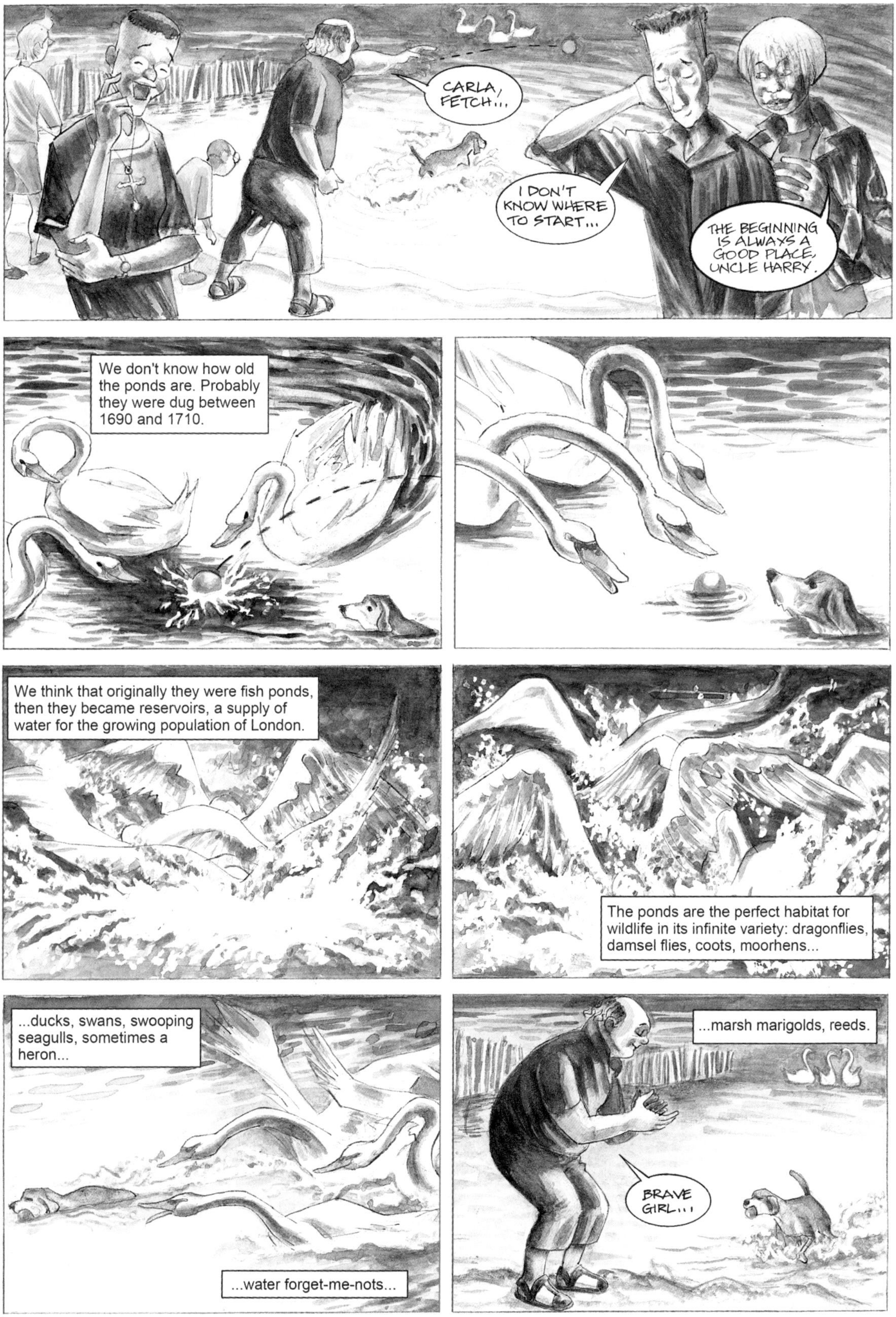
CARLA, FETCH...
I DON'T KNOW WHERE TO START...
THE BEGINNING IS ALWAYS A GOOD PLACE, UNCLE HARRY.
We don't know how old the ponds are. Probably they were dug between 1690 and 1710.
We think that originally they were fish ponds, then they became reservoirs, a supply of water for the growing population of London.
The ponds are the perfect habitat for wildlife in its infinite variety: dragonflies, damsel flies, coots, moorhens...
...ducks, swans, swooping seagulls, sometimes a heron...
...water forget-me-nots...
...marsh marigolds, reeds.
BRAVE GIRL...

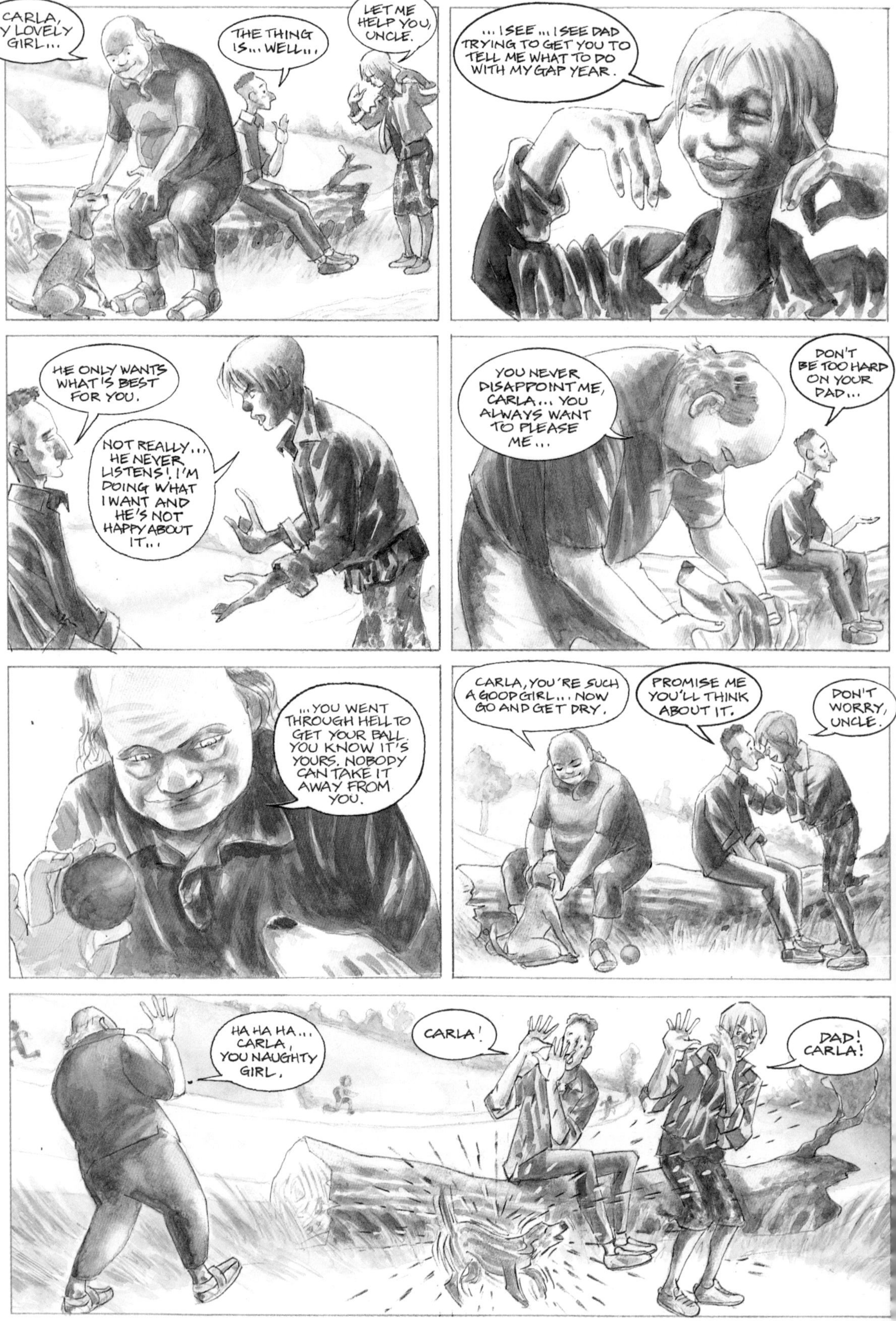
CARLA, MY LOVELY GIRL...
THE THING IS... WELL...
LET ME HELP YOU, UNCLE.
...I SEE... I SEE DAD TRYING TO GET YOU TO TELL ME WHAT TO DO WITH MY GAP YEAR.
HE ONLY WANTS WHAT'S BEST FOR YOU.
NOT REALLY... HE NEVER LISTENS! I'M DOING WHAT I WANT AND HE'S NOT HAPPY ABOUT IT...
YOU NEVER DISAPPOINT ME, CARLA... YOU ALWAYS WANT TO PLEASE ME...
DON'T BE TOO HARD ON YOUR DAD...
...YOU WENT THROUGH HELL TO GET YOUR BALL. YOU KNOW IT'S YOURS. NOBODY CAN TAKE IT AWAY FROM YOU.
CARLA, YOU'RE SUCH A GOOD GIRL... NOW GO AND GET DRY.
PROMISE ME YOU'LL THINK ABOUT IT.
DON'T WORRY, UNCLE.
HA HA HA... CARLA, YOU NAUGHTY GIRL.
CARLA!
DAD! CARLA!

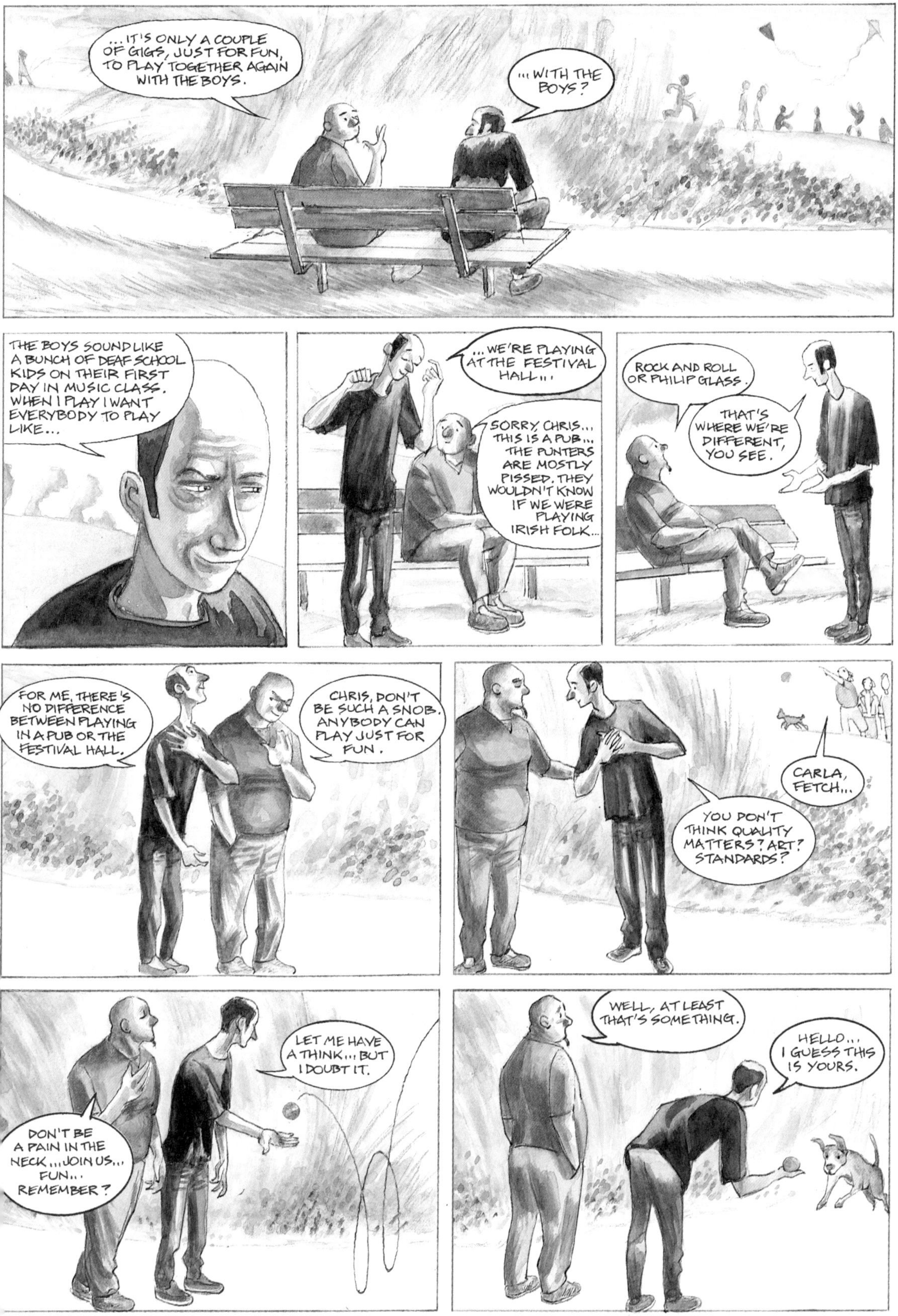
...IT'S ONLY A COUPLE OF GIGS, JUST FOR FUN, TO PLAY TOGETHER AGAIN WITH THE BOYS.
...WITH THE BOYS?
THE BOYS SOUND LIKE A BUNCH OF DEAF SCHOOL KIDS ON THEIR FIRST DAY IN MUSIC CLASS. WHEN I PLAY I WANT EVERYBODY TO PLAY LIKE...
...WE'RE PLAYING AT THE FESTIVAL HALL...
SORRY, CHRIS... THIS IS A PUB... THE PUNTERS ARE MOSTLY PISSED. THEY WOULDN'T KNOW IF WE WERE PLAYING IRISH FOLK...
ROCK AND ROLL OR PHILIP GLASS.
THAT'S WHERE WE'RE DIFFERENT, YOU SEE.
FOR ME, THERE'S NO DIFFERENCE BETWEEN PLAYING IN A PUB OR THE FESTIVAL HALL.
CHRIS, DON'T BE SUCH A SNOB. ANYBODY CAN PLAY JUST FOR FUN.
CARLA, FETCH...
YOU DON'T THINK QUALITY MATTERS? ART? STANDARDS?
LET ME HAVE A THINK... BUT I DOUBT IT.
DON'T BE A PAIN IN THE NECK... JOIN US... FUN... REMEMBER?
WELL, AT LEAST THAT'S SOMETHING.
HELLO... I GUESS THIS IS YOURS.

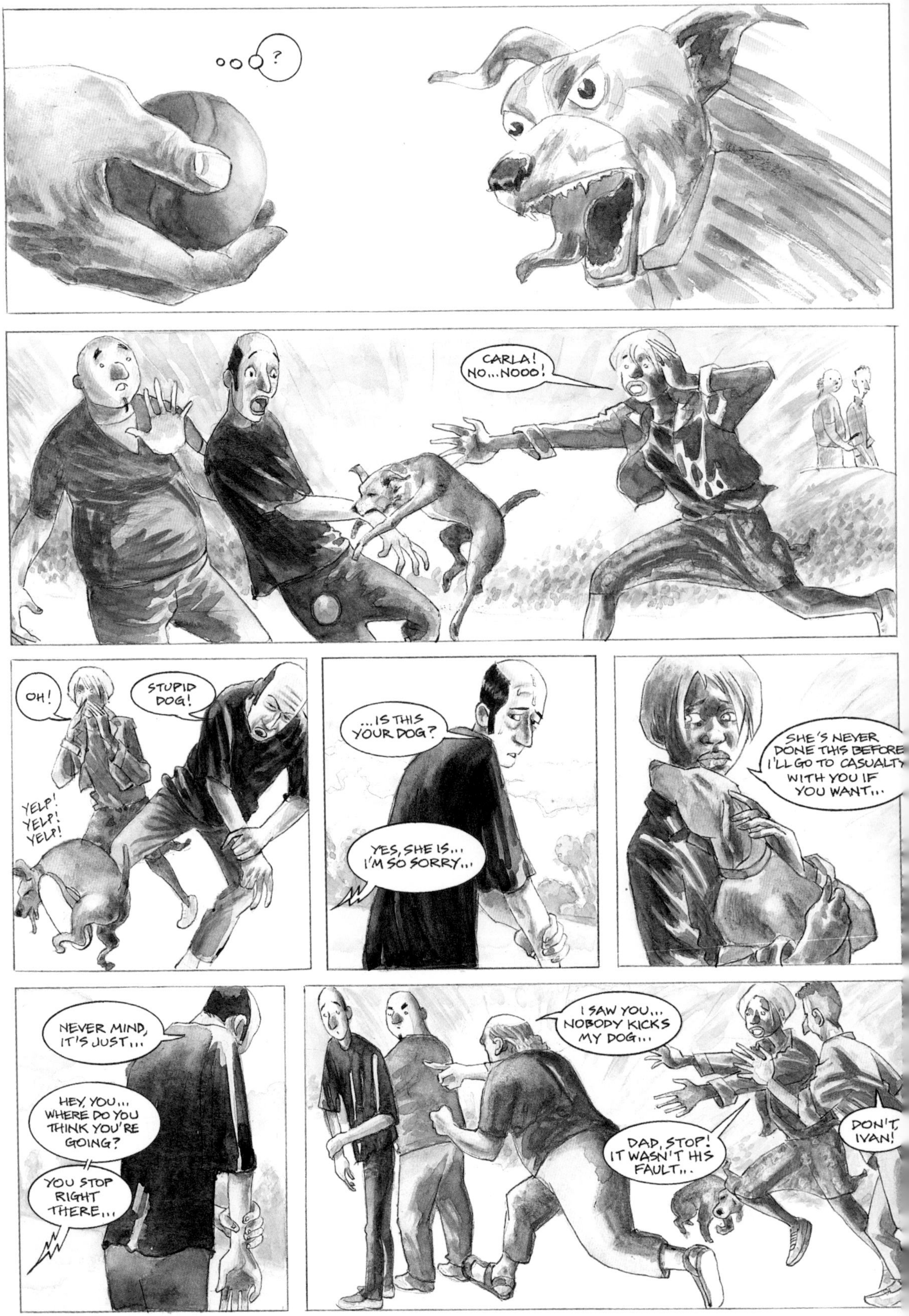
?
CARLA! NO...NOOO!
OH!
STUPID DOG!
YELP! YELP! YELP!
...IS THIS YOUR DOG?
YES, SHE IS... I'M SO SORRY...
SHE'S NEVER DONE THIS BEFORE I'LL GO TO CASUALTY WITH YOU IF YOU WANT...
NEVER MIND, IT'S JUST...
HEY, YOU... WHERE DO YOU THINK YOU'RE GOING?
YOU STOP RIGHT THERE...
I SAW YOU... NOBODY KICKS MY DOG...
DAD, STOP! IT WASN'T HIS FAULT...
DON'T, IVAN!

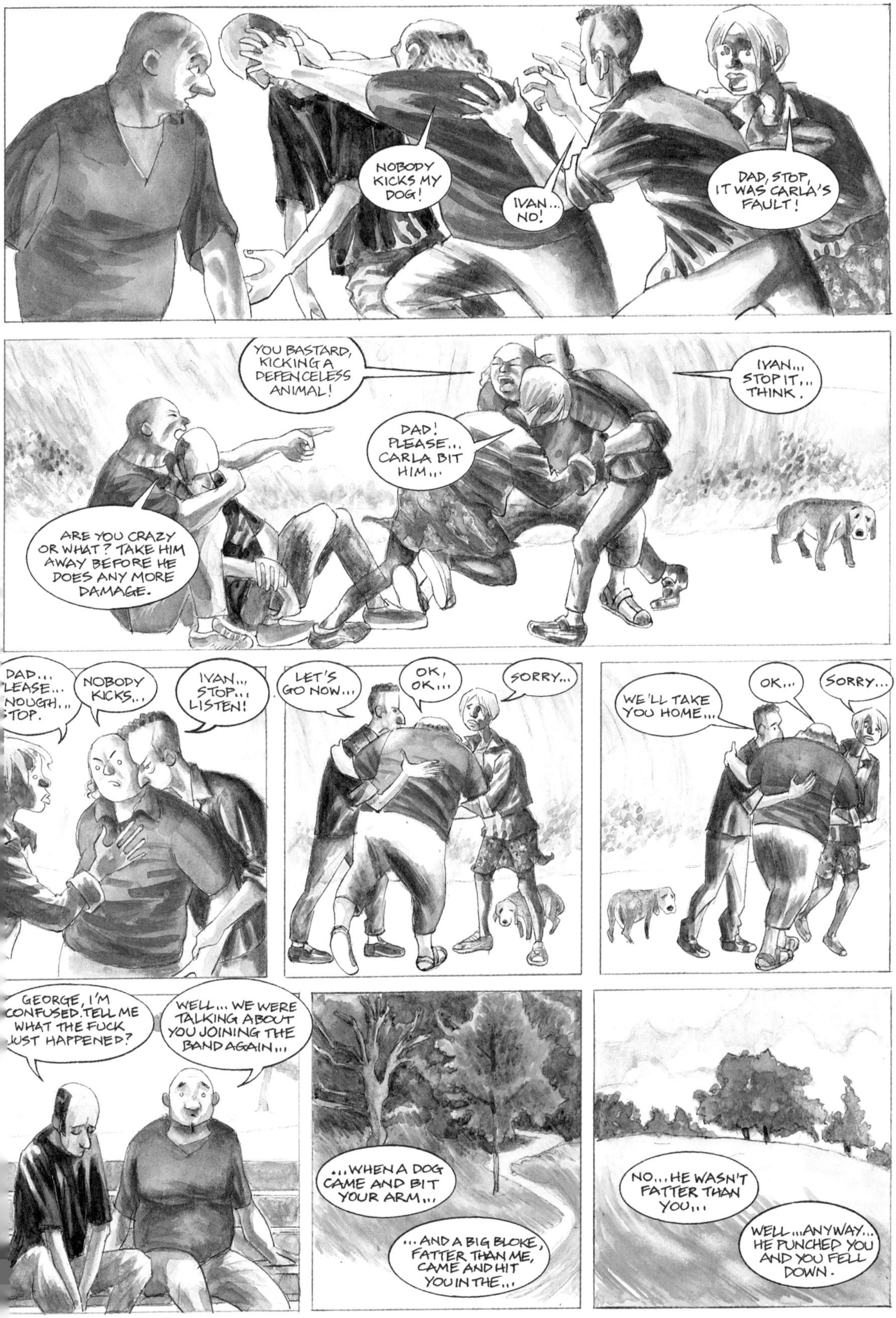
NOBODY KICKS MY DOG!
IVAN... NO!
DAD, STOP, IT WAS CARLA'S FAULT!
YOU BASTARD, KICKING A DEFENCELESS ANIMAL!
IVAN... STOP IT... THINK.
DAD! PLEASE... CARLA BIT HIM...
ARE YOU CRAZY OR WHAT? TAKE HIM AWAY BEFORE HE DOES ANY MORE DAMAGE.
DAD... PLEASE... ENOUGH... STOP.
NOBODY KICKS...
IVAN... STOP... LISTEN!
LET'S GO NOW...
OK, OK...
SORRY...
WE'LL TAKE YOU HOME...
OK...
SORRY...
GEORGE, I'M CONFUSED. TELL ME WHAT THE FUCK JUST HAPPENED?
WELL... WE WERE TALKING ABOUT YOU JOINING THE BAND AGAIN...
...WHEN A DOG CAME AND BIT YOUR ARM...
...AND A BIG BLOKE, FATTER THAN ME, CAME AND HIT YOU IN THE...
NO... HE WASN'T FATTER THAN YOU...
WELL... ANYWAY... HE PUNCHED YOU AND YOU FELL DOWN.

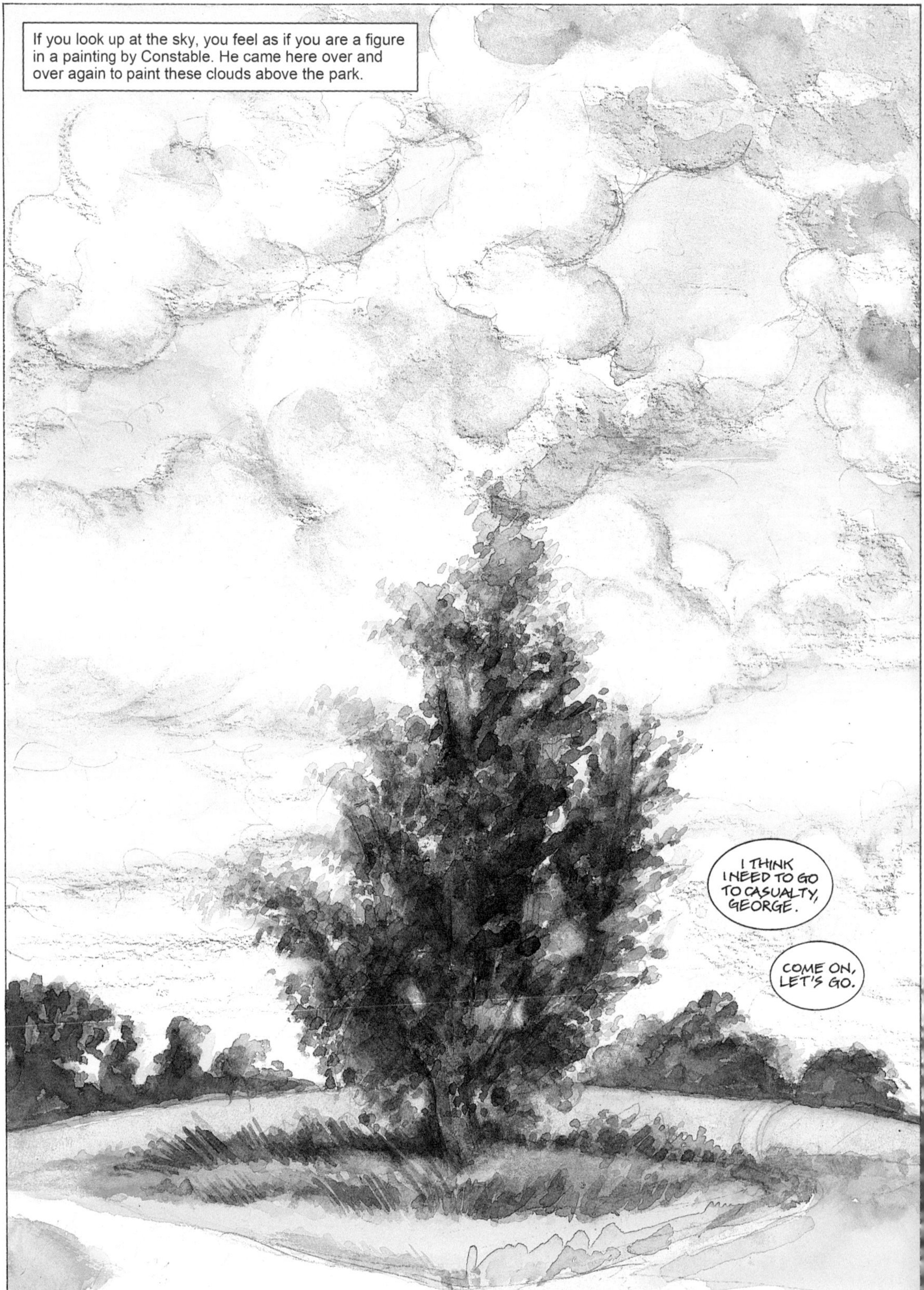
If you look up at the sky, you feel as if you are a figure in a painting by Constable. He came here over and over again to paint these clouds above the park.
I THINK I NEED TO GO TO CASUALTY, GEORGE.
COME ON, LET'S GO.

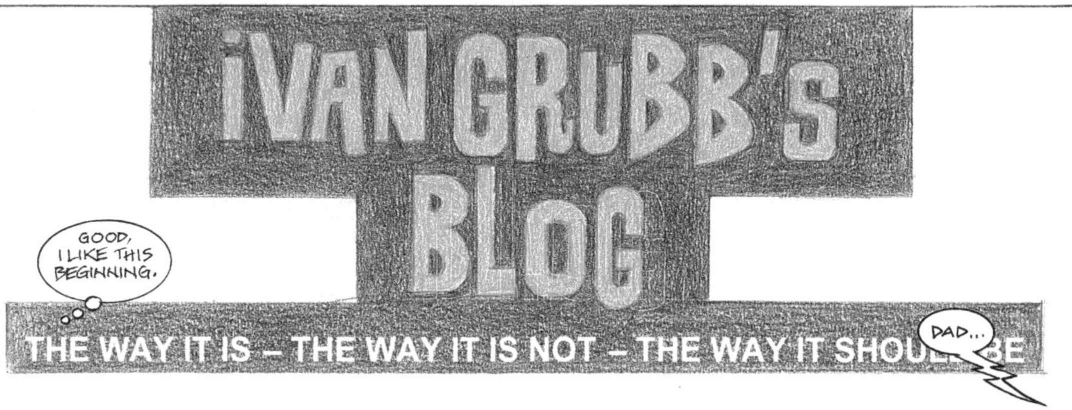
IVAN GRUBB'S BLOG
GOOD, I LIKE THIS BEGINNING.
THE WAY IT IS – THE WAY IT IS NOT – THE WAY IT SHOU BE
DAD...

The way it is. Our neighbourhood's filled with beautiful things, the park, the lovely buildings, the old pubs and cafes. Most of the beautiful things seem to have come down to us from our noble ancestors in their top hats and crinoline skirts. All the bad things seem to have come from today. The mobile phones and the forests of traffic lights on every corner and the ugly graffiti pretending to be art and most of the people who are so full of their own sense of all their so-called rights.

The way it isn't. All this liberalitis was supposed to make our city some sort of a paradise, everybody safe and happy, with kids given their own hi-viz vest and prozac in the maternity ward. But yesterday in the park a man high on his own self-importance like some kind of middle-class crack addict kicked my dog.

What was I supposed to do? Take him to the small claims court? No way! I sorted that man out good and proper. I punched him and that's **The Way It Should Be**.

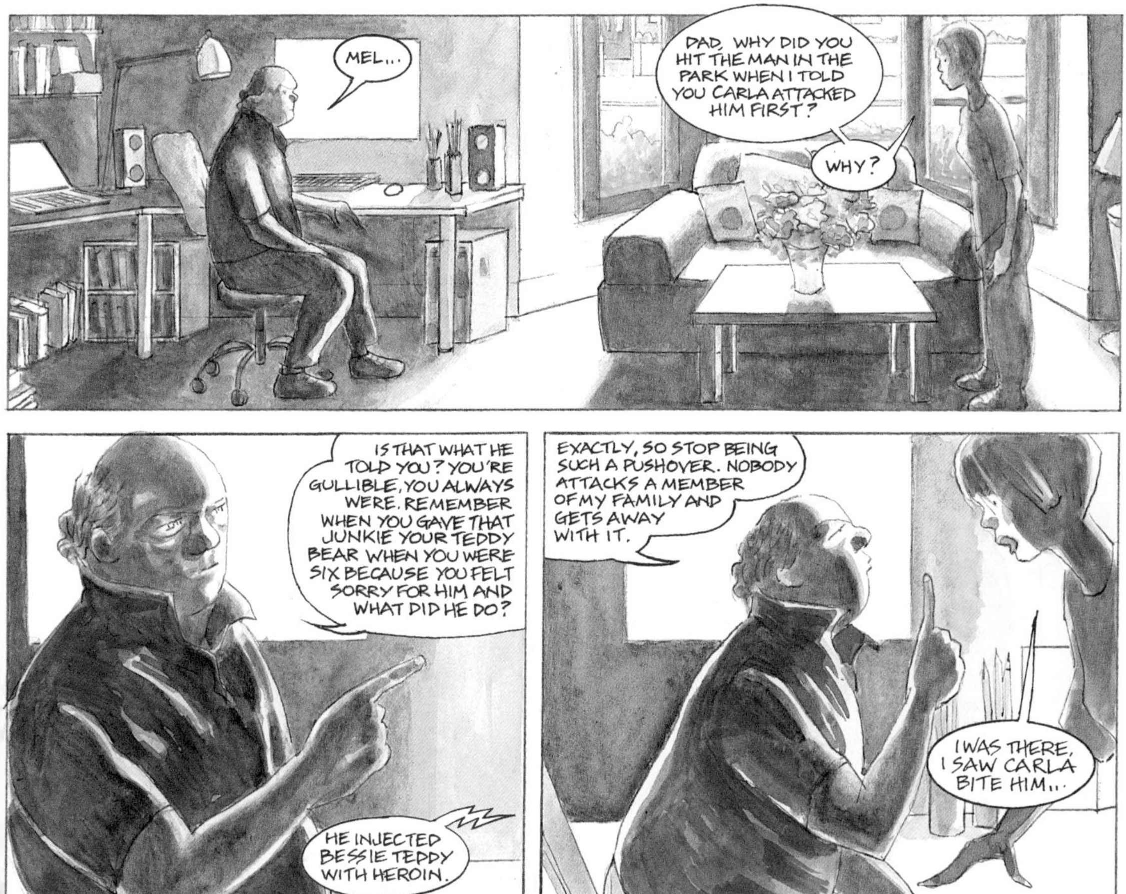
MEL...
DAD, WHY DID YOU HIT THE MAN IN THE PARK WHEN I TOLD YOU CARLA ATTACKED HIM FIRST?
WHY?
IS THAT WHAT HE TOLD YOU? YOU'RE GULLIBLE, YOU ALWAYS WERE. REMEMBER WHEN YOU GAVE THAT JUNKIE YOUR TEDDY BEAR WHEN YOU WERE SIX BECAUSE YOU FELT SORRY FOR HIM AND WHAT DID HE DO?
HE INJECTED BESSIE TEDDY WITH HEROIN.
EXACTLY, SO STOP BEING SUCH A PUSHOVER. NOBODY ATTACKS A MEMBER OF MY FAMILY AND GETS AWAY WITH IT.
I WAS THERE, I SAW CARLA BITE HIM...

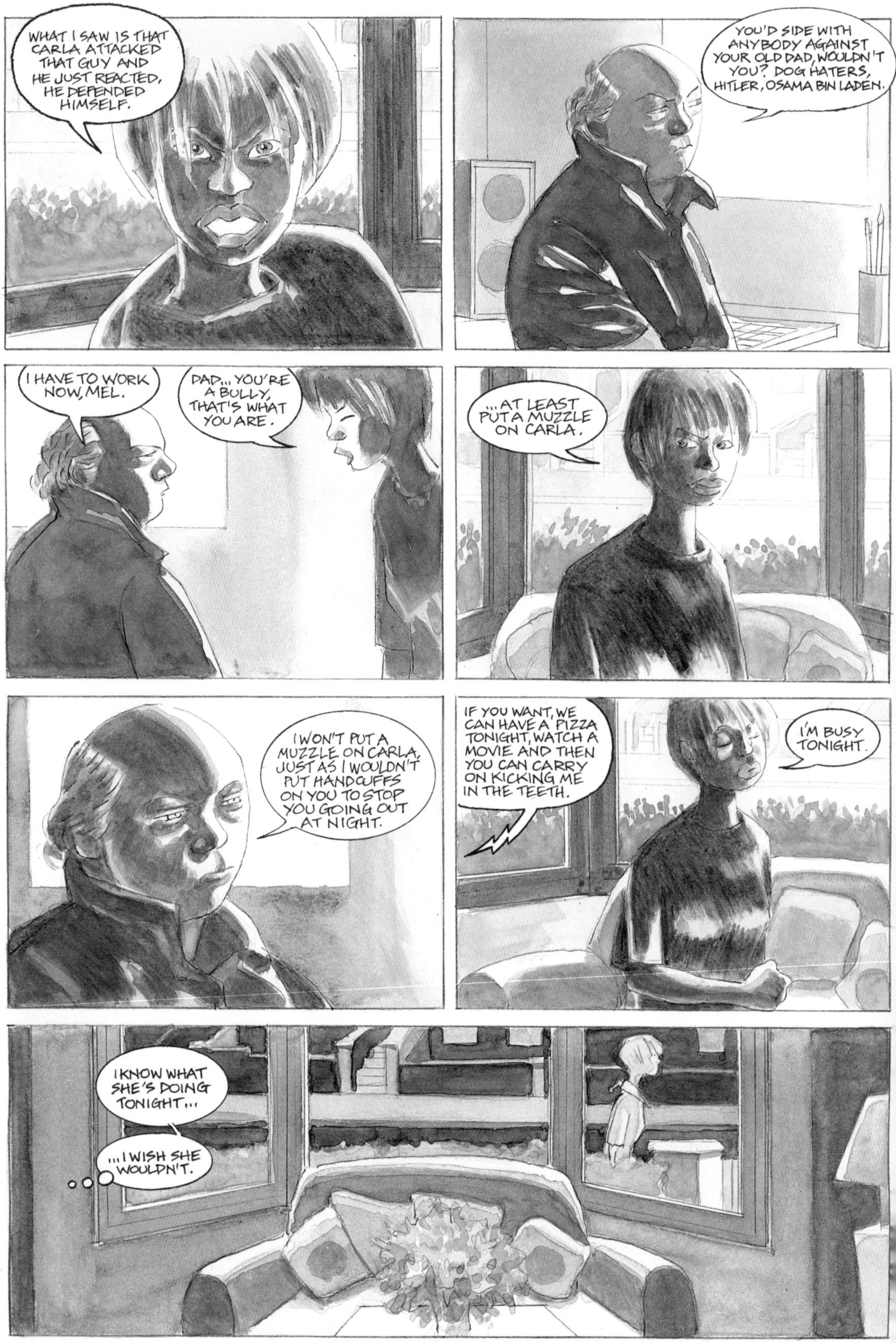
WHAT I SAW IS THAT CARLA ATTACKED THAT GUY AND HE JUST REACTED, HE DEFENDED HIMSELF.
YOU'D SIDE WITH ANYBODY AGAINST YOUR OLD DAD, WOULDN'T YOU? DOG HATERS, HITLER, OSAMA BIN LADEN.
I HAVE TO WORK NOW, MEL.
DAD... YOU'RE A BULLY, THAT'S WHAT YOU ARE.
...AT LEAST PUT A MUZZLE ON CARLA.
I WON'T PUT A MUZZLE ON CARLA, JUST AS I WOULDN'T PUT HANDCUFFS ON YOU TO STOP YOU GOING OUT AT NIGHT.
IF YOU WANT, WE CAN HAVE A PIZZA TONIGHT, WATCH A MOVIE AND THEN YOU CAN CARRY ON KICKING ME IN THE TEETH.
I'M BUSY TONIGHT.
I KNOW WHAT SHE'S DOING TONIGHT...
...I WISH SHE WOULDN'T.

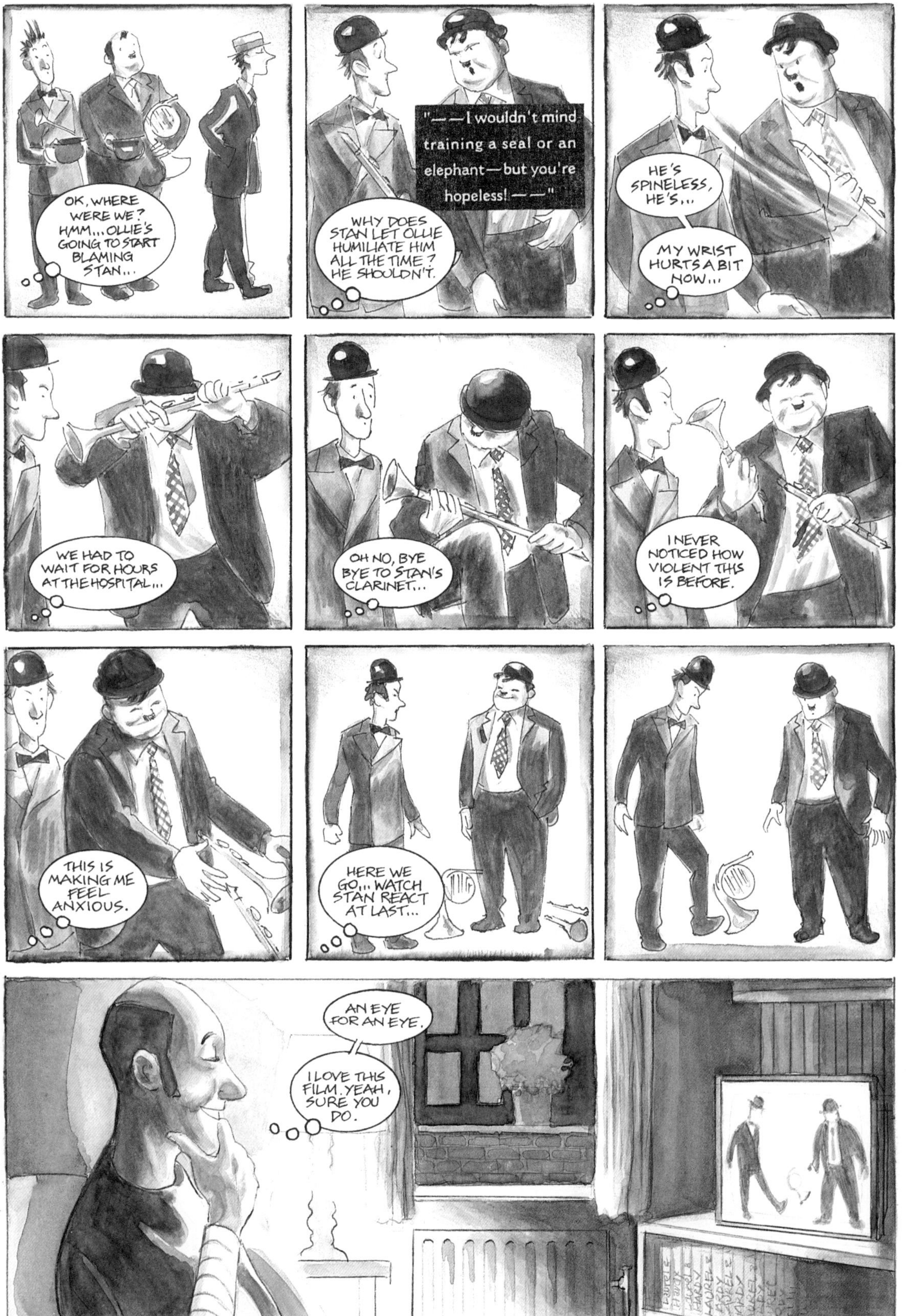
OK, WHERE WERE WE? HMM... OLLIE'S GOING TO START BLAMING STAN...
"— —I wouldn't mind training a seal or an elephant—but you're hopeless! — —"
WHY DOES STAN LET OLLIE HUMILIATE HIM ALL THE TIME? HE SHOULDN'T.
HE'S SPINELESS, HE'S...
MY WRIST HURTS A BIT NOW...
WE HAD TO WAIT FOR HOURS AT THE HOSPITAL...
OH NO, BYE BYE TO STAN'S CLARINET...
I NEVER NOTICED HOW VIOLENT THIS IS BEFORE.
THIS IS MAKING ME FEEL ANXIOUS.
HERE WE GO... WATCH STAN REACT AT LAST...
AN EYE FOR AN EYE.
I LOVE THIS FILM. YEAH, SURE YOU DO.

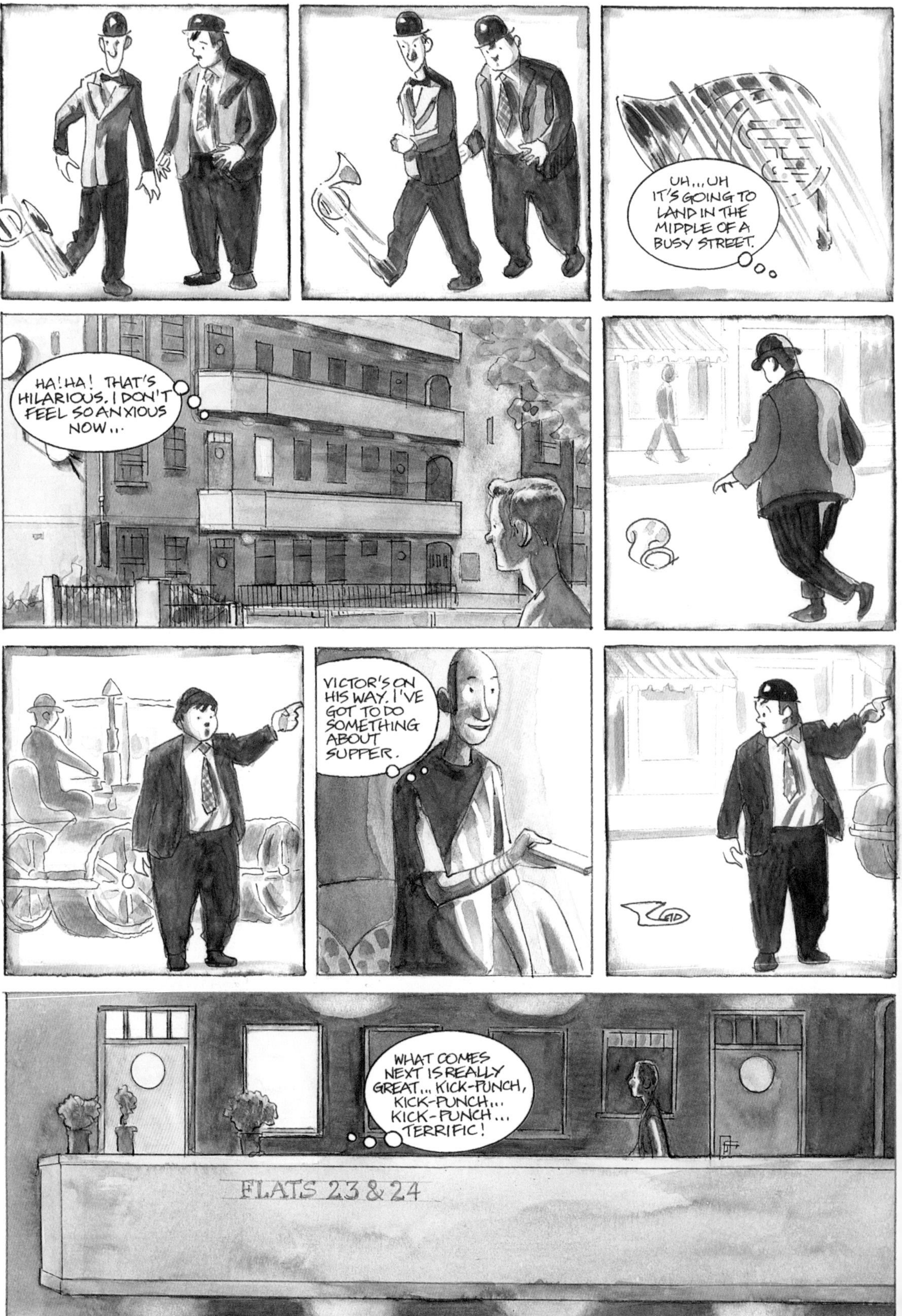
UH... UH IT'S GOING TO LAND IN THE MIDDLE OF A BUSY STREET.
HA! HA! THAT'S HILARIOUS. I DON'T FEEL SO ANXIOUS NOW...
VICTOR'S ON HIS WAY. I'VE GOT TO DO SOMETHING ABOUT SUPPER.
WHAT COMES NEXT IS REALLY GREAT... KICK-PUNCH, KICK-PUNCH... KICK-PUNCH... TERRIFIC!
FLATS 23 & 24

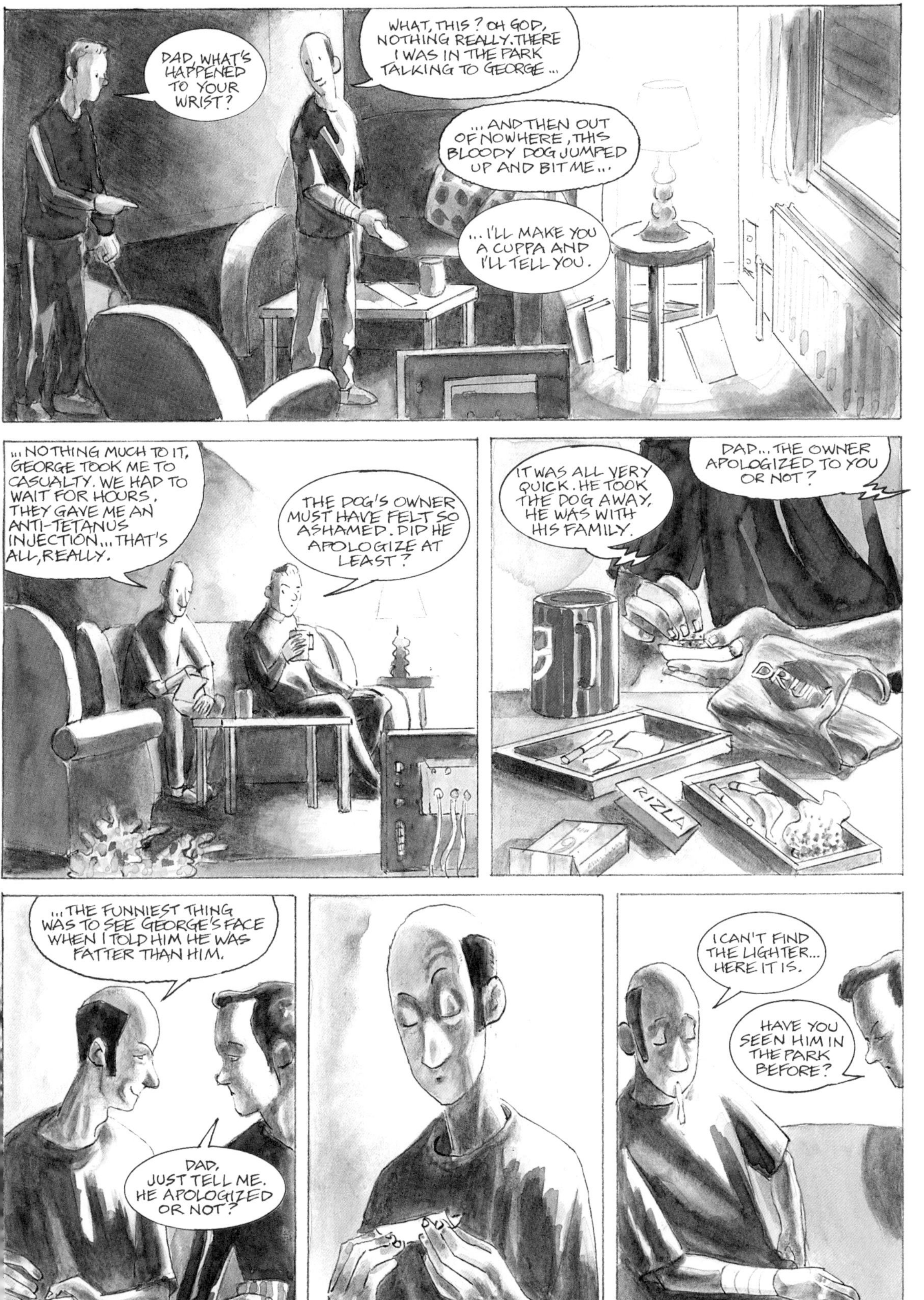
DAD, WHAT'S HAPPENED TO YOUR WRIST?
WHAT, THIS? OH GOD, NOTHING REALLY. THERE I WAS IN THE PARK TALKING TO GEORGE...
...AND THEN OUT OF NOWHERE, THIS BLOODY DOG JUMPED UP AND BIT ME...
...I'LL MAKE YOU A CUPPA AND I'LL TELL YOU.
...NOTHING MUCH TO IT, GEORGE TOOK ME TO CASUALTY. WE HAD TO WAIT FOR HOURS. THEY GAVE ME AN ANTI-TETANUS INJECTION... THAT'S ALL, REALLY.
THE DOG'S OWNER MUST HAVE FELT SO ASHAMED. DID HE APOLOGIZE AT LEAST?
IT WAS ALL VERY QUICK. HE TOOK THE DOG AWAY. HE WAS WITH HIS FAMILY.
DAD... THE OWNER APOLOGIZED TO YOU OR NOT?
RIZLA
...THE FUNNIEST THING WAS TO SEE GEORGE'S FACE WHEN I TOLD HIM HE WAS FATTER THAN HIM.
DAD, JUST TELL ME. HE APOLOGIZED OR NOT?
I CAN'T FIND THE LIGHTER... HERE IT IS.
HAVE YOU SEEN HIM IN THE PARK BEFORE?

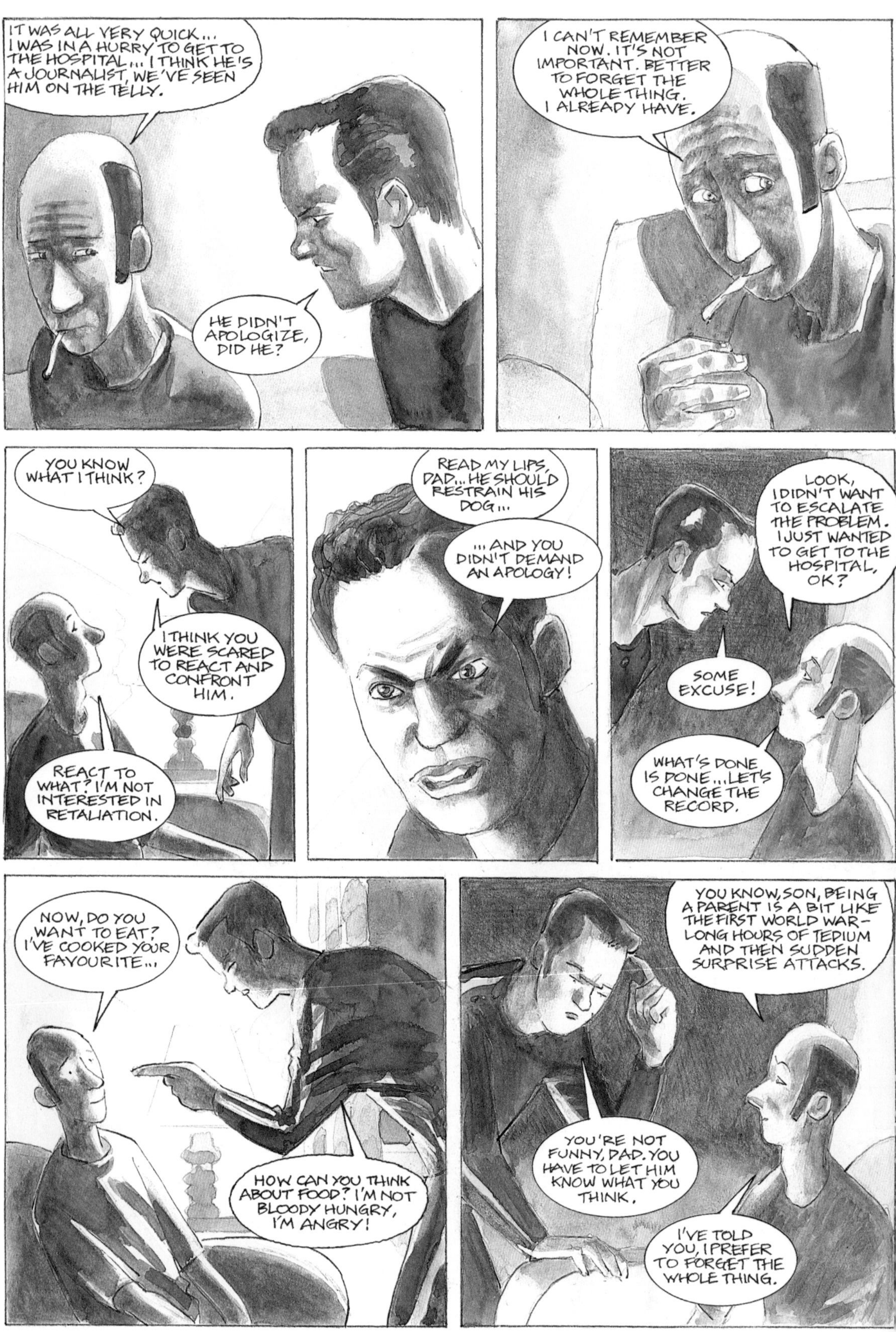
IT WAS ALL VERY QUICK... I WAS IN A HURRY TO GET TO THE HOSPITAL... I THINK HE'S A JOURNALIST, WE'VE SEEN HIM ON THE TELLY.
HE DIDN'T APOLOGIZE, DID HE?
I CAN'T REMEMBER NOW. IT'S NOT IMPORTANT. BETTER TO FORGET THE WHOLE THING. I ALREADY HAVE.
YOU KNOW WHAT I THINK?
I THINK YOU WERE SCARED TO REACT AND CONFRONT HIM.
REACT TO WHAT? I'M NOT INTERESTED IN RETALIATION.
READ MY LIPS, DAD... HE SHOULD RESTRAIN HIS DOG...
... AND YOU DIDN'T DEMAND AN APOLOGY!
LOOK, I DIDN'T WANT TO ESCALATE THE PROBLEM. I JUST WANTED TO GET TO THE HOSPITAL, OK?
SOME EXCUSE!
WHAT'S DONE IS DONE... LET'S CHANGE THE RECORD.
NOW, DO YOU WANT TO EAT? I'VE COOKED YOUR FAVOURITE...
HOW CAN YOU THINK ABOUT FOOD? I'M NOT BLOODY HUNGRY, I'M ANGRY!
YOU KNOW, SON, BEING A PARENT IS A BIT LIKE THE FIRST WORLD WAR - LONG HOURS OF TEDIUM AND THEN SUDDEN SURPRISE ATTACKS.
YOU'RE NOT FUNNY, DAD. YOU HAVE TO LET HIM KNOW WHAT YOU THINK.
I'VE TOLD YOU, I PREFER TO FORGET THE WHOLE THING.

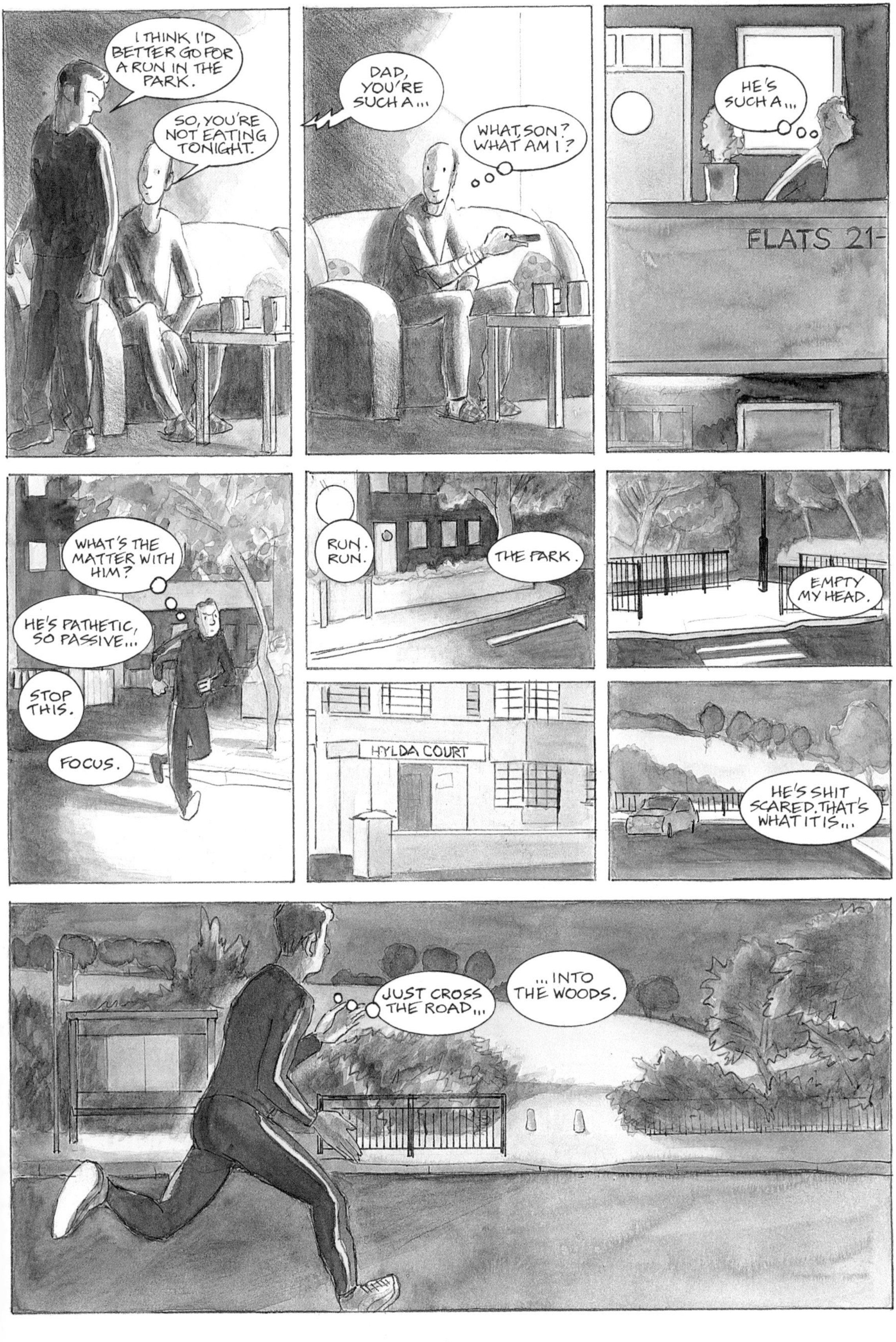
I THINK I'D BETTER GO FOR A RUN IN THE PARK.
SO, YOU'RE NOT EATING TONIGHT.
DAD, YOU'RE SUCH A...
WHAT, SON? WHAT AM I?
HE'S SUCH A...
FLATS 21-
WHAT'S THE MATTER WITH HIM?
HE'S PATHETIC, SO PASSIVE...
STOP THIS.
FOCUS.
RUN. RUN.
THE PARK.
EMPTY MY HEAD.
HYLDA COURT
HE'S SHIT SCARED, THAT'S WHAT IT IS...
JUST CROSS THE ROAD...
...INTO THE WOODS.

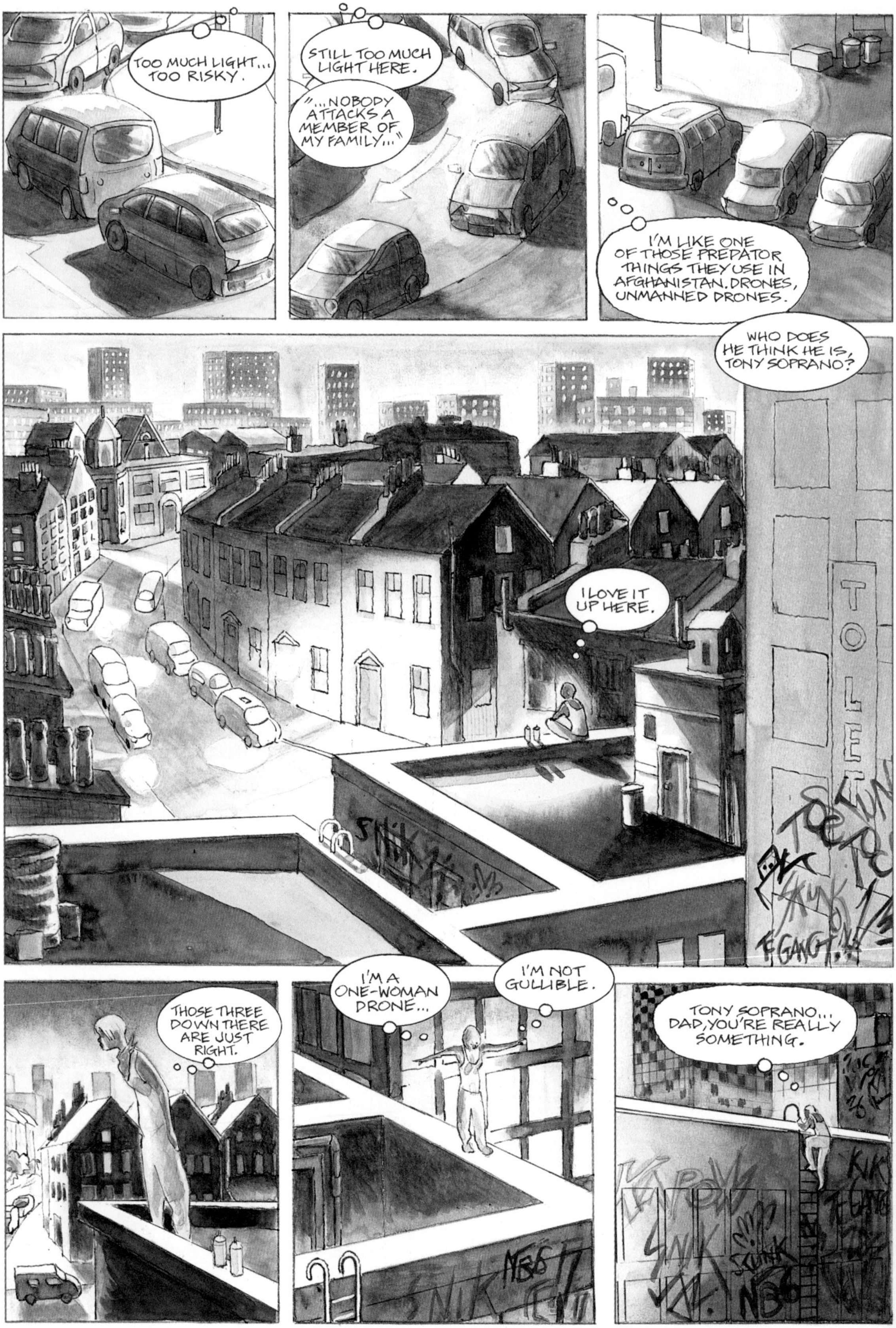
TOO MUCH LIGHT... TOO RISKY.
STILL TOO MUCH LIGHT HERE.
"...NOBODY ATTACKS A MEMBER OF MY FAMILY..."
I'M LIKE ONE OF THOSE PREDATOR THINGS THEY USE IN AFGHANISTAN. DRONES, UNMANNED DRONES.
WHO DOES HE THINK HE IS, TONY SOPRANO?
I LOVE IT UP HERE.
TO LET
THOSE THREE DOWN THERE ARE JUST RIGHT.
I'M A ONE-WOMAN DRONE...
I'M NOT GULLIBLE.
TONY SOPRANO... DAD, YOU'RE REALLY SOMETHING.

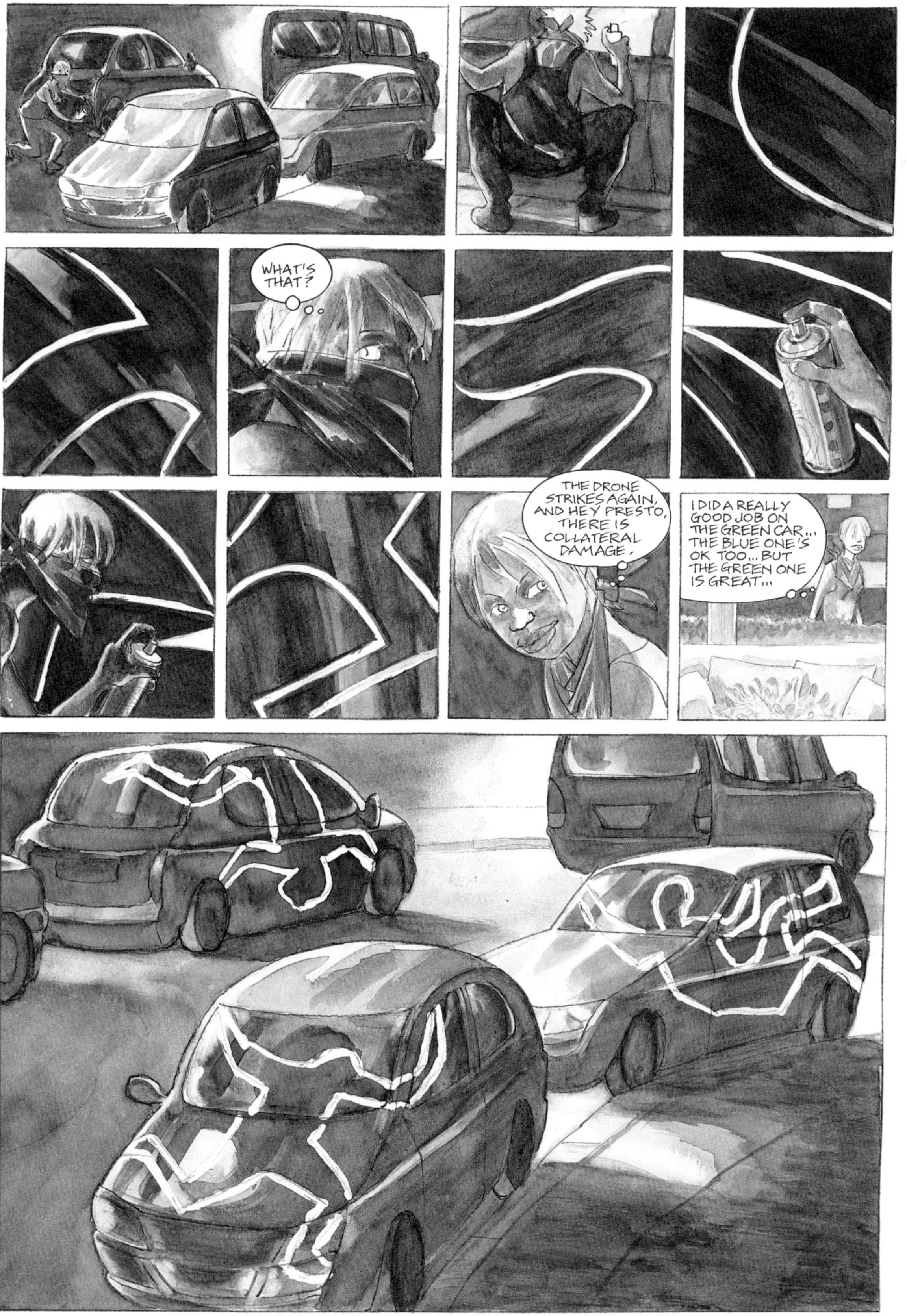
WHAT'S THAT?
THE DRONE STRIKES AGAIN, AND HEY PRESTO, THERE IS COLLATERAL DAMAGE.
I DID A REALLY GOOD JOB ON THE GREEN CAR... THE BLUE ONE'S OK TOO... BUT THE GREEN ONE IS GREAT...

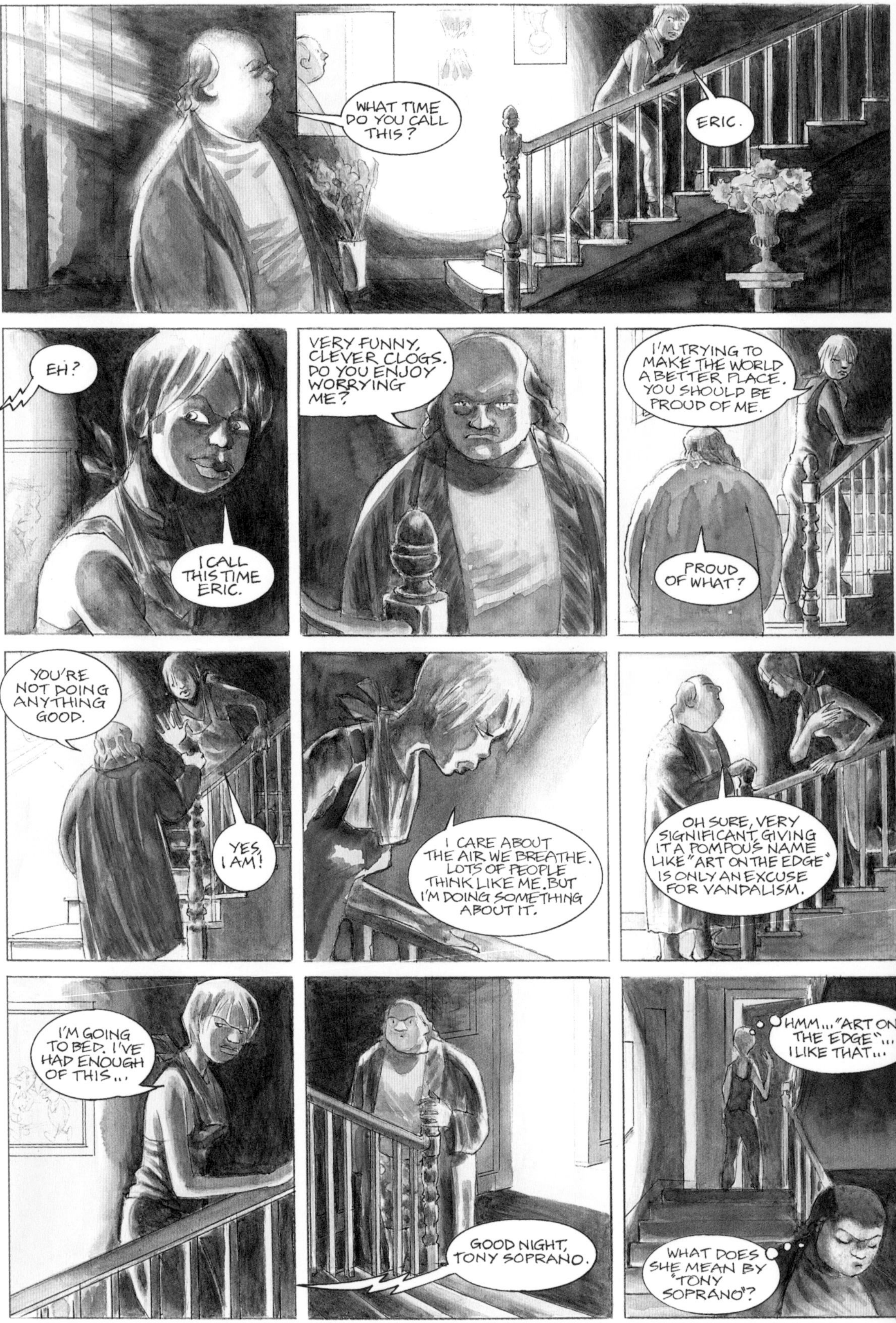
WHAT TIME DO YOU CALL THIS?
ERIC.
EH?
I CALL THIS TIME ERIC.
VERY FUNNY, CLEVER CLOGS. DO YOU ENJOY WORRYING ME?
I'M TRYING TO MAKE THE WORLD A BETTER PLACE. YOU SHOULD BE PROUD OF ME.
PROUD OF WHAT?
YOU'RE NOT DOING ANYTHING GOOD.
YES, I AM!
I CARE ABOUT THE AIR WE BREATHE. LOTS OF PEOPLE THINK LIKE ME. BUT I'M DOING SOMETHING ABOUT IT.
OH SURE, VERY SIGNIFICANT, GIVING IT A POMPOUS NAME LIKE "ART ON THE EDGE" IS ONLY AN EXCUSE FOR VANDALISM.
I'M GOING TO BED. I'VE HAD ENOUGH OF THIS...
GOOD NIGHT, TONY SOPRANO.
HMM... "ART ON THE EDGE"... I LIKE THAT...
WHAT DOES SHE MEAN BY "TONY SOPRANO"?

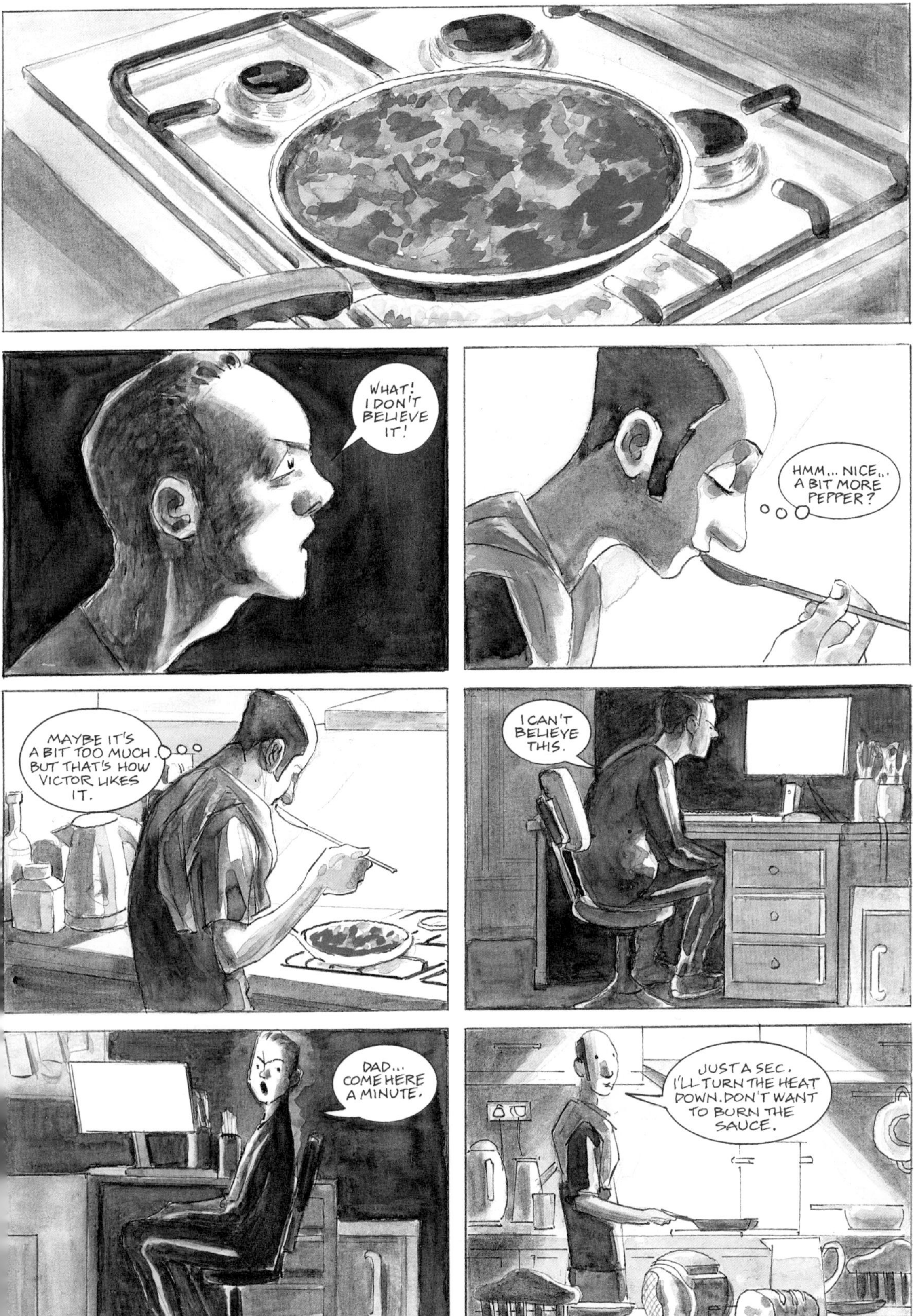
WHAT! I DON'T BELIEVE IT!
HMM... NICE... A BIT MORE PEPPER?
MAYBE IT'S A BIT TOO MUCH. BUT THAT'S HOW VICTOR LIKES IT.
I CAN'T BELIEVE THIS.
DAD... COME HERE A MINUTE.
JUST A SEC. I'LL TURN THE HEAT DOWN. DON'T WANT TO BURN THE SAUCE.

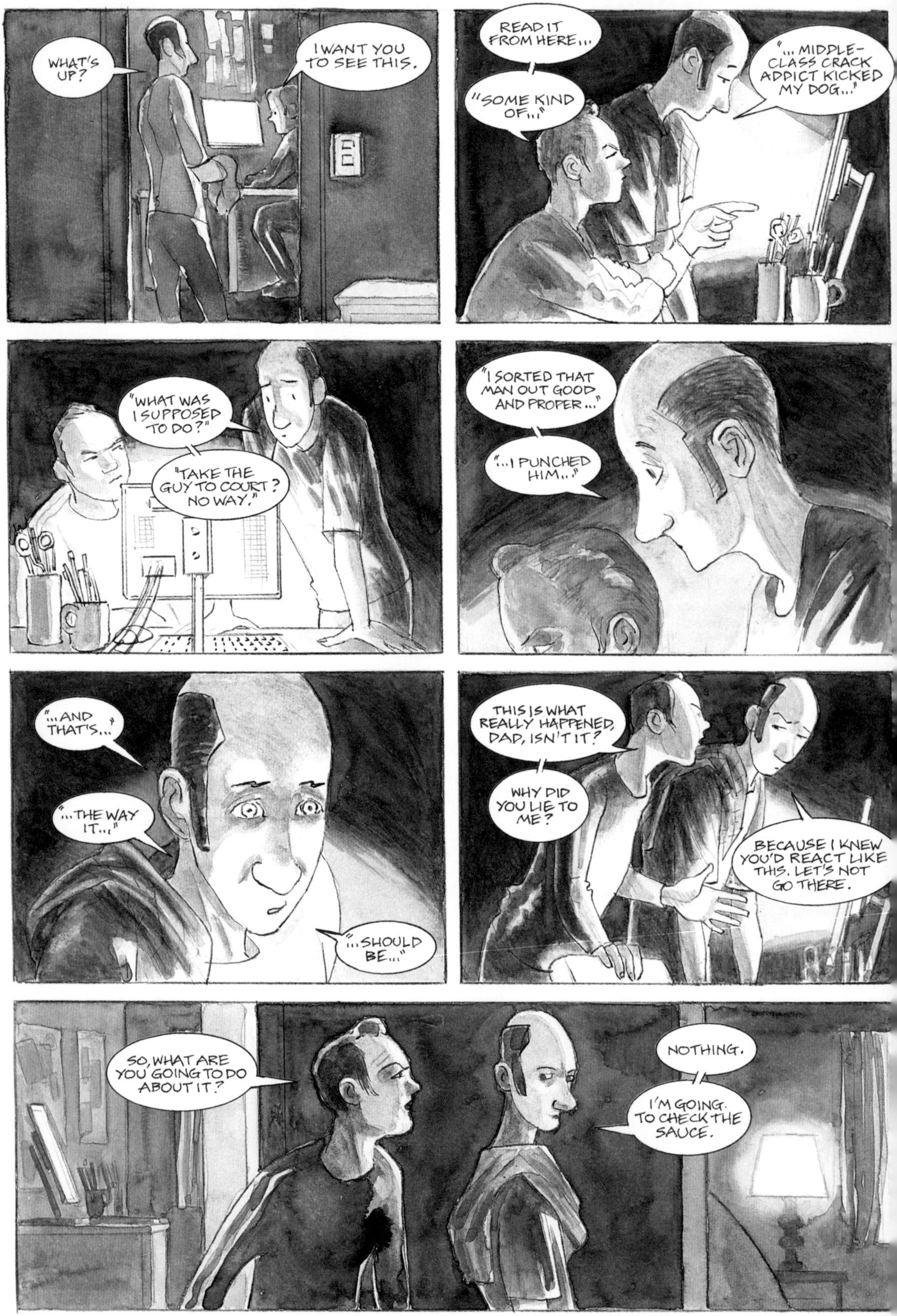
WHAT'S UP?
I WANT YOU TO SEE THIS.
READ IT FROM HERE...
"SOME KIND OF..."
"... MIDDLE-CLASS CRACK ADDICT KICKED MY DOG..."
"WHAT WAS I SUPPOSED TO DO?"
"TAKE THE GUY TO COURT? NO WAY."
"I SORTED THAT MAN OUT GOOD AND PROPER..."
"...I PUNCHED HIM..."
"...AND THAT'S..."
"...THE WAY IT..."
"...SHOULD BE..."
THIS IS WHAT REALLY HAPPENED, DAD, ISN'T IT?
WHY DID YOU LIE TO ME?
BECAUSE I KNEW YOU'D REACT LIKE THIS. LET'S NOT GO THERE.
SO, WHAT ARE YOU GOING TO DO ABOUT IT?
NOTHING.
I'M GOING TO CHECK THE SAUCE.

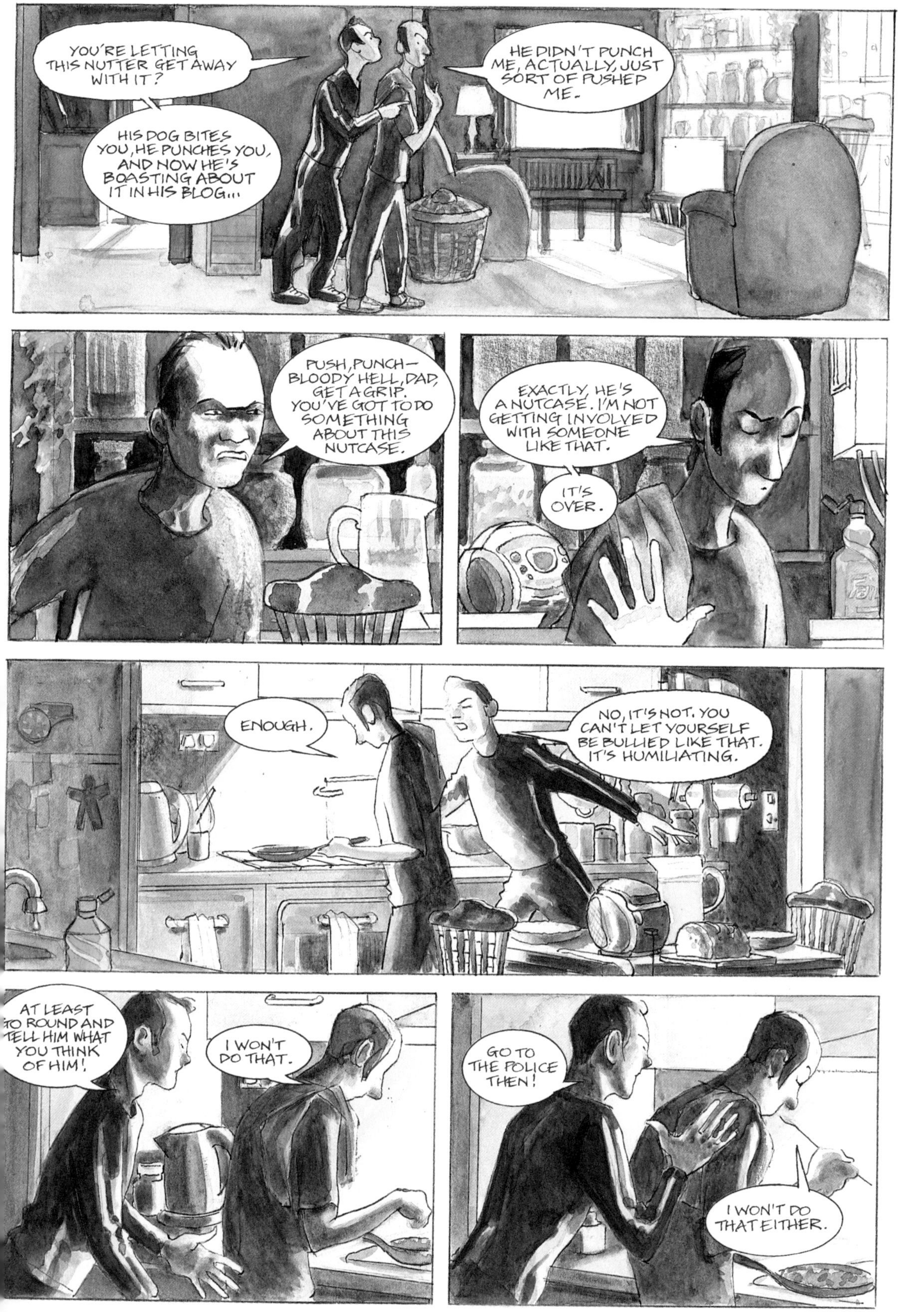

YOU'RE LETTING THIS NUTTER GET AWAY WITH IT?
HIS DOG BITES YOU, HE PUNCHES YOU, AND NOW HE'S BOASTING ABOUT IT IN HIS BLOG...
HE DIDN'T PUNCH ME, ACTUALLY, JUST SORT OF PUSHED ME.
PUSH, PUNCH— BLOODY HELL, DAD, GET A GRIP. YOU'VE GOT TO DO SOMETHING ABOUT THIS NUTCASE.
EXACTLY, HE'S A NUTCASE. I'M NOT GETTING INVOLVED WITH SOMEONE LIKE THAT.
IT'S OVER.
ENOUGH.
NO, IT'S NOT. YOU CAN'T LET YOURSELF BE BULLIED LIKE THAT. IT'S HUMILIATING.
AT LEAST GO ROUND AND TELL HIM WHAT YOU THINK OF HIM!
I WON'T DO THAT.
GO TO THE POLICE THEN!
I WON'T DO THAT EITHER.

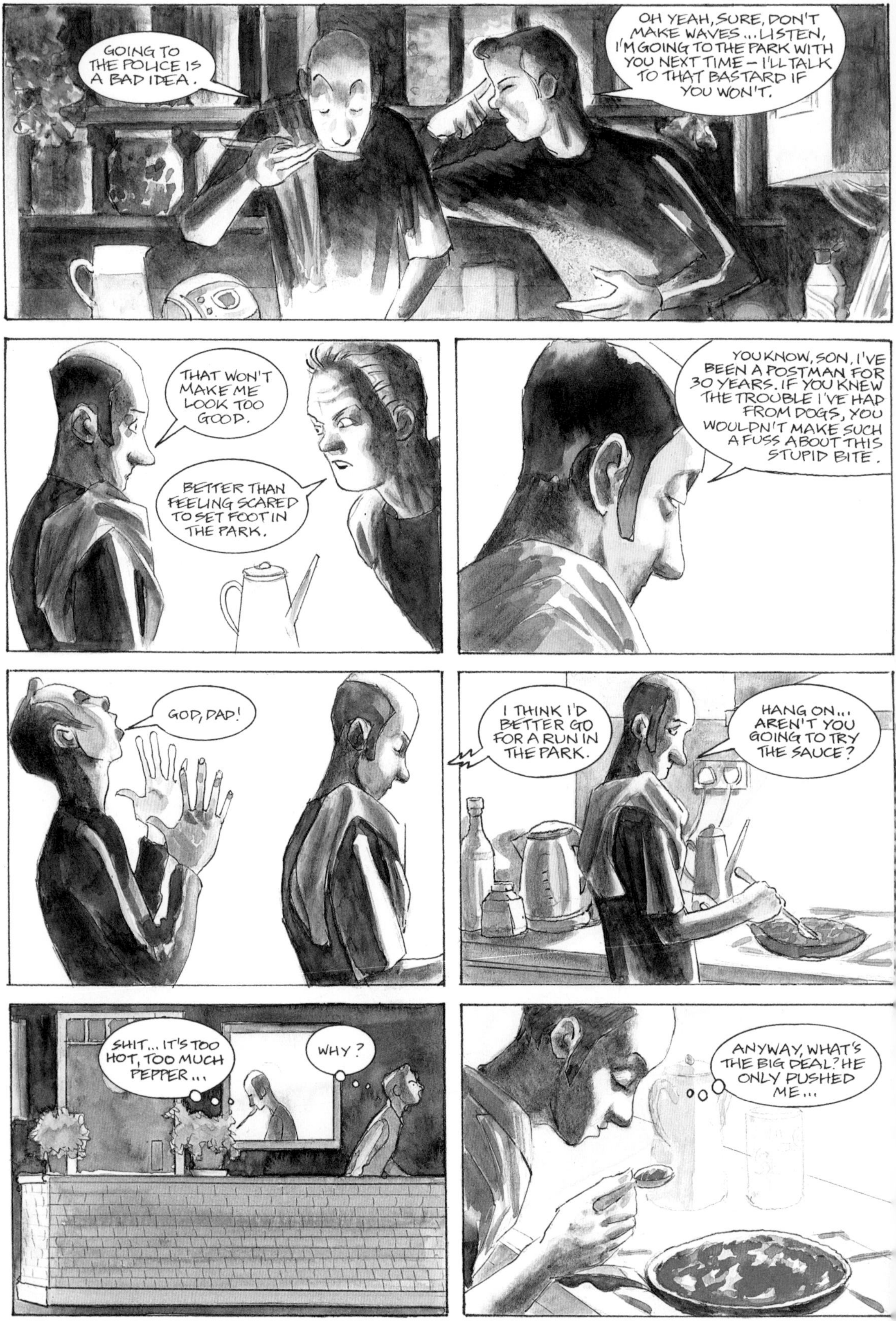
GOING TO THE POLICE IS A BAD IDEA.
OH YEAH, SURE, DON'T MAKE WAVES... LISTEN, I'M GOING TO THE PARK WITH YOU NEXT TIME – I'LL TALK TO THAT BASTARD IF YOU WON'T.
THAT WON'T MAKE ME LOOK TOO GOOD.
BETTER THAN FEELING SCARED TO SET FOOT IN THE PARK.
YOU KNOW, SON, I'VE BEEN A POSTMAN FOR 30 YEARS. IF YOU KNEW THE TROUBLE I'VE HAD FROM DOGS, YOU WOULDN'T MAKE SUCH A FUSS ABOUT THIS STUPID BITE.
GOD, DAD!
I THINK I'D BETTER GO FOR A RUN IN THE PARK.
HANG ON... AREN'T YOU GOING TO TRY THE SAUCE?
SHIT... IT'S TOO HOT, TOO MUCH PEPPER...
WHY?
ANYWAY, WHAT'S THE BIG DEAL? HE ONLY PUSHED ME...

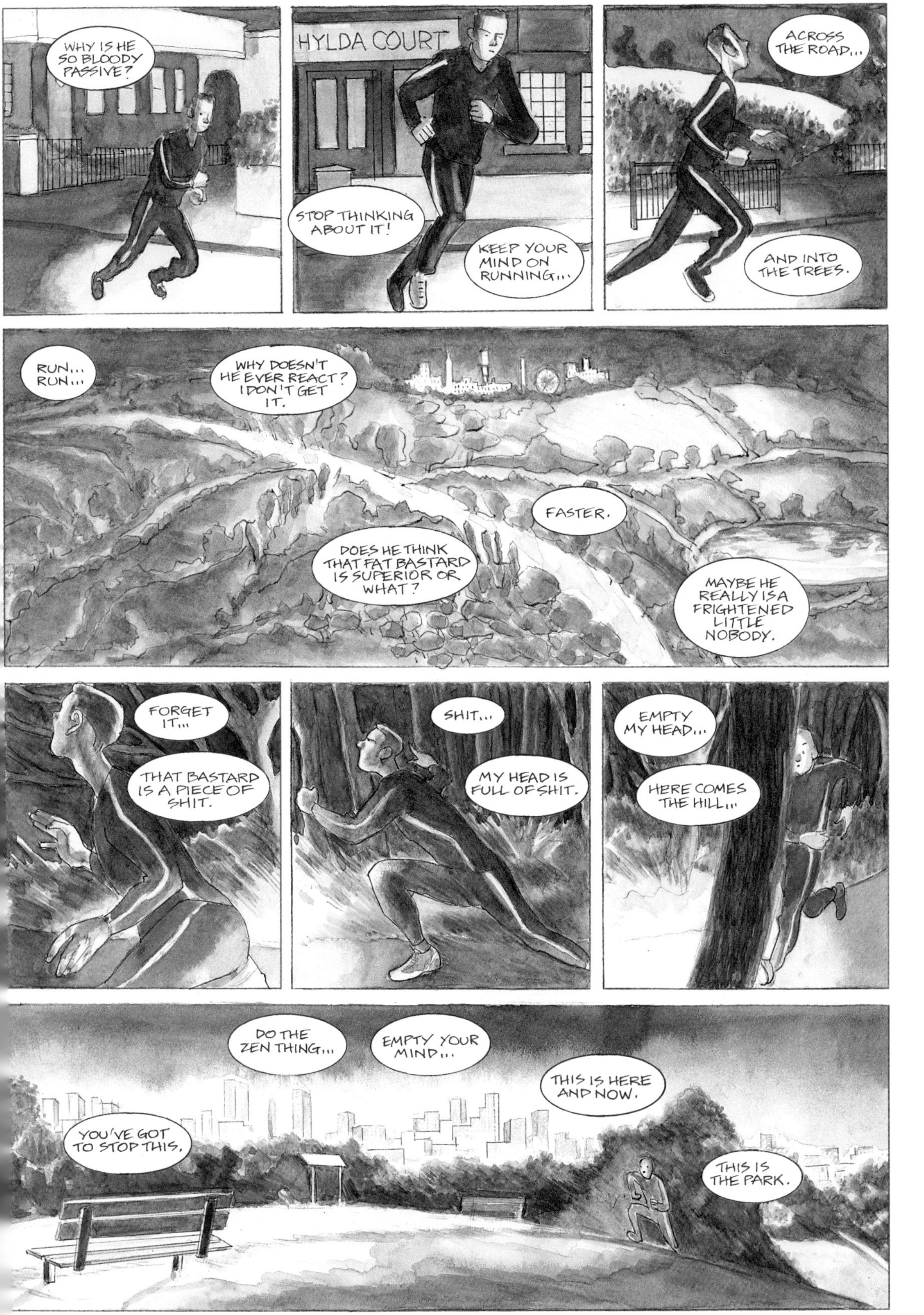
WHY IS HE SO BLOODY PASSIVE?
HYLDA COURT
STOP THINKING ABOUT IT!
KEEP YOUR MIND ON RUNNING...
ACROSS THE ROAD...
AND INTO THE TREES.
RUN... RUN...
WHY DOESN'T HE EVER REACT? I DON'T GET IT.
FASTER.
DOES HE THINK THAT FAT BASTARD IS SUPERIOR OR WHAT?
MAYBE HE REALLY IS A FRIGHTENED LITTLE NOBODY.
FORGET IT...
THAT BASTARD IS A PIECE OF SHIT.
SHIT...
MY HEAD IS FULL OF SHIT.
EMPTY MY HEAD...
HERE COMES THE HILL...
DO THE ZEN THING...
EMPTY YOUR MIND...
THIS IS HERE AND NOW.
YOU'VE GOT TO STOP THIS.
THIS IS THE PARK.

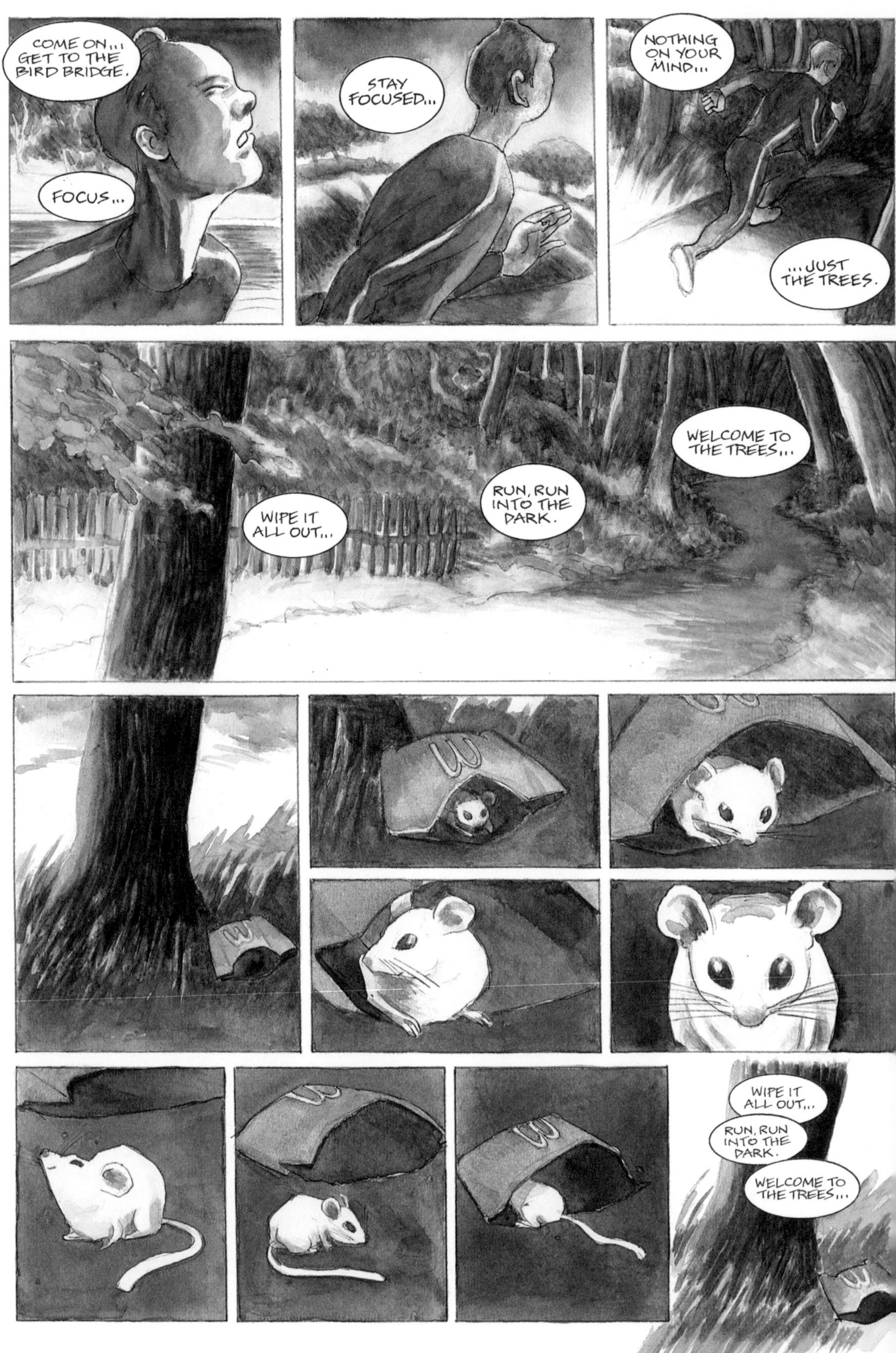
COME ON... GET TO THE BIRD BRIDGE.
FOCUS...
STAY FOCUSED...
NOTHING ON YOUR MIND...
...JUST THE TREES.
WIPE IT ALL OUT...
RUN, RUN INTO THE DARK.
WELCOME TO THE TREES...
WIPE IT ALL OUT...
RUN, RUN INTO THE DARK.
WELCOME TO THE TREES...

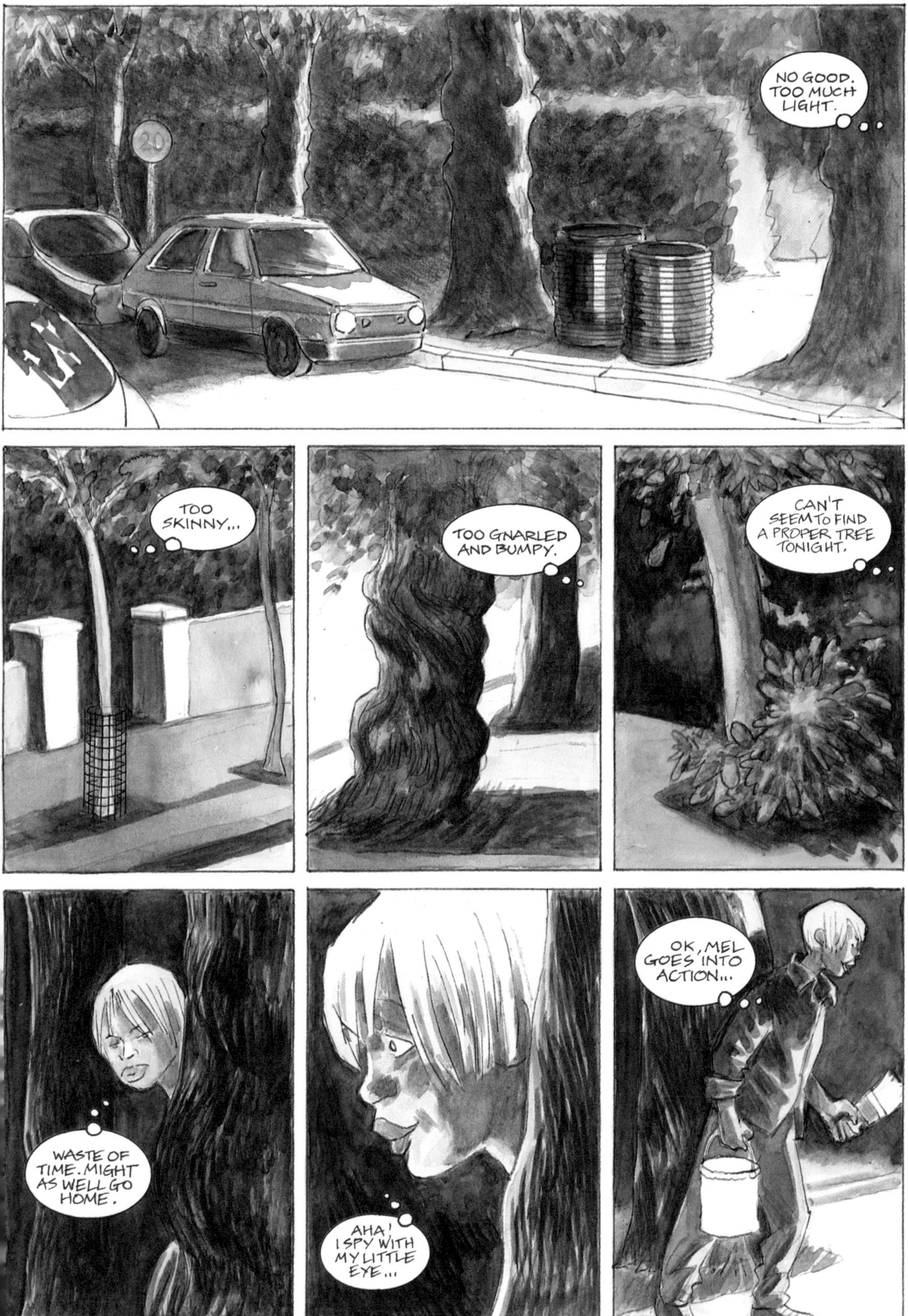
NO GOOD. TOO MUCH LIGHT.
TOO SKINNY...
TOO GNARLED AND BUMPY.
CAN'T SEEM TO FIND A PROPER TREE TONIGHT.
WASTE OF TIME. MIGHT AS WELL GO HOME.
AHA! I SPY WITH MY LITTLE EYE...
OK, MEL GOES INTO ACTION...

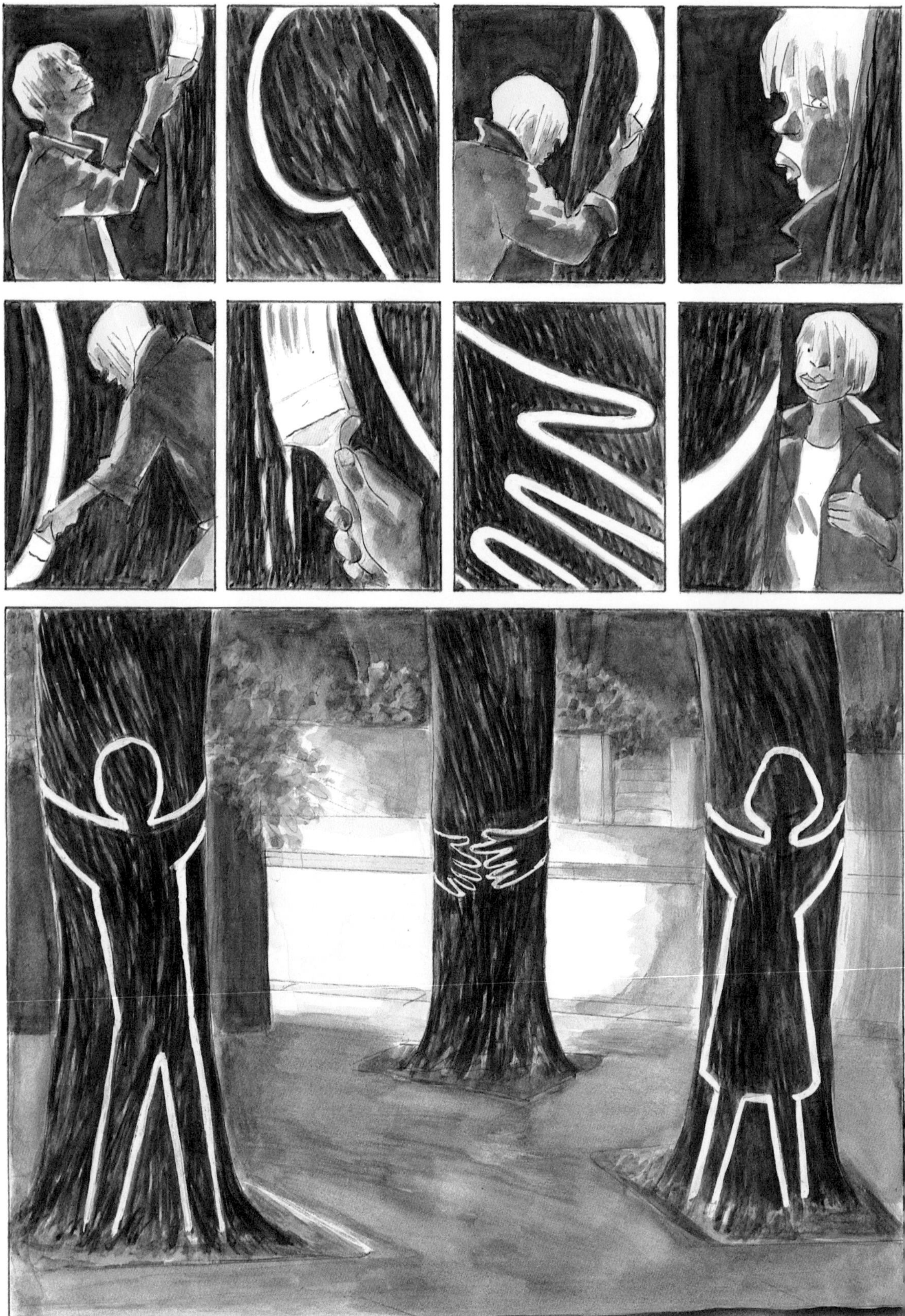

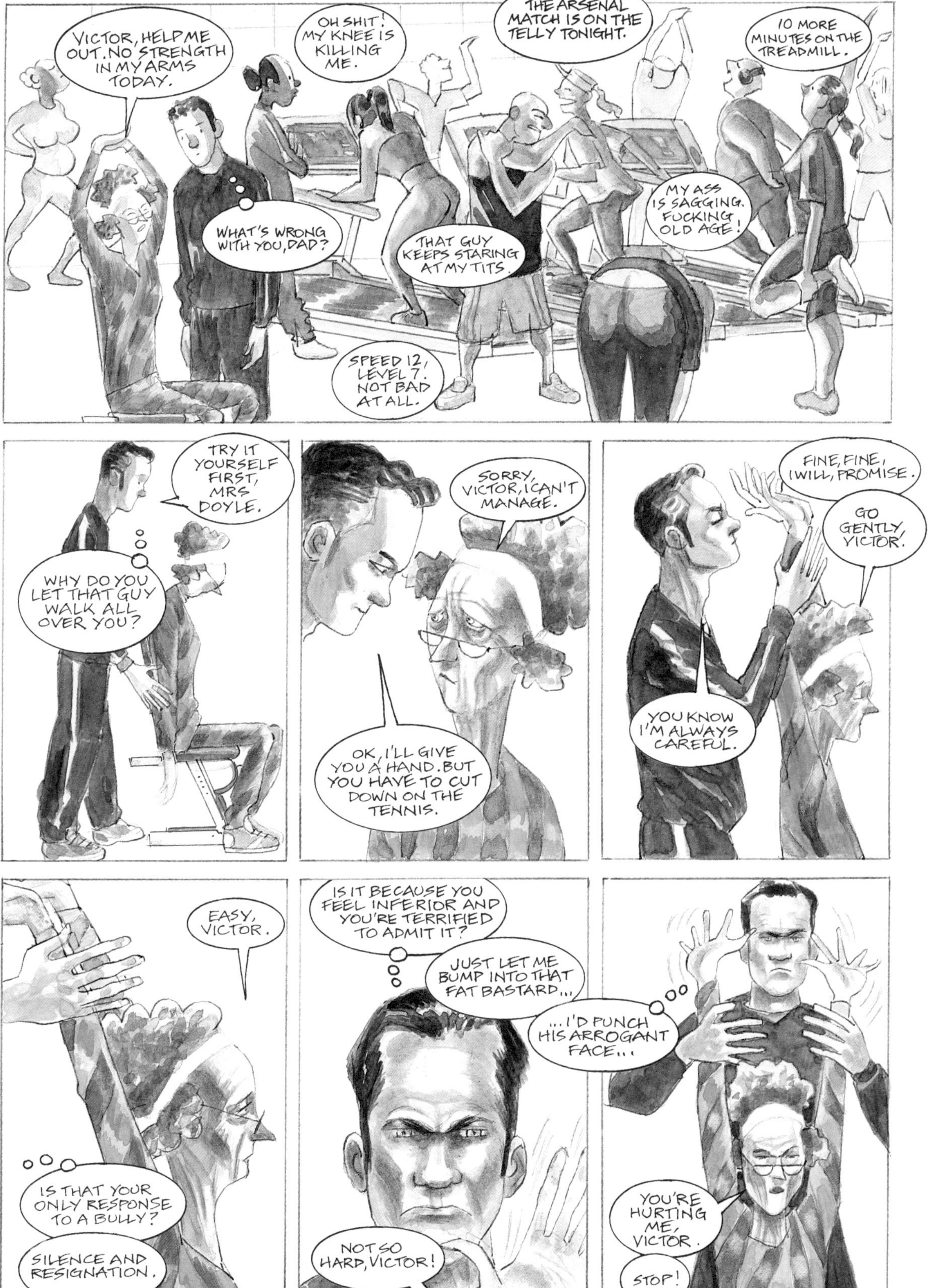
VICTOR, HELP ME OUT. NO STRENGTH IN MY ARMS TODAY.
OH SHIT! MY KNEE IS KILLING ME.
THE ARSENAL MATCH IS ON THE TELLY TONIGHT.
10 MORE MINUTES ON THE TREADMILL.
WHAT'S WRONG WITH YOU, DAD?
THAT GUY KEEPS STARING AT MY TITS.
MY ASS IS SAGGING. FUCKING OLD AGE!
SPEED 12, LEVEL 7. NOT BAD AT ALL.
TRY IT YOURSELF FIRST, MRS DOYLE.
WHY DO YOU LET THAT GUY WALK ALL OVER YOU?
SORRY, VICTOR, I CAN'T MANAGE.
OK, I'LL GIVE YOU A HAND. BUT YOU HAVE TO CUT DOWN ON THE TENNIS.
FINE, FINE, I WILL, PROMISE.
GO GENTLY, VICTOR.
YOU KNOW I'M ALWAYS CAREFUL.
EASY, VICTOR.
IS THAT YOUR ONLY RESPONSE TO A BULLY?
SILENCE AND RESIGNATION.
IS IT BECAUSE YOU FEEL INFERIOR AND YOU'RE TERRIFIED TO ADMIT IT?
JUST LET ME BUMP INTO THAT FAT BASTARD...
...I'D PUNCH HIS ARROGANT FACE...
NOT SO HARD, VICTOR!
YOU'RE HURTING ME, VICTOR.
STOP!

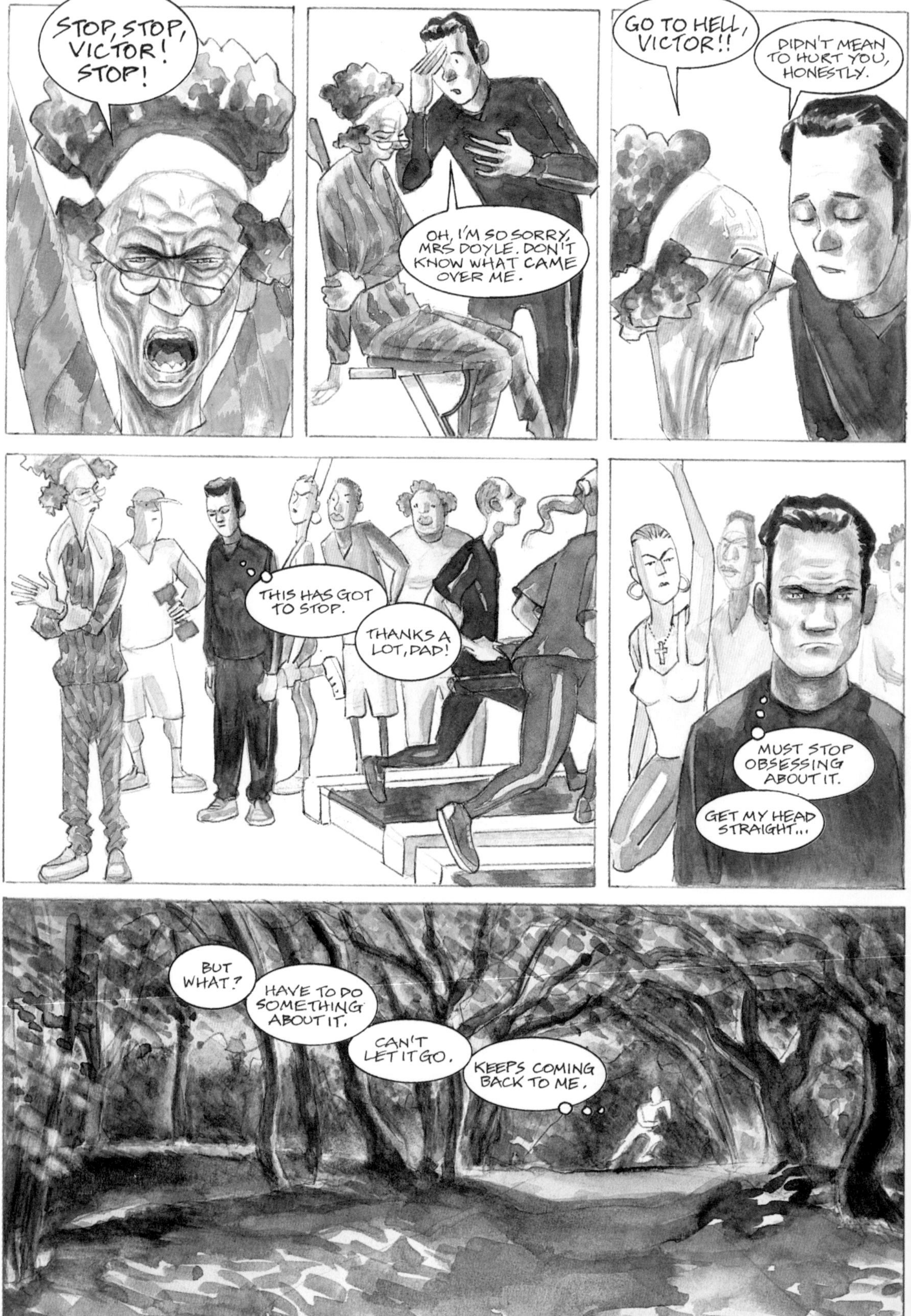
STOP, STOP, VICTOR! STOP!
OH, I'M SO SORRY, MRS DOYLE. DON'T KNOW WHAT CAME OVER ME.
GO TO HELL, VICTOR!!
DIDN'T MEAN TO HURT YOU, HONESTLY.
THIS HAS GOT TO STOP.
THANKS A LOT, DAD!
MUST STOP OBSESSING ABOUT IT.
GET MY HEAD STRAIGHT...
BUT WHAT?
HAVE TO DO SOMETHING ABOUT IT.
CAN'T LET IT GO.
KEEPS COMING BACK TO ME.

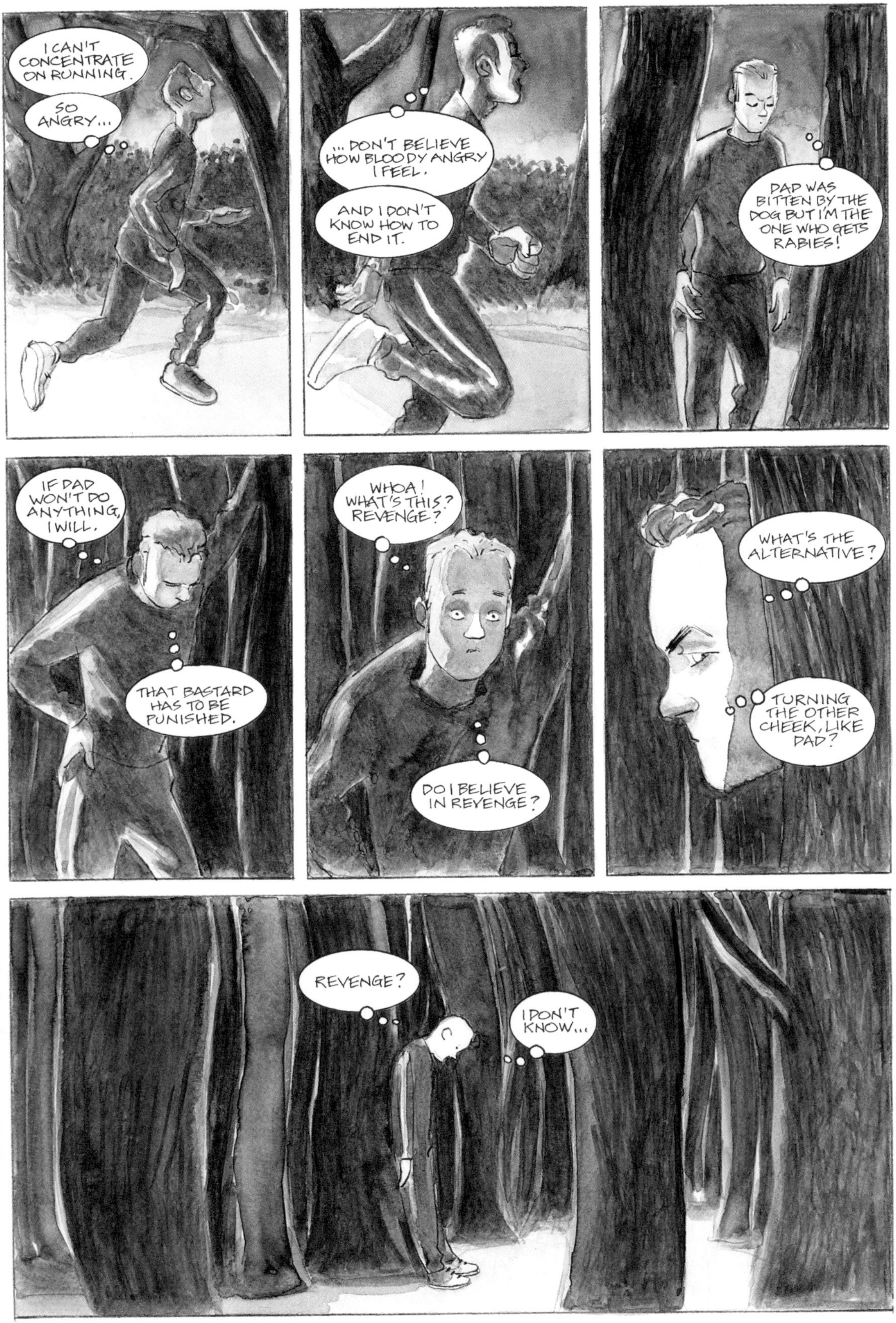
I CAN'T CONCENTRATE ON RUNNING.
SO ANGRY...
... DON'T BELIEVE HOW BLOODY ANGRY I FEEL.
AND I DON'T KNOW HOW TO END IT.
DAD WAS BITTEN BY THE DOG BUT I'M THE ONE WHO GETS RABIES!
IF DAD WON'T DO ANYTHING, I WILL.
THAT BASTARD HAS TO BE PUNISHED.
WHOA! WHAT'S THIS? REVENGE?
DO I BELIEVE IN REVENGE?
WHAT'S THE ALTERNATIVE?
TURNING THE OTHER CHEEK, LIKE DAD?
REVENGE?
I DON'T KNOW...

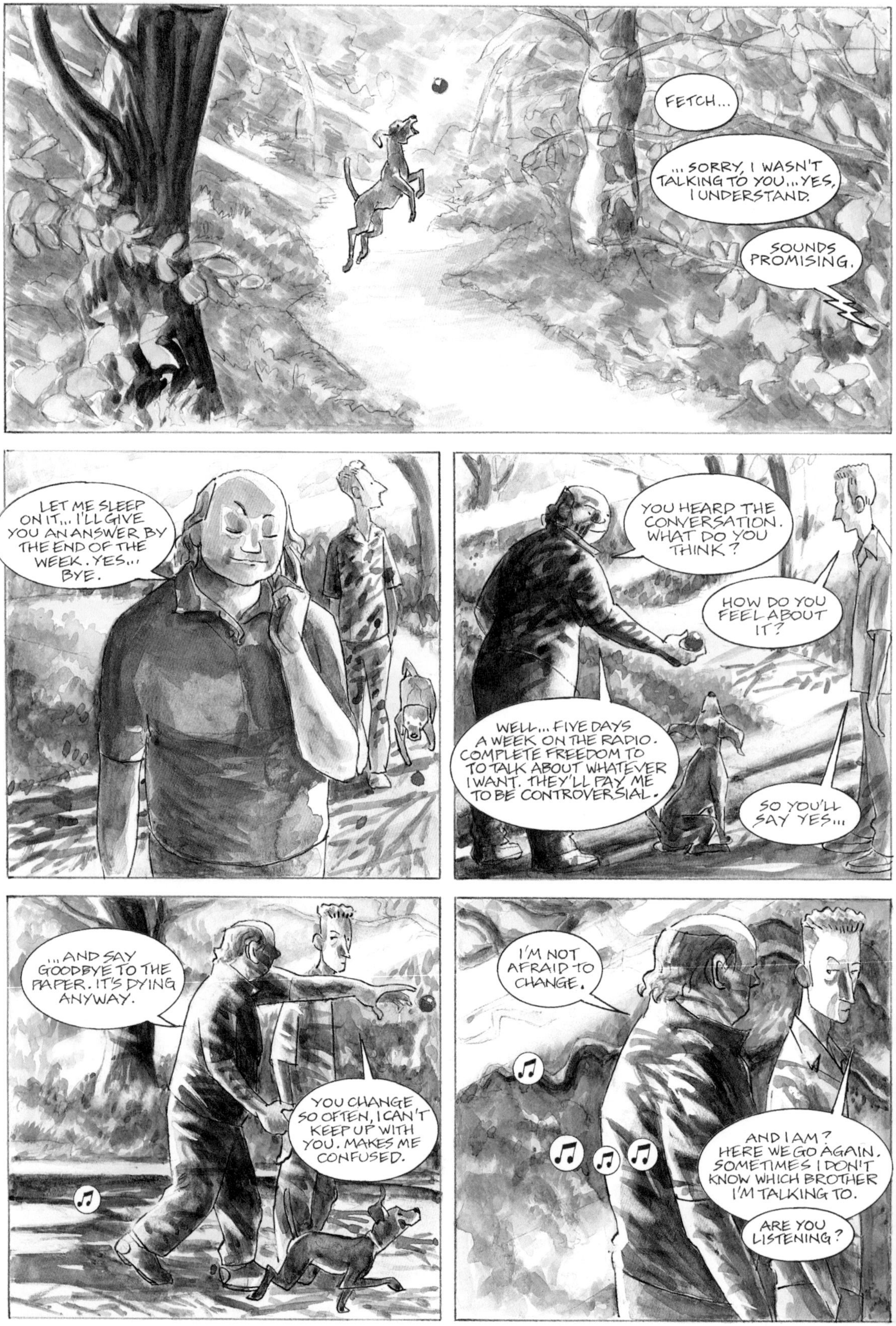
FETCH...
... SORRY, I WASN'T TALKING TO YOU... YES, I UNDERSTAND.
SOUNDS PROMISING.
LET ME SLEEP ON IT... I'LL GIVE YOU AN ANSWER BY THE END OF THE WEEK. YES... BYE.
YOU HEARD THE CONVERSATION. WHAT DO YOU THINK?
HOW DO YOU FEEL ABOUT IT?
WELL... FIVE DAYS A WEEK ON THE RADIO. COMPLETE FREEDOM TO TO TALK ABOUT WHATEVER I WANT. THEY'LL PAY ME TO BE CONTROVERSIAL.
SO YOU'LL SAY YES...
... AND SAY GOODBYE TO THE PAPER. IT'S DYING ANYWAY.
YOU CHANGE SO OFTEN, I CAN'T KEEP UP WITH YOU. MAKES ME CONFUSED.
I'M NOT AFRAID TO CHANGE.
AND I AM? HERE WE GO AGAIN. SOMETIMES I DON'T KNOW WHICH BROTHER I'M TALKING TO.
ARE YOU LISTENING?

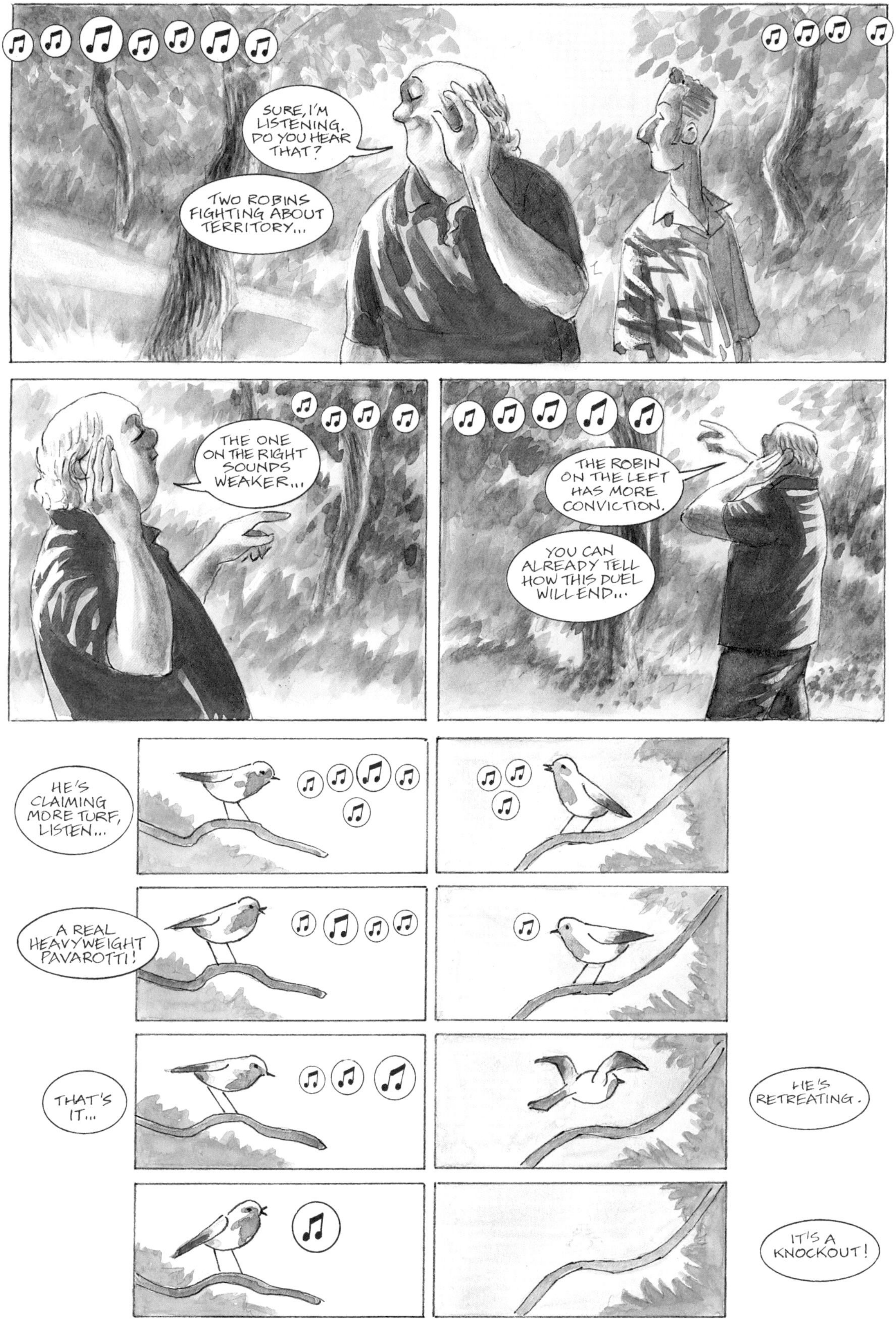
SURE, I'M LISTENING. DO YOU HEAR THAT?
TWO ROBINS FIGHTING ABOUT TERRITORY...
THE ONE ON THE RIGHT SOUNDS WEAKER...
THE ROBIN ON THE LEFT HAS MORE CONVICTION.
YOU CAN ALREADY TELL HOW THIS DUEL WILL END...
HE'S CLAIMING MORE TURF, LISTEN...
A REAL HEAVYWEIGHT PAVAROTTI!
THAT'S IT...
HE'S RETREATING.
IT'S A KNOCKOUT!

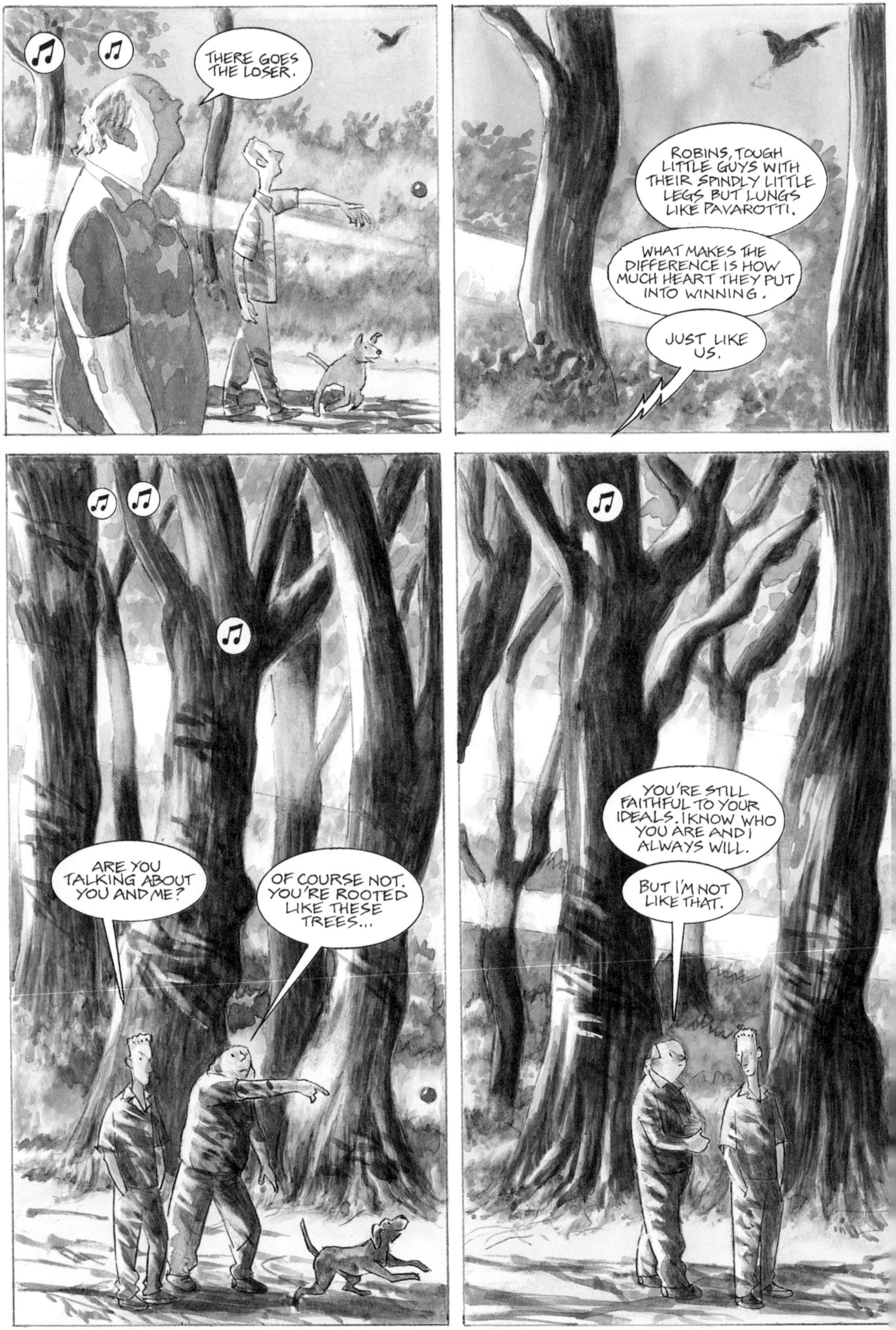
THERE GOES THE LOSER.
ROBINS, TOUGH LITTLE GUYS WITH THEIR SPINDLY LITTLE LEGS BUT LUNGS LIKE PAVAROTTI.
WHAT MAKES THE DIFFERENCE IS HOW MUCH HEART THEY PUT INTO WINNING.
JUST LIKE US.
ARE YOU TALKING ABOUT YOU AND ME?
OF COURSE NOT. YOU'RE ROOTED LIKE THESE TREES...
YOU'RE STILL FAITHFUL TO YOUR IDEALS. I KNOW WHO YOU ARE AND I ALWAYS WILL.
BUT I'M NOT LIKE THAT.

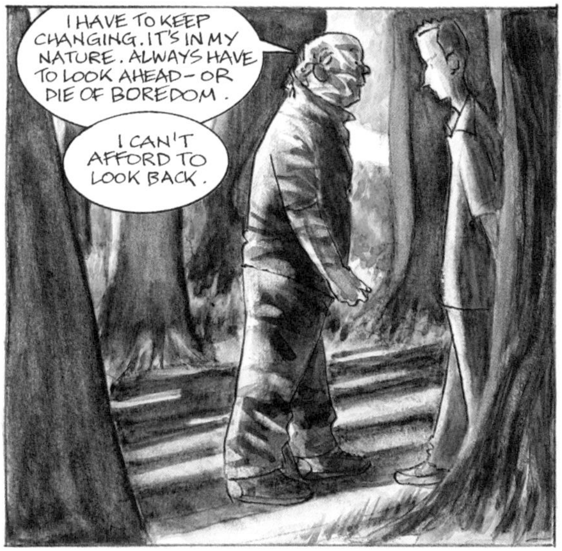
I HAVE TO KEEP CHANGING. IT'S IN MY NATURE. ALWAYS HAVE TO LOOK AHEAD - OR DIE OF BOREDOM.
I CAN'T AFFORD TO LOOK BACK.

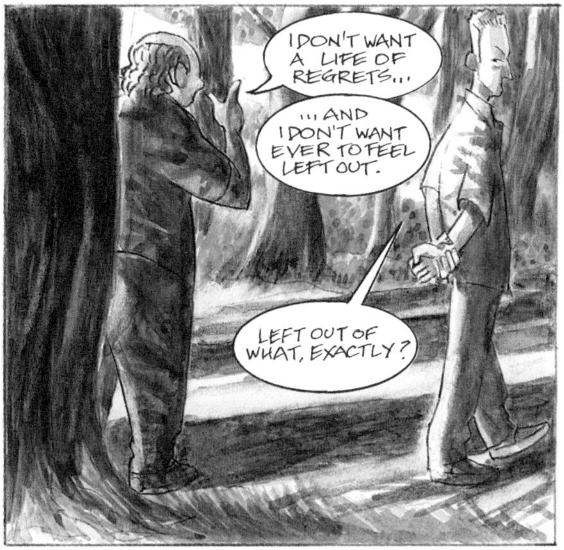
I DON'T WANT A LIFE OF REGRETS...
...AND I DON'T WANT EVER TO FEEL LEFT OUT.
LEFT OUT OF WHAT, EXACTLY?

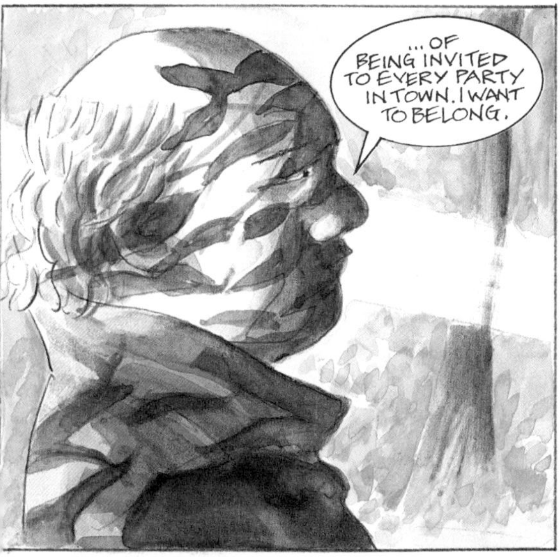
...OF BEING INVITED TO EVERY PARTY IN TOWN. I WANT TO BELONG.

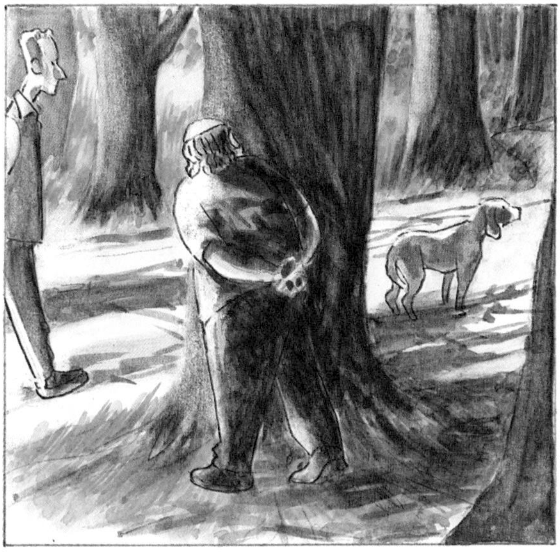

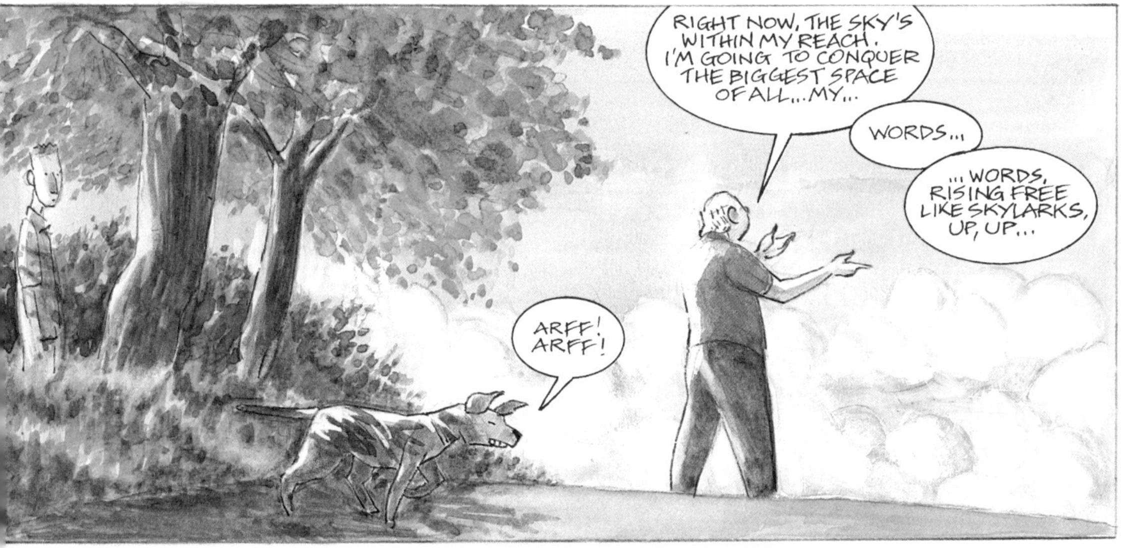
RIGHT NOW, THE SKY'S WITHIN MY REACH. I'M GOING TO CONQUER THE BIGGEST SPACE OF ALL... MY...
WORDS...
...WORDS, RISING FREE LIKE SKYLARKS, UP, UP...
ARFF! ARFF!

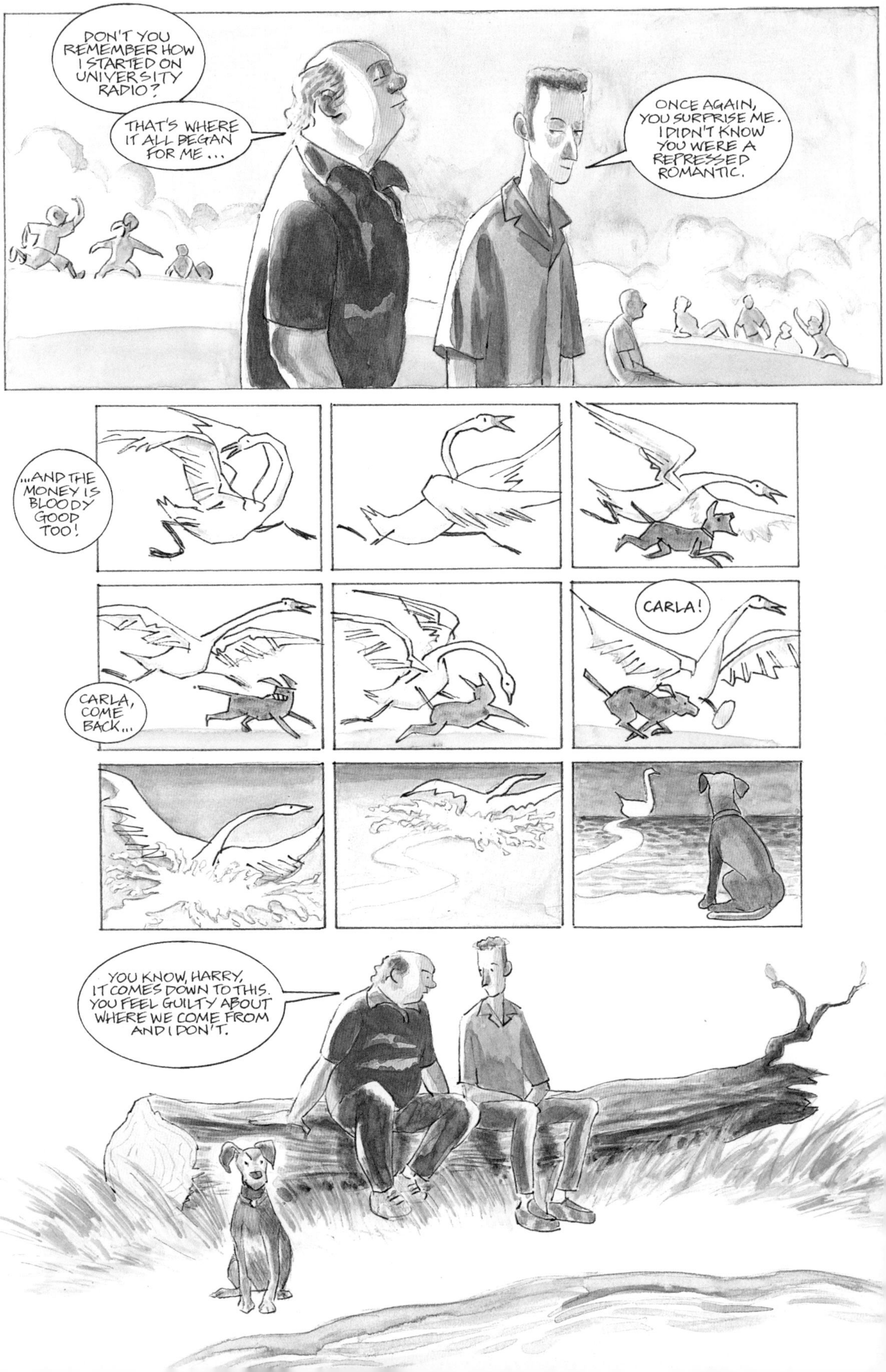
DON'T YOU REMEMBER HOW I STARTED ON UNIVERSITY RADIO?
THAT'S WHERE IT ALL BEGAN FOR ME...
ONCE AGAIN, YOU SURPRISE ME. I DIDN'T KNOW YOU WERE A REPRESSED ROMANTIC.
...AND THE MONEY IS BLOODY GOOD TOO!
CARLA, COME BACK...
CARLA!
YOU KNOW, HARRY, IT COMES DOWN TO THIS. YOU FEEL GUILTY ABOUT WHERE WE COME FROM AND I DON'T.

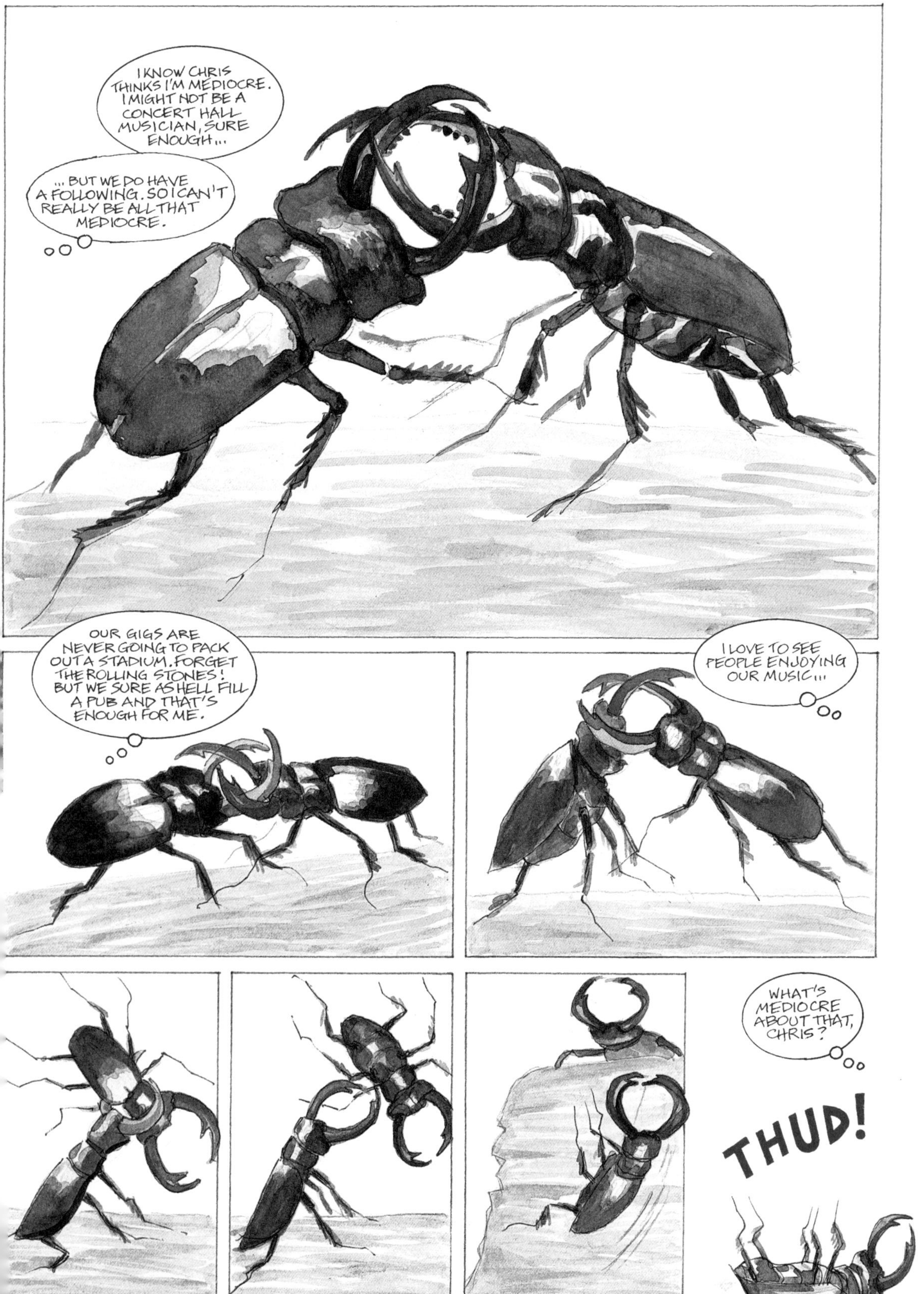
I KNOW CHRIS THINKS I'M MEDIOCRE. I MIGHT NOT BE A CONCERT HALL MUSICIAN, SURE ENOUGH...
... BUT WE DO HAVE A FOLLOWING. SO I CAN'T REALLY BE ALL THAT MEDIOCRE.
OUR GIGS ARE NEVER GOING TO PACK OUT A STADIUM. FORGET THE ROLLING STONES! BUT WE SURE AS HELL FILL A PUB AND THAT'S ENOUGH FOR ME.
I LOVE TO SEE PEOPLE ENJOYING OUR MUSIC...
WHAT'S MEDIOCRE ABOUT THAT, CHRIS?
THUD!

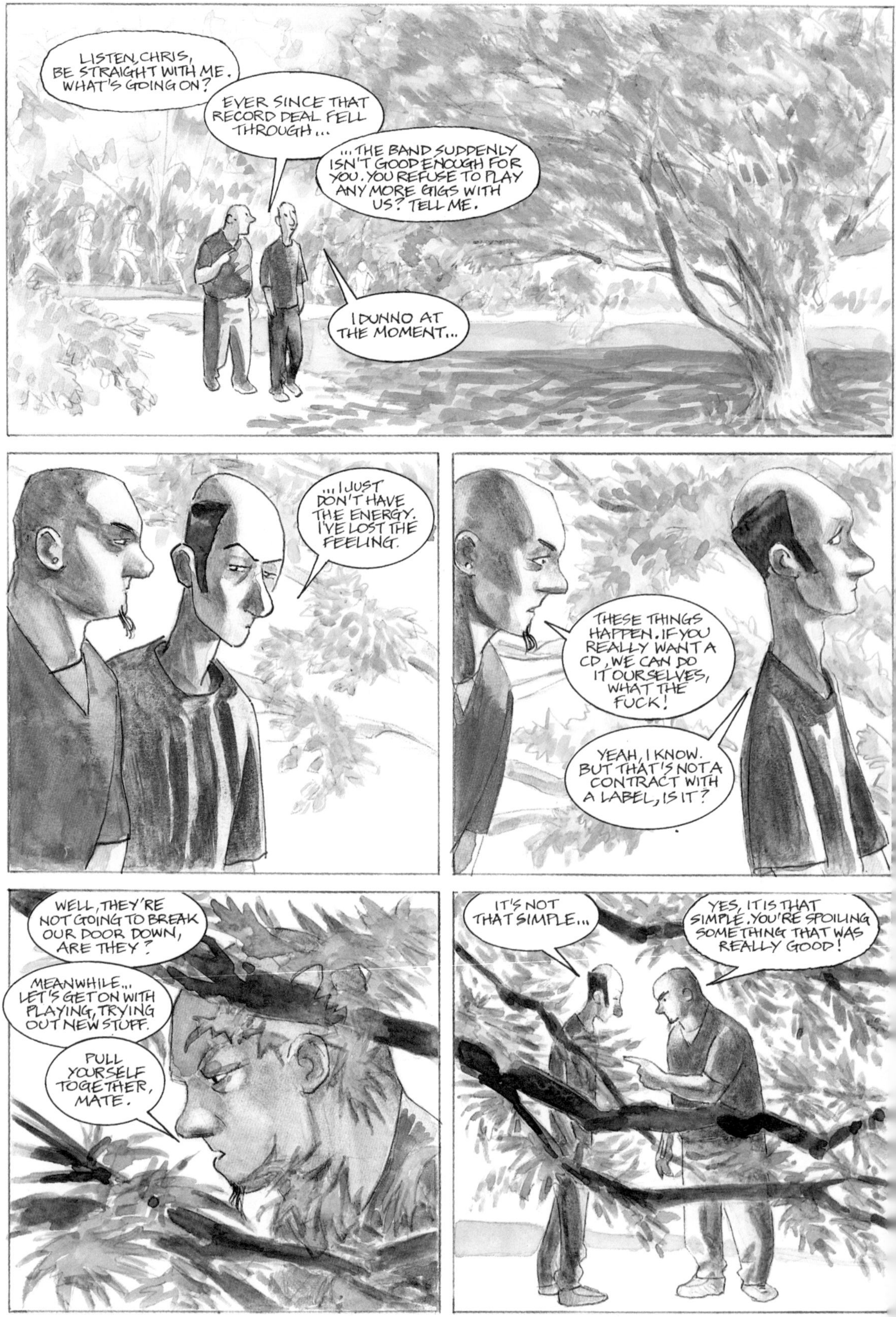
LISTEN, CHRIS, BE STRAIGHT WITH ME. WHAT'S GOING ON?
EVER SINCE THAT RECORD DEAL FELL THROUGH...
...THE BAND SUDDENLY ISN'T GOOD ENOUGH FOR YOU. YOU REFUSE TO PLAY ANY MORE GIGS WITH US? TELL ME.
I DUNNO AT THE MOMENT...
...I JUST DON'T HAVE THE ENERGY. I'VE LOST THE FEELING.
THESE THINGS HAPPEN. IF YOU REALLY WANT A CD, WE CAN DO IT OURSELVES, WHAT THE FUCK!
YEAH, I KNOW. BUT THAT'S NOT A CONTRACT WITH A LABEL, IS IT?
WELL, THEY'RE NOT GOING TO BREAK OUR DOOR DOWN, ARE THEY?
MEANWHILE... LET'S GET ON WITH PLAYING, TRYING OUT NEW STUFF.
PULL YOURSELF TOGETHER, MATE.
IT'S NOT THAT SIMPLE...
YES, IT IS THAT SIMPLE. YOU'RE SPOILING SOMETHING THAT WAS REALLY GOOD!

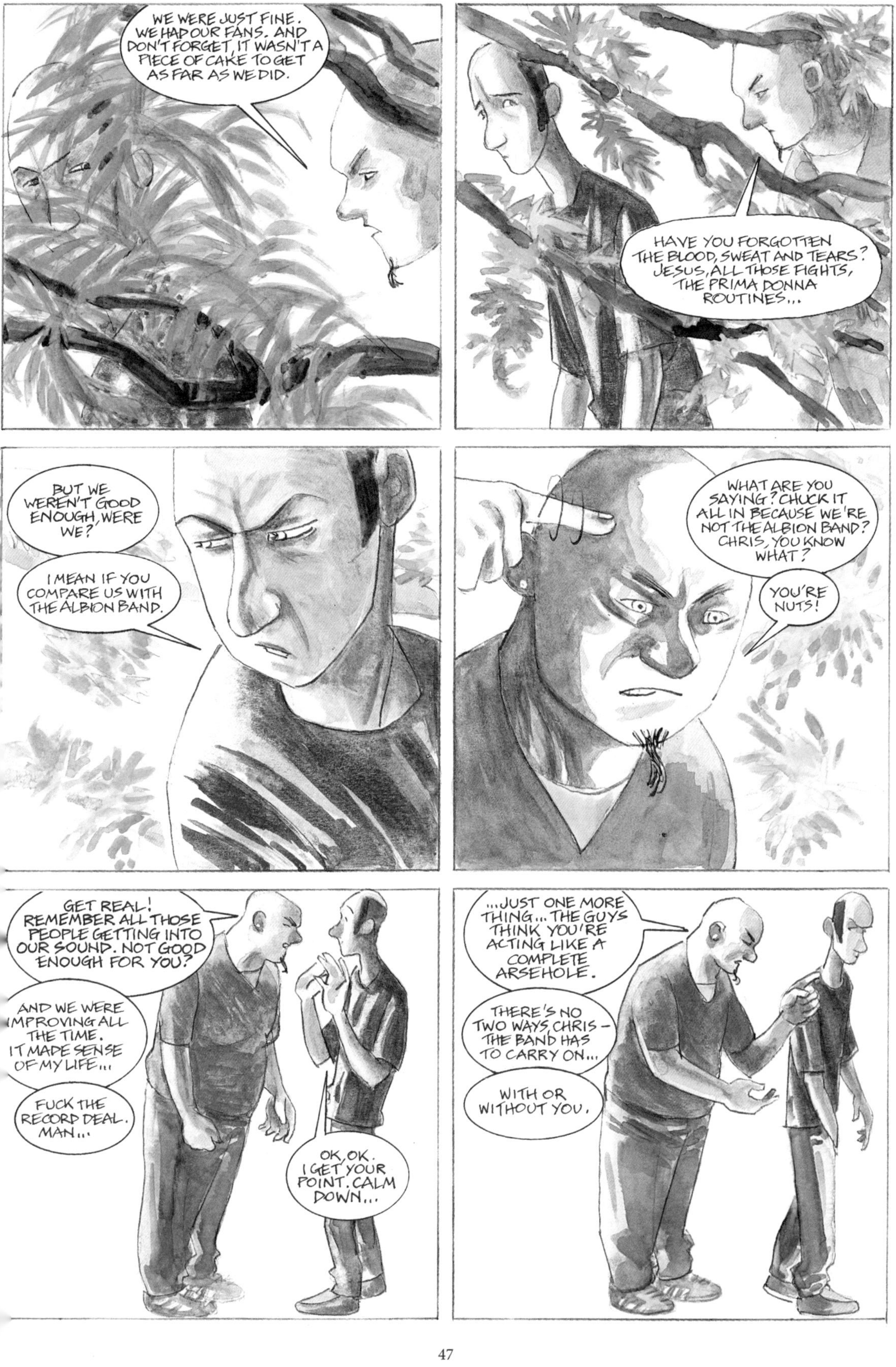
WE WERE JUST FINE. WE HAD OUR FANS. AND DON'T FORGET, IT WASN'T A PIECE OF CAKE TO GET AS FAR AS WE DID.
HAVE YOU FORGOTTEN THE BLOOD, SWEAT AND TEARS? JESUS, ALL THOSE FIGHTS, THE PRIMA DONNA ROUTINES...
BUT WE WEREN'T GOOD ENOUGH, WERE WE?
I MEAN IF YOU COMPARE US WITH THE ALBION BAND.
WHAT ARE YOU SAYING? CHUCK IT ALL IN BECAUSE WE'RE NOT THE ALBION BAND? CHRIS, YOU KNOW WHAT?
YOU'RE NUTS!
GET REAL! REMEMBER ALL THOSE PEOPLE GETTING INTO OUR SOUND. NOT GOOD ENOUGH FOR YOU?
AND WE WERE IMPROVING ALL THE TIME. IT MADE SENSE OF MY LIFE...
FUCK THE RECORD DEAL. MAN...
OK, OK. I GET YOUR POINT. CALM DOWN...
...JUST ONE MORE THING... THE GUYS THINK YOU'RE ACTING LIKE A COMPLETE ARSEHOLE.
THERE'S NO TWO WAYS, CHRIS – THE BAND HAS TO CARRY ON...
WITH OR WITHOUT YOU.

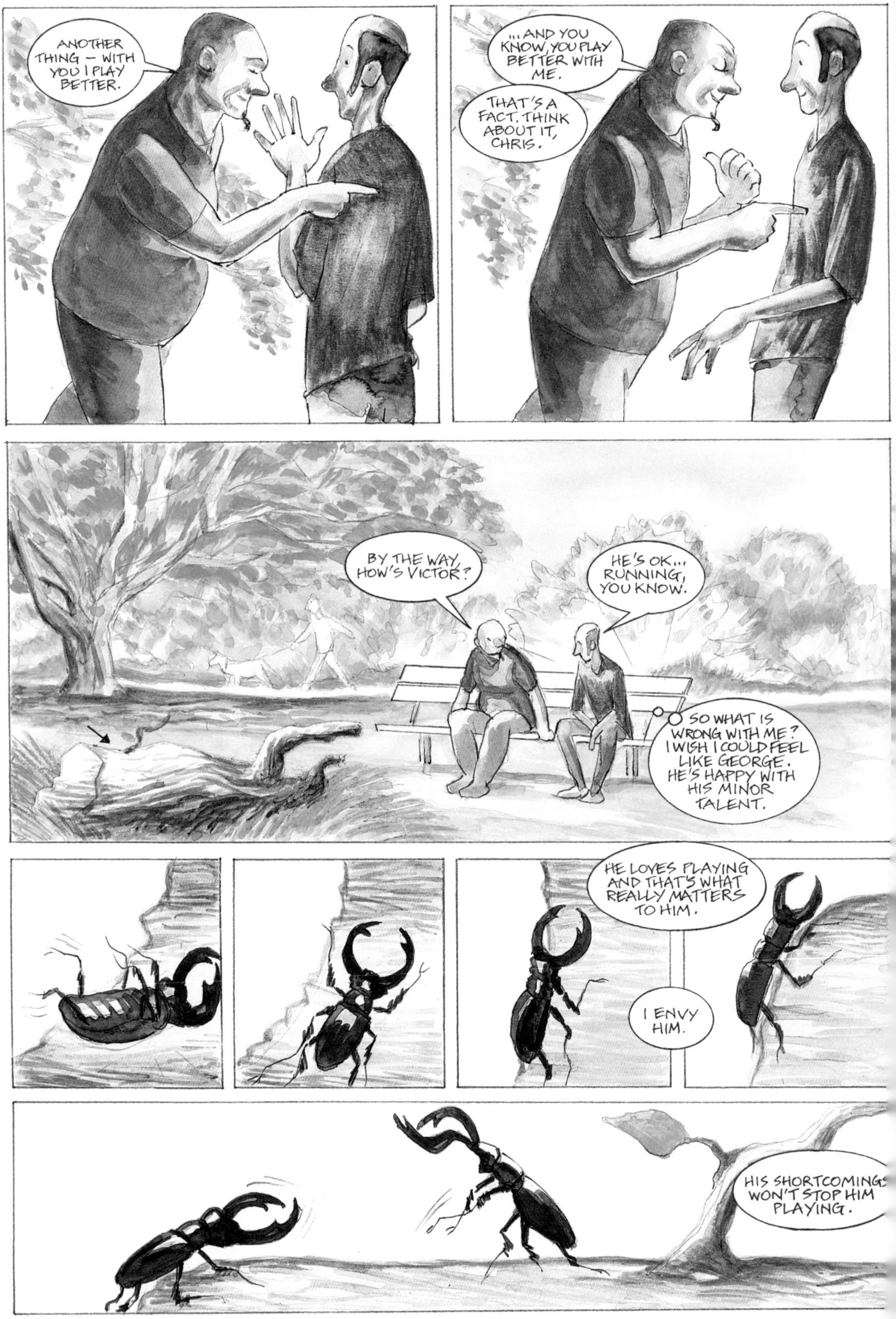
ANOTHER THING – WITH YOU I PLAY BETTER.
...AND YOU KNOW, YOU PLAY BETTER WITH ME.
THAT'S A FACT. THINK ABOUT IT, CHRIS.
BY THE WAY, HOW'S VICTOR?
HE'S OK... RUNNING, YOU KNOW.
SO WHAT IS WRONG WITH ME? I WISH I COULD FEEL LIKE GEORGE. HE'S HAPPY WITH HIS MINOR TALENT.
HE LOVES PLAYING AND THAT'S WHAT REALLY MATTERS TO HIM.
I ENVY HIM.
HIS SHORTCOMINGS WON'T STOP HIM PLAYING.

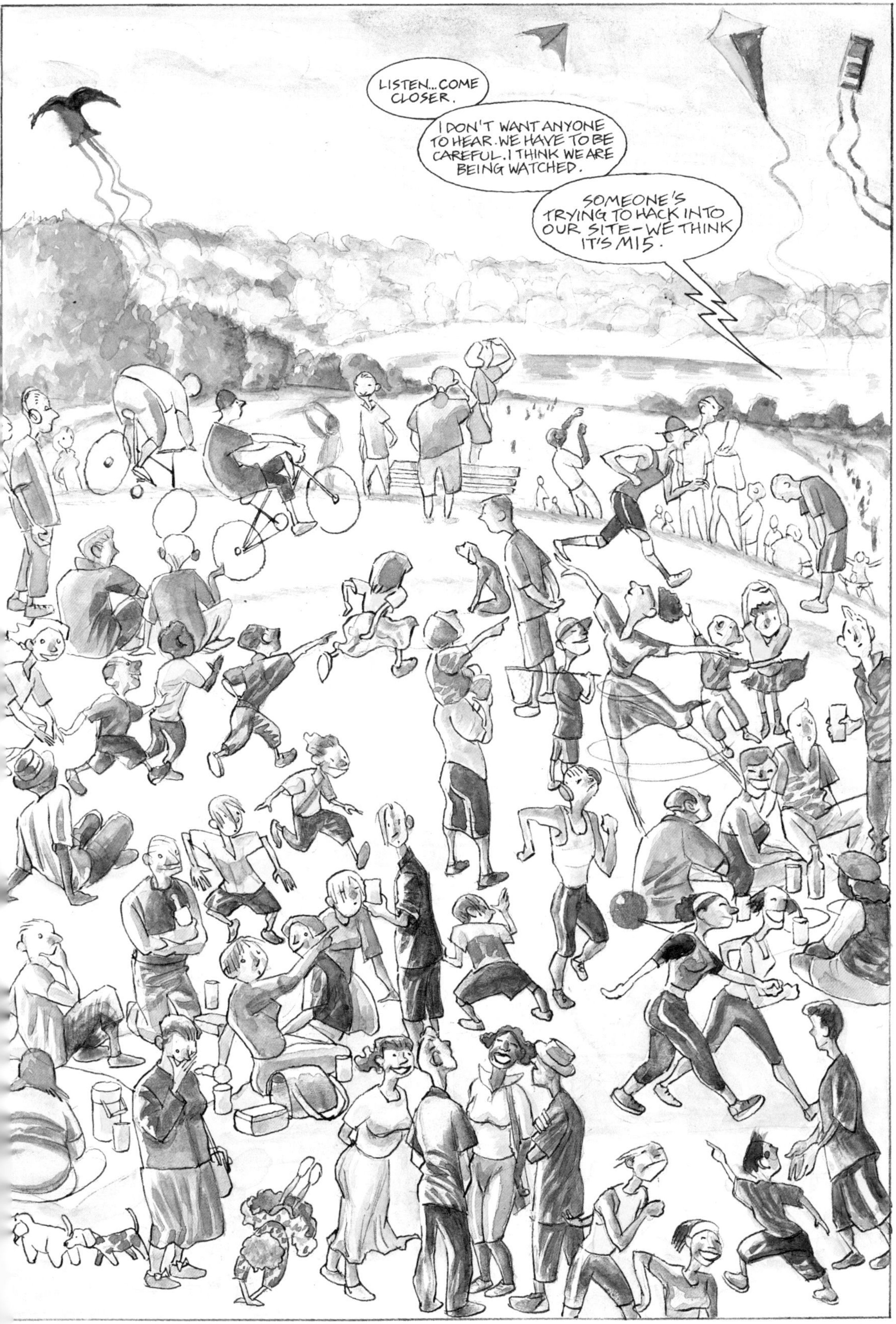
LISTEN...COME CLOSER.
I DON'T WANT ANYONE TO HEAR. WE HAVE TO BE CAREFUL. I THINK WE ARE BEING WATCHED.
SOMEONE'S TRYING TO HACK INTO OUR SITE– WE THINK IT'S MI5.

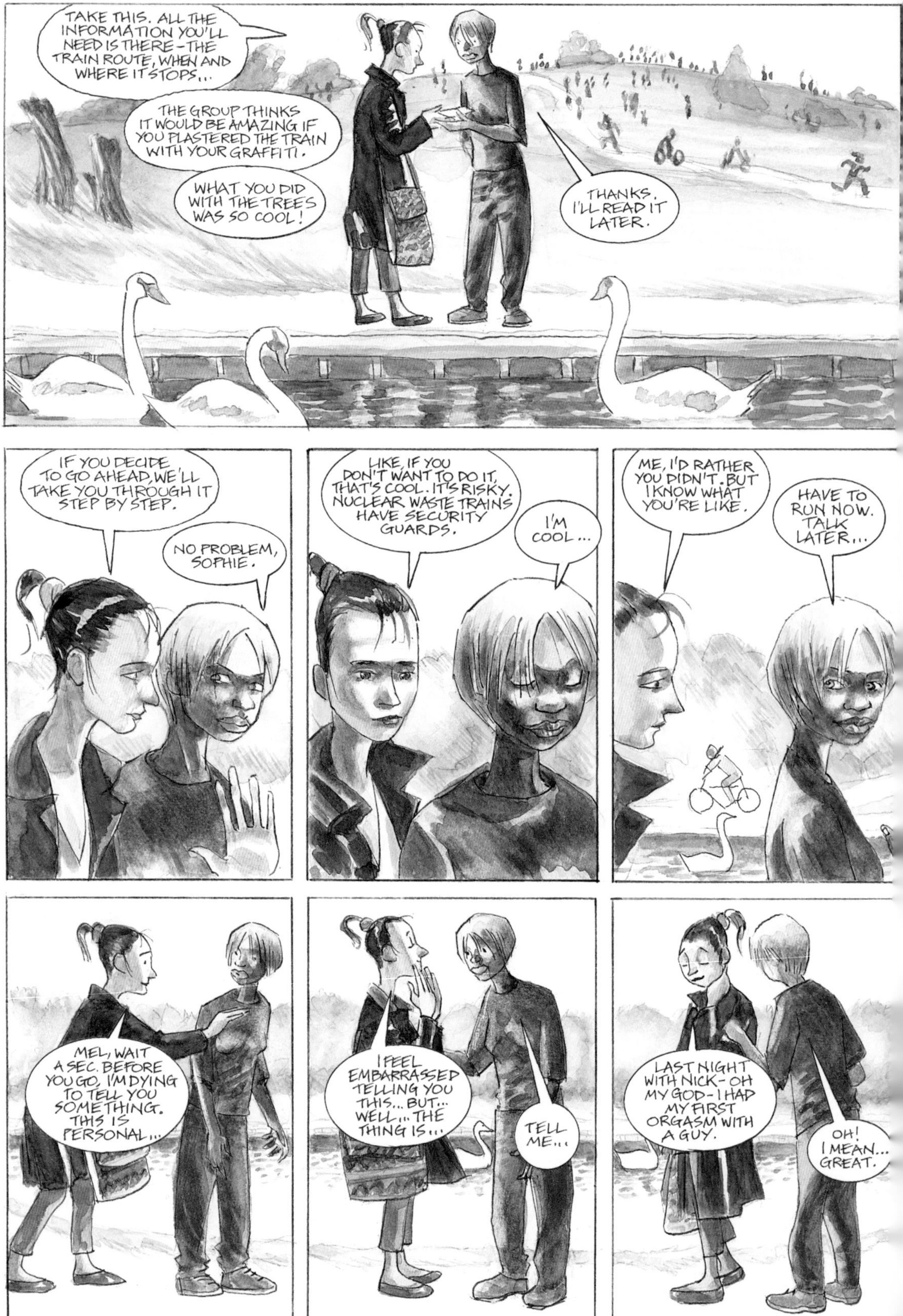
TAKE THIS. ALL THE INFORMATION YOU'LL NEED IS THERE - THE TRAIN ROUTE, WHEN AND WHERE IT STOPS...
THE GROUP THINKS IT WOULD BE AMAZING IF YOU PLASTERED THE TRAIN WITH YOUR GRAFFITI.
WHAT YOU DID WITH THE TREES WAS SO COOL!
THANKS. I'LL READ IT LATER.
IF YOU DECIDE TO GO AHEAD, WE'LL TAKE YOU THROUGH IT STEP BY STEP.
NO PROBLEM, SOPHIE.
LIKE, IF YOU DON'T WANT TO DO IT, THAT'S COOL. IT'S RISKY. NUCLEAR WASTE TRAINS HAVE SECURITY GUARDS.
I'M COOL...
ME, I'D RATHER YOU DIDN'T. BUT I KNOW WHAT YOU'RE LIKE.
HAVE TO RUN NOW. TALK LATER...
MEL, WAIT A SEC. BEFORE YOU GO, I'M DYING TO TELL YOU SOMETHING. THIS IS PERSONAL...
I FEEL EMBARRASSED TELLING YOU THIS... BUT... WELL... THE THING IS...
TELL ME...
LAST NIGHT WITH NICK - OH MY GOD - I HAD MY FIRST ORGASM WITH A GUY.
OH! I MEAN... GREAT.

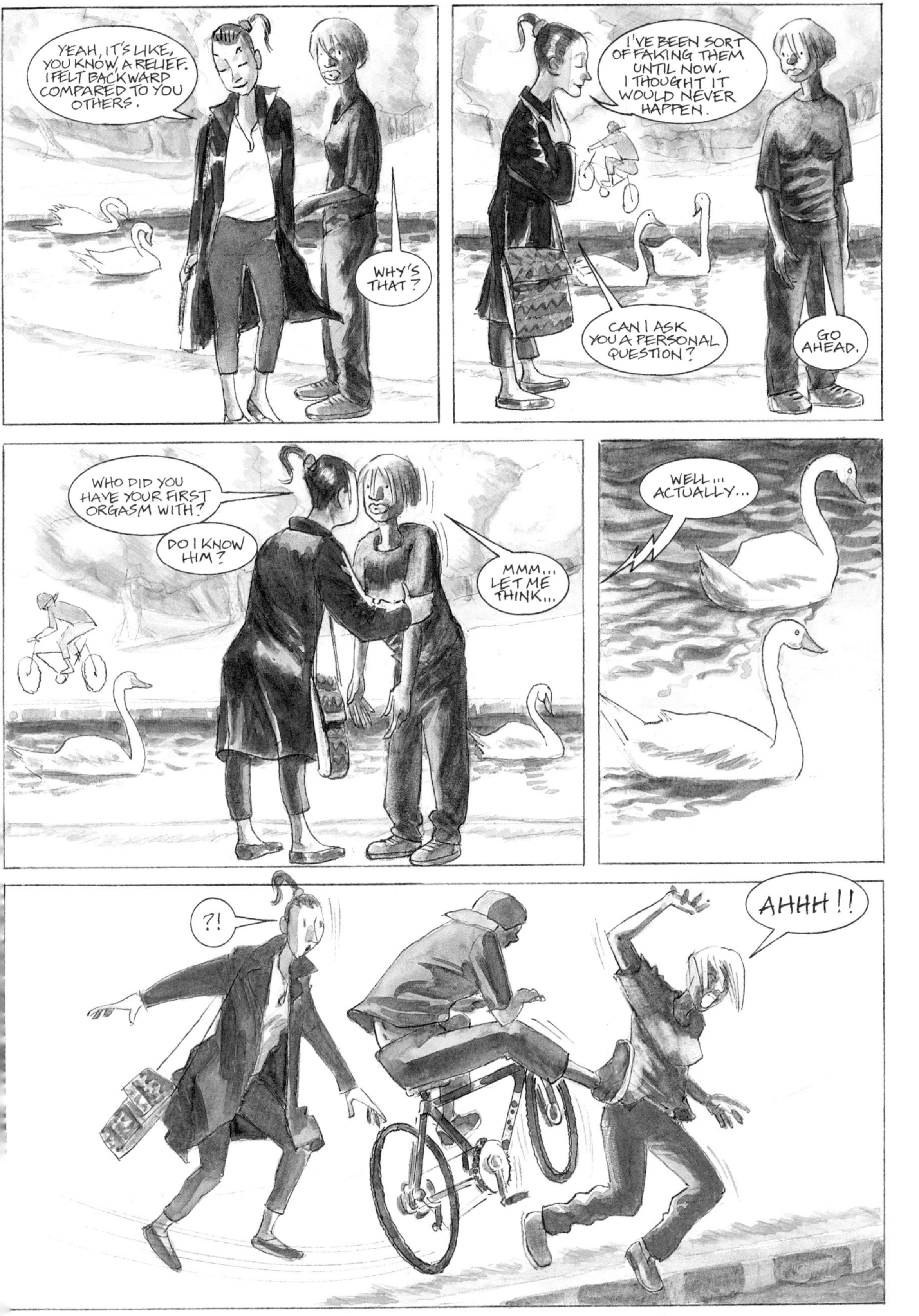
YEAH, IT'S LIKE, YOU KNOW, A RELIEF. I FELT BACKWARD COMPARED TO YOU OTHERS.
WHY'S THAT?
I'VE BEEN SORT OF FAKING THEM UNTIL NOW. I THOUGHT IT WOULD NEVER HAPPEN.
CAN I ASK YOU A PERSONAL QUESTION?
GO AHEAD.
WHO DID YOU HAVE YOUR FIRST ORGASM WITH?
DO I KNOW HIM?
MMM... LET ME THINK...
WELL... ACTUALLY...
?!
AHHH!!

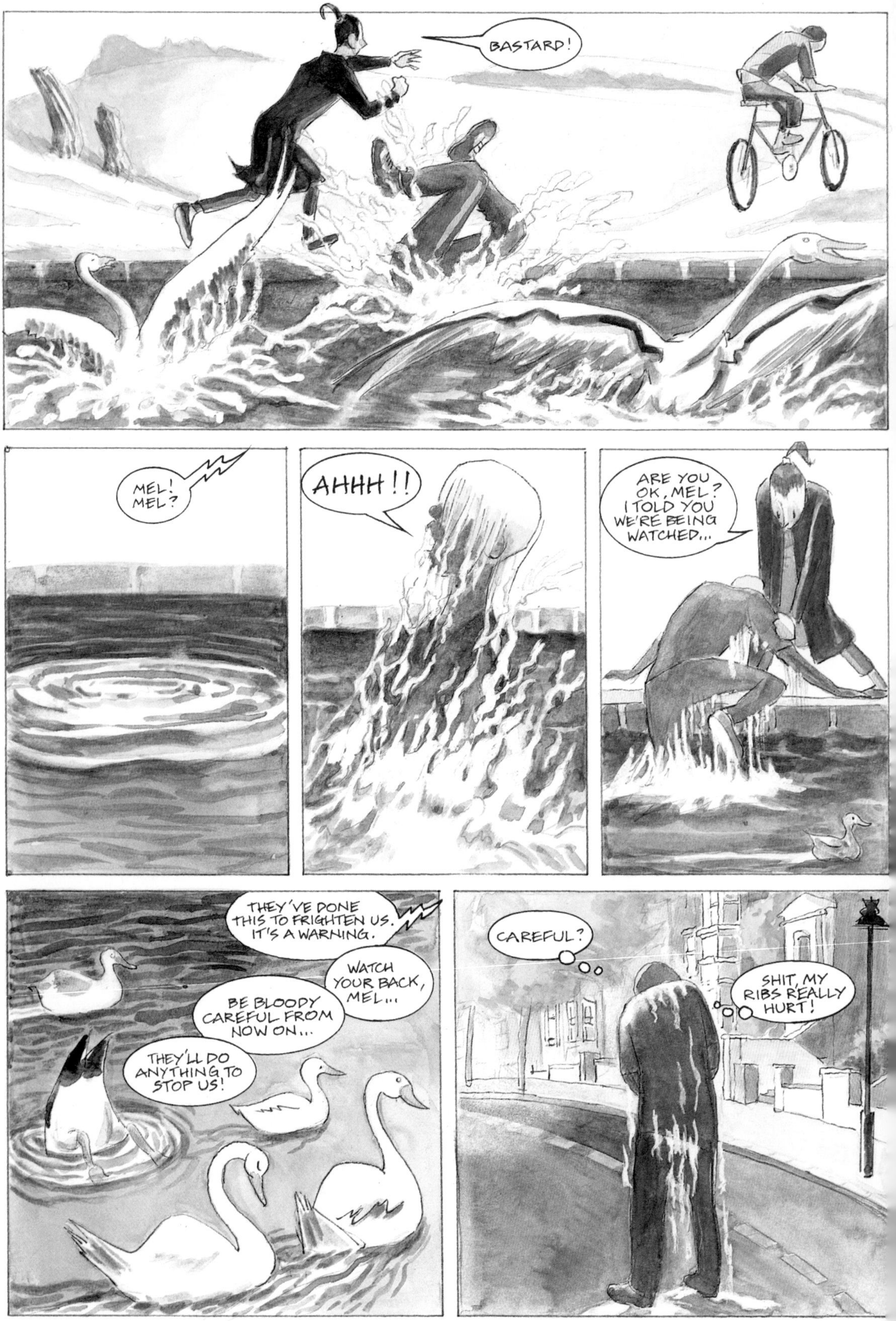
BASTARD!
MEL! MEL?
AHHH!!
ARE YOU OK, MEL? I TOLD YOU WE'RE BEING WATCHED...
THEY'VE DONE THIS TO FRIGHTEN US. IT'S A WARNING.
WATCH YOUR BACK, MEL...
BE BLOODY CAREFUL FROM NOW ON...
THEY'LL DO ANYTHING TO STOP US!
CAREFUL?
SHIT, MY RIBS REALLY HURT!

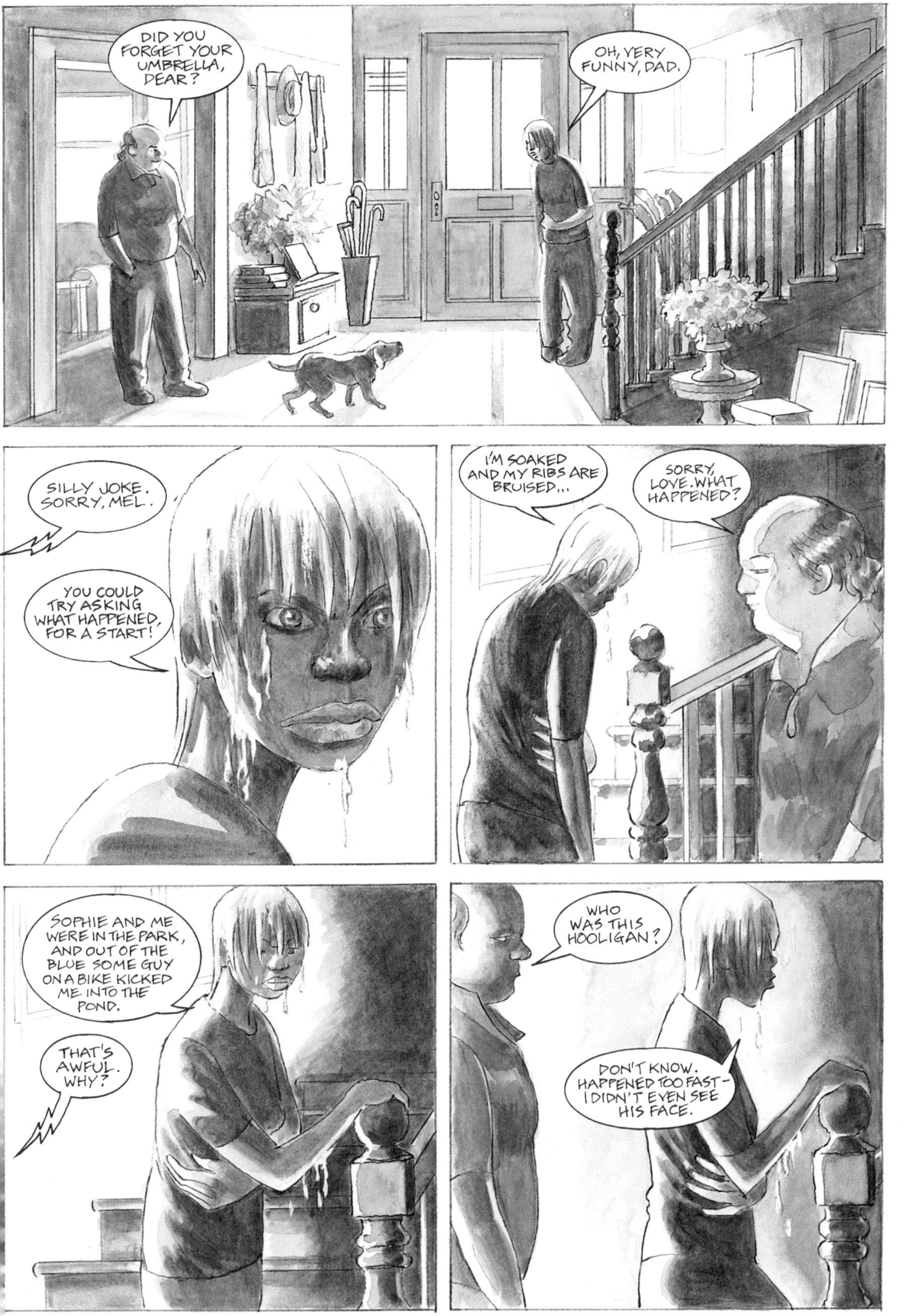
DID YOU FORGET YOUR UMBRELLA, DEAR?
OH, VERY FUNNY, DAD.
SILLY JOKE. SORRY, MEL.
YOU COULD TRY ASKING WHAT HAPPENED, FOR A START!
I'M SOAKED AND MY RIBS ARE BRUISED...
SORRY, LOVE. WHAT HAPPENED?
SOPHIE AND ME WERE IN THE PARK, AND OUT OF THE BLUE SOME GUY ON A BIKE KICKED ME INTO THE POND.
THAT'S AWFUL. WHY?
WHO WAS THIS HOOLIGAN?
DON'T KNOW. HAPPENED TOO FAST- I DIDN'T EVEN SEE HIS FACE.

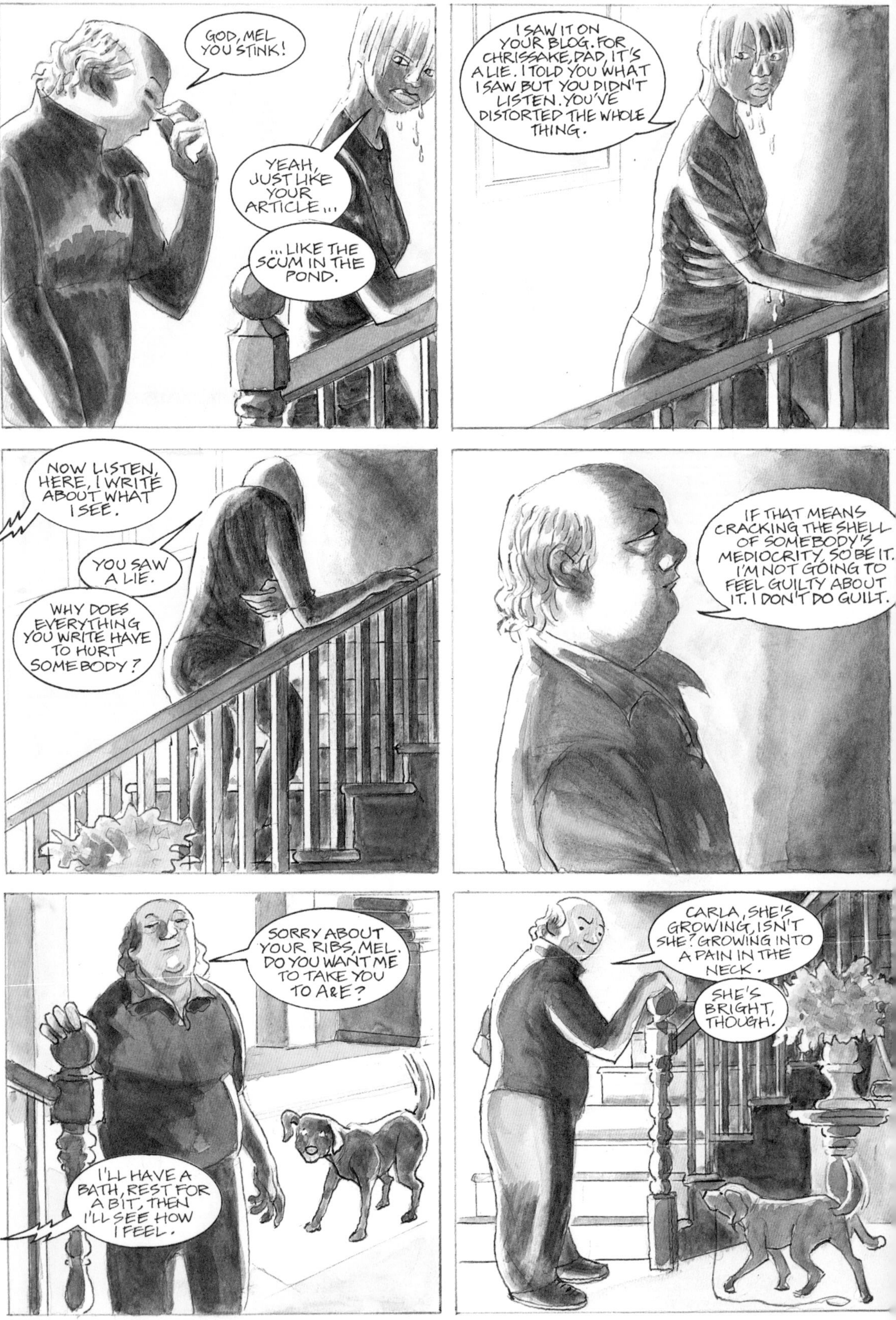
GOD, MEL YOU STINK!
YEAH, JUST LIKE YOUR ARTICLE...
...LIKE THE SCUM IN THE POND.
I SAW IT ON YOUR BLOG. FOR CHRISSAKE, DAD, IT'S A LIE. I TOLD YOU WHAT I SAW BUT YOU DIDN'T LISTEN. YOU'VE DISTORTED THE WHOLE THING.
NOW LISTEN, HERE, I WRITE ABOUT WHAT I SEE.
YOU SAW A LIE.
WHY DOES EVERYTHING YOU WRITE HAVE TO HURT SOMEBODY?
IF THAT MEANS CRACKING THE SHELL OF SOMEBODY'S MEDIOCRITY, SO BE IT. I'M NOT GOING TO FEEL GUILTY ABOUT IT. I DON'T DO GUILT.
SORRY ABOUT YOUR RIBS, MEL. DO YOU WANT ME TO TAKE YOU TO A&E?
I'LL HAVE A BATH, REST FOR A BIT, THEN I'LL SEE HOW I FEEL.
CARLA, SHE'S GROWING, ISN'T SHE? GROWING INTO A PAIN IN THE NECK.
SHE'S BRIGHT, THOUGH.

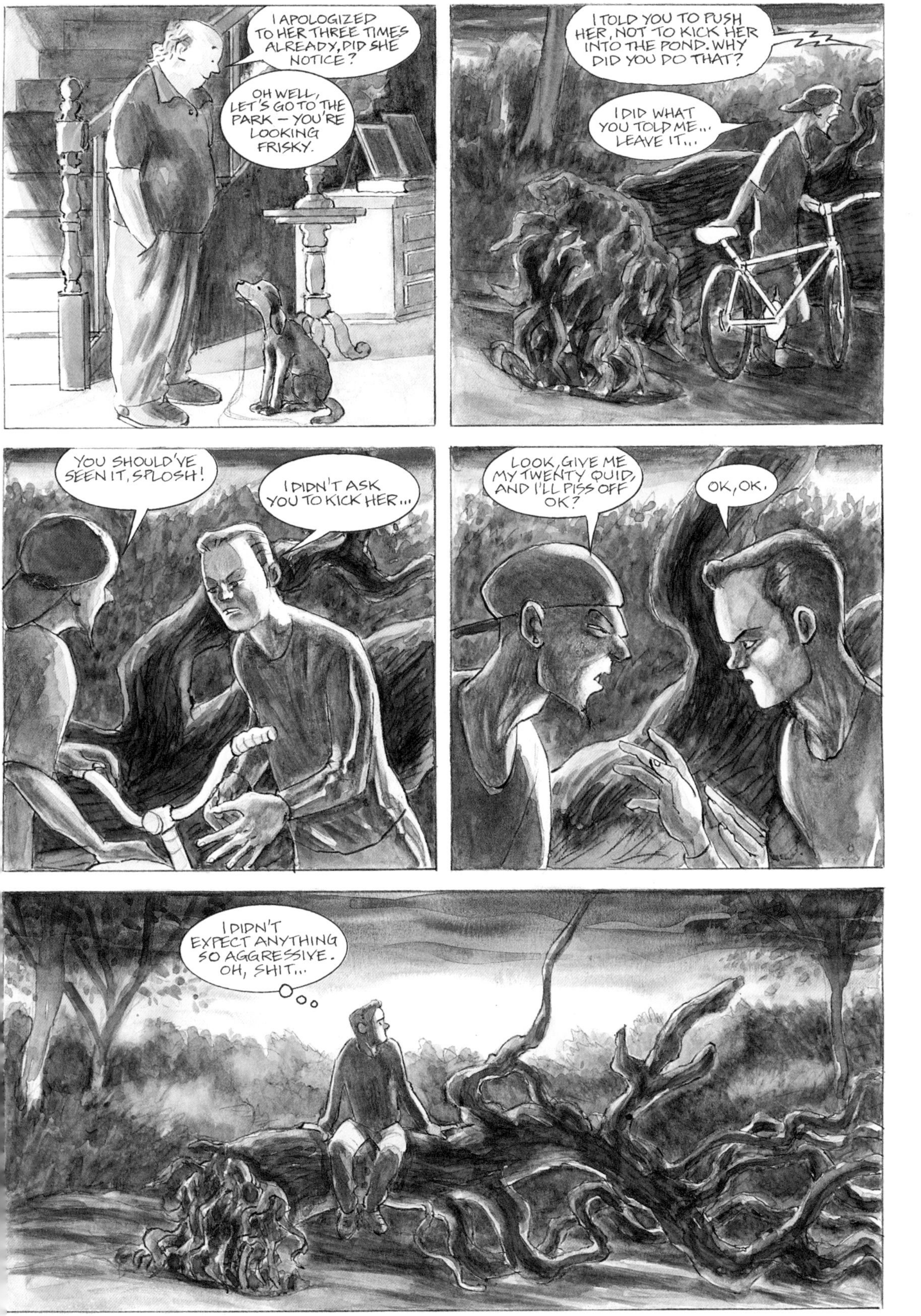
I APOLOGIZED TO HER THREE TIMES ALREADY, DID SHE NOTICE?
OH WELL, LET'S GO TO THE PARK – YOU'RE LOOKING FRISKY.
I TOLD YOU TO PUSH HER, NOT TO KICK HER INTO THE POND. WHY DID YOU DO THAT?
I DID WHAT YOU TOLD ME... LEAVE IT...
YOU SHOULD'VE SEEN IT, SPLOSH!
I DIDN'T ASK YOU TO KICK HER...
LOOK, GIVE ME MY TWENTY QUID, AND I'LL PISS OFF OK?
OK, OK.
I DIDN'T EXPECT ANYTHING SO AGGRESSIVE. OH, SHIT...

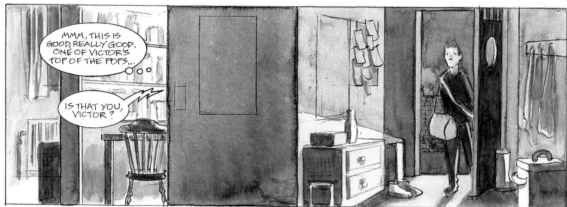

MMM, THIS IS GOOD, REALLY GOOD, ONE OF VICTOR'S TOP OF THE POPS...

IS THAT YOU, VICTOR?

SUPPER'S READY, ONE OF YOUR SPECIALS.

I'M NOT HUNGRY, DAD. I HAD SOMETHING TO EAT WITH FRIENDS AFTER THE GYM.

...NIGHT, DAD.

BUT I DID ONE OF YOUR SPECIALS...

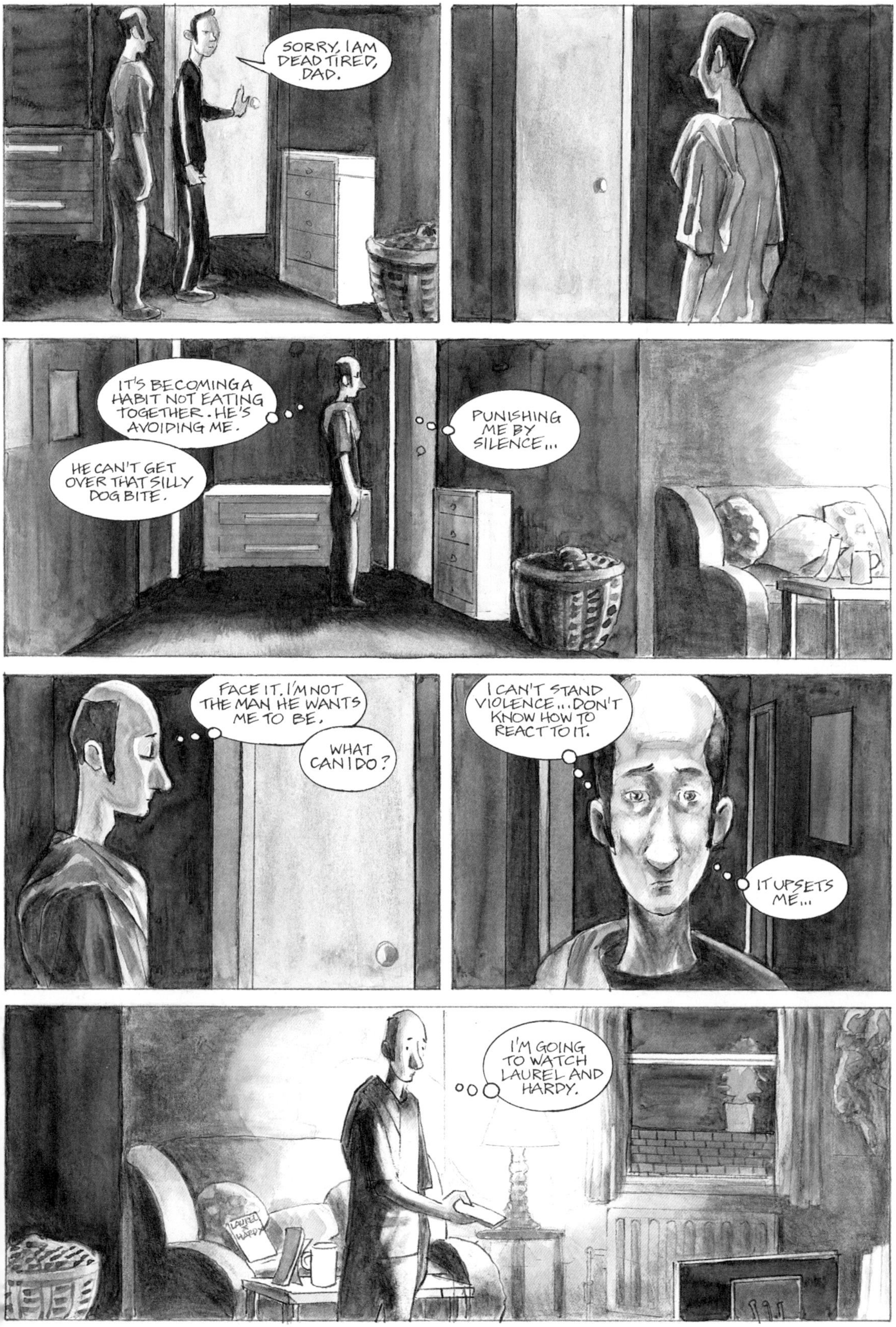
SORRY, I AM DEAD TIRED, DAD.
IT'S BECOMING A HABIT NOT EATING TOGETHER. HE'S AVOIDING ME.
HE CAN'T GET OVER THAT SILLY DOG BITE.
PUNISHING ME BY SILENCE...
FACE IT. I'M NOT THE MAN HE WANTS ME TO BE.
WHAT CAN I DO?
I CAN'T STAND VIOLENCE... DON'T KNOW HOW TO REACT TO IT.
IT UPSETS ME...
I'M GOING TO WATCH LAUREL AND HARDY.
LAUREL & HARDY

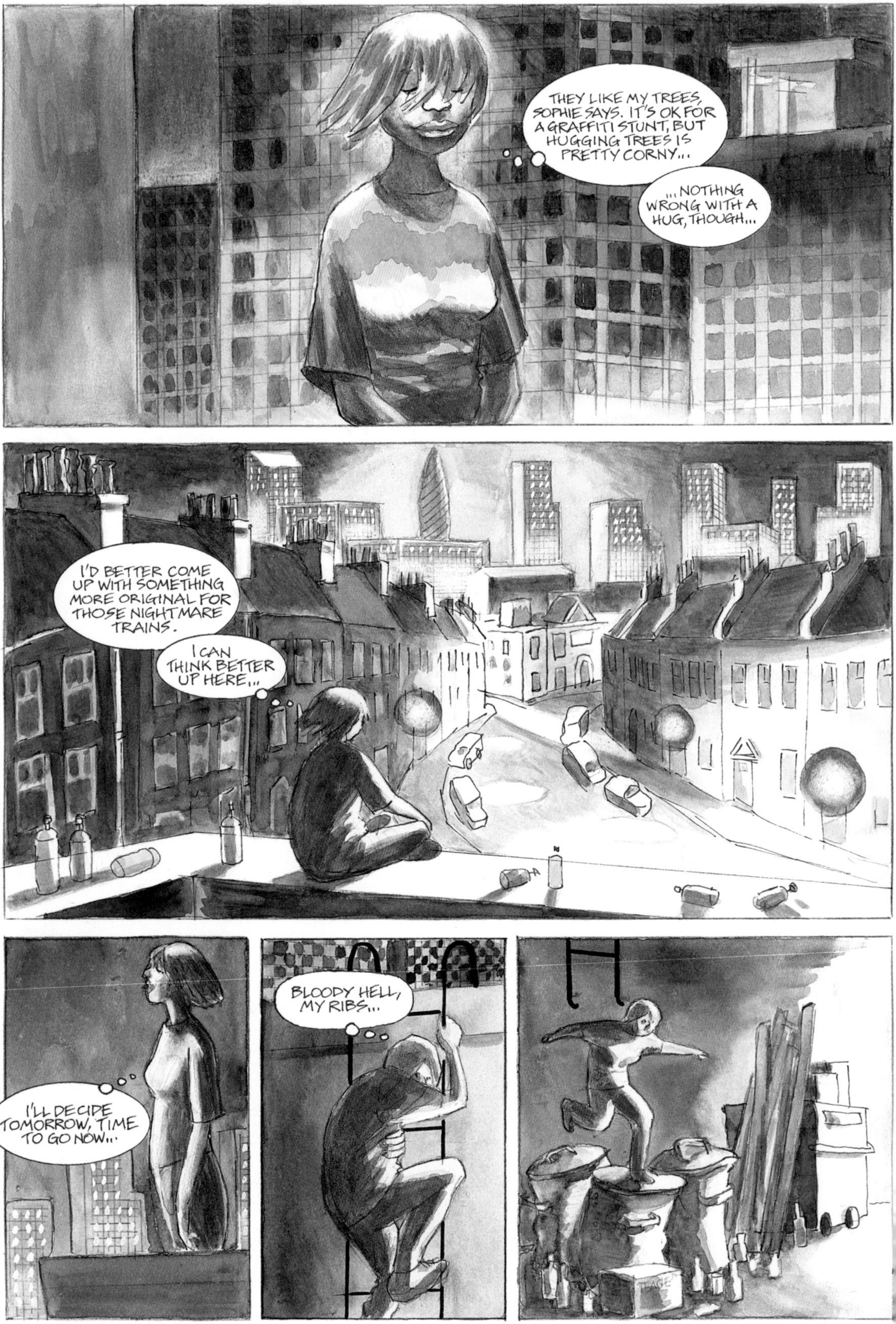
THEY LIKE MY TREES, SOPHIE SAYS. IT'S OK FOR A GRAFFITI STUNT, BUT HUGGING TREES IS PRETTY CORNY...
...NOTHING WRONG WITH A HUG, THOUGH...
I'D BETTER COME UP WITH SOMETHING MORE ORIGINAL FOR THOSE NIGHTMARE TRAINS.
I CAN THINK BETTER UP HERE...
I'LL DECIDE TOMORROW, TIME TO GO NOW...
BLOODY HELL, MY RIBS...

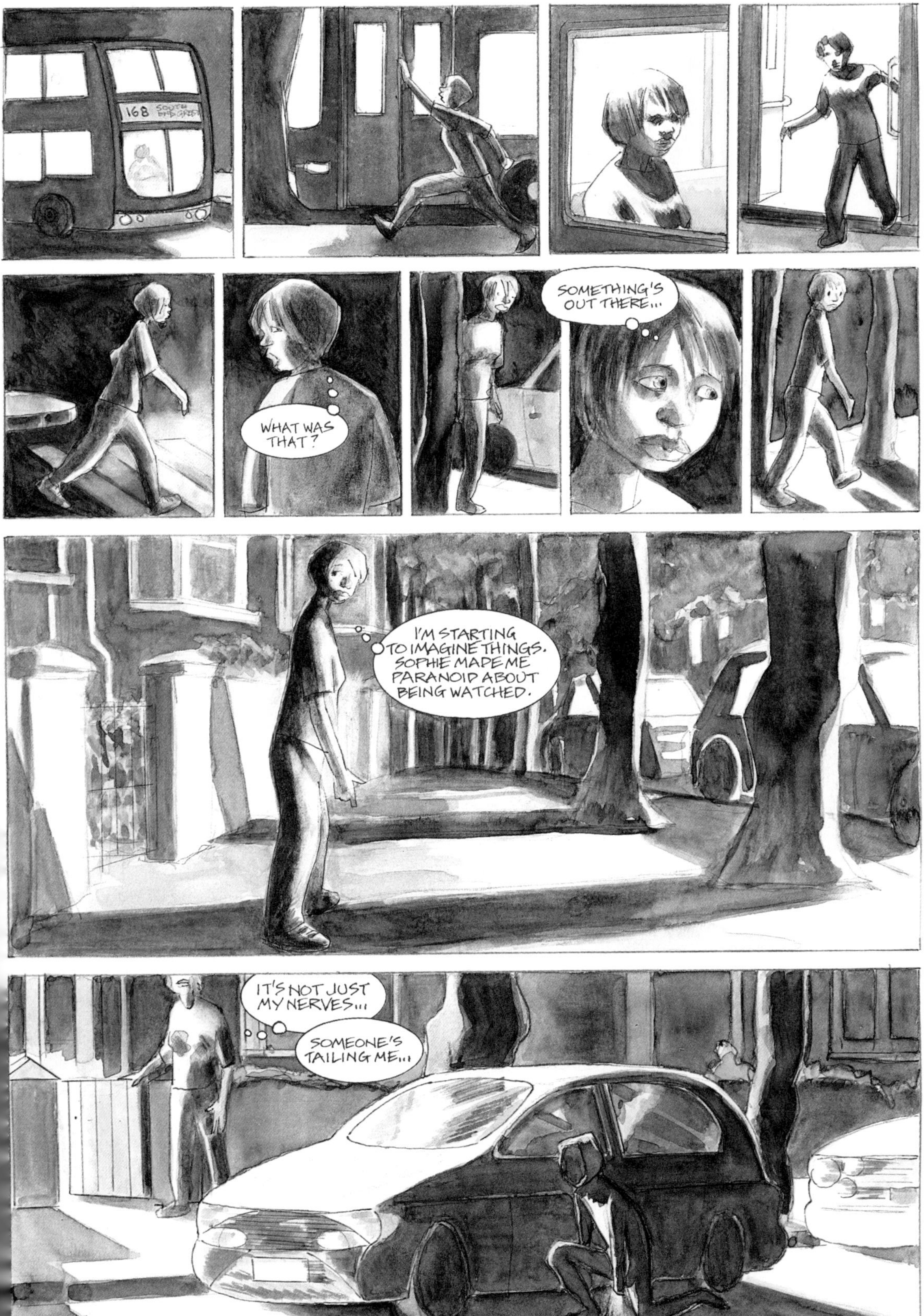
168 SOUTH END GREEN
WHAT WAS THAT?
SOMETHING'S OUT THERE...
I'M STARTING TO IMAGINE THINGS. SOPHIE MADE ME PARANOID ABOUT BEING WATCHED.
IT'S NOT JUST MY NERVES...
SOMEONE'S TAILING ME...

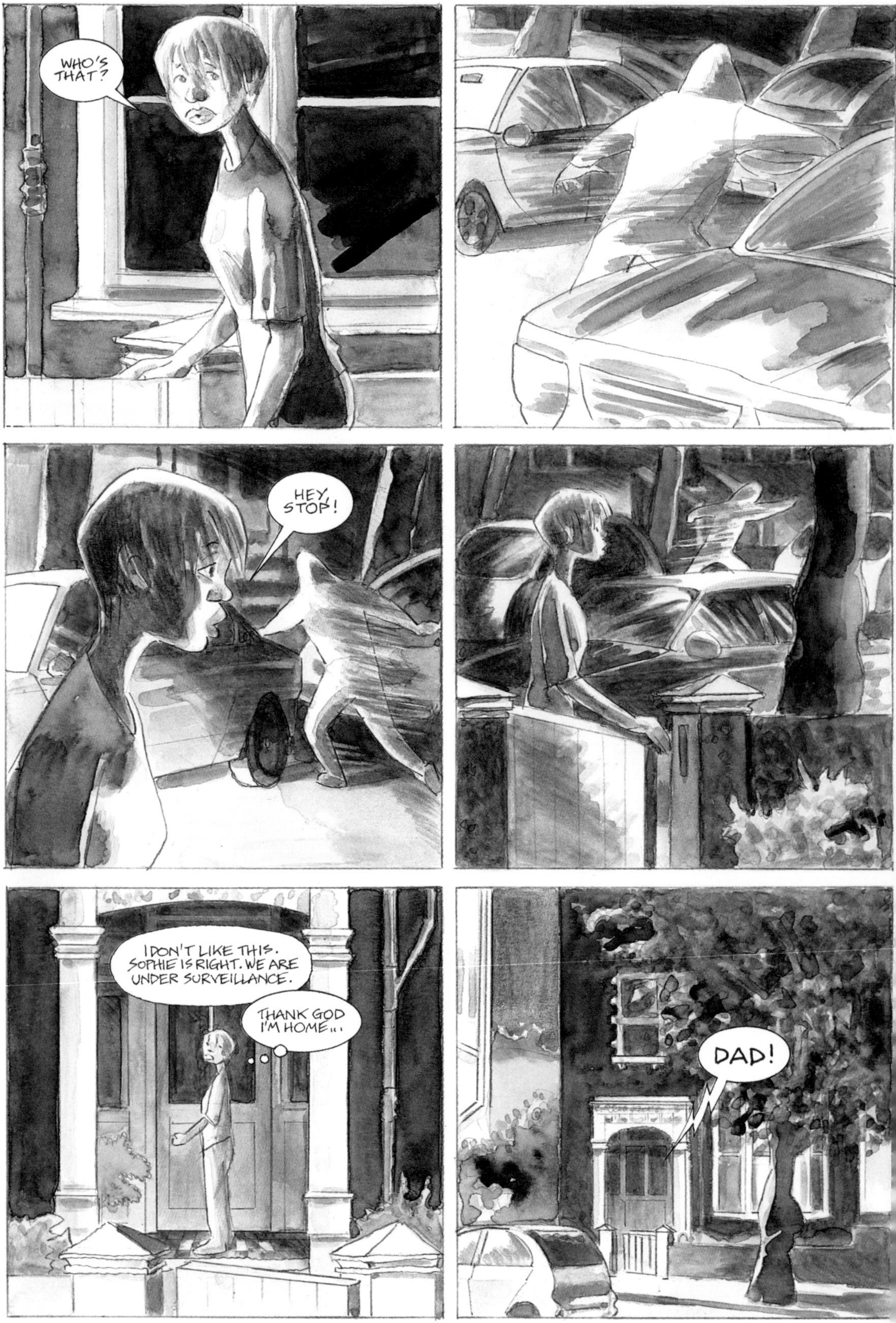
WHO'S THAT?
HEY, STOP!
I DON'T LIKE THIS. SOPHIE IS RIGHT. WE ARE UNDER SURVEILLANCE.
THANK GOD I'M HOME...
DAD!

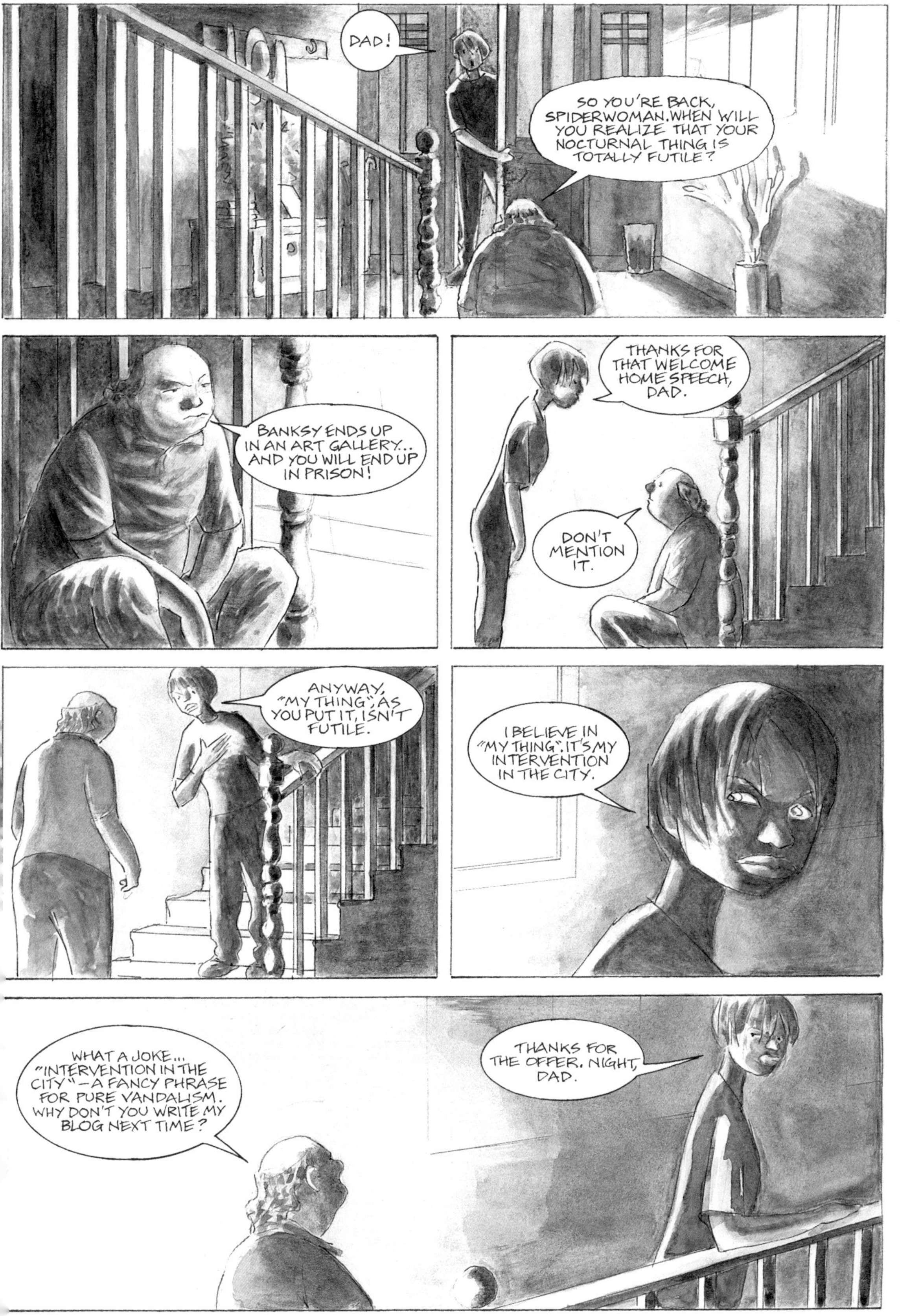
DAD!
SO YOU'RE BACK, SPIDERWOMAN. WHEN WILL YOU REALIZE THAT YOUR NOCTURNAL THING IS TOTALLY FUTILE?
BANKSY ENDS UP IN AN ART GALLERY... AND YOU WILL END UP IN PRISON!
THANKS FOR THAT WELCOME HOME SPEECH, DAD.
DON'T MENTION IT.
ANYWAY, "MY THING", AS YOU PUT IT, ISN'T FUTILE.
I BELIEVE IN "MY THING". IT'S MY INTERVENTION IN THE CITY.
WHAT A JOKE... "INTERVENTION IN THE CITY" – A FANCY PHRASE FOR PURE VANDALISM. WHY DON'T YOU WRITE MY BLOG NEXT TIME?
THANKS FOR THE OFFER. NIGHT, DAD.

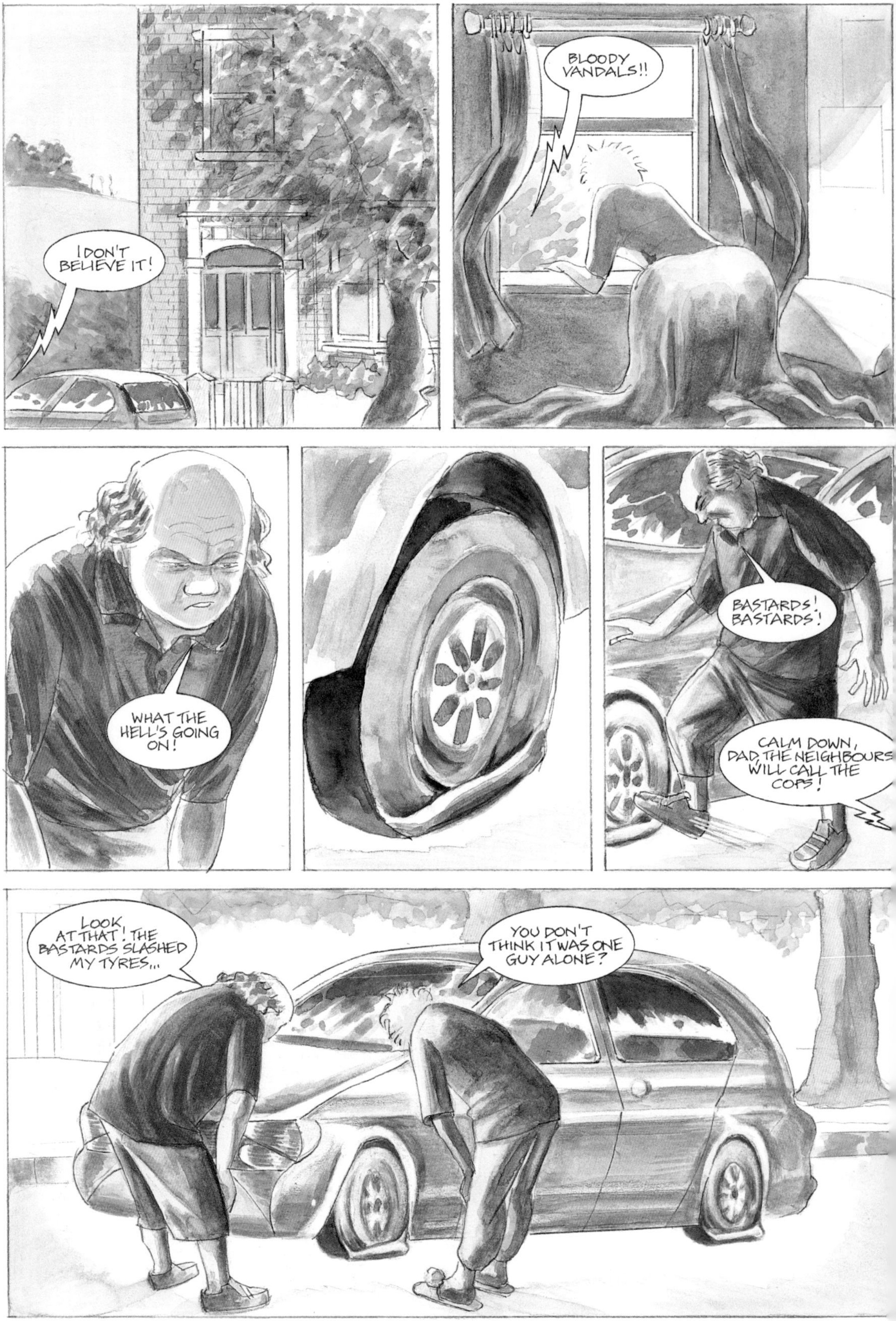
I DON'T BELIEVE IT!
BLOODY VANDALS!!
WHAT THE HELL'S GOING ON!
BASTARDS! BASTARDS!
CALM DOWN, DAD, THE NEIGHBOURS WILL CALL THE COPS!
LOOK AT THAT! THE BASTARDS SLASHED MY TYRES...
YOU DON'T THINK IT WAS ONE GUY ALONE?

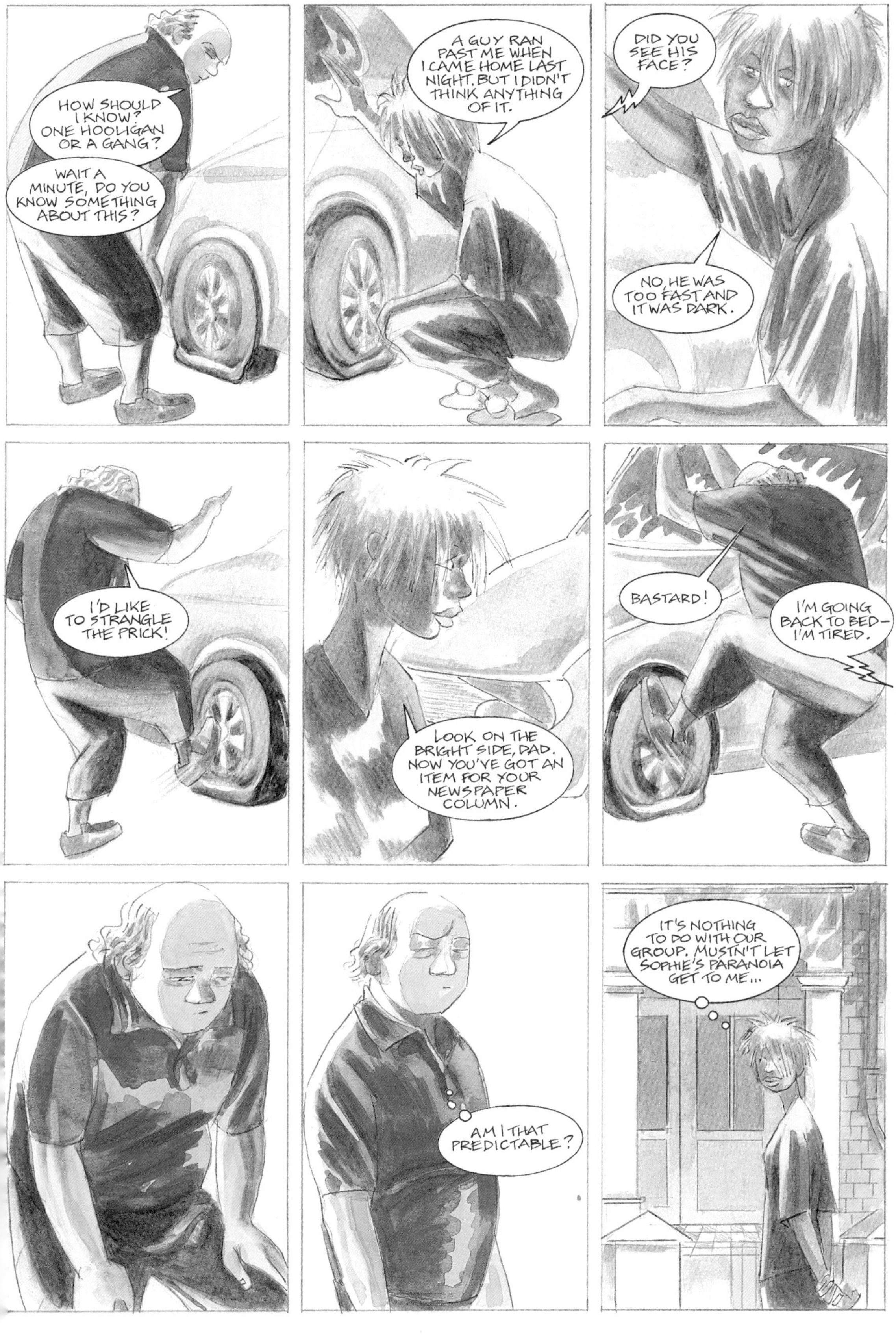
HOW SHOULD I KNOW? ONE HOOLIGAN OR A GANG?
WAIT A MINUTE, DO YOU KNOW SOMETHING ABOUT THIS?
A GUY RAN PAST ME WHEN I CAME HOME LAST NIGHT. BUT I DIDN'T THINK ANYTHING OF IT.
DID YOU SEE HIS FACE?
NO, HE WAS TOO FAST AND IT WAS DARK.
I'D LIKE TO STRANGLE THE PRICK!
LOOK ON THE BRIGHT SIDE, DAD. NOW YOU'VE GOT AN ITEM FOR YOUR NEWSPAPER COLUMN.
BASTARD!
I'M GOING BACK TO BED- I'M TIRED.
AM I THAT PREDICTABLE?
IT'S NOTHING TO DO WITH OUR GROUP. MUSTN'T LET SOPHIE'S PARANOIA GET TO ME...

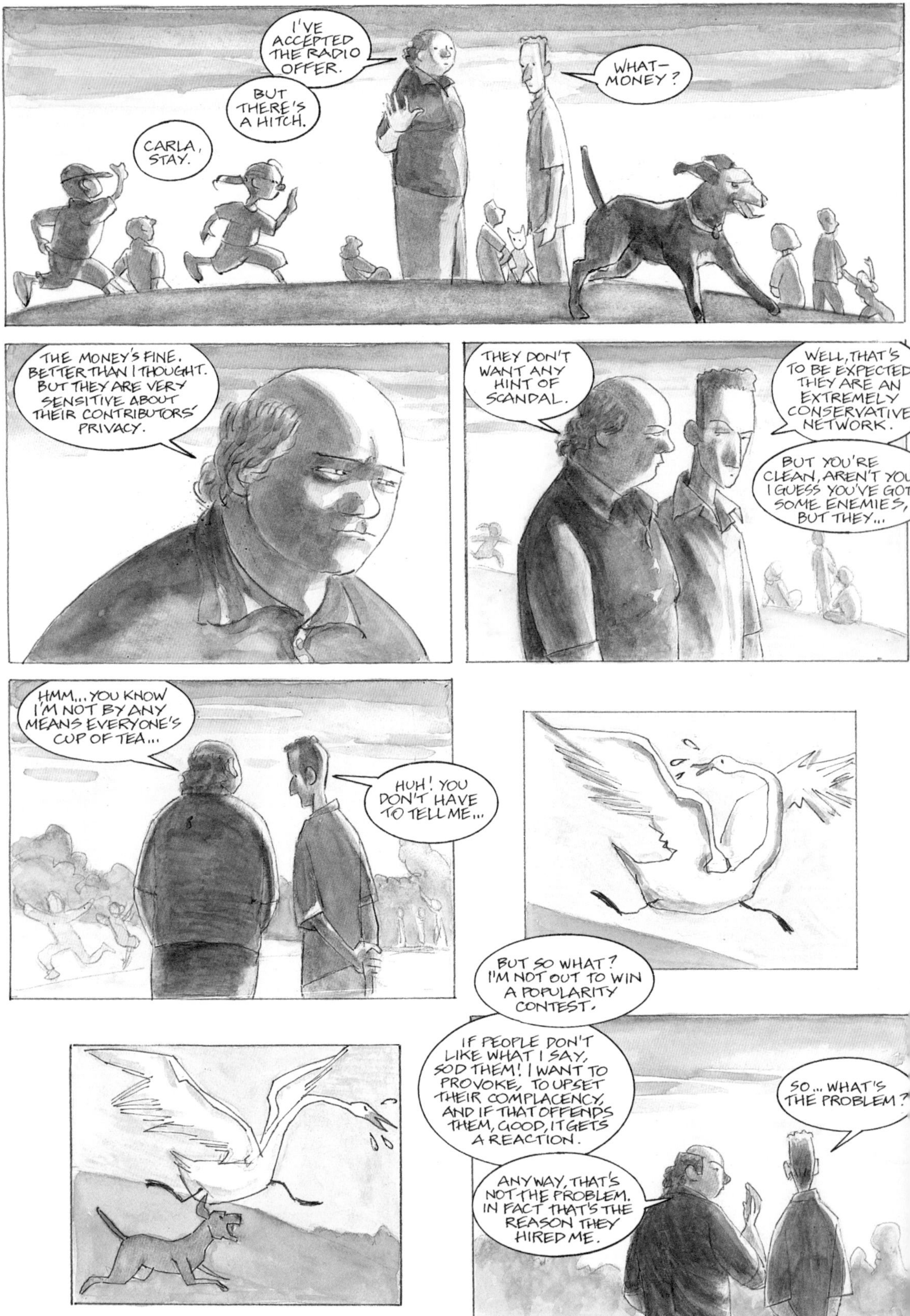
I'VE ACCEPTED THE RADIO OFFER.
BUT THERE'S A HITCH.
CARLA, STAY.
WHAT— MONEY?
THE MONEY'S FINE. BETTER THAN I THOUGHT. BUT THEY ARE VERY SENSITIVE ABOUT THEIR CONTRIBUTORS' PRIVACY.
THEY DON'T WANT ANY HINT OF SCANDAL.
WELL, THAT'S TO BE EXPECTED THEY ARE AN EXTREMELY CONSERVATIVE NETWORK.
BUT YOU'RE CLEAN, AREN'T YOU
I GUESS YOU'VE GOT SOME ENEMIES, BUT THEY...
HMM... YOU KNOW I'M NOT BY ANY MEANS EVERYONE'S CUP OF TEA...
HUH! YOU DON'T HAVE TO TELL ME...
BUT SO WHAT? I'M NOT OUT TO WIN A POPULARITY CONTEST.
IF PEOPLE DON'T LIKE WHAT I SAY, SOD THEM! I WANT TO PROVOKE, TO UPSET THEIR COMPLACENCY, AND IF THAT OFFENDS THEM, GOOD, IT GETS A REACTION.
ANYWAY, THAT'S NOT THE PROBLEM. IN FACT THAT'S THE REASON THEY HIRED ME.
SO... WHAT'S THE PROBLEM?

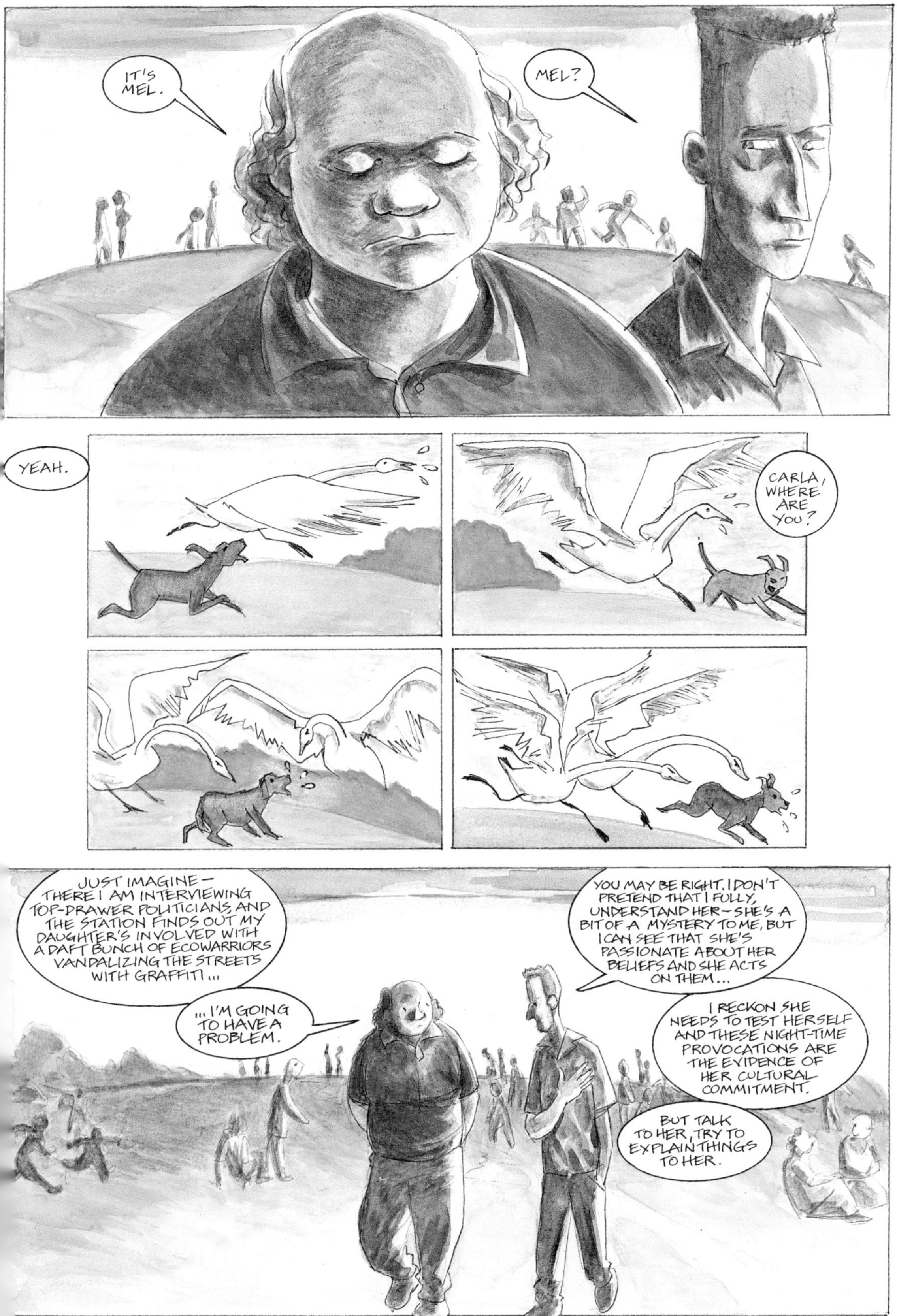
IT'S MEL.
MEL?
YEAH.
CARLA, WHERE ARE YOU?
JUST IMAGINE— THERE I AM INTERVIEWING TOP-DRAWER POLITICIANS, AND THE STATION FINDS OUT MY DAUGHTER'S INVOLVED WITH A DAFT BUNCH OF ECOWARRIORS VANDALIZING THE STREETS WITH GRAFFITI...
...I'M GOING TO HAVE A PROBLEM.
YOU MAY BE RIGHT. I DON'T PRETEND THAT I FULLY UNDERSTAND HER—SHE'S A BIT OF A MYSTERY TO ME, BUT I CAN SEE THAT SHE'S PASSIONATE ABOUT HER BELIEFS AND SHE ACTS ON THEM...
I RECKON SHE NEEDS TO TEST HERSELF AND THESE NIGHT-TIME PROVOCATIONS ARE THE EVIDENCE OF HER CULTURAL COMMITMENT.
BUT TALK TO HER, TRY TO EXPLAIN THINGS TO HER.

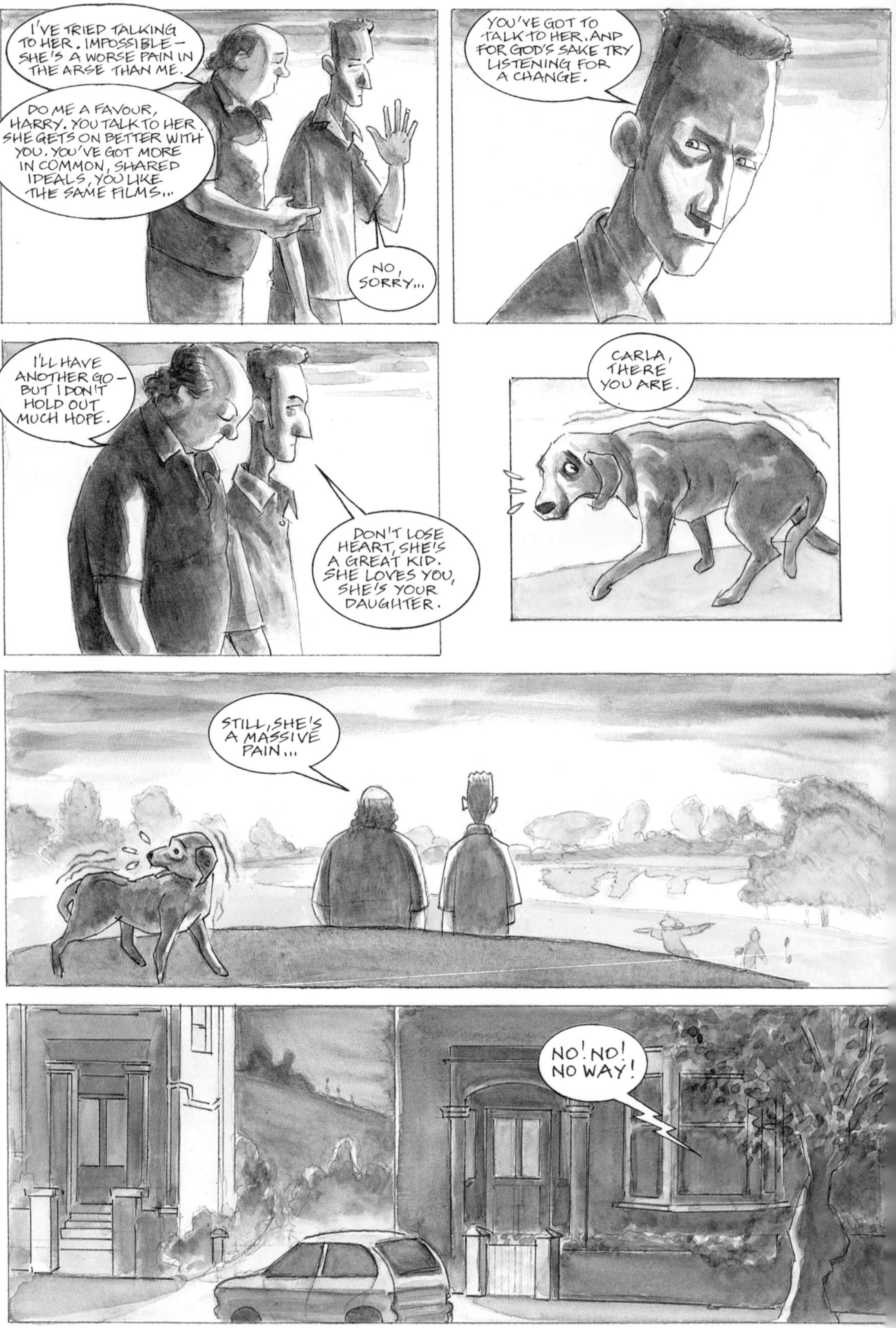
I'VE TRIED TALKING TO HER. IMPOSSIBLE - SHE'S A WORSE PAIN IN THE ARSE THAN ME.
DO ME A FAVOUR, HARRY. YOU TALK TO HER. SHE GETS ON BETTER WITH YOU. YOU'VE GOT MORE IN COMMON, SHARED IDEALS, YOU LIKE THE SAME FILMS...
NO, SORRY...
YOU'VE GOT TO TALK TO HER. AND FOR GOD'S SAKE TRY LISTENING FOR A CHANGE.
I'LL HAVE ANOTHER GO - BUT I DON'T HOLD OUT MUCH HOPE.
DON'T LOSE HEART, SHE'S A GREAT KID. SHE LOVES YOU, SHE'S YOUR DAUGHTER.
CARLA, THERE YOU ARE.
STILL, SHE'S A MASSIVE PAIN...
NO! NO! NO WAY!

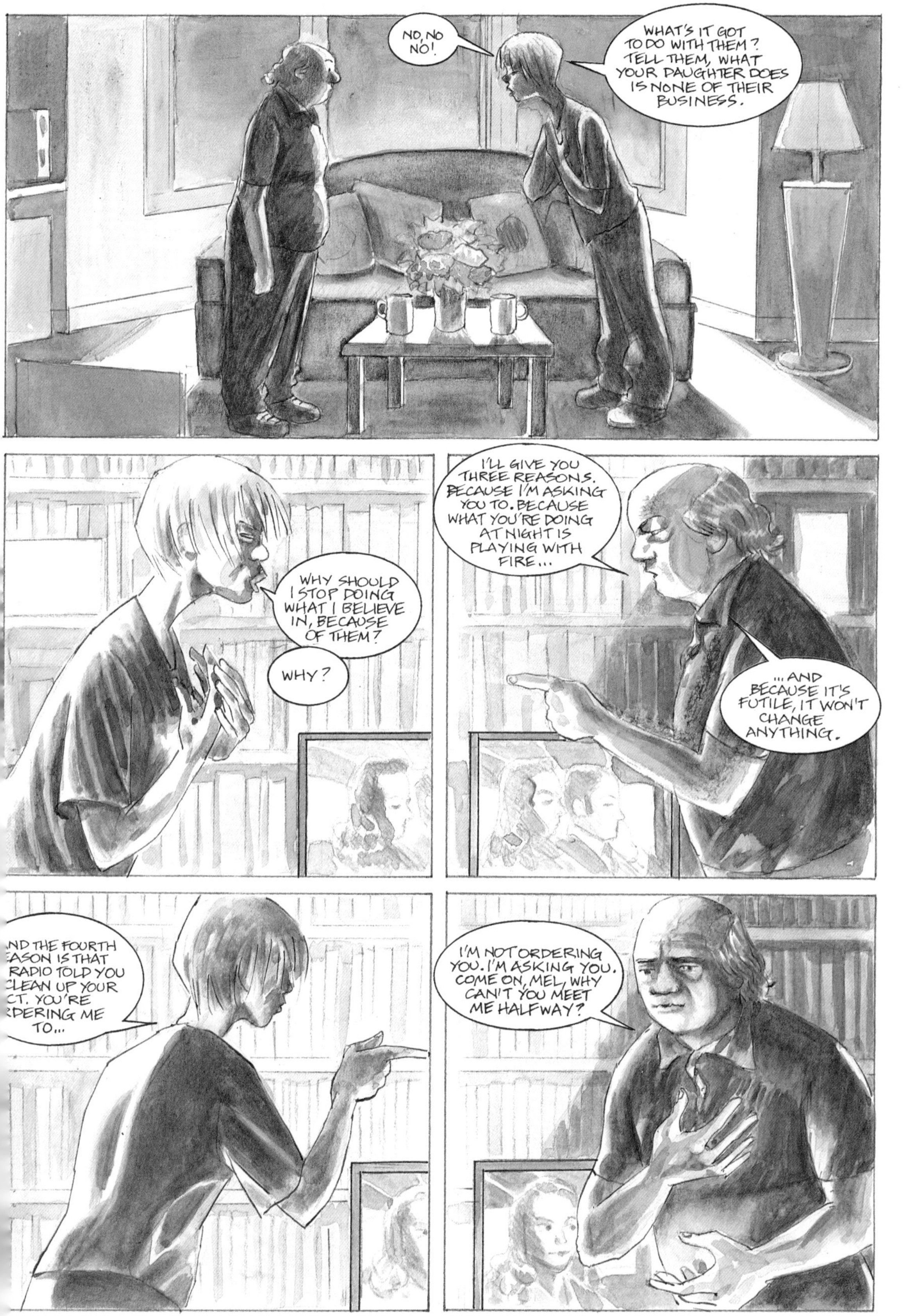
NO, NO NO!
WHAT'S IT GOT TO DO WITH THEM? TELL THEM, WHAT YOUR DAUGHTER DOES IS NONE OF THEIR BUSINESS.
WHY SHOULD I STOP DOING WHAT I BELIEVE IN, BECAUSE OF THEM?
WHY?
I'LL GIVE YOU THREE REASONS. BECAUSE I'M ASKING YOU TO. BECAUSE WHAT YOU'RE DOING AT NIGHT IS PLAYING WITH FIRE...
...AND BECAUSE IT'S FUTILE, IT WON'T CHANGE ANYTHING.
ND THE FOURTH EASON IS THAT RADIO TOLD YOU CLEAN UP YOUR CT. YOU'RE RDERING ME TO...
I'M NOT ORDERING YOU. I'M ASKING YOU. COME ON, MEL, WHY CAN'T YOU MEET ME HALFWAY?

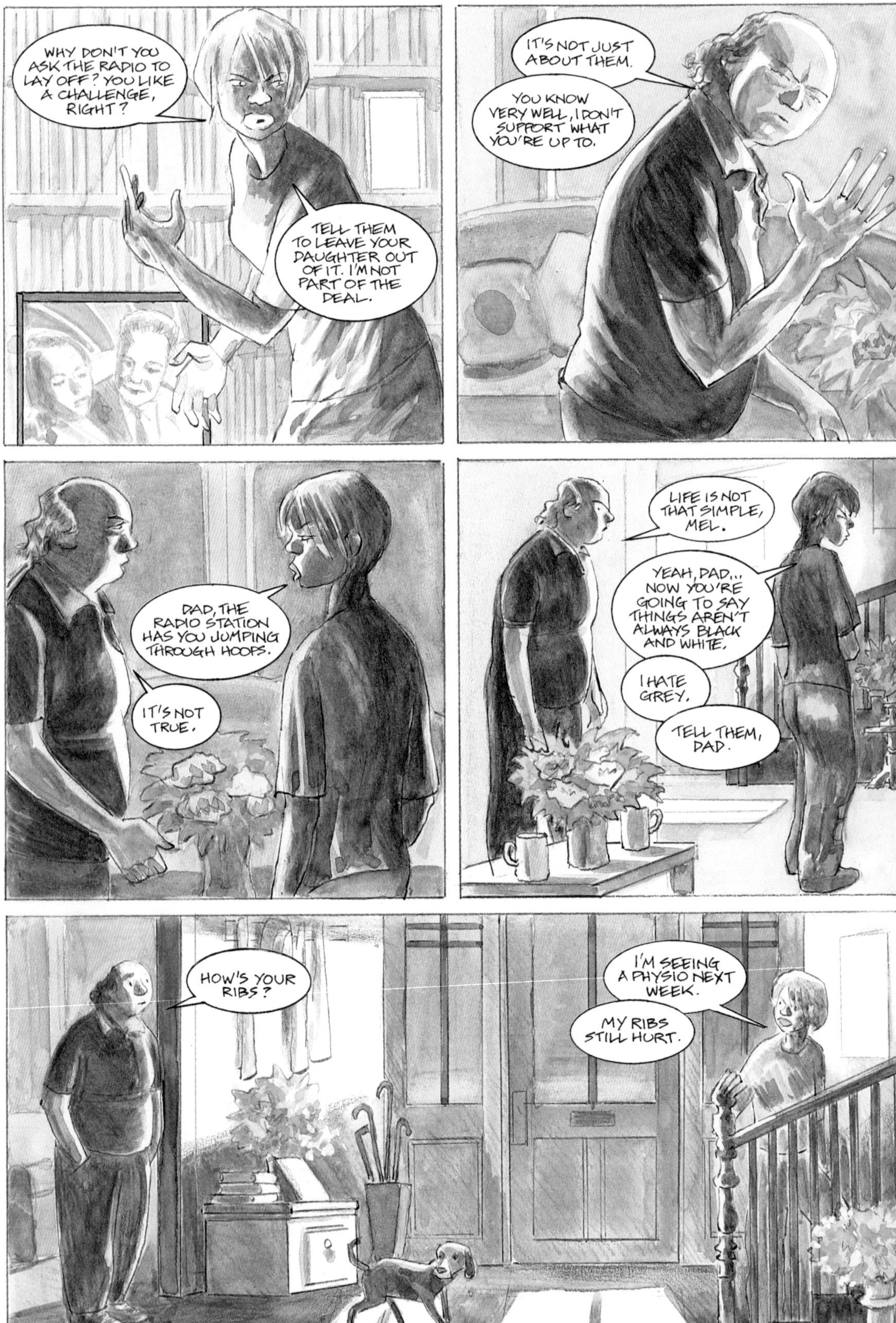
WHY DON'T YOU ASK THE RADIO TO LAY OFF? YOU LIKE A CHALLENGE, RIGHT?
TELL THEM TO LEAVE YOUR DAUGHTER OUT OF IT. I'M NOT PART OF THE DEAL.
IT'S NOT JUST ABOUT THEM.
YOU KNOW VERY WELL, I DON'T SUPPORT WHAT YOU'RE UP TO.
DAD, THE RADIO STATION HAS YOU JUMPING THROUGH HOOPS.
IT'S NOT TRUE.
LIFE IS NOT THAT SIMPLE, MEL.
YEAH, DAD... NOW YOU'RE GOING TO SAY THINGS AREN'T ALWAYS BLACK AND WHITE.
I HATE GREY.
TELL THEM, DAD.
HOW'S YOUR RIBS?
I'M SEEING A PHYSIO NEXT WEEK.
MY RIBS STILL HURT.

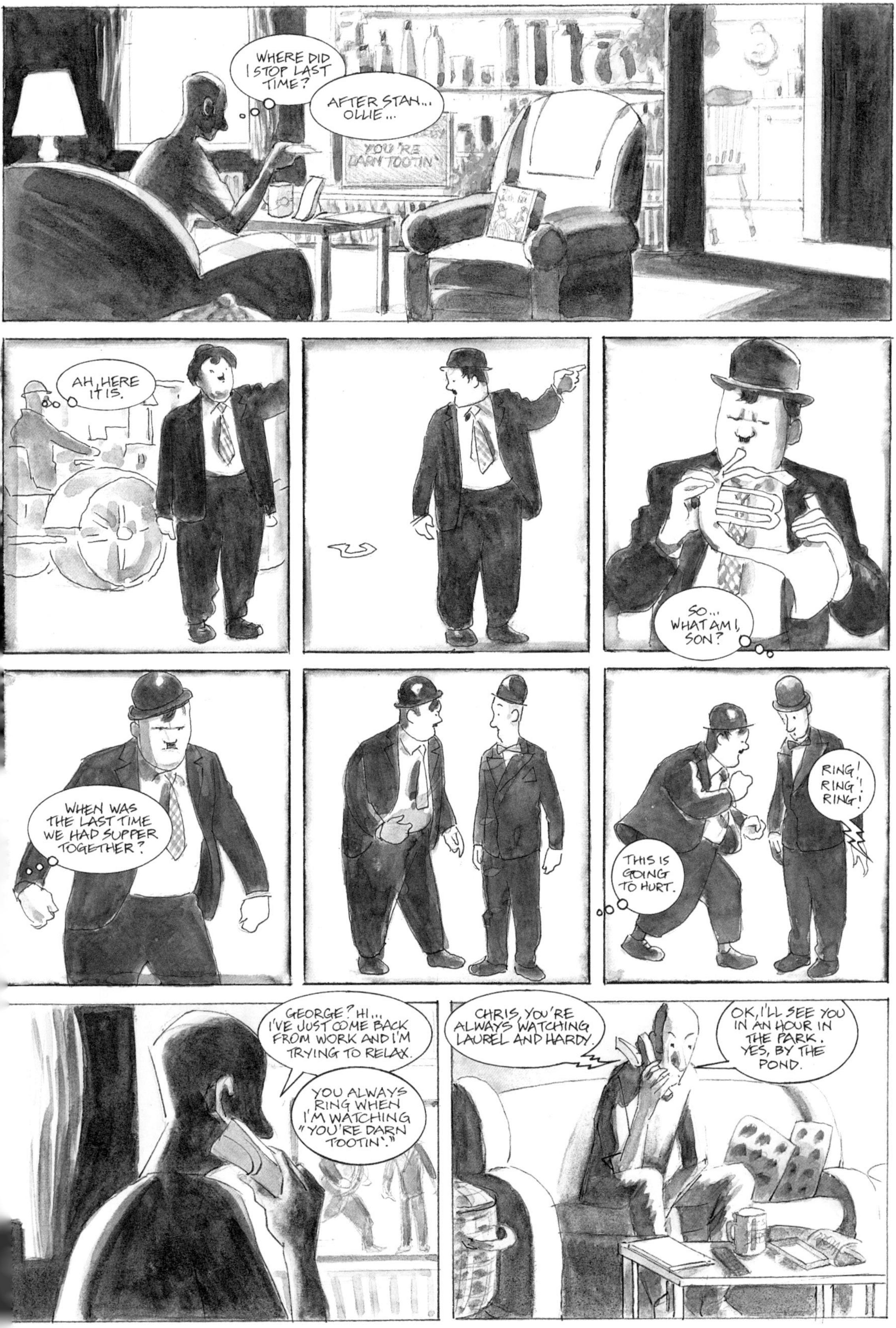
WHERE DID I STOP LAST TIME?
AFTER STAN... OLLIE...
YOU'RE DARN TOOTIN'
AH, HERE IT IS.
SO... WHAT AM I, SON?
WHEN WAS THE LAST TIME WE HAD SUPPER TOGETHER?
RING! RING! RING!
THIS IS GOING TO HURT.
GEORGE? HI... I'VE JUST COME BACK FROM WORK AND I'M TRYING TO RELAX.
YOU ALWAYS RING WHEN I'M WATCHING "YOU'RE DARN TOOTIN'."
CHRIS, YOU'RE ALWAYS WATCHING LAUREL AND HARDY.
OK, I'LL SEE YOU IN AN HOUR IN THE PARK. YES, BY THE POND.

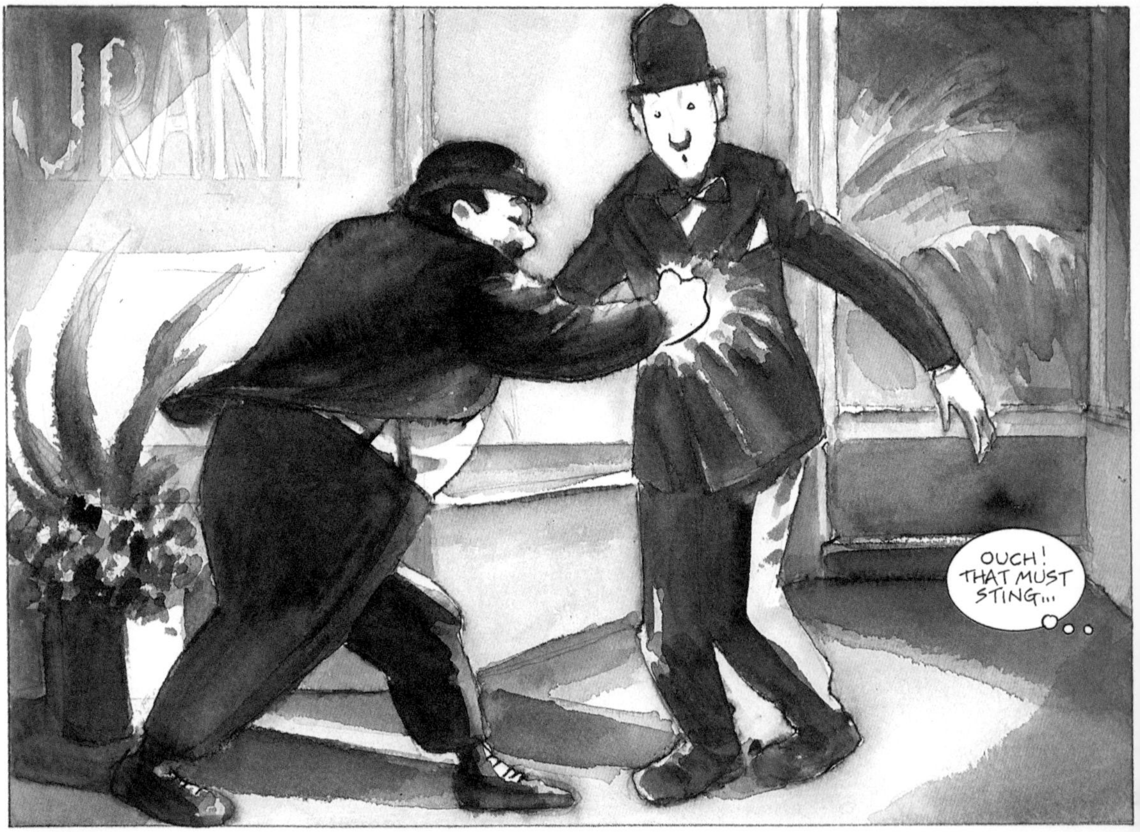
URANT
OUCH! THAT MUST STING...

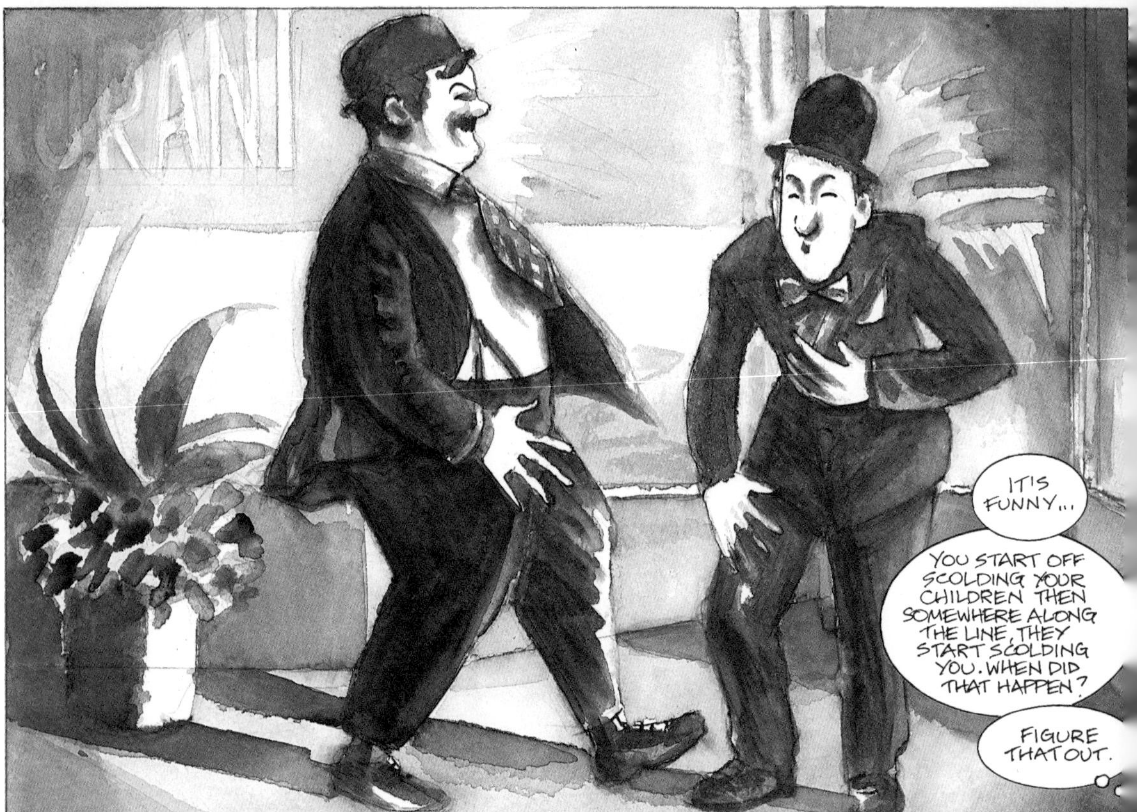
URANT
IT'S FUNNY...
YOU START OFF SCOLDING YOUR CHILDREN THEN SOMEWHERE ALONG THE LINE, THEY START SCOLDING YOU. WHEN DID THAT HAPPEN?
FIGURE THAT OUT.

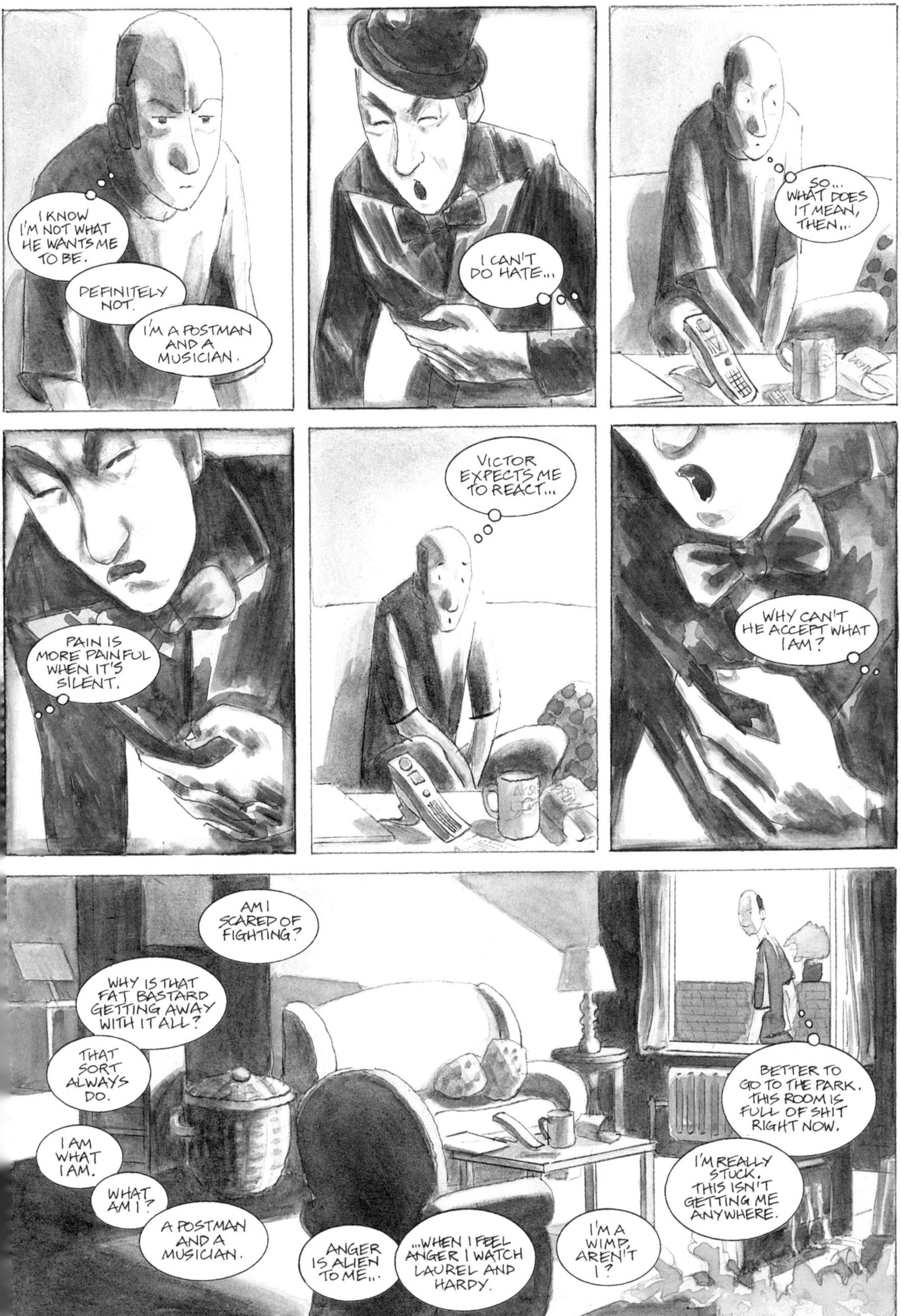
I KNOW I'M NOT WHAT HE WANTS ME TO BE.
DEFINITELY NOT.
I'M A POSTMAN AND A MUSICIAN.
I CAN'T DO HATE...
SO... WHAT DOES IT MEAN, THEN...
PAIN IS MORE PAINFUL WHEN IT'S SILENT.
VICTOR EXPECTS ME TO REACT...
WHY CAN'T HE ACCEPT WHAT I AM?
AM I SCARED OF FIGHTING?
WHY IS THAT FAT BASTARD GETTING AWAY WITH IT ALL?
THAT SORT ALWAYS DO.
I AM WHAT I AM.
WHAT AM I?
A POSTMAN AND A MUSICIAN.
ANGER IS ALIEN TO ME...
...WHEN I FEEL ANGER I WATCH LAUREL AND HARDY.
I'M A WIMP, AREN'T I?
I'M REALLY STUCK. THIS ISN'T GETTING ME ANYWHERE.
BETTER TO GO TO THE PARK. THIS ROOM IS FULL OF SHIT RIGHT NOW.

The ladder's wobbly...

I hope nobody's up there... I want to be by myself.

That's better...

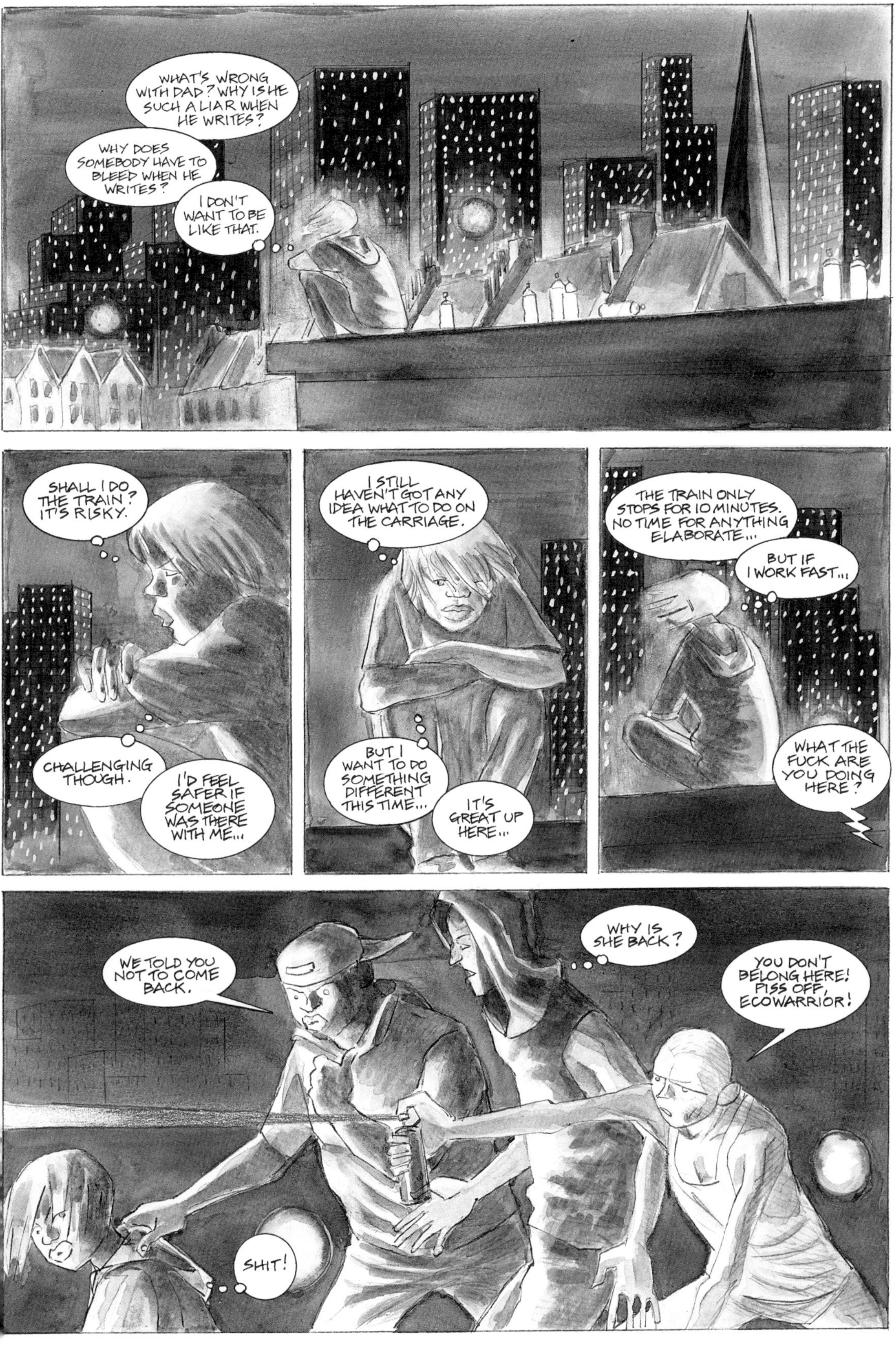
WHAT'S WRONG WITH DAD? WHY IS HE SUCH A LIAR WHEN HE WRITES?
WHY DOES SOMEBODY HAVE TO BLEED WHEN HE WRITES?
I DON'T WANT TO BE LIKE THAT.
SHALL I DO THE TRAIN? IT'S RISKY.
CHALLENGING THOUGH.
I'D FEEL SAFER IF SOMEONE WAS THERE WITH ME...
I STILL HAVEN'T GOT ANY IDEA WHAT TO DO ON THE CARRIAGE.
BUT I WANT TO DO SOMETHING DIFFERENT THIS TIME...
IT'S GREAT UP HERE...
THE TRAIN ONLY STOPS FOR 10 MINUTES. NO TIME FOR ANYTHING ELABORATE...
BUT IF I WORK FAST...
WHAT THE FUCK ARE YOU DOING HERE?
WE TOLD YOU NOT TO COME BACK.
WHY IS SHE BACK?
YOU DON'T BELONG HERE! PISS OFF, ECOWARRIOR!
SHIT!

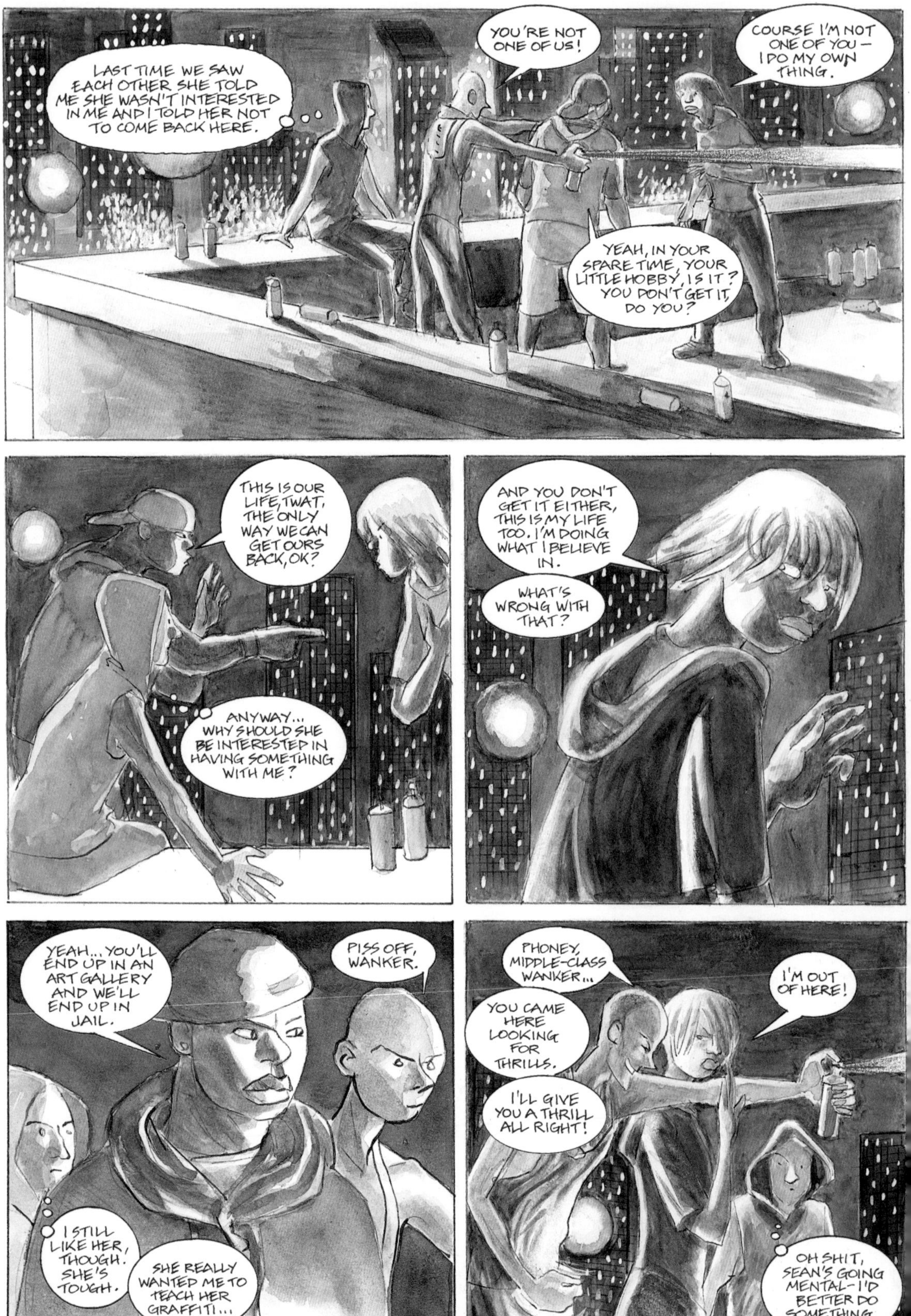
LAST TIME WE SAW EACH OTHER SHE TOLD ME SHE WASN'T INTERESTED IN ME AND I TOLD HER NOT TO COME BACK HERE.
YOU'RE NOT ONE OF US!
COURSE I'M NOT ONE OF YOU – I DO MY OWN THING.
YEAH, IN YOUR SPARE TIME, YOUR LITTLE HOBBY, IS IT? YOU DON'T GET IT, DO YOU?
THIS IS OUR LIFE, TWAT, THE ONLY WAY WE CAN GET OURS BACK, OK?
ANYWAY... WHY SHOULD SHE BE INTERESTED IN HAVING SOMETHING WITH ME?
AND YOU DON'T GET IT EITHER, THIS IS MY LIFE TOO. I'M DOING WHAT I BELIEVE IN.
WHAT'S WRONG WITH THAT?
YEAH... YOU'LL END UP IN AN ART GALLERY AND WE'LL END UP IN JAIL.
PISS OFF, WANKER.
I STILL LIKE HER, THOUGH. SHE'S TOUGH.
SHE REALLY WANTED ME TO TEACH HER GRAFFITI...
PHONEY, MIDDLE-CLASS WANKER...
YOU CAME HERE LOOKING FOR THRILLS.
I'LL GIVE YOU A THRILL ALL RIGHT!
I'M OUT OF HERE!
OH SHIT, SEAN'S GOING MENTAL – I'D BETTER DO SOMETHING.

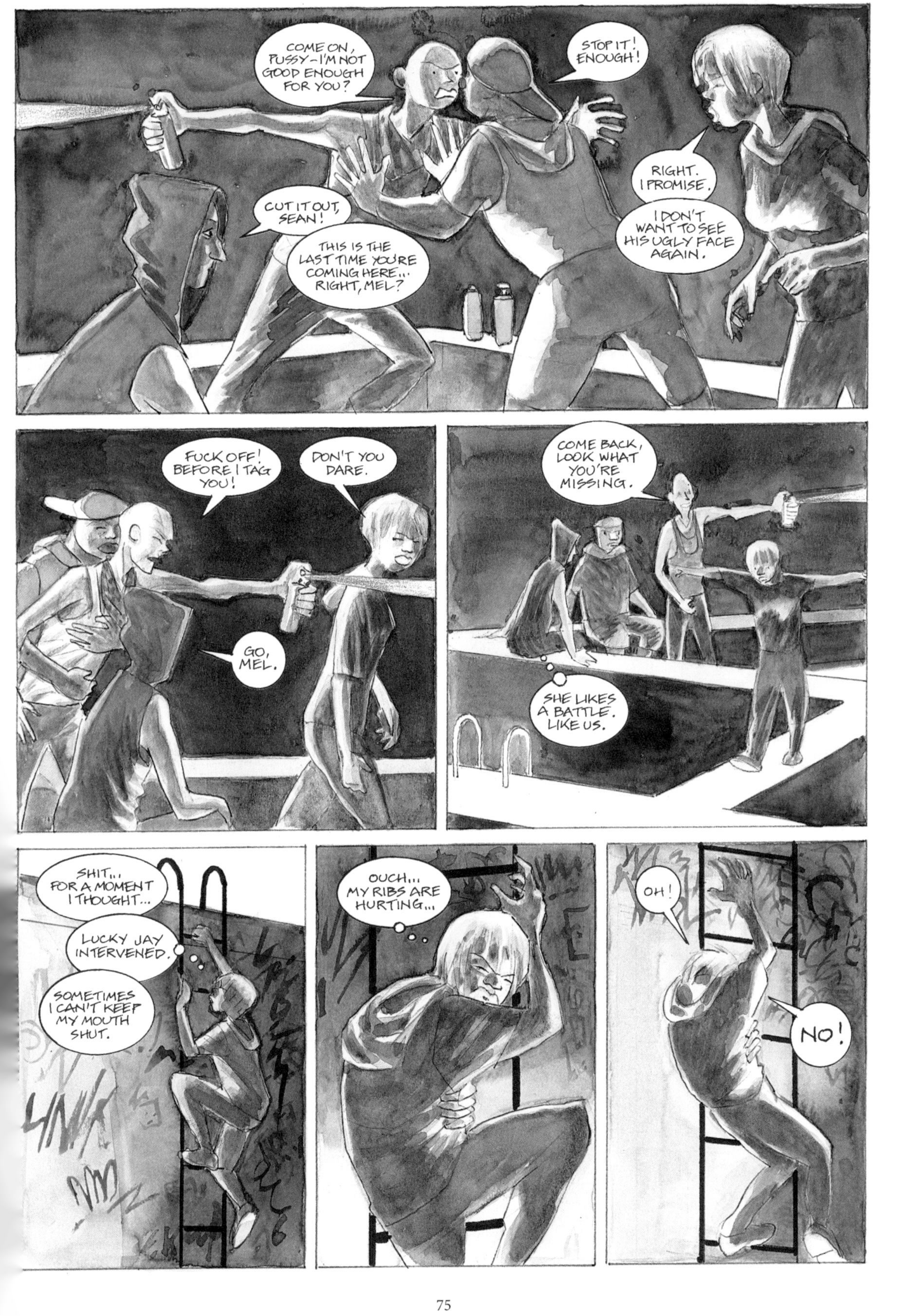
COME ON, PUSSY - I'M NOT GOOD ENOUGH FOR YOU?
STOP IT! ENOUGH!
RIGHT. I PROMISE.
I DON'T WANT TO SEE HIS UGLY FACE AGAIN.
CUT IT OUT, SEAN!
THIS IS THE LAST TIME YOU'RE COMING HERE... RIGHT, MEL?
FUCK OFF! BEFORE I TAG YOU!
DON'T YOU DARE.
GO, MEL.
COME BACK, LOOK WHAT YOU'RE MISSING.
SHE LIKES A BATTLE. LIKE US.
SHIT... FOR A MOMENT I THOUGHT...
LUCKY JAY INTERVENED.
SOMETIMES I CAN'T KEEP MY MOUTH SHUT.
OUCH... MY RIBS ARE HURTING...
OH!
NO!

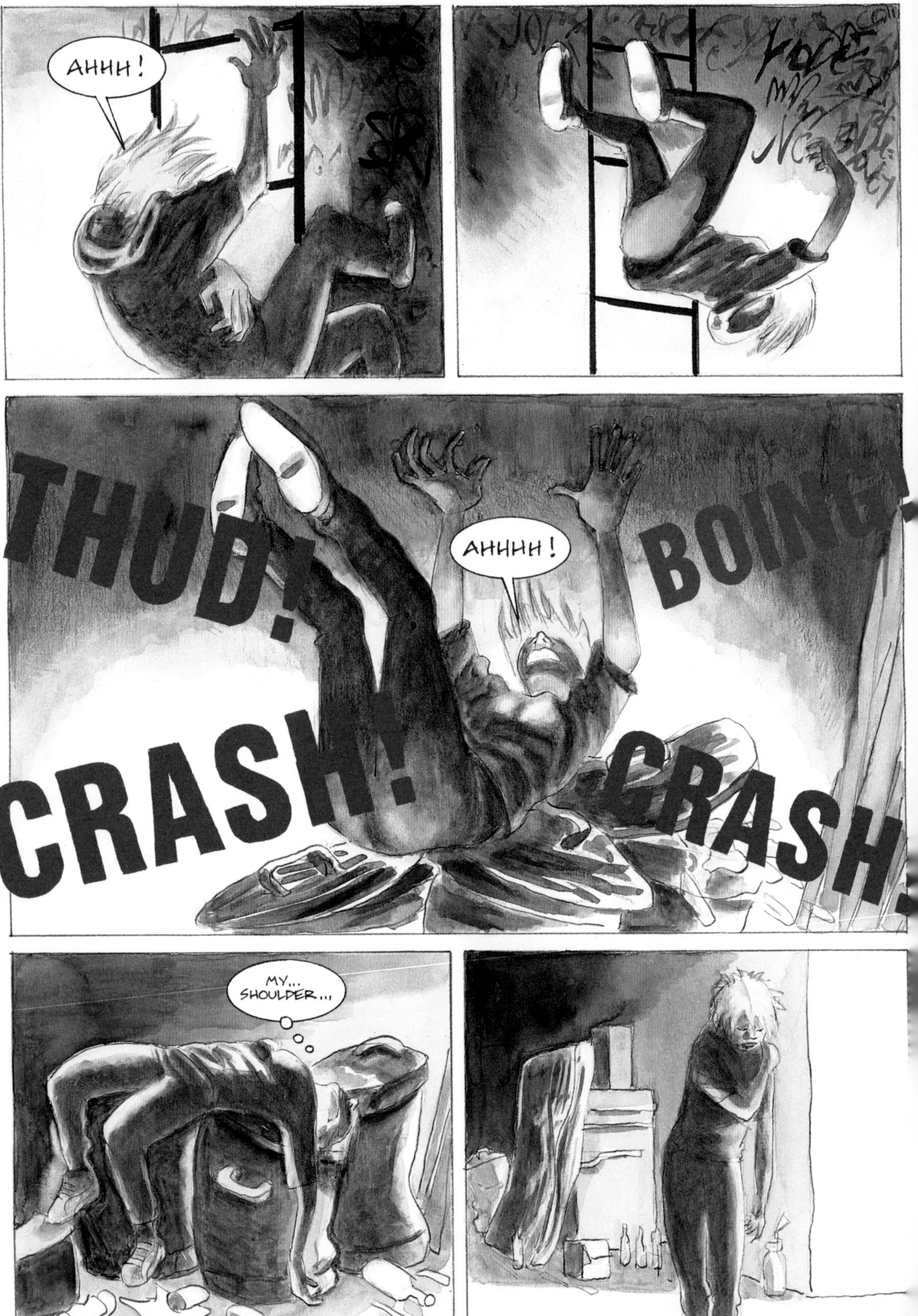
AHHH!
THUD!
AHHHH!
BOING!
CRASH!
CRASH!
MY... SHOULDER...

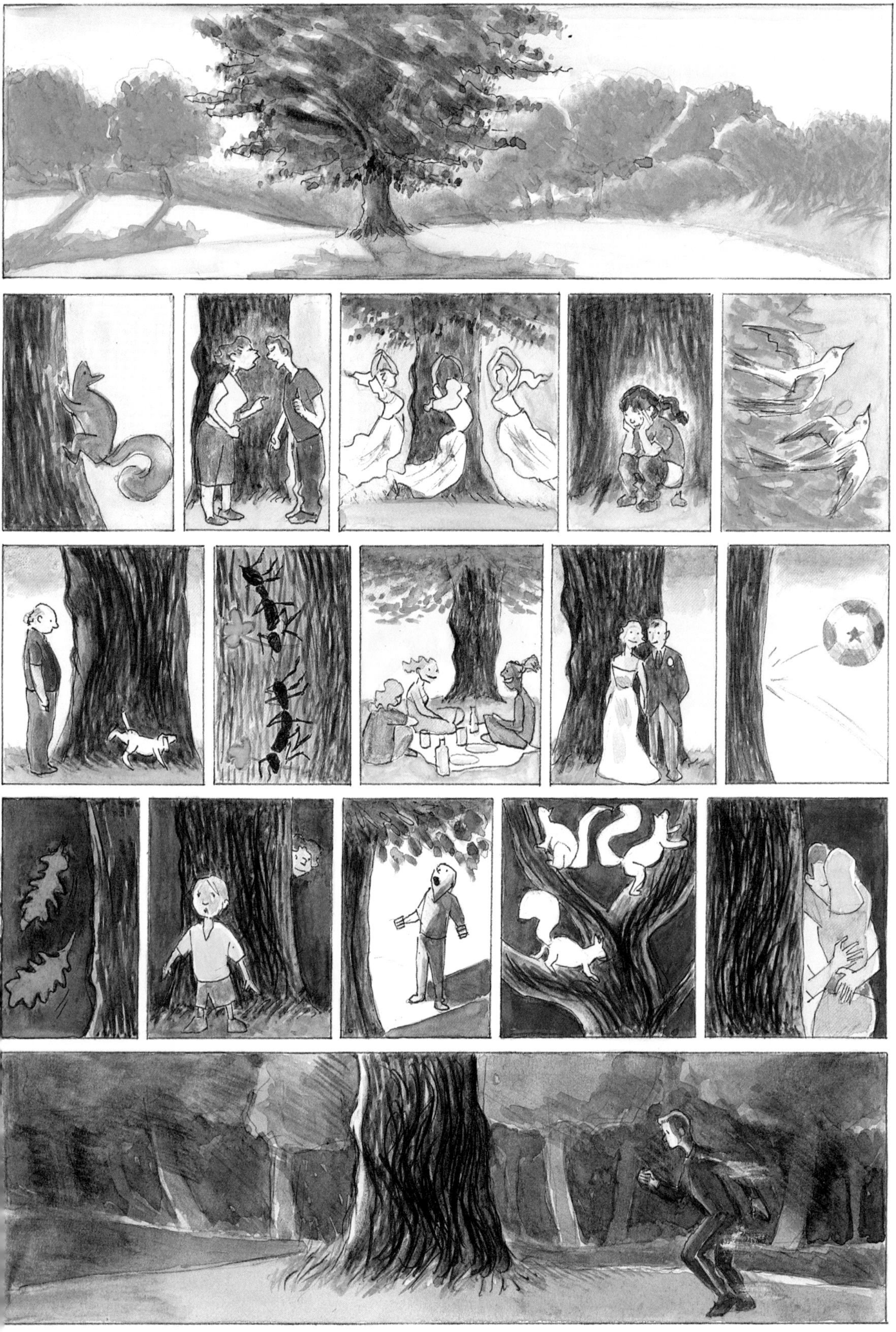

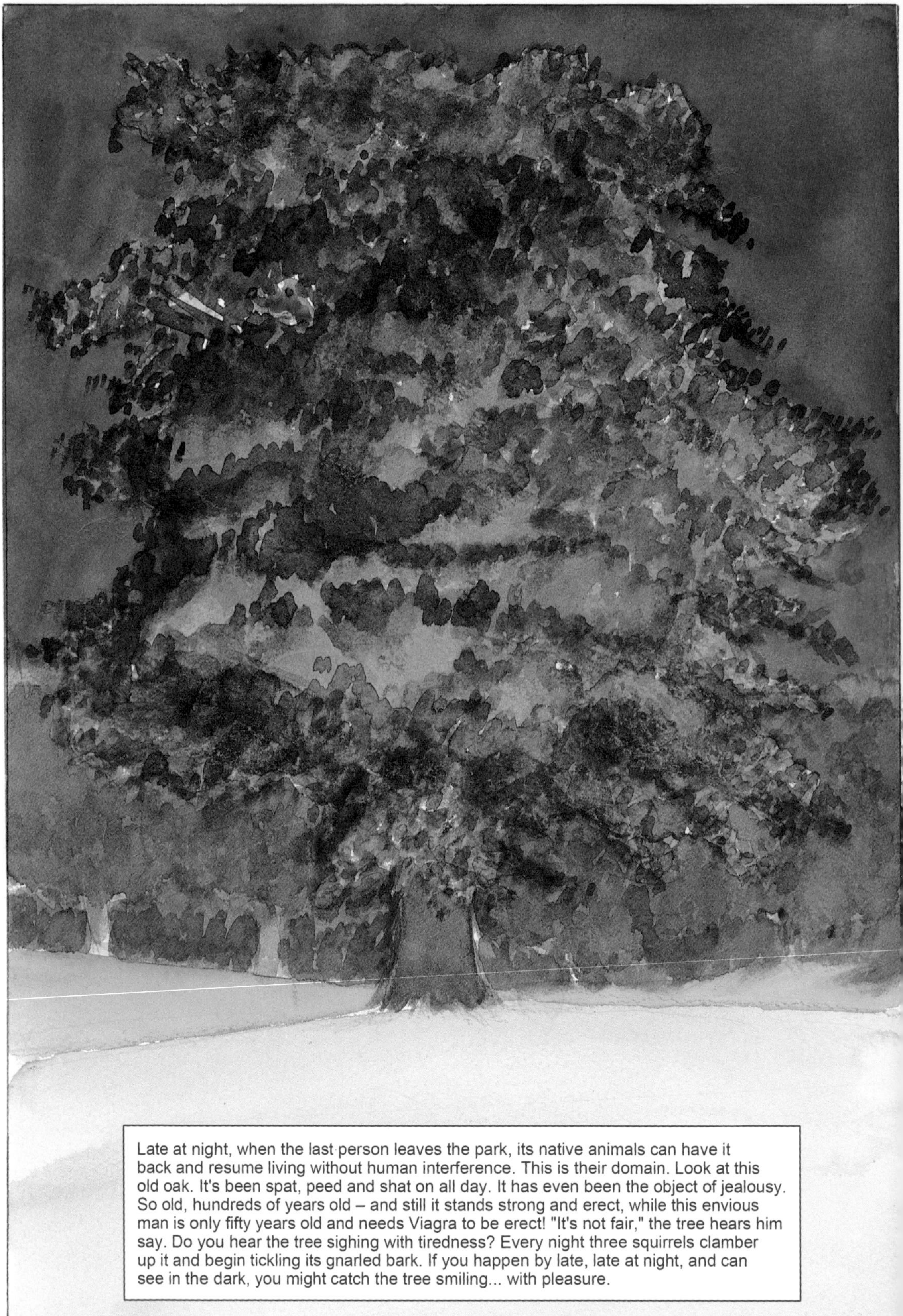
Late at night, when the last person leaves the park, its native animals can have it back and resume living without human interference. This is their domain. Look at this old oak. It's been spat, peed and shat on all day. It has even been the object of jealousy. So old, hundreds of years old – and still it stands strong and erect, while this envious man is only fifty years old and needs Viagra to be erect! "It's not fair," the tree hears him say. Do you hear the tree sighing with tiredness? Every night three squirrels clamber up it and begin tickling its gnarled bark. If you happen by late, late at night, and can see in the dark, you might catch the tree smiling... with pleasure.

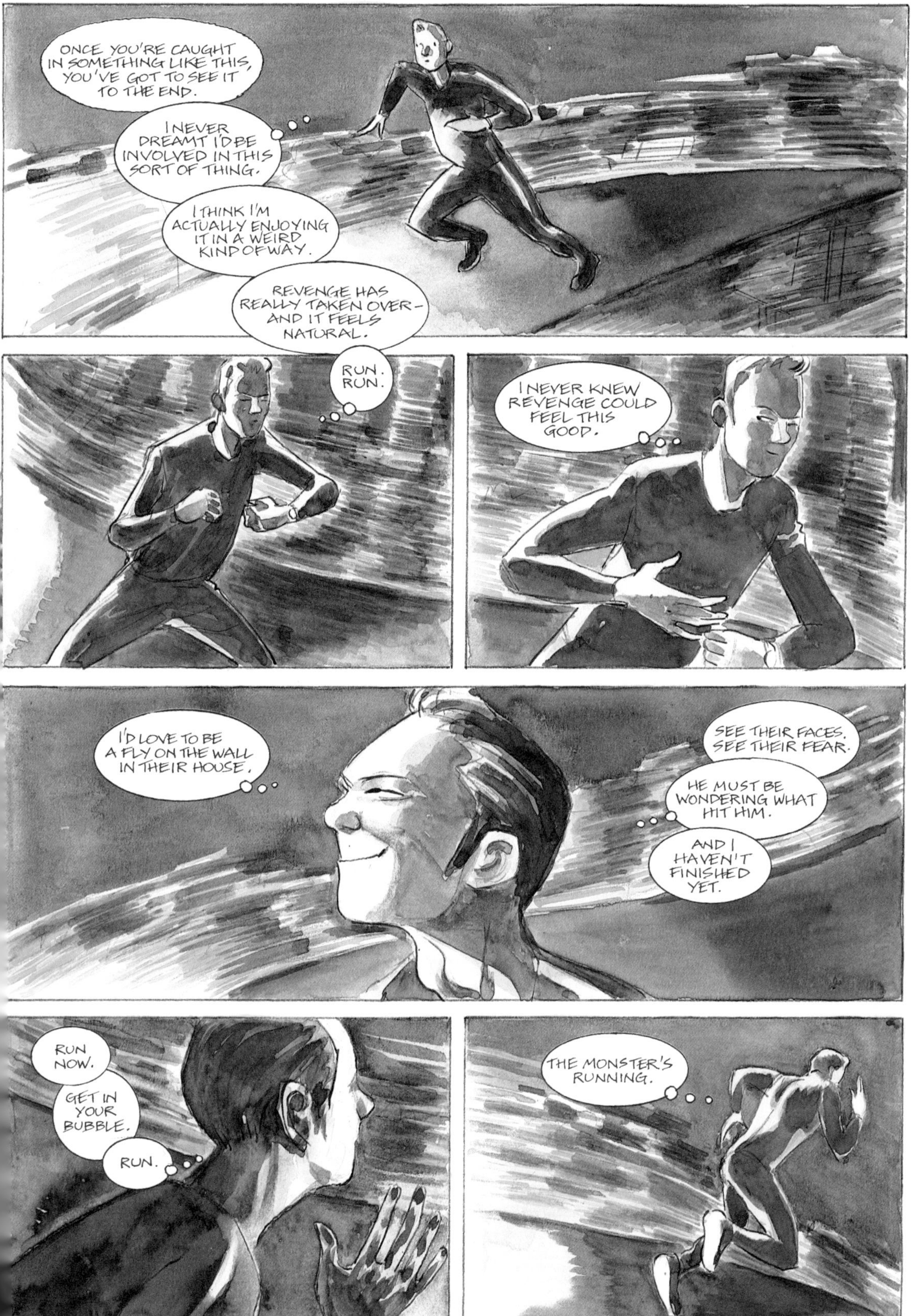
ONCE YOU'RE CAUGHT IN SOMETHING LIKE THIS, YOU'VE GOT TO SEE IT TO THE END.
I NEVER DREAMT I'D BE INVOLVED IN THIS SORT OF THING.
I THINK I'M ACTUALLY ENJOYING IT IN A WEIRD KIND OF WAY.
REVENGE HAS REALLY TAKEN OVER - AND IT FEELS NATURAL.
RUN. RUN.
I NEVER KNEW REVENGE COULD FEEL THIS GOOD.
I'D LOVE TO BE A FLY ON THE WALL IN THEIR HOUSE.
SEE THEIR FACES. SEE THEIR FEAR.
HE MUST BE WONDERING WHAT HIT HIM.
AND I HAVEN'T FINISHED YET.
RUN NOW.
GET IN YOUR BUBBLE.
RUN.
THE MONSTER'S RUNNING.

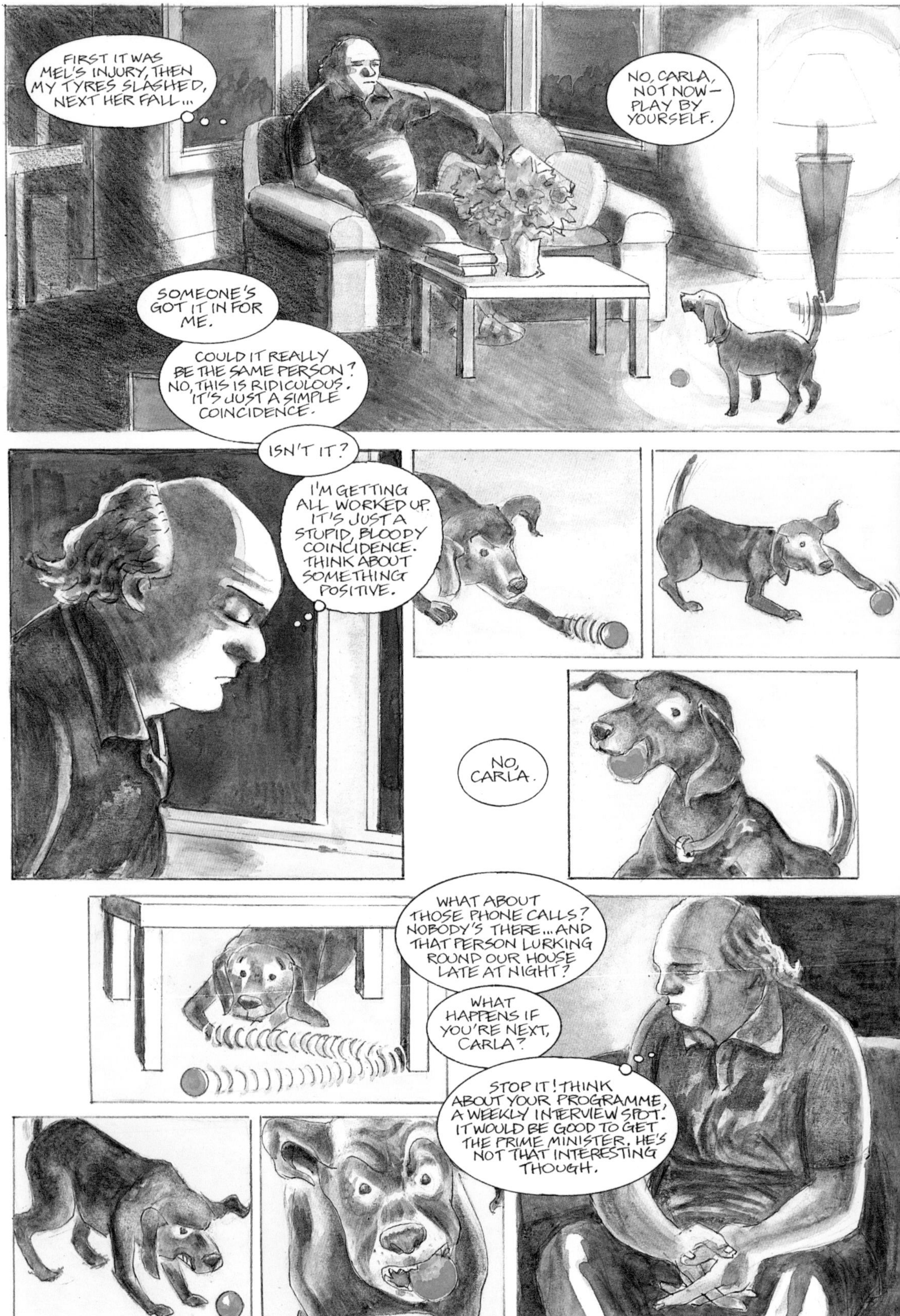
FIRST IT WAS MEL'S INJURY, THEN MY TYRES SLASHED, NEXT HER FALL...
NO, CARLA, NOT NOW— PLAY BY YOURSELF.
SOMEONE'S GOT IT IN FOR ME.
COULD IT REALLY BE THE SAME PERSON? NO, THIS IS RIDICULOUS. IT'S JUST A SIMPLE COINCIDENCE.
ISN'T IT?
I'M GETTING ALL WORKED UP. IT'S JUST A STUPID, BLOODY COINCIDENCE. THINK ABOUT SOMETHING POSITIVE.
NO, CARLA.
WHAT ABOUT THOSE PHONE CALLS? NOBODY'S THERE... AND THAT PERSON LURKING ROUND OUR HOUSE LATE AT NIGHT?
WHAT HAPPENS IF YOU'RE NEXT, CARLA?
STOP IT! THINK ABOUT YOUR PROGRAMME, A WEEKLY INTERVIEW SPOT. IT WOULD BE GOOD TO GET THE PRIME MINISTER. HE'S NOT THAT INTERESTING THOUGH.

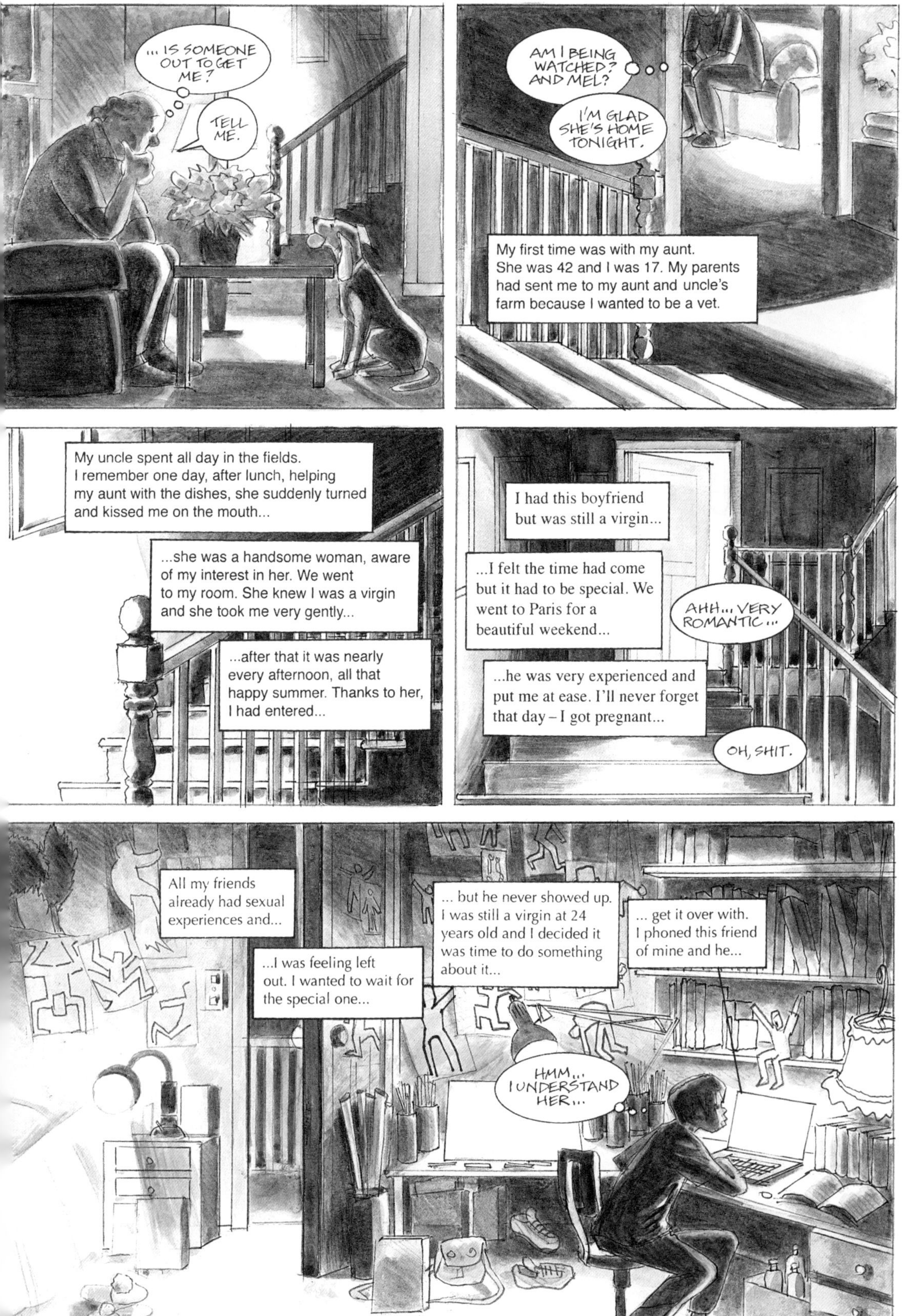
... IS SOMEONE OUT TO GET ME?
TELL ME.
AM I BEING WATCHED? AND MEL?
I'M GLAD SHE'S HOME TONIGHT.
My first time was with my aunt. She was 42 and I was 17. My parents had sent me to my aunt and uncle's farm because I wanted to be a vet.
My uncle spent all day in the fields. I remember one day, after lunch, helping my aunt with the dishes, she suddenly turned and kissed me on the mouth...
...she was a handsome woman, aware of my interest in her. We went to my room. She knew I was a virgin and she took me very gently...
...after that it was nearly every afternoon, all that happy summer. Thanks to her, I had entered...
I had this boyfriend but was still a virgin...
...I felt the time had come but it had to be special. We went to Paris for a beautiful weekend...
AHH... VERY ROMANTIC...
...he was very experienced and put me at ease. I'll never forget that day – I got pregnant...
OH, SHIT.
All my friends already had sexual experiences and...
...I was feeling left out. I wanted to wait for the special one...
... but he never showed up. I was still a virgin at 24 years old and I decided it was time to do something about it...
... get it over with. I phoned this friend of mine and he...
HMM... I UNDERSTAND HER...

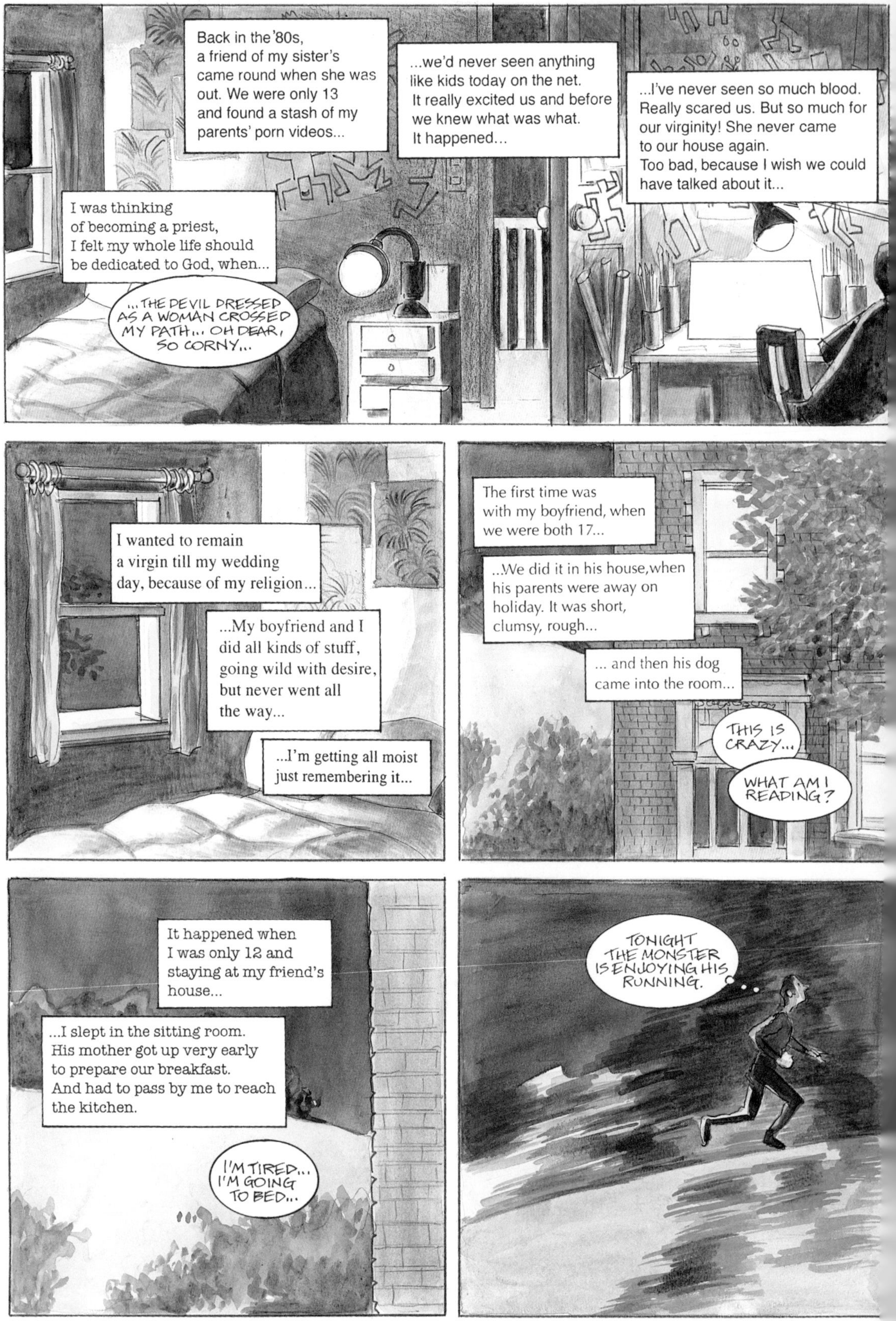
Back in the '80s, a friend of my sister's came round when she was out. We were only 13 and found a stash of my parents' porn videos...
...we'd never seen anything like kids today on the net. It really excited us and before we knew what was what. It happened...
...I've never seen so much blood. Really scared us. But so much for our virginity! She never came to our house again. Too bad, because I wish we could have talked about it...
I was thinking of becoming a priest, I felt my whole life should be dedicated to God, when...
...THE DEVIL DRESSED AS A WOMAN CROSSED MY PATH... OH DEAR, SO CORNY...
I wanted to remain a virgin till my wedding day, because of my religion...
...My boyfriend and I did all kinds of stuff, going wild with desire, but never went all the way...
...I'm getting all moist just remembering it...
The first time was with my boyfriend, when we were both 17...
...We did it in his house, when his parents were away on holiday. It was short, clumsy, rough...
... and then his dog came into the room...
THIS IS CRAZY...
WHAT AM I READING?
It happened when I was only 12 and staying at my friend's house...
...I slept in the sitting room. His mother got up very early to prepare our breakfast. And had to pass by me to reach the kitchen.
I'M TIRED... I'M GOING TO BED...
TONIGHT THE MONSTER IS ENJOYING HIS RUNNING.

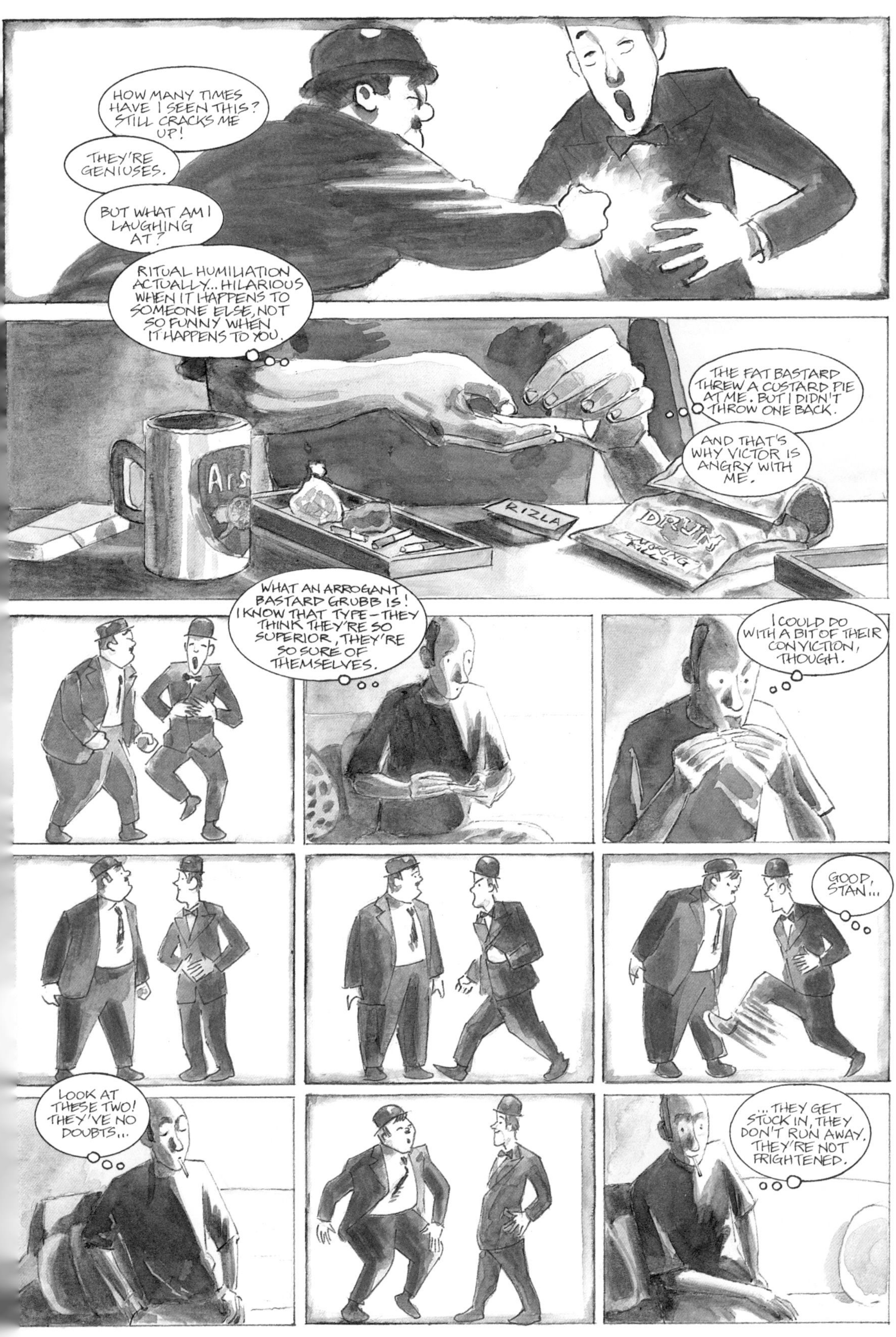
HOW MANY TIMES HAVE I SEEN THIS? STILL CRACKS ME UP!
THEY'RE GENIUSES.
BUT WHAT AM I LAUGHING AT?
RITUAL HUMILIATION ACTUALLY... HILARIOUS WHEN IT HAPPENS TO SOMEONE ELSE, NOT SO FUNNY WHEN IT HAPPENS TO YOU.
THE FAT BASTARD THREW A CUSTARD PIE AT ME. BUT I DIDN'T THROW ONE BACK.
AND THAT'S WHY VICTOR IS ANGRY WITH ME.
RIZLA
DRUM
WHAT AN ARROGANT BASTARD GRUBB IS! I KNOW THAT TYPE – THEY THINK THEY'RE SO SUPERIOR, THEY'RE SO SURE OF THEMSELVES.
I COULD DO WITH A BIT OF THEIR CONVICTION, THOUGH.
GOOD, STAN...
LOOK AT THESE TWO! THEY'VE NO DOUBTS...
... THEY GET STUCK IN, THEY DON'T RUN AWAY. THEY'RE NOT FRIGHTENED.

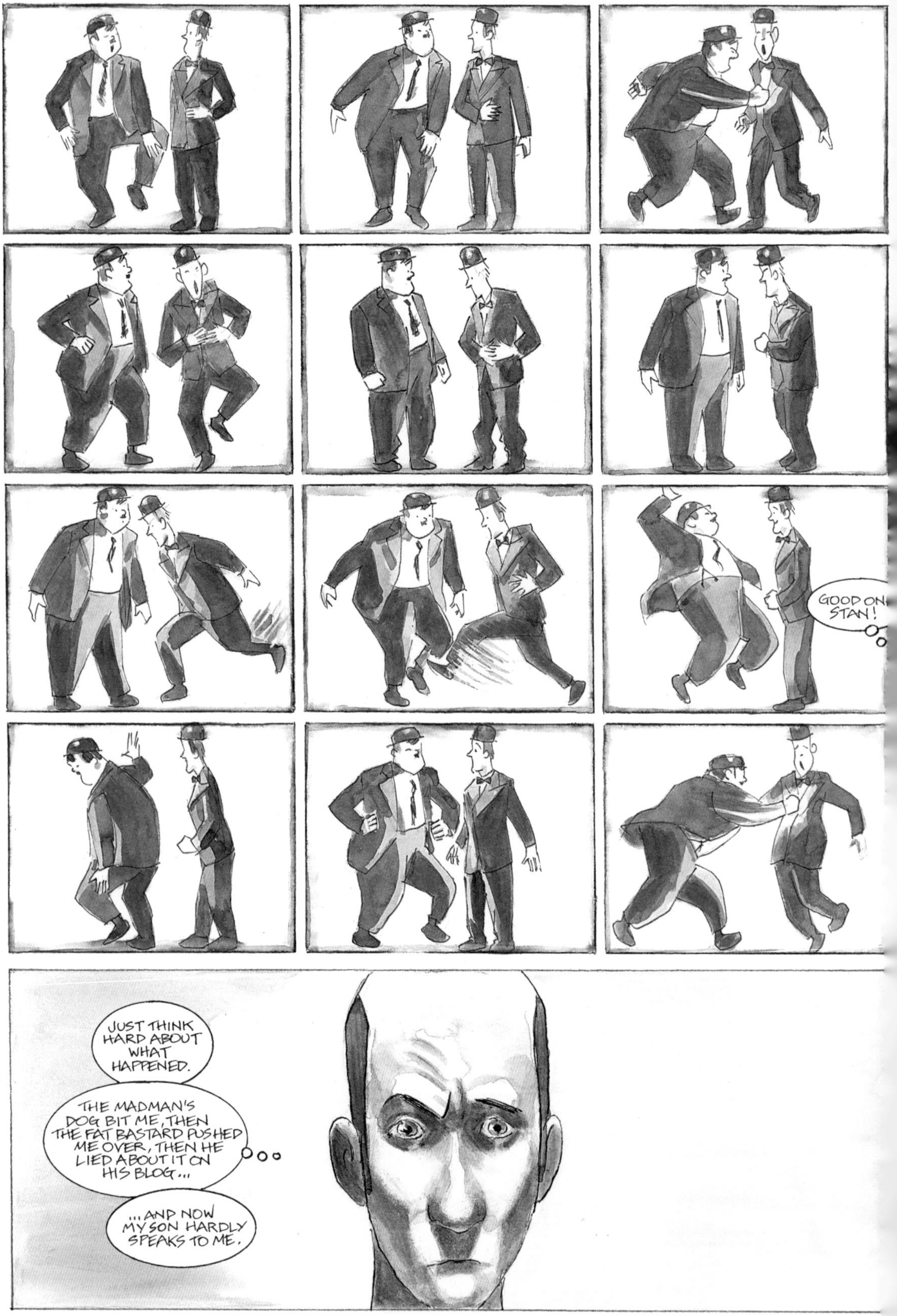
GOOD ON STAN!
JUST THINK HARD ABOUT WHAT HAPPENED.
THE MADMAN'S DOG BIT ME, THEN THE FAT BASTARD PUSHED ME OVER, THEN HE LIED ABOUT IT ON HIS BLOG...
...AND NOW MY SON HARDLY SPEAKS TO ME.

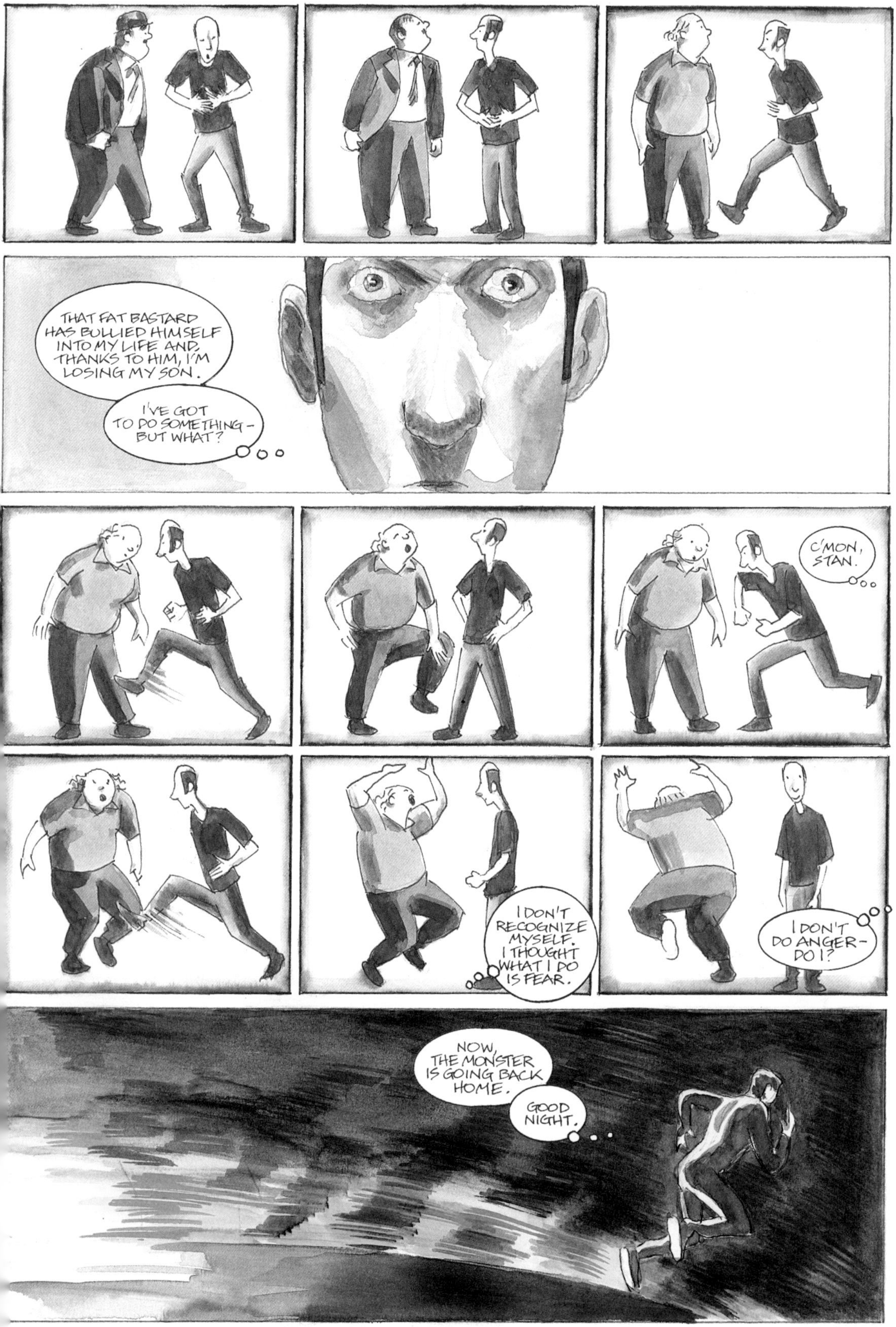
THAT FAT BASTARD HAS BULLIED HIMSELF INTO MY LIFE AND, THANKS TO HIM, I'M LOSING MY SON.
I'VE GOT TO DO SOMETHING - BUT WHAT?
C'MON, STAN.
I DON'T RECOGNIZE MYSELF. I THOUGHT WHAT I DO IS FEAR.
I DON'T DO ANGER - DO I?
NOW, THE MONSTER IS GOING BACK HOME.
GOOD NIGHT.

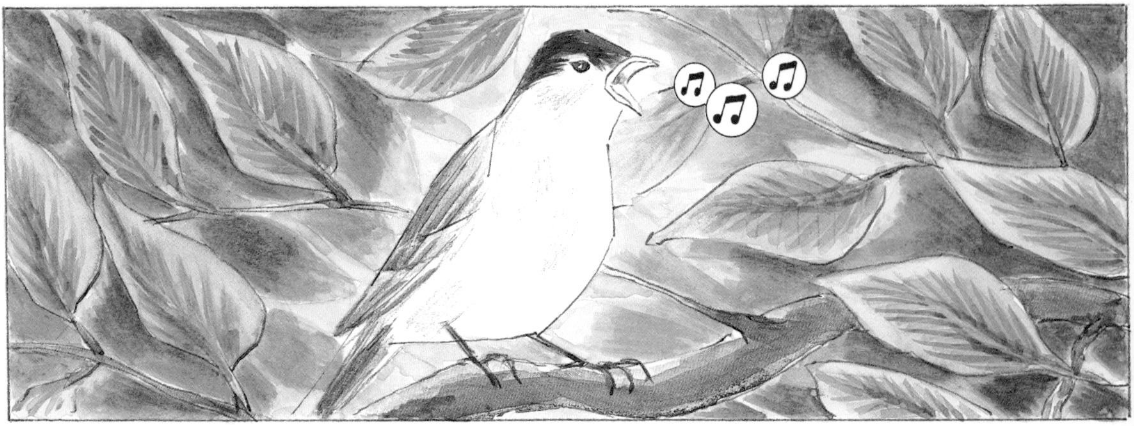

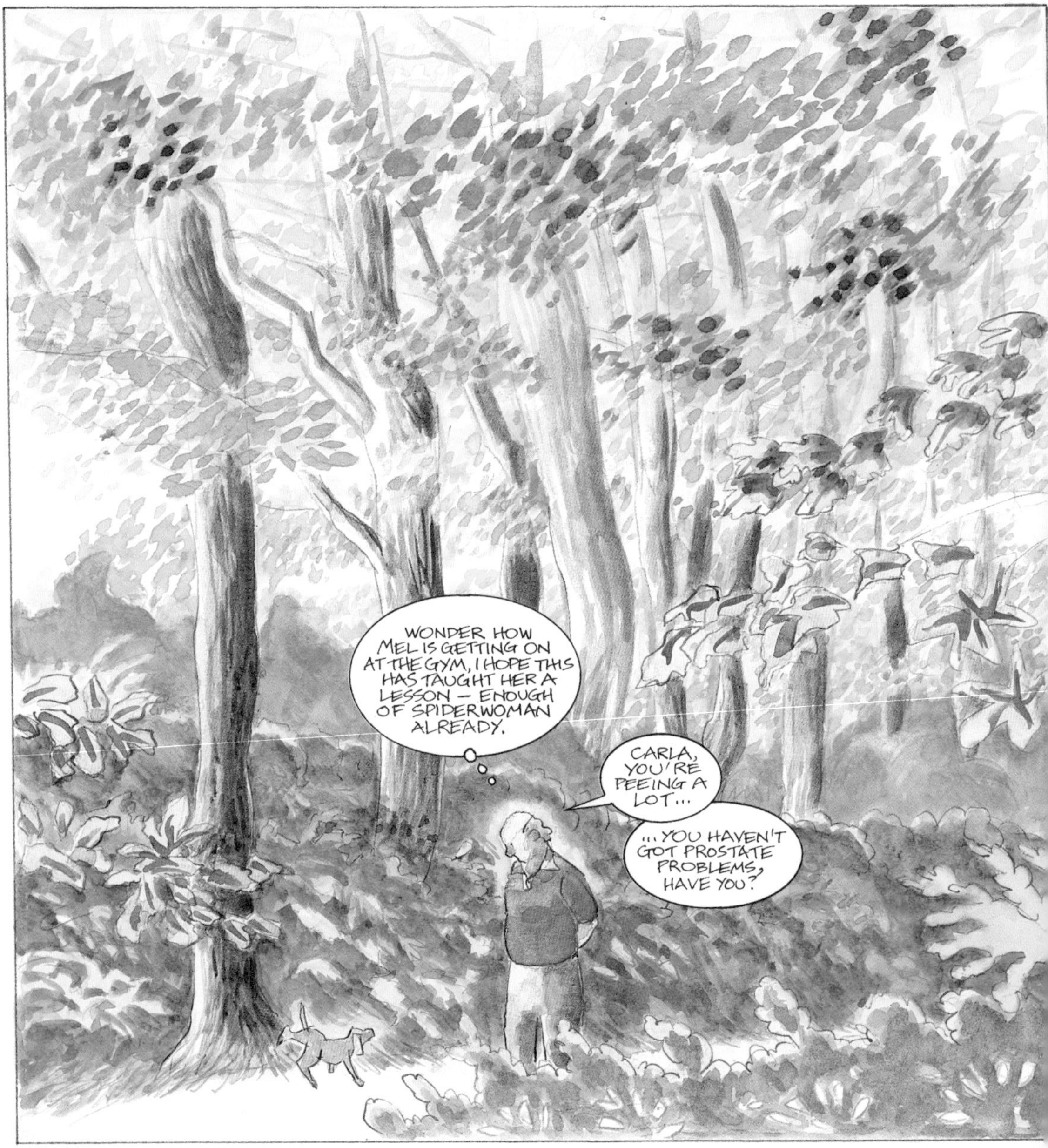
WONDER HOW MEL IS GETTING ON AT THE GYM, I HOPE THIS HAS TAUGHT HER A LESSON — ENOUGH OF SPIDERWOMAN ALREADY.
CARLA, YOU'RE PEEING A LOT...
...YOU HAVEN'T GOT PROSTATE PROBLEMS, HAVE YOU?

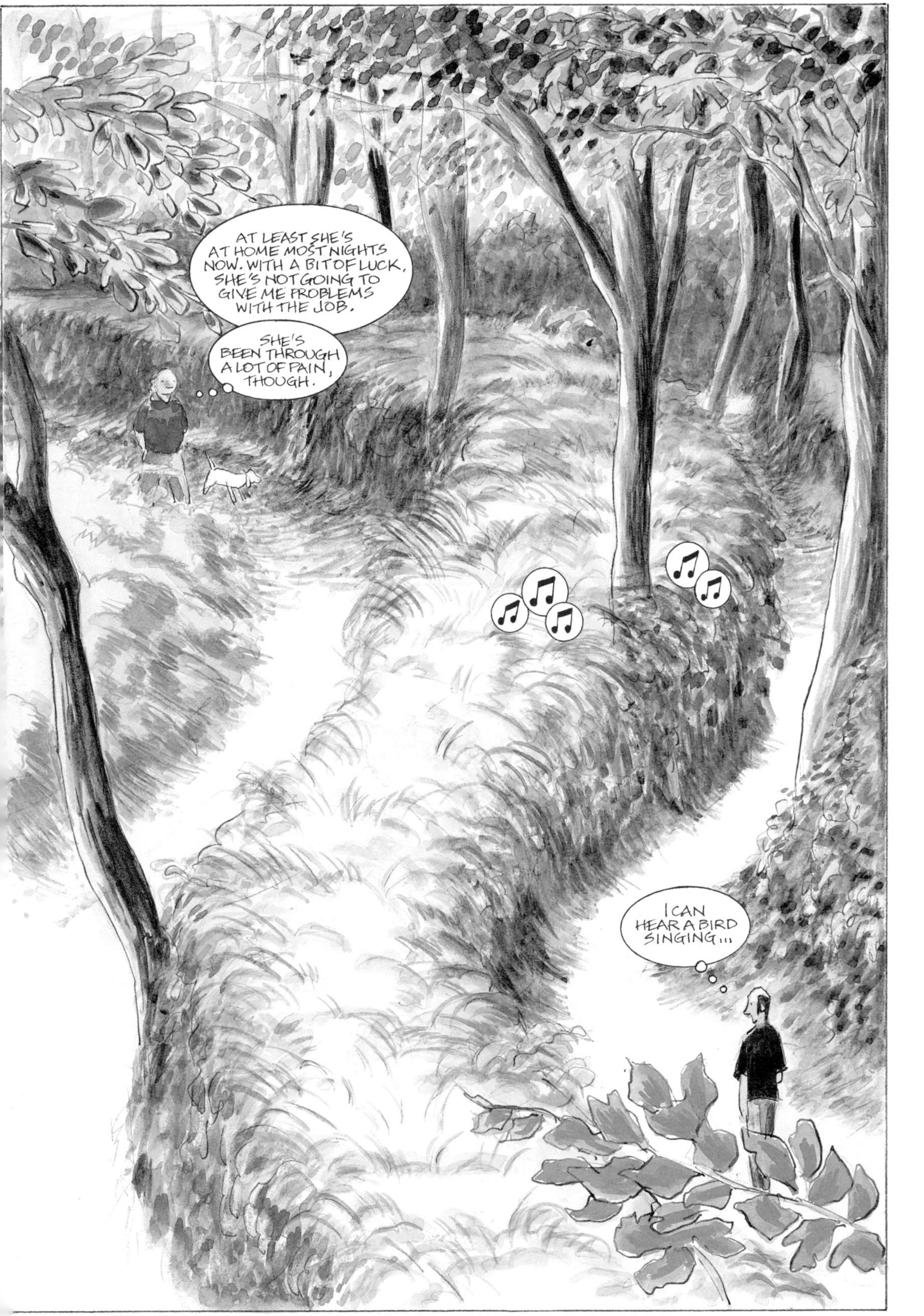
AT LEAST SHE'S AT HOME MOST NIGHTS NOW. WITH A BIT OF LUCK, SHE'S NOT GOING TO GIVE ME PROBLEMS WITH THE JOB.
SHE'S BEEN THROUGH A LOT OF PAIN, THOUGH.
I CAN HEAR A BIRD SINGING...

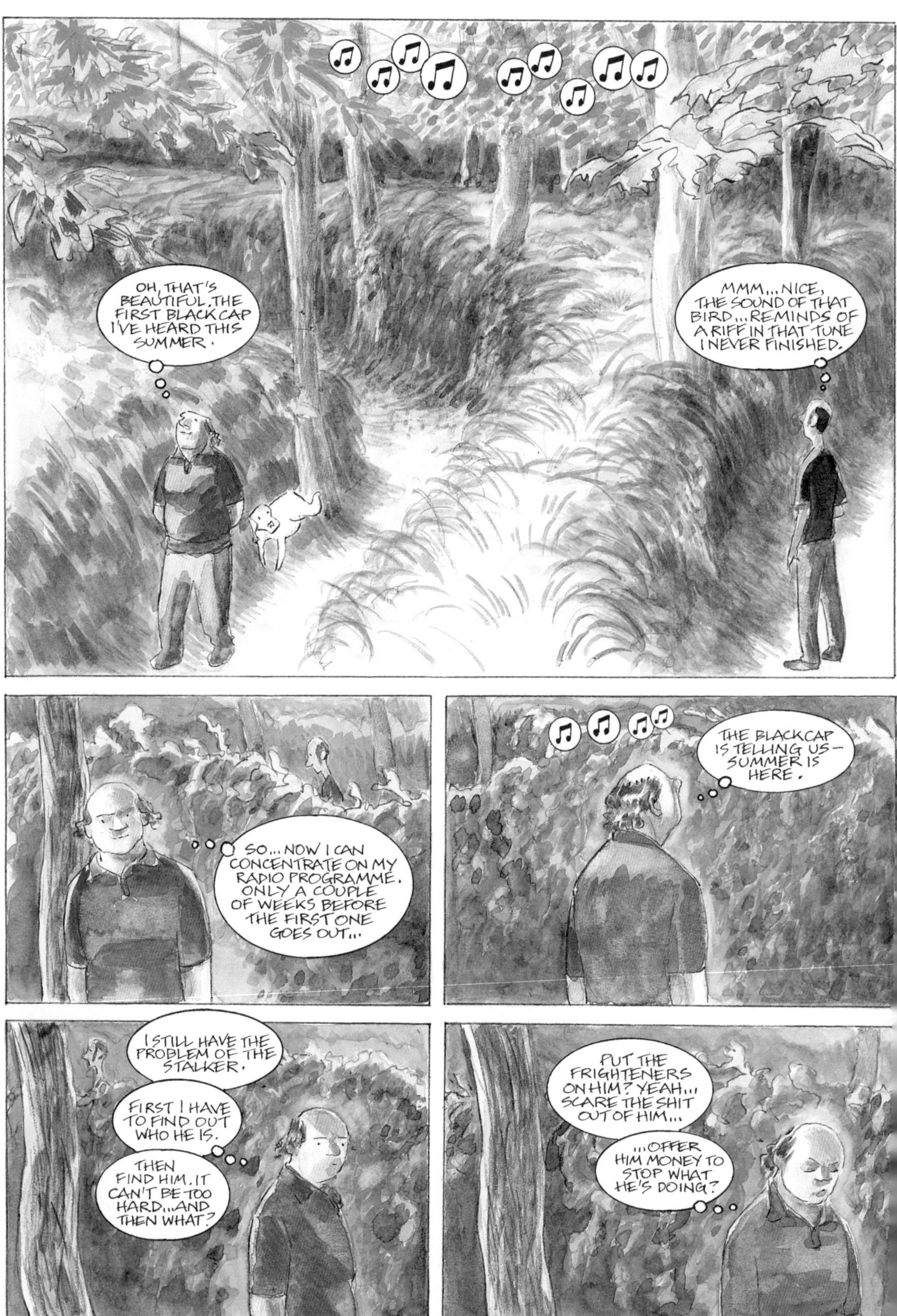
OH, THAT'S BEAUTIFUL. THE FIRST BLACKCAP I'VE HEARD THIS SUMMER.
MMM... NICE, THE SOUND OF THAT BIRD... REMINDS OF A RIFF IN THAT TUNE I NEVER FINISHED.
SO... NOW I CAN CONCENTRATE ON MY RADIO PROGRAMME. ONLY A COUPLE OF WEEKS BEFORE THE FIRST ONE GOES OUT...
THE BLACKCAP IS TELLING US— SUMMER IS HERE.
I STILL HAVE THE PROBLEM OF THE STALKER.
FIRST I HAVE TO FIND OUT WHO HE IS.
THEN FIND HIM. IT CAN'T BE TOO HARD... AND THEN WHAT?
PUT THE FRIGHTENERS ON HIM? YEAH... SCARE THE SHIT OUT OF HIM...
...OFFER HIM MONEY TO STOP WHAT HE'S DOING?

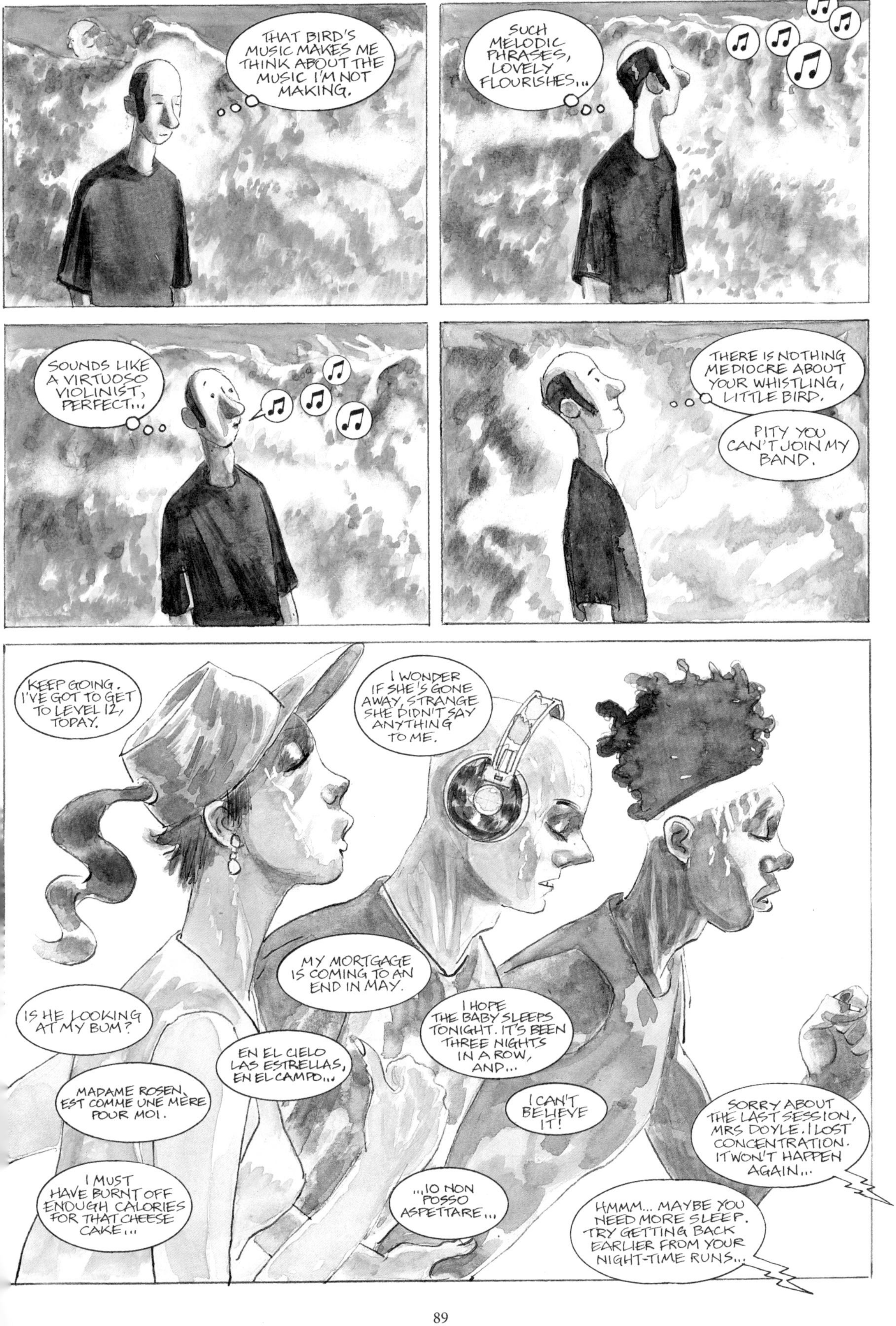
THAT BIRD'S MUSIC MAKES ME THINK ABOUT THE MUSIC I'M NOT MAKING.
SUCH MELODIC PHRASES, LOVELY FLOURISHES...
SOUNDS LIKE A VIRTUOSO VIOLINIST, PERFECT...
THERE IS NOTHING MEDIOCRE ABOUT YOUR WHISTLING, LITTLE BIRD.
PITY YOU CAN'T JOIN MY BAND.
KEEP GOING. I'VE GOT TO GET TO LEVEL 12, TODAY.
I WONDER IF SHE'S GONE AWAY, STRANGE SHE DIDN'T SAY ANYTHING TO ME.
MY MORTGAGE IS COMING TO AN END IN MAY.
IS HE LOOKING AT MY BUM?
I HOPE THE BABY SLEEPS TONIGHT. IT'S BEEN THREE NIGHTS IN A ROW, AND...
EN EL CIELO LAS ESTRELLAS, EN EL CAMPO...
MADAME ROSEN, EST COMME UNE MÈRE POUR MOI.
I CAN'T BELIEVE IT!
SORRY ABOUT THE LAST SESSION, MRS DOYLE. I LOST CONCENTRATION. IT WON'T HAPPEN AGAIN...
I MUST HAVE BURNT OFF ENOUGH CALORIES FOR THAT CHEESE CAKE...
...IO NON POSSO ASPETTARE...
HMMM... MAYBE YOU NEED MORE SLEEP. TRY GETTING BACK EARLIER FROM YOUR NIGHT-TIME RUNS...

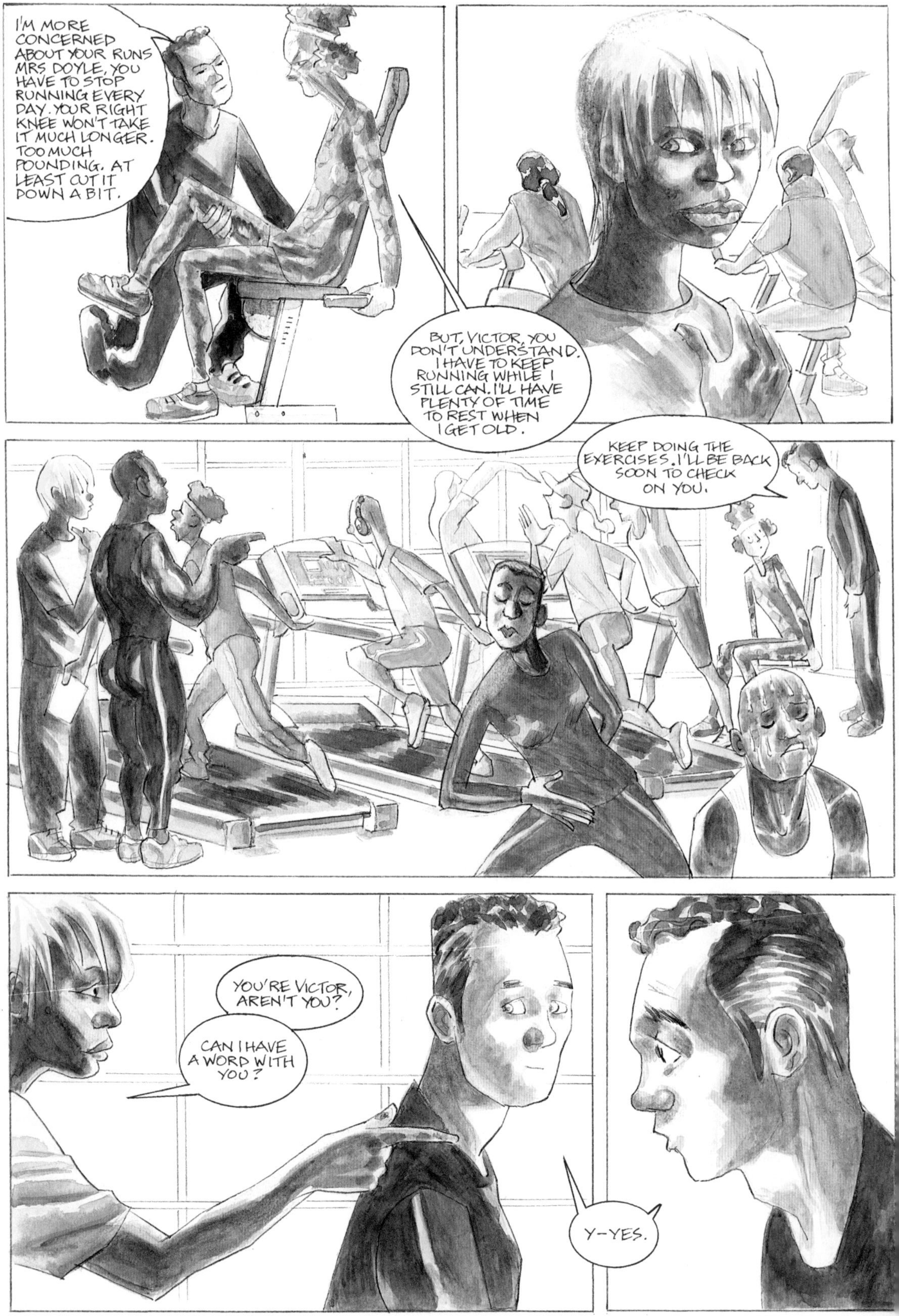

I'M MORE CONCERNED ABOUT YOUR RUNS MRS DOYLE, YOU HAVE TO STOP RUNNING EVERY DAY. YOUR RIGHT KNEE WON'T TAKE IT MUCH LONGER. TOO MUCH POUNDING. AT LEAST CUT IT DOWN A BIT.
BUT, VICTOR, YOU DON'T UNDERSTAND. I HAVE TO KEEP RUNNING WHILE I STILL CAN. I'LL HAVE PLENTY OF TIME TO REST WHEN I GET OLD.
KEEP DOING THE EXERCISES. I'LL BE BACK SOON TO CHECK ON YOU.
YOU'RE VICTOR, AREN'T YOU?
CAN I HAVE A WORD WITH YOU?
Y-YES.

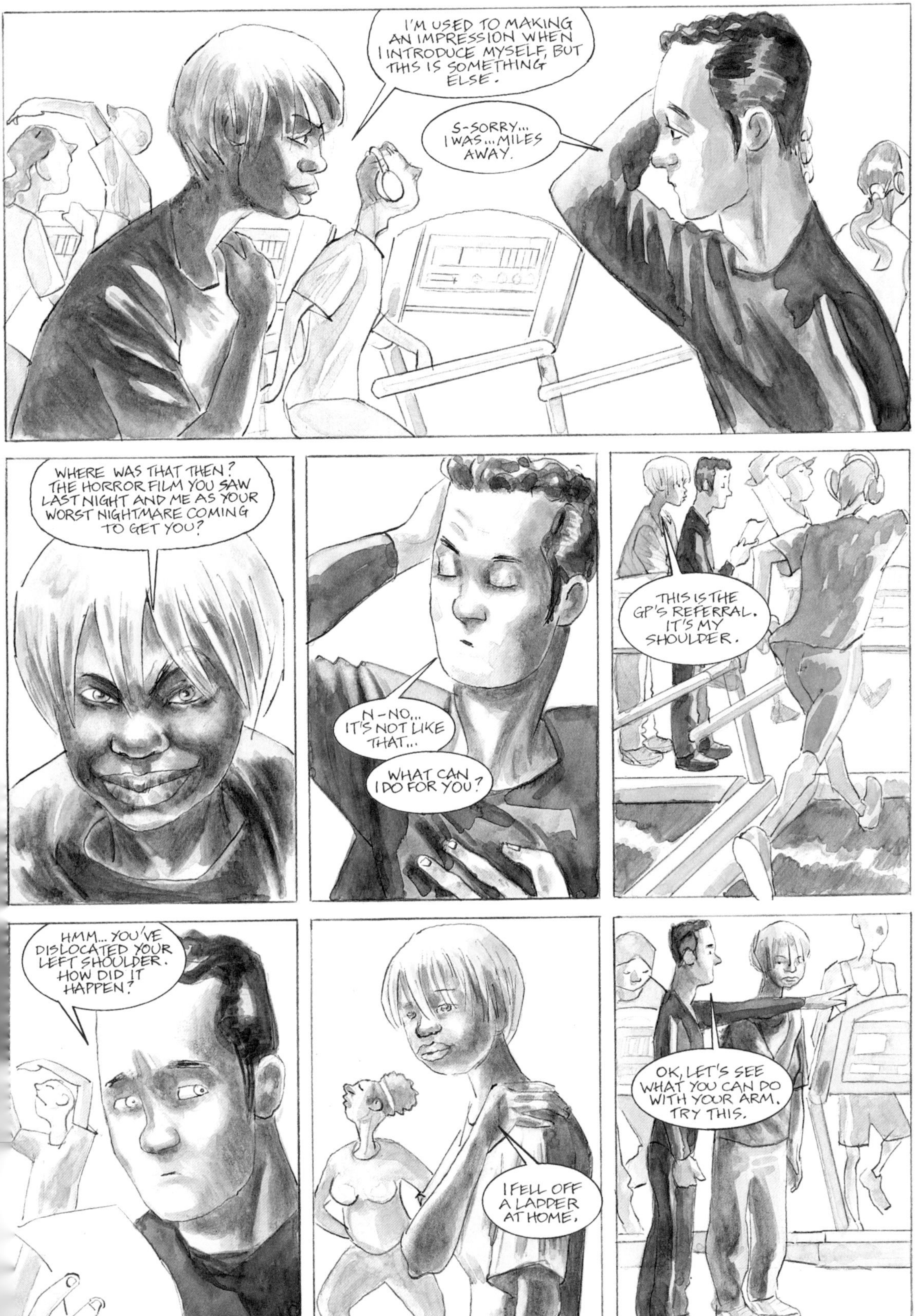
I'M USED TO MAKING AN IMPRESSION WHEN I INTRODUCE MYSELF, BUT THIS IS SOMETHING ELSE.
S-SORRY... I WAS... MILES AWAY.
WHERE WAS THAT THEN? THE HORROR FILM YOU SAW LAST NIGHT AND ME AS YOUR WORST NIGHTMARE COMING TO GET YOU?
N-NO... IT'S NOT LIKE THAT...
WHAT CAN I DO FOR YOU?
THIS IS THE GP'S REFERRAL. IT'S MY SHOULDER.
HMM... YOU'VE DISLOCATED YOUR LEFT SHOULDER. HOW DID IT HAPPEN?
I FELL OFF A LADDER AT HOME.
OK, LET'S SEE WHAT YOU CAN DO WITH YOUR ARM. TRY THIS.

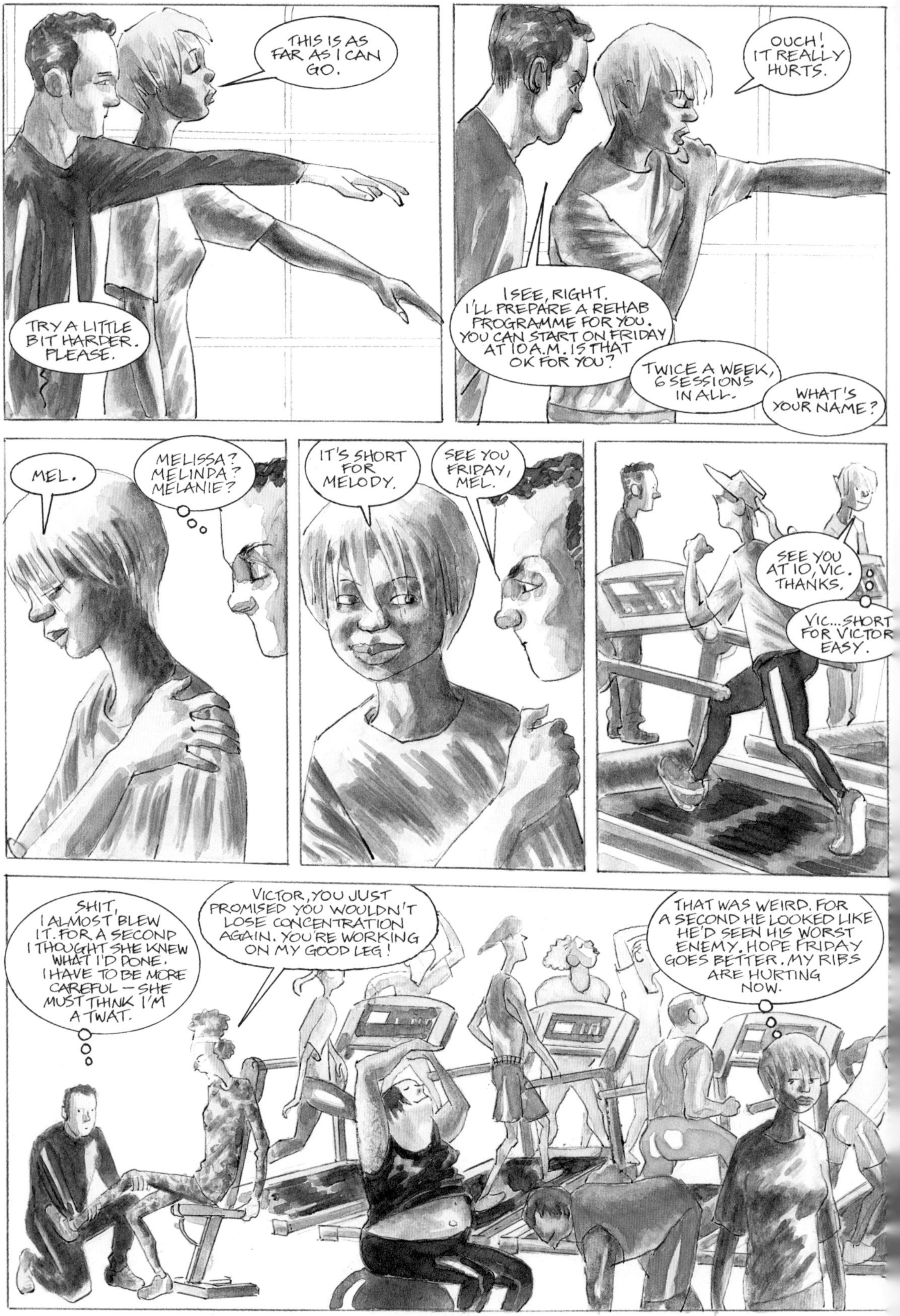
THIS IS AS FAR AS I CAN GO.
TRY A LITTLE BIT HARDER. PLEASE.
OUCH! IT REALLY HURTS.
I SEE, RIGHT. I'LL PREPARE A REHAB PROGRAMME FOR YOU. YOU CAN START ON FRIDAY AT 10 A.M. IS THAT OK FOR YOU?
TWICE A WEEK, 6 SESSIONS IN ALL.
WHAT'S YOUR NAME?
MEL.
MELISSA? MELINDA? MELANIE?
IT'S SHORT FOR MELODY.
SEE YOU FRIDAY, MEL.
SEE YOU AT 10, VIC. THANKS.
VIC... SHORT FOR VICTOR EASY.
SHIT, I ALMOST BLEW IT. FOR A SECOND I THOUGHT SHE KNEW WHAT I'D DONE. I HAVE TO BE MORE CAREFUL — SHE MUST THINK I'M A TWAT.
VICTOR, YOU JUST PROMISED YOU WOULDN'T LOSE CONCENTRATION AGAIN. YOU'RE WORKING ON MY GOOD LEG!
THAT WAS WEIRD. FOR A SECOND HE LOOKED LIKE HE'D SEEN HIS WORST ENEMY. HOPE FRIDAY GOES BETTER. MY RIBS ARE HURTING NOW.

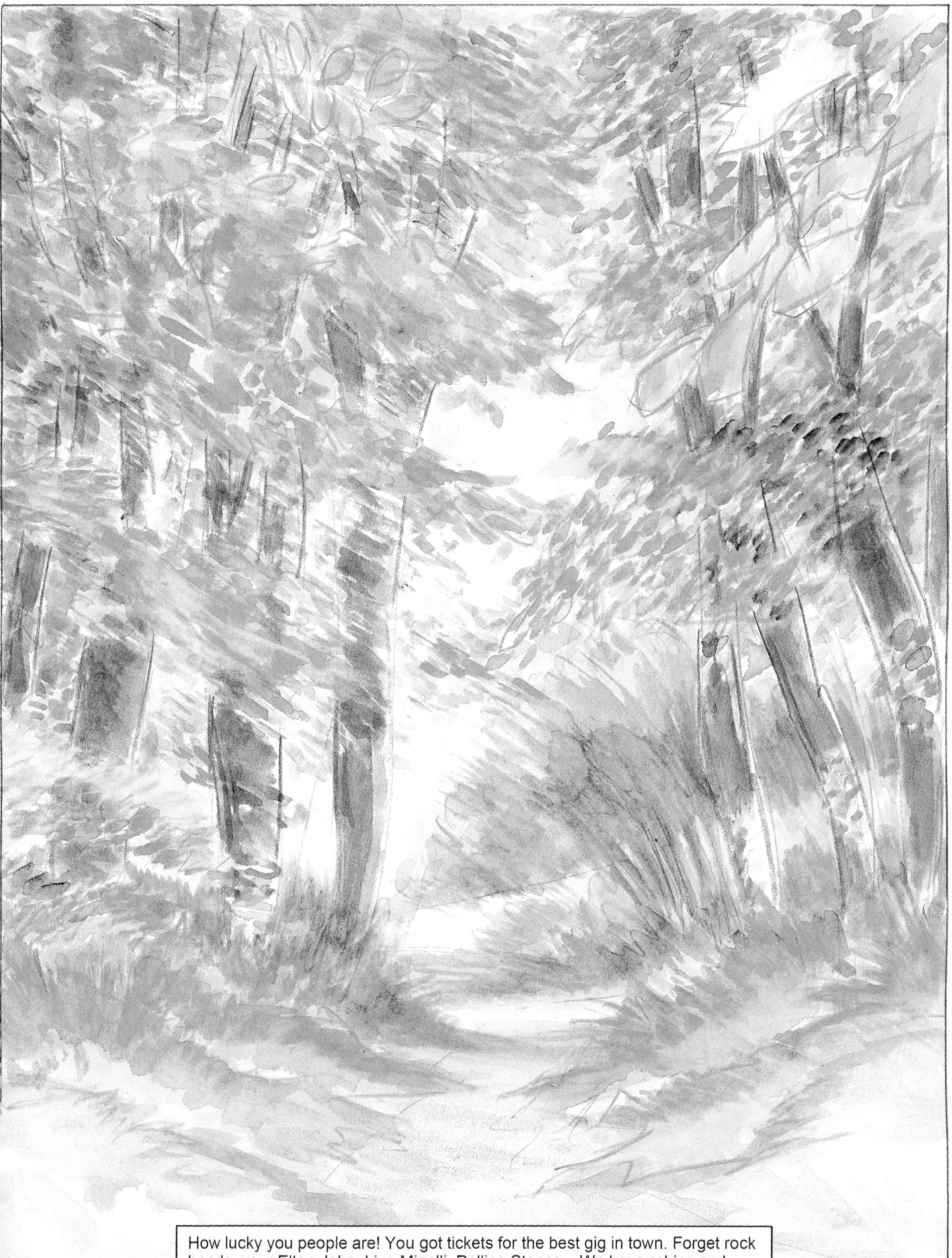
How lucky you people are! You got tickets for the best gig in town. Forget rock bands, your Elton John, Liza Minelli, Rolling Stones... We have robins and wrens, thrushes and blackbirds, blue tits, starlings, jays, nuthatches and treecreepers. There may even be a guest appearance from a parakeet. The trees are their stage, and they are the most beautiful performers you'll ever hear. Amazing harmonies, stunning duets, rocking trios, incredible quartets. This is the real concert in the park.

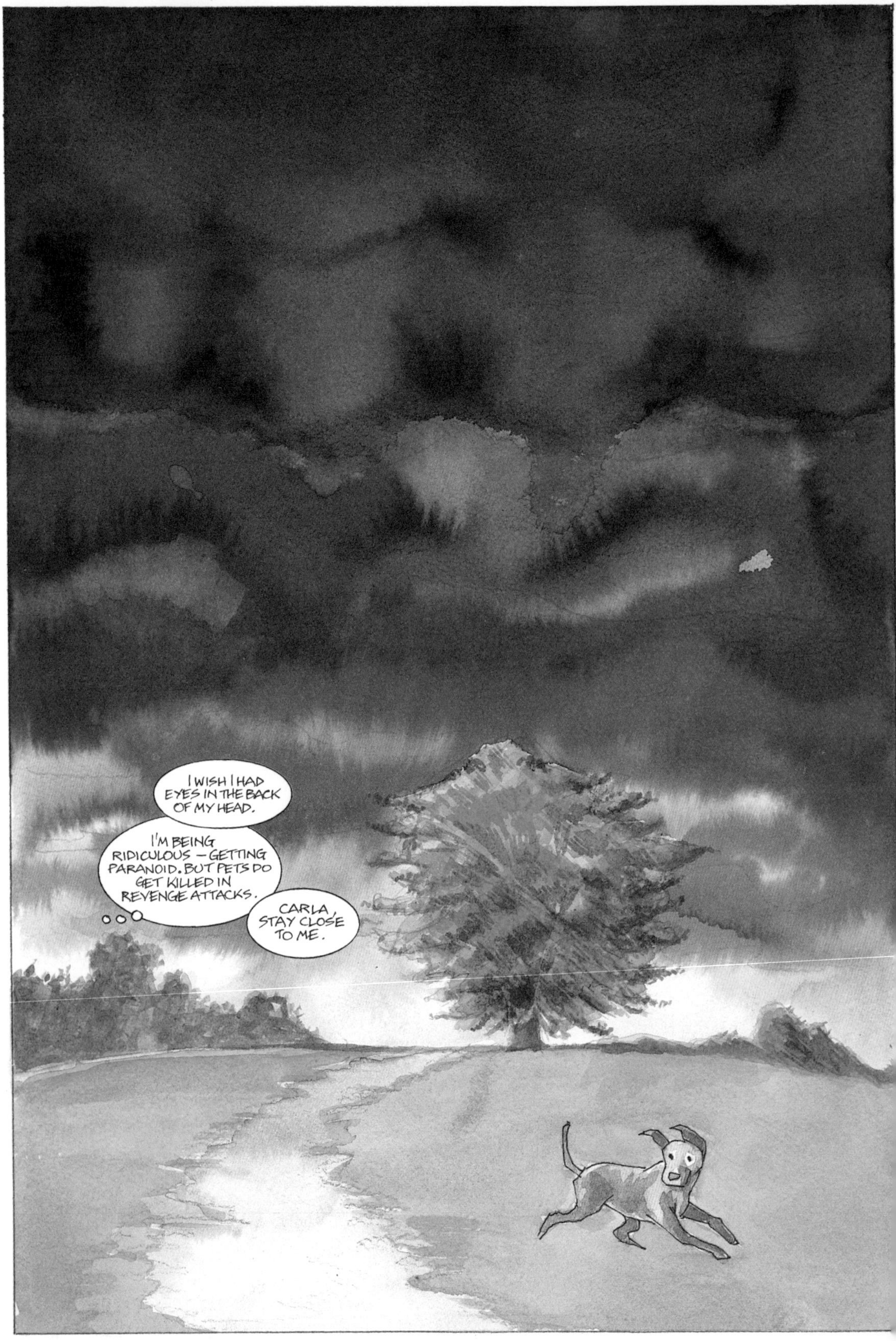
I WISH I HAD EYES IN THE BACK OF MY HEAD.
I'M BEING RIDICULOUS — GETTING PARANOID. BUT PETS DO GET KILLED IN REVENGE ATTACKS.
CARLA, STAY CLOSE TO ME.

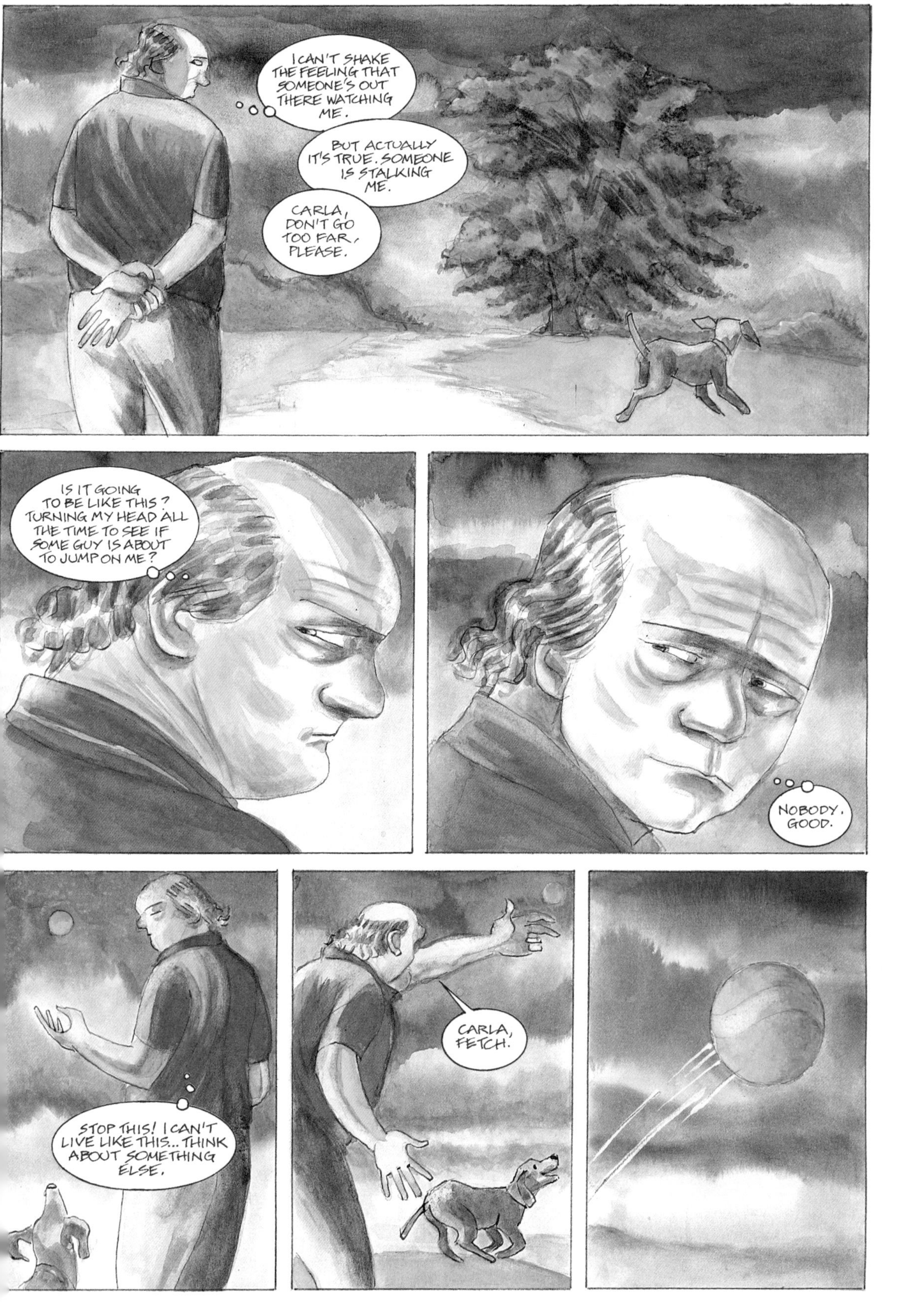
I CAN'T SHAKE THE FEELING THAT SOMEONE'S OUT THERE WATCHING ME.
BUT ACTUALLY IT'S TRUE. SOMEONE IS STALKING ME.
CARLA, DON'T GO TOO FAR, PLEASE.
IS IT GOING TO BE LIKE THIS? TURNING MY HEAD ALL THE TIME TO SEE IF SOME GUY IS ABOUT TO JUMP ON ME?
NOBODY. GOOD.
STOP THIS! I CAN'T LIVE LIKE THIS... THINK ABOUT SOMETHING ELSE.
CARLA, FETCH.

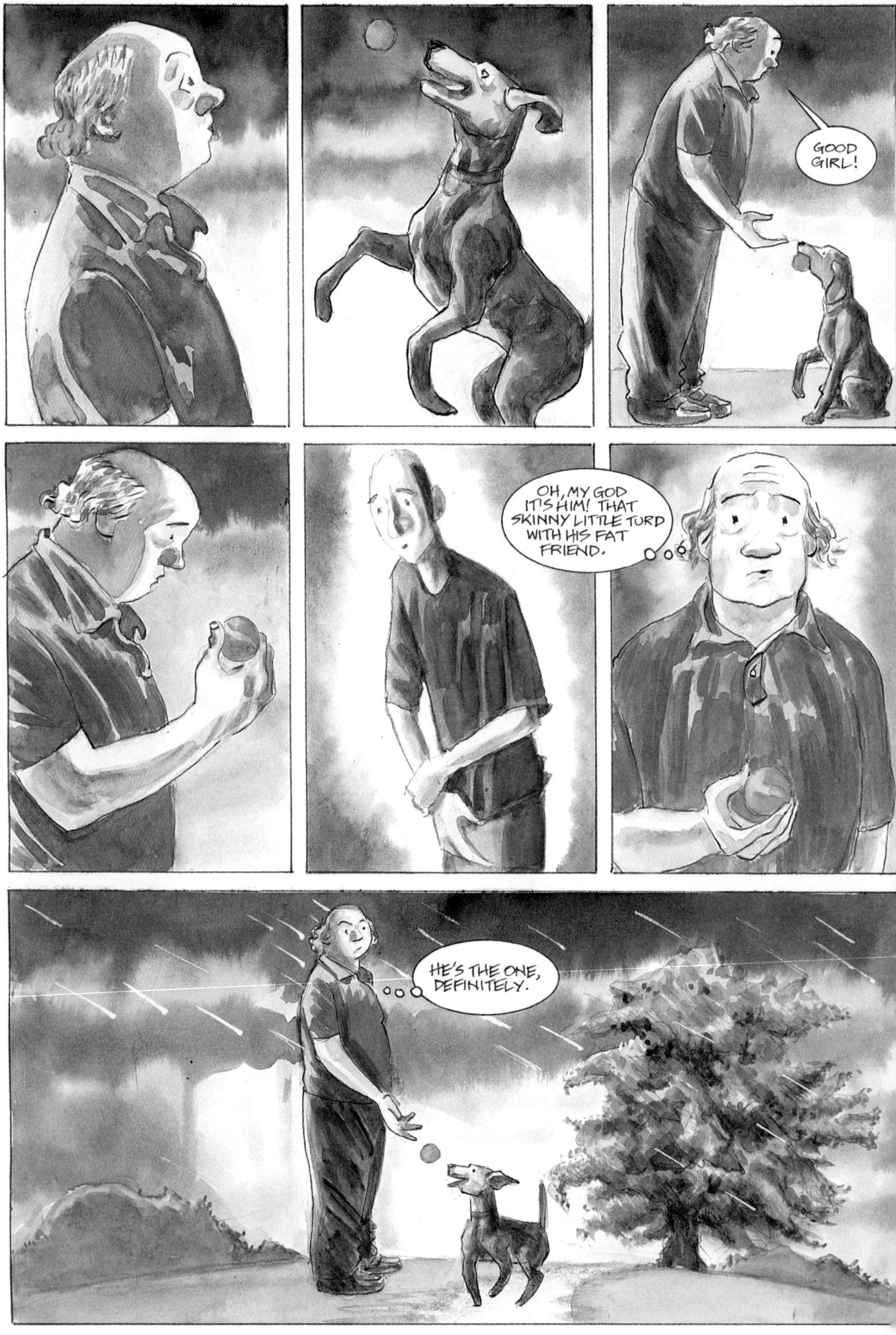
GOOD GIRL!
OH, MY GOD IT'S HIM! THAT SKINNY LITTLE TURD WITH HIS FAT FRIEND.
HE'S THE ONE, DEFINITELY.

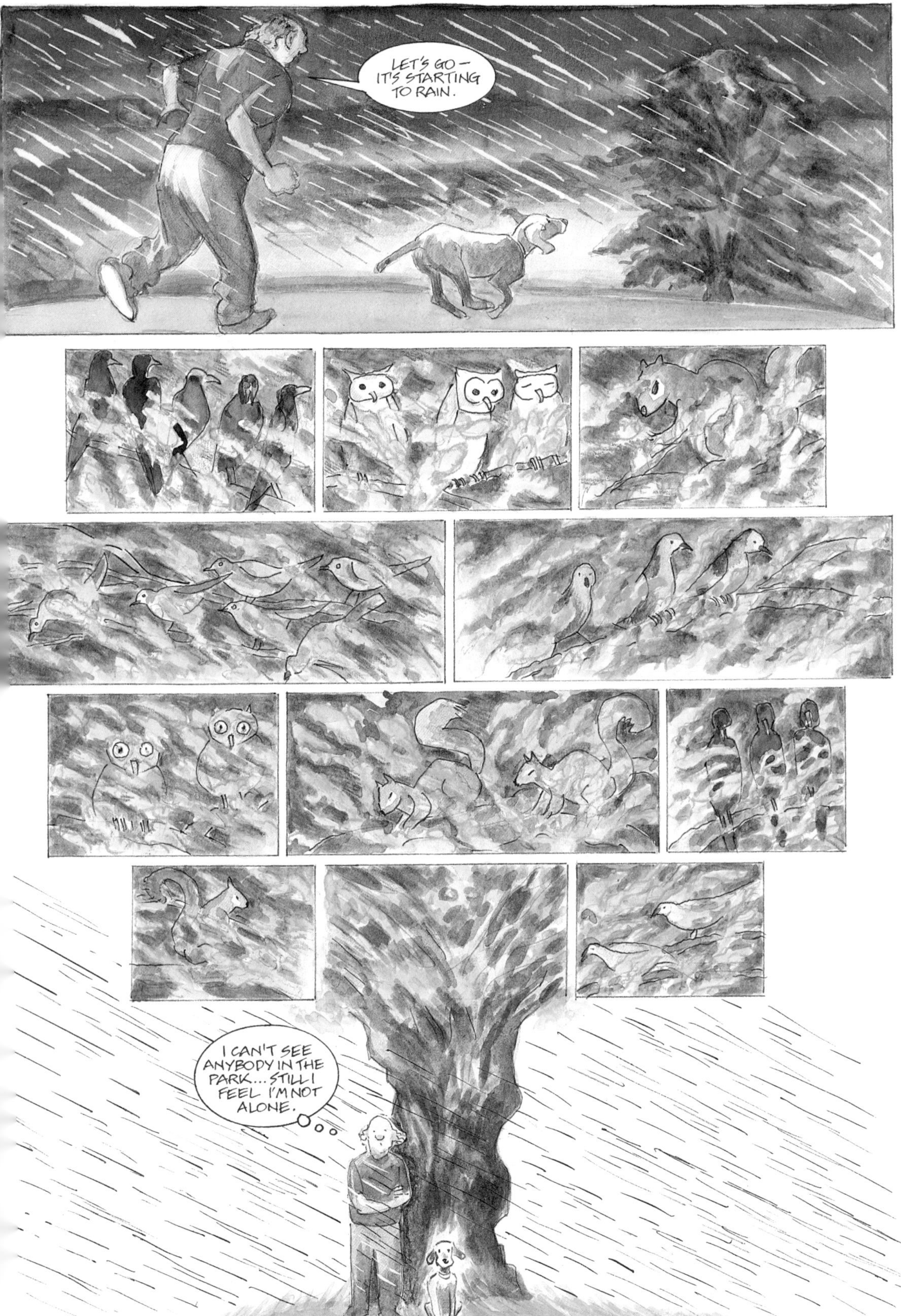
LET'S GO — IT'S STARTING TO RAIN.
I CAN'T SEE ANYBODY IN THE PARK... STILL I FEEL I'M NOT ALONE.

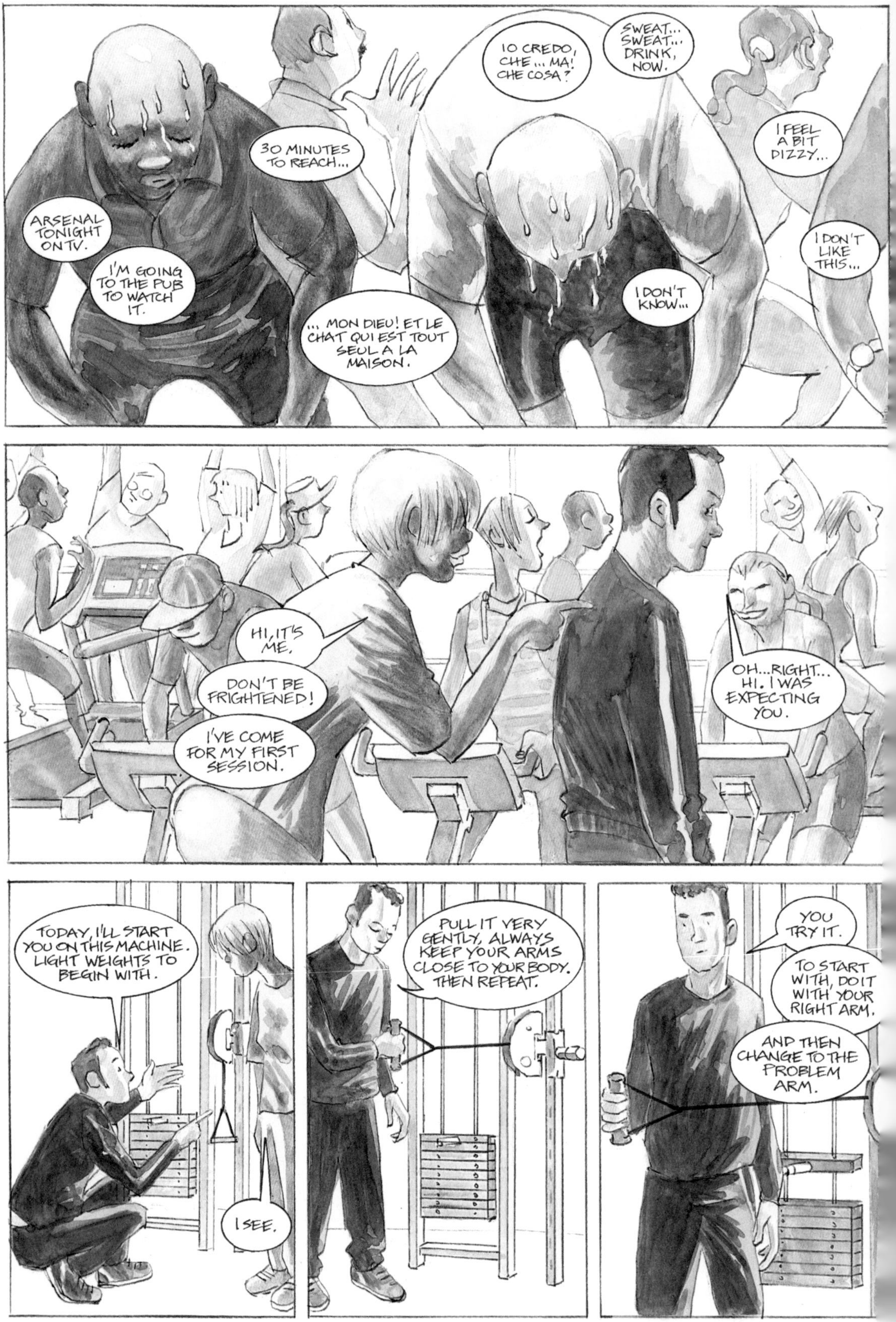
ARSENAL TONIGHT ON TV.
I'M GOING TO THE PUB TO WATCH IT.
30 MINUTES TO REACH...
... MON DIEU! ET LE CHAT QUI EST TOUT SEUL A LA MAISON.
IO CREDO, CHE ... MA! CHE COSA?
SWEAT... SWEAT... DRINK, NOW.
I DON'T KNOW...
I FEEL A BIT DIZZY...
I DON'T LIKE THIS...
HI, IT'S ME.
DON'T BE FRIGHTENED!
I'VE COME FOR MY FIRST SESSION.
OH...RIGHT... HI. I WAS EXPECTING YOU.
TODAY, I'LL START YOU ON THIS MACHINE. LIGHT WEIGHTS TO BEGIN WITH.
I SEE.
PULL IT VERY GENTLY, ALWAYS KEEP YOUR ARMS CLOSE TO YOUR BODY. THEN REPEAT.
YOU TRY IT.
TO START WITH, DO IT WITH YOUR RIGHT ARM.
AND THEN CHANGE TO THE PROBLEM ARM.

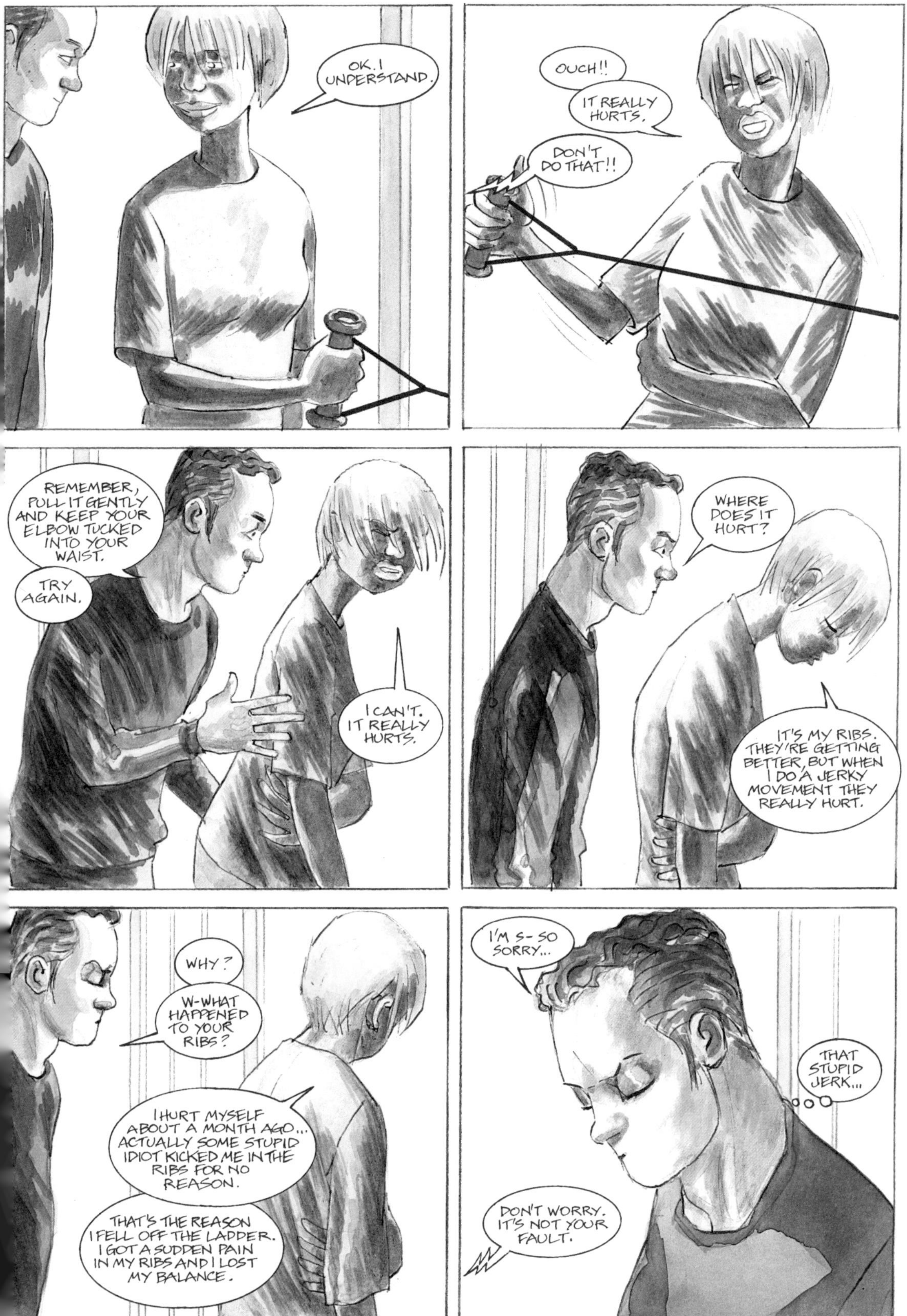
OK. I UNDERSTAND.
OUCH!!
IT REALLY HURTS.
DON'T DO THAT!!
REMEMBER, PULL IT GENTLY AND KEEP YOUR ELBOW TUCKED INTO YOUR WAIST.
TRY AGAIN.
I CAN'T. IT REALLY HURTS.
WHERE DOES IT HURT?
IT'S MY RIBS. THEY'RE GETTING BETTER, BUT WHEN I DO A JERKY MOVEMENT THEY REALLY HURT.
WHY?
W-WHAT HAPPENED TO YOUR RIBS?
I HURT MYSELF ABOUT A MONTH AGO... ACTUALLY SOME STUPID IDIOT KICKED ME IN THE RIBS FOR NO REASON.
THAT'S THE REASON I FELL OFF THE LADDER. I GOT A SUDDEN PAIN IN MY RIBS AND I LOST MY BALANCE.
I'M S-SO SORRY...
THAT STUPID JERK...
DON'T WORRY. IT'S NOT YOUR FAULT.

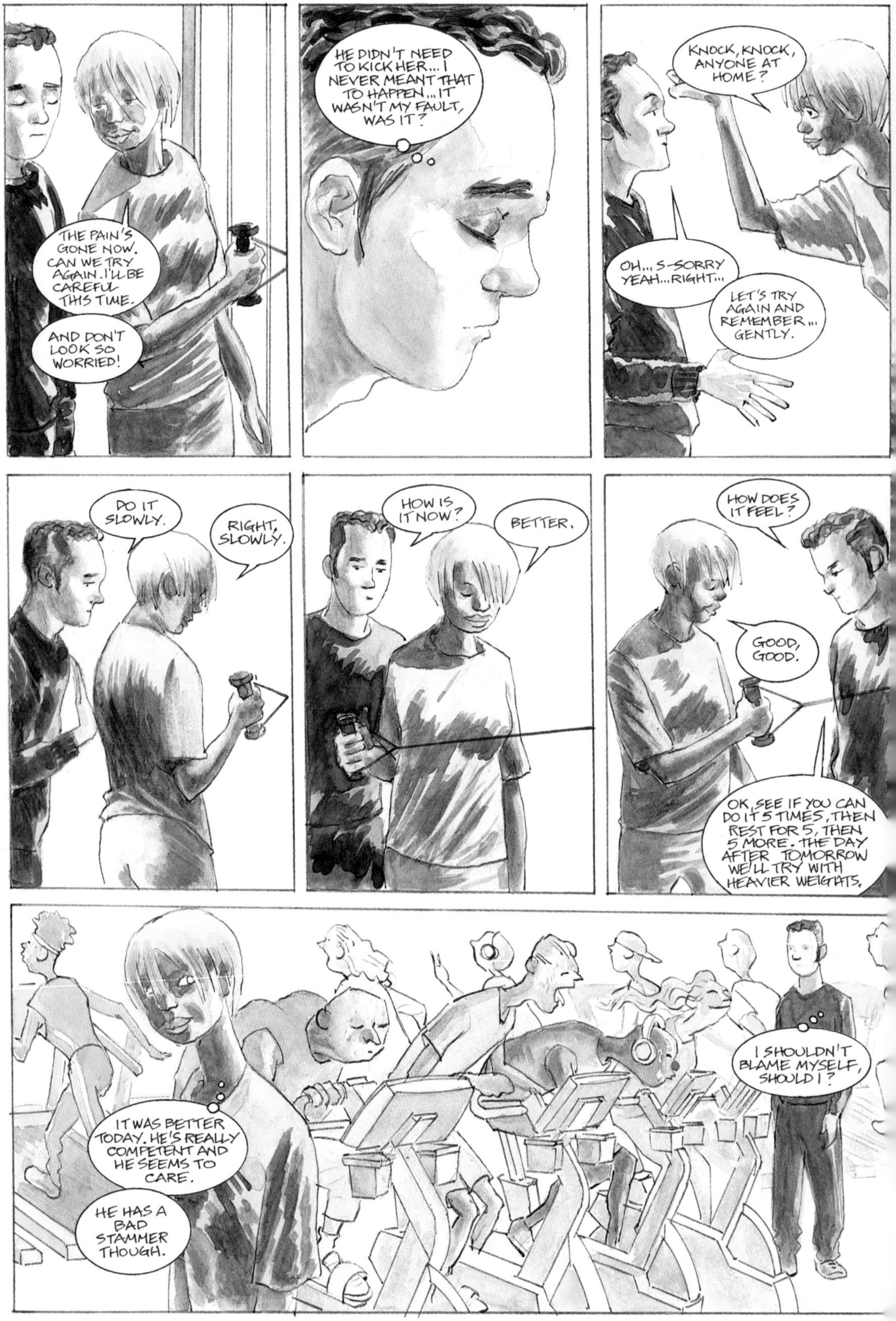
THE PAIN'S GONE NOW. CAN WE TRY AGAIN. I'LL BE CAREFUL THIS TIME.
AND DON'T LOOK SO WORRIED!
HE DIDN'T NEED TO KICK HER... I NEVER MEANT THAT TO HAPPEN... IT WASN'T MY FAULT, WAS IT?
KNOCK, KNOCK, ANYONE AT HOME?
OH... S-SORRY YEAH... RIGHT...
LET'S TRY AGAIN AND REMEMBER... GENTLY.
DO IT SLOWLY.
RIGHT, SLOWLY.
HOW IS IT NOW?
BETTER.
HOW DOES IT FEEL?
GOOD, GOOD.
OK, SEE IF YOU CAN DO IT 5 TIMES, THEN REST FOR 5, THEN 5 MORE. THE DAY AFTER TOMORROW WE'LL TRY WITH HEAVIER WEIGHTS.
IT WAS BETTER TODAY. HE'S REALLY COMPETENT AND HE SEEMS TO CARE.
HE HAS A BAD STAMMER THOUGH.
I SHOULDN'T BLAME MYSELF, SHOULD I?

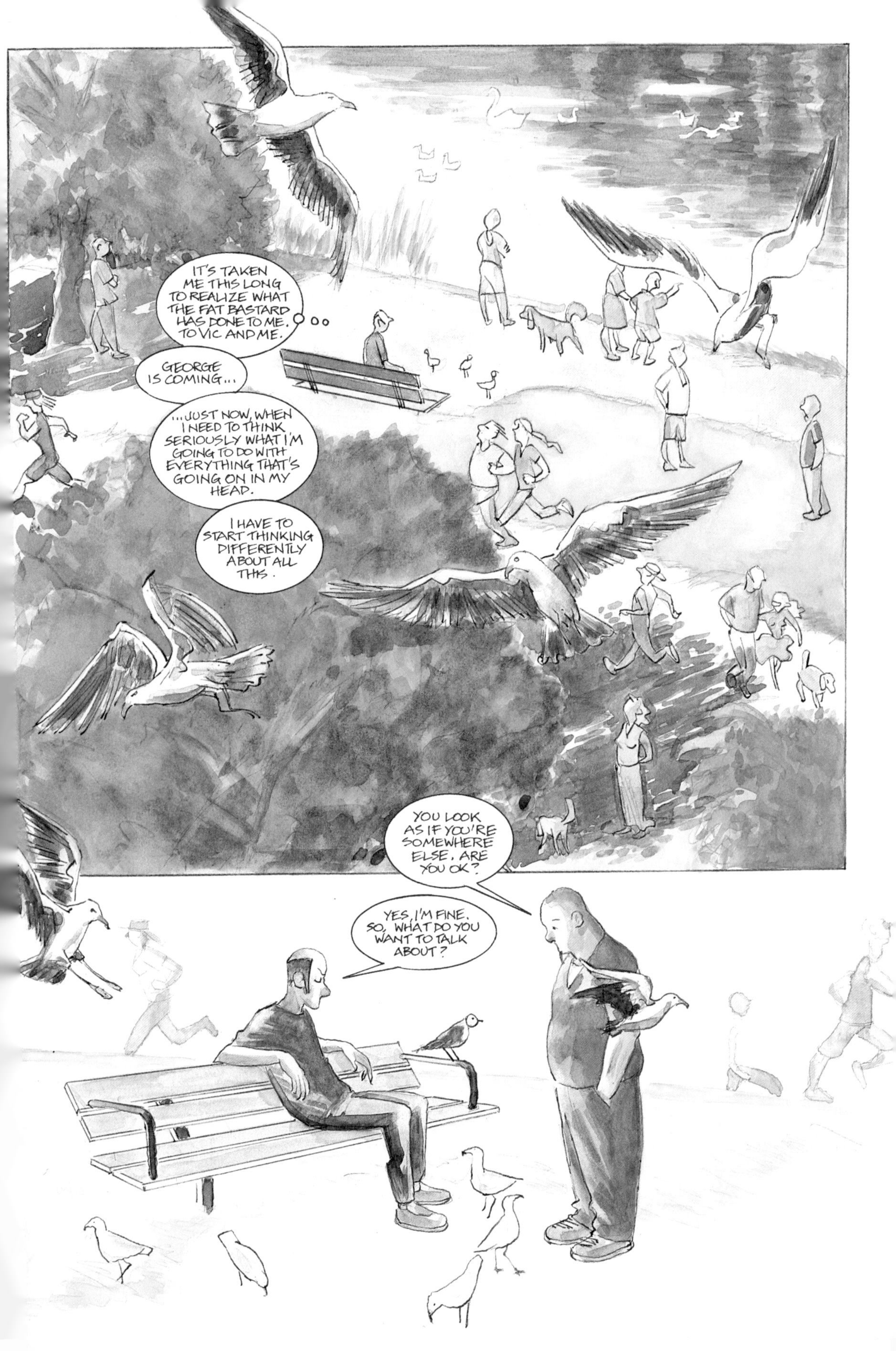
IT'S TAKEN ME THIS LONG TO REALIZE WHAT THE FAT BASTARD HAS DONE TO ME. TO VIC AND ME.
GEORGE IS COMING...
...JUST NOW, WHEN I NEED TO THINK SERIOUSLY WHAT I'M GOING TO DO WITH EVERYTHING THAT'S GOING ON IN MY HEAD.
I HAVE TO START THINKING DIFFERENTLY ABOUT ALL THIS.
YOU LOOK AS IF YOU'RE SOMEWHERE ELSE. ARE YOU OK?
YES, I'M FINE. SO, WHAT DO YOU WANT TO TALK ABOUT?

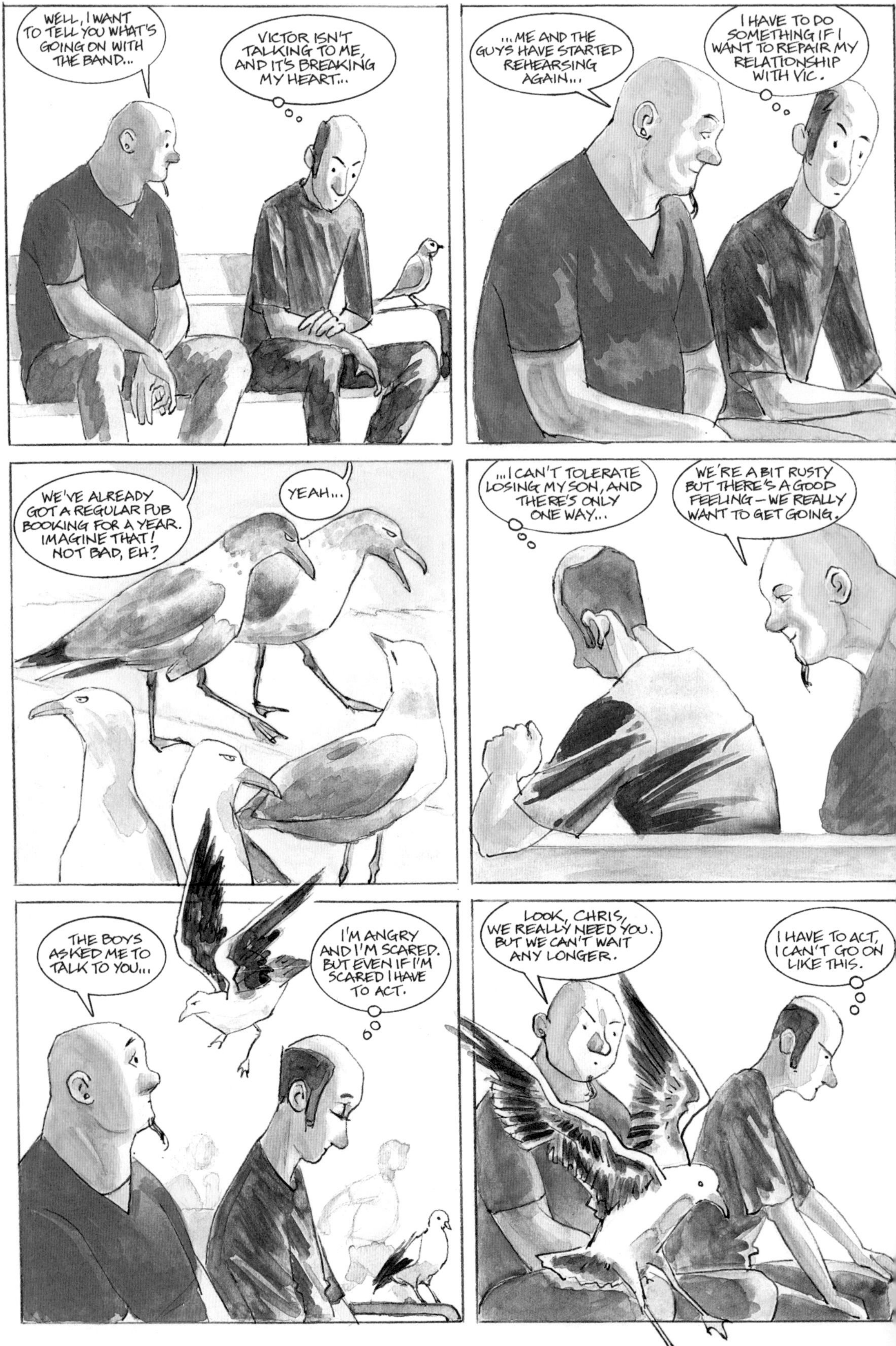
WELL, I WANT TO TELL YOU WHAT'S GOING ON WITH THE BAND...
VICTOR ISN'T TALKING TO ME, AND IT'S BREAKING MY HEART...
...ME AND THE GUYS HAVE STARTED REHEARSING AGAIN...
I HAVE TO DO SOMETHING IF I WANT TO REPAIR MY RELATIONSHIP WITH VIC.
WE'VE ALREADY GOT A REGULAR PUB BOOKING FOR A YEAR. IMAGINE THAT! NOT BAD, EH?
YEAH...
...I CAN'T TOLERATE LOSING MY SON, AND THERE'S ONLY ONE WAY...
WE'RE A BIT RUSTY BUT THERE'S A GOOD FEELING – WE REALLY WANT TO GET GOING.
THE BOYS ASKED ME TO TALK TO YOU...
I'M ANGRY AND I'M SCARED. BUT EVEN IF I'M SCARED I HAVE TO ACT.
LOOK, CHRIS, WE REALLY NEED YOU. BUT WE CAN'T WAIT ANY LONGER.
I HAVE TO ACT, I CAN'T GO ON LIKE THIS.

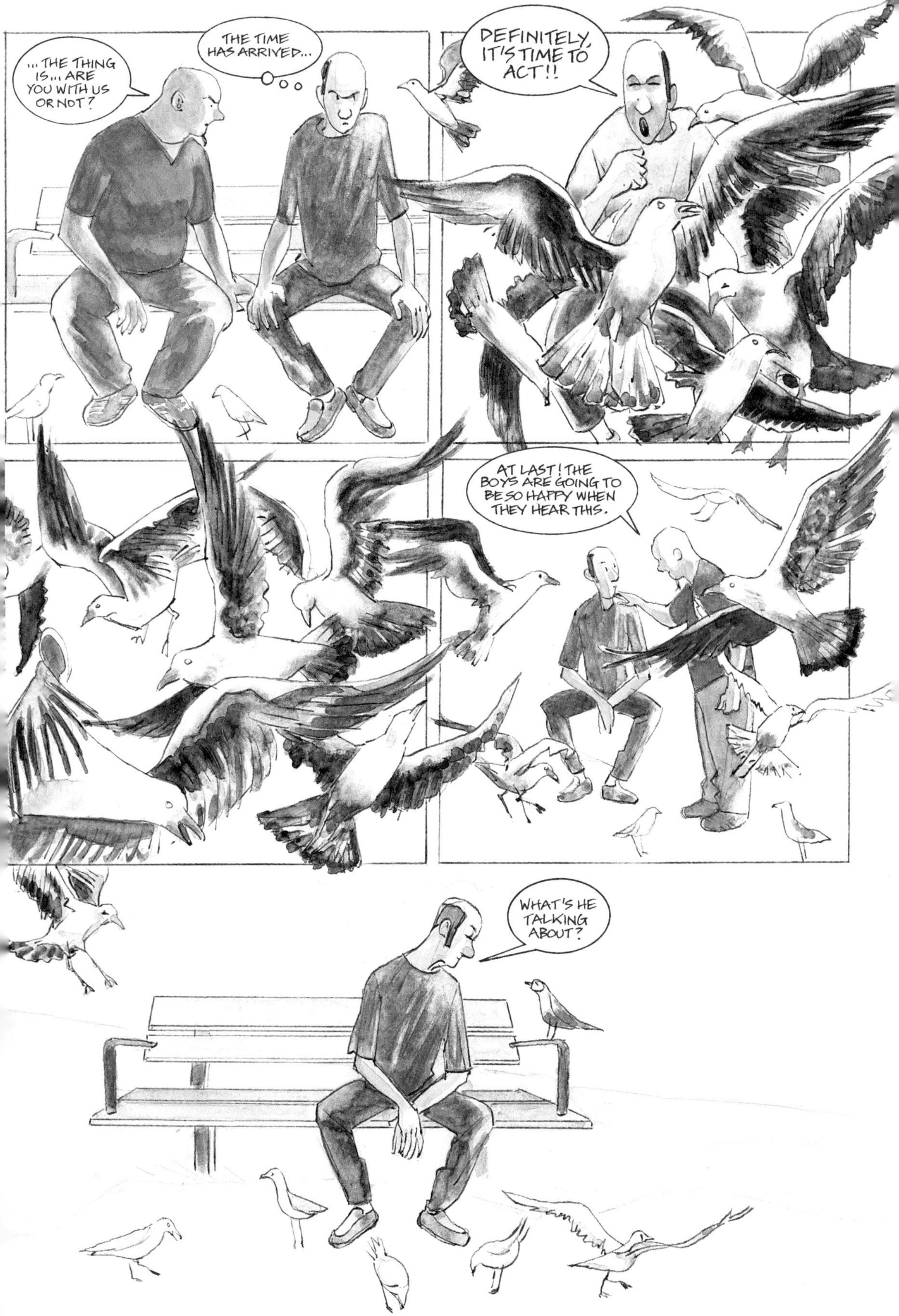
...THE THING IS... ARE YOU WITH US OR NOT?
THE TIME HAS ARRIVED...
DEFINITELY, IT'S TIME TO ACT!!
AT LAST! THE BOYS ARE GOING TO BE SO HAPPY WHEN THEY HEAR THIS.
WHAT'S HE TALKING ABOUT?

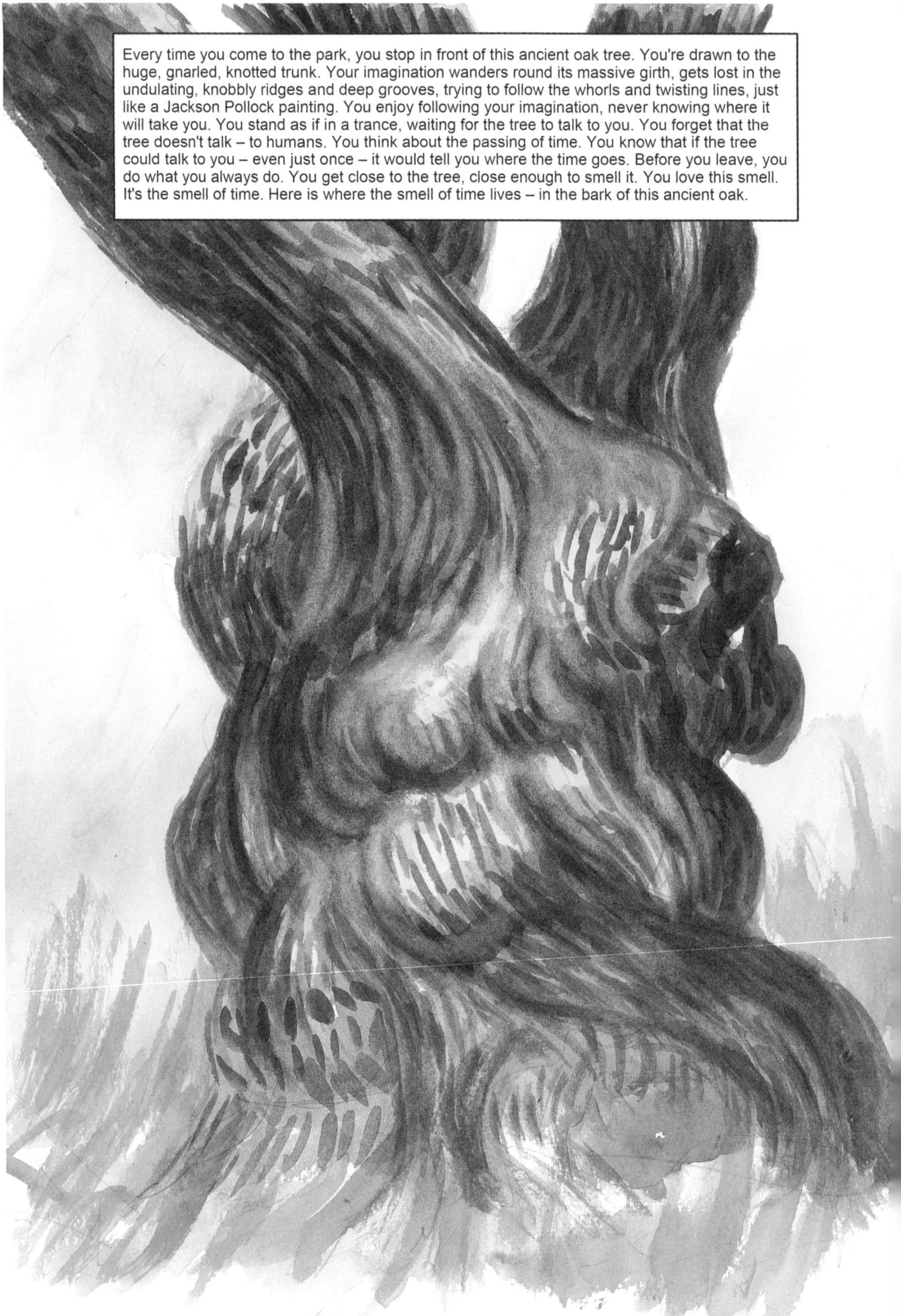
Every time you come to the park, you stop in front of this ancient oak tree. You're drawn to the huge, gnarled, knotted trunk. Your imagination wanders round its massive girth, gets lost in the undulating, knobbly ridges and deep grooves, trying to follow the whorls and twisting lines, just like a Jackson Pollock painting. You enjoy following your imagination, never knowing where it will take you. You stand as if in a trance, waiting for the tree to talk to you. You forget that the tree doesn't talk – to humans. You think about the passing of time. You know that if the tree could talk to you – even just once – it would tell you where the time goes. Before you leave, you do what you always do. You get close to the tree, close enough to smell it. You love this smell. It's the smell of time. Here is where the smell of time lives – in the bark of this ancient oak.

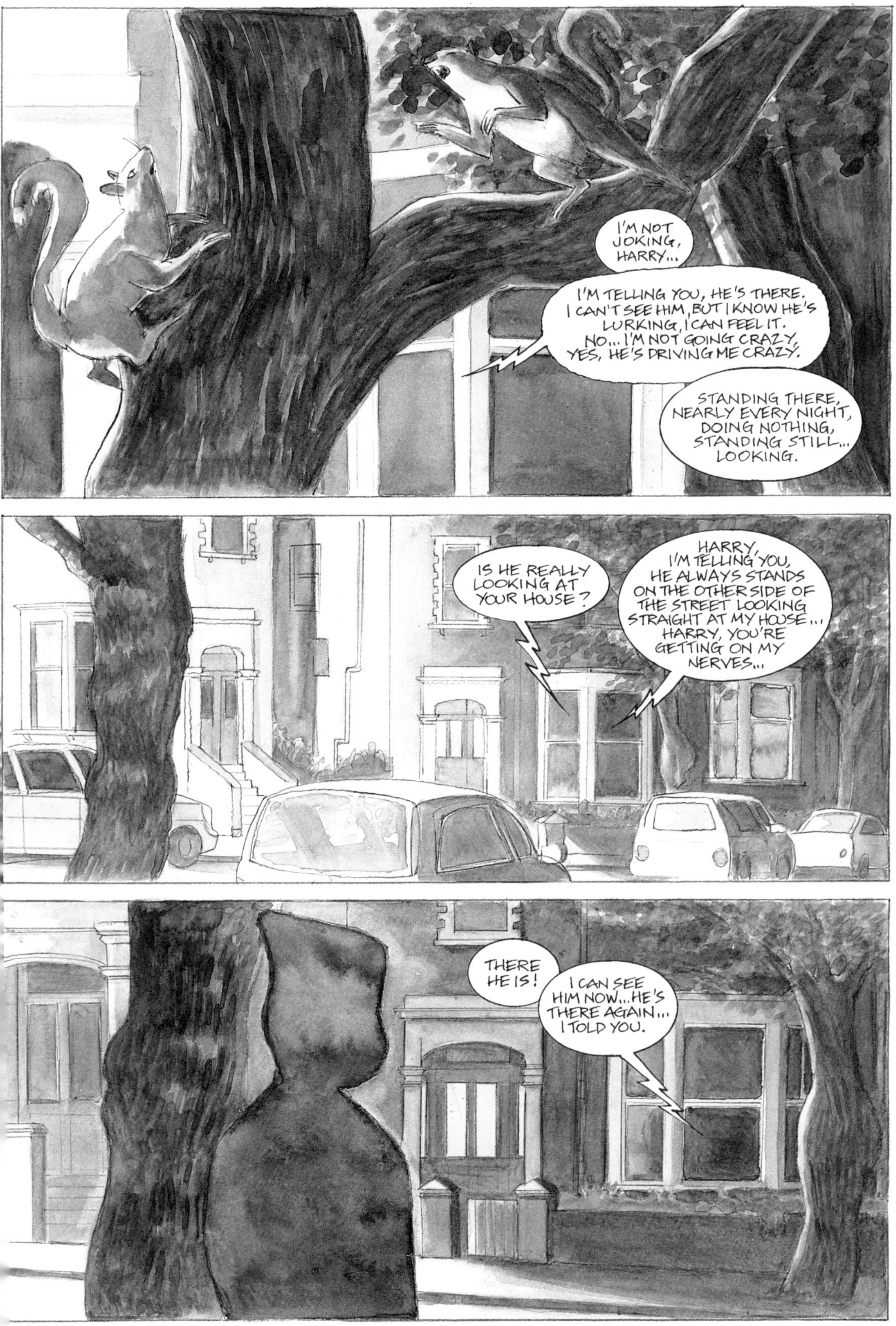
I'M NOT JOKING, HARRY...
I'M TELLING YOU, HE'S THERE. I CAN'T SEE HIM, BUT I KNOW HE'S LURKING, I CAN FEEL IT. NO... I'M NOT GOING CRAZY, YES, HE'S DRIVING ME CRAZY.
STANDING THERE, NEARLY EVERY NIGHT, DOING NOTHING, STANDING STILL... LOOKING.
IS HE REALLY LOOKING AT YOUR HOUSE?
HARRY, I'M TELLING YOU, HE ALWAYS STANDS ON THE OTHER SIDE OF THE STREET LOOKING STRAIGHT AT MY HOUSE... HARRY, YOU'RE GETTING ON MY NERVES...
THERE HE IS!
I CAN SEE HIM NOW... HE'S THERE AGAIN... I TOLD YOU.

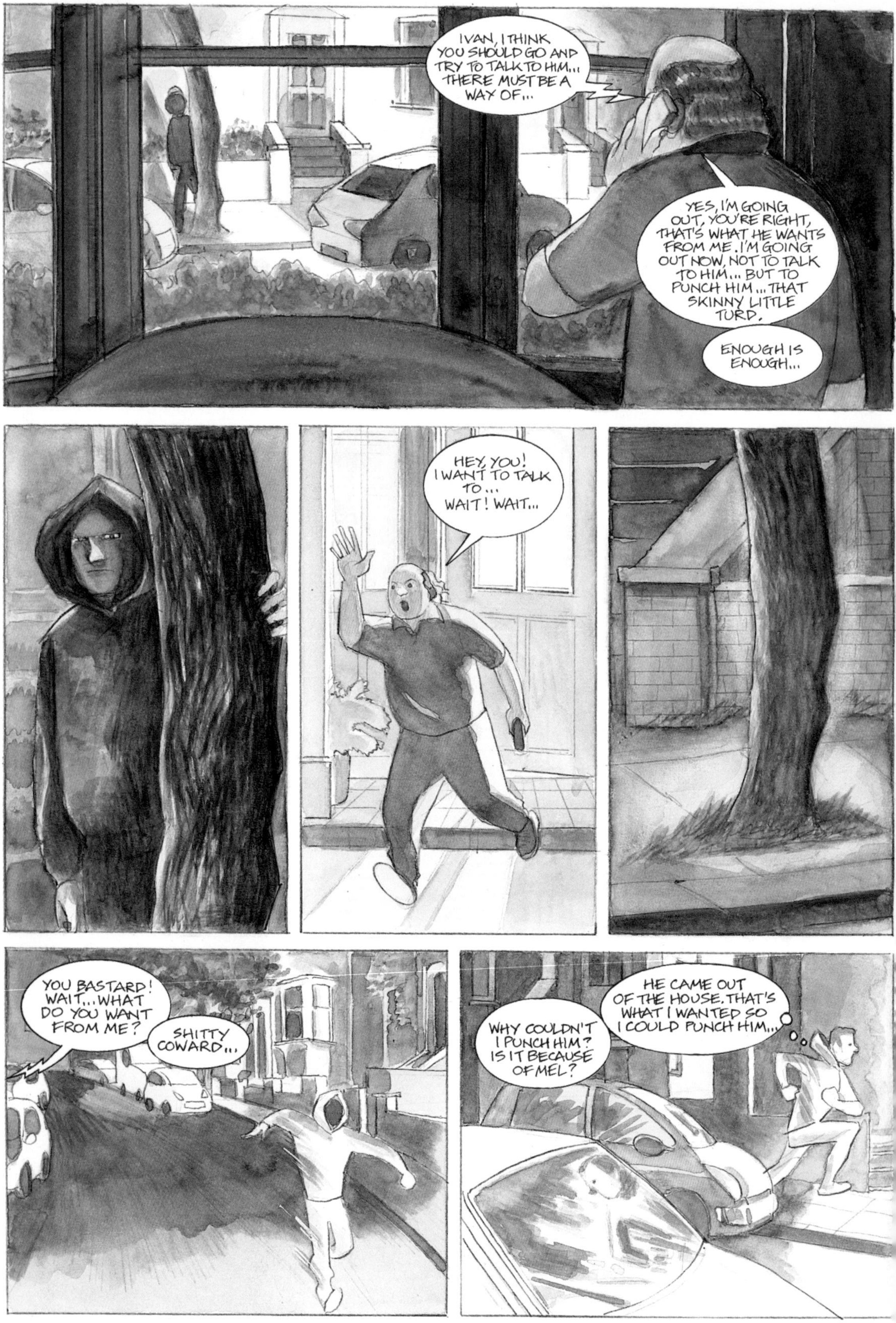
IVAN, I THINK YOU SHOULD GO AND TRY TO TALK TO HIM... THERE MUST BE A WAY OF...
YES, I'M GOING OUT, YOU'RE RIGHT, THAT'S WHAT HE WANTS FROM ME. I'M GOING OUT NOW, NOT TO TALK TO HIM... BUT TO PUNCH HIM... THAT SKINNY LITTLE TURD.
ENOUGH IS ENOUGH...
HEY, YOU! I WANT TO TALK TO... WAIT! WAIT...
YOU BASTARD! WAIT... WHAT DO YOU WANT FROM ME?
SHITTY COWARD...
WHY COULDN'T I PUNCH HIM? IS IT BECAUSE OF MEL?
HE CAME OUT OF THE HOUSE. THAT'S WHAT I WANTED SO I COULD PUNCH HIM...

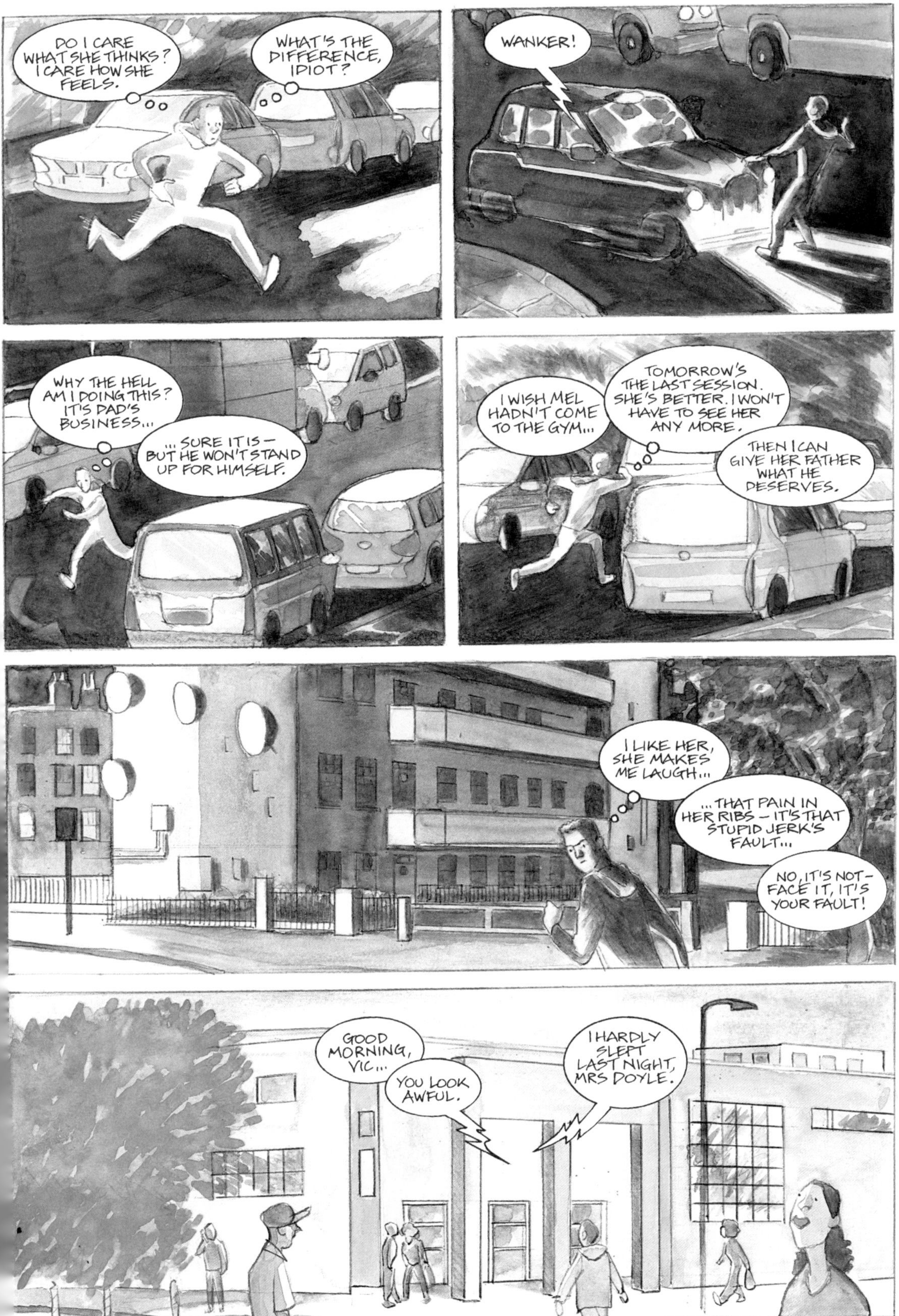
DO I CARE WHAT SHE THINKS? I CARE HOW SHE FEELS.
WHAT'S THE DIFFERENCE, IDIOT?
WANKER!
WHY THE HELL AM I DOING THIS? IT'S DAD'S BUSINESS...
...SURE IT IS — BUT HE WON'T STAND UP FOR HIMSELF.
I WISH MEL HADN'T COME TO THE GYM...
TOMORROW'S THE LAST SESSION. SHE'S BETTER. I WON'T HAVE TO SEE HER ANY MORE.
THEN I CAN GIVE HER FATHER WHAT HE DESERVES.
I LIKE HER, SHE MAKES ME LAUGH...
...THAT PAIN IN HER RIBS — IT'S THAT STUPID JERK'S FAULT...
NO, IT'S NOT — FACE IT, IT'S YOUR FAULT!
GOOD MORNING, VIC...
YOU LOOK AWFUL.
I HARDLY SLEPT LAST NIGHT, MRS DOYLE.

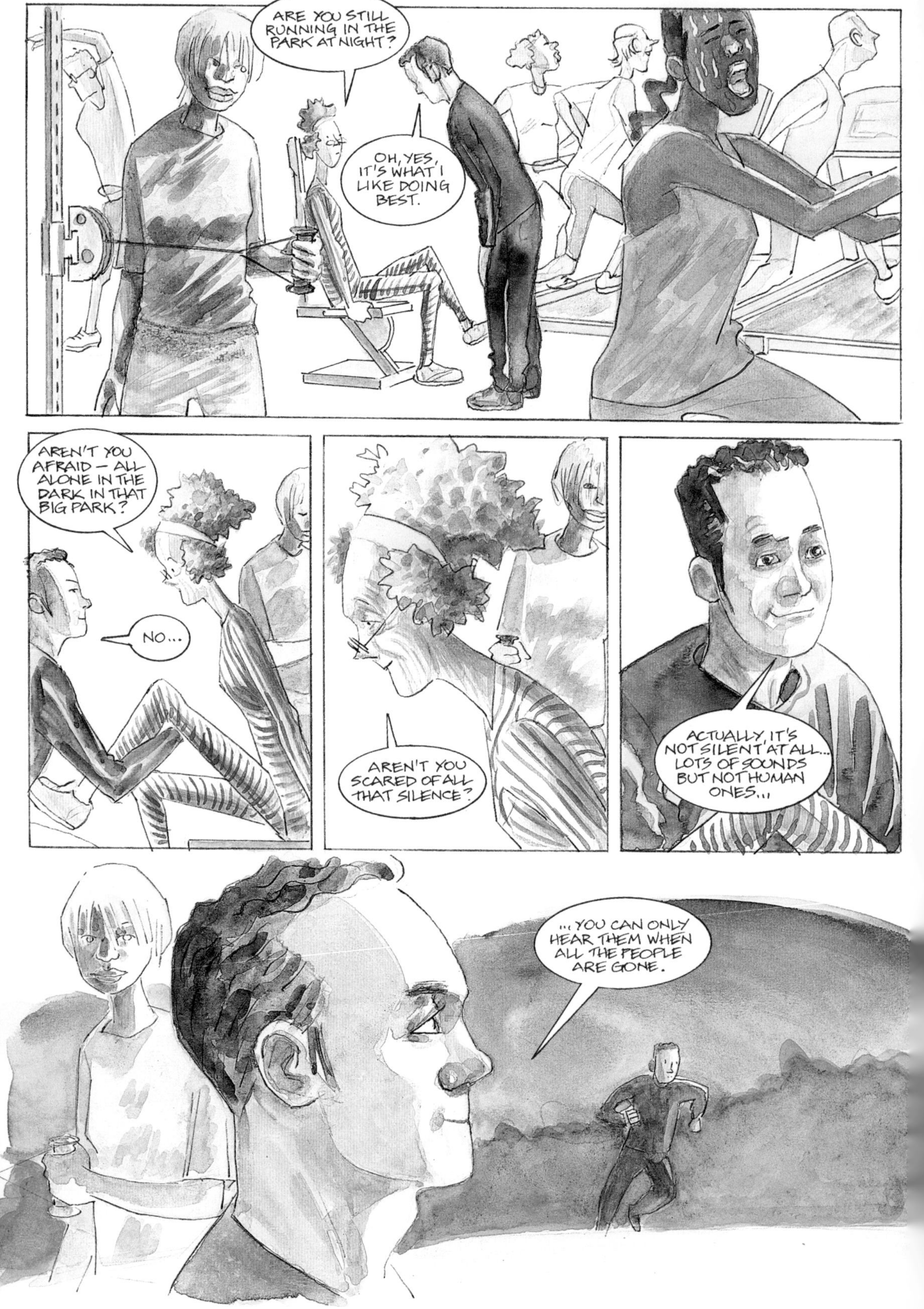
ARE YOU STILL RUNNING IN THE PARK AT NIGHT?
OH, YES, IT'S WHAT I LIKE DOING BEST.
AREN'T YOU AFRAID — ALL ALONE IN THE DARK IN THAT BIG PARK?
NO...
AREN'T YOU SCARED OF ALL THAT SILENCE?
ACTUALLY, IT'S NOT SILENT AT ALL... LOTS OF SOUNDS BUT NOT HUMAN ONES...
...YOU CAN ONLY HEAR THEM WHEN ALL THE PEOPLE ARE GONE.

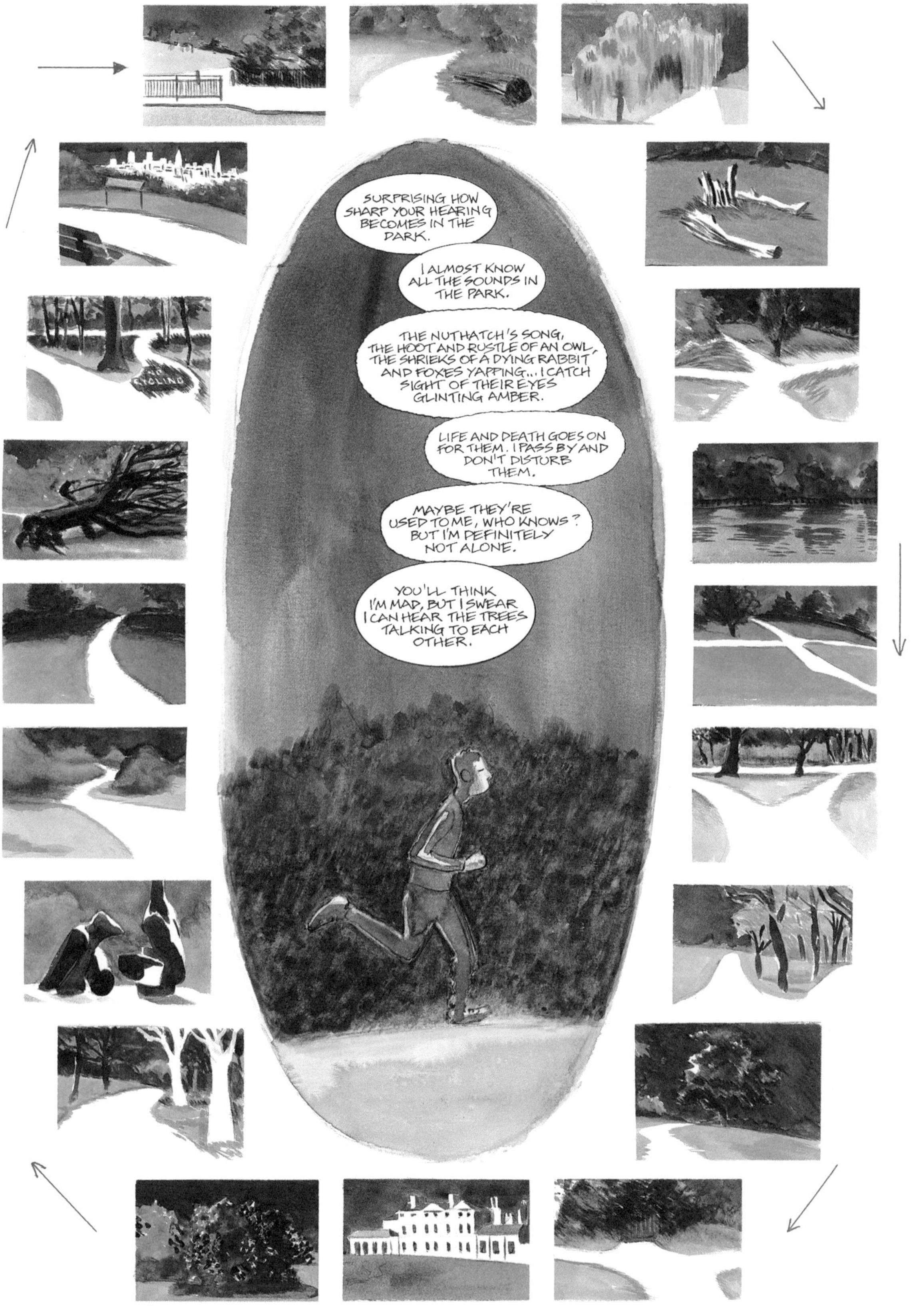
NO CYCLING
SURPRISING HOW SHARP YOUR HEARING BECOMES IN THE DARK.
I ALMOST KNOW ALL THE SOUNDS IN THE PARK.
THE NUTHATCH'S SONG, THE HOOT AND RUSTLE OF AN OWL, THE SHRIEKS OF A DYING RABBIT AND FOXES YAPPING... I CATCH SIGHT OF THEIR EYES GLINTING AMBER.
LIFE AND DEATH GOES ON FOR THEM. I PASS BY AND DON'T DISTURB THEM.
MAYBE THEY'RE USED TO ME, WHO KNOWS? BUT I'M DEFINITELY NOT ALONE.
YOU'LL THINK I'M MAD, BUT I SWEAR I CAN HEAR THE TREES TALKING TO EACH OTHER.

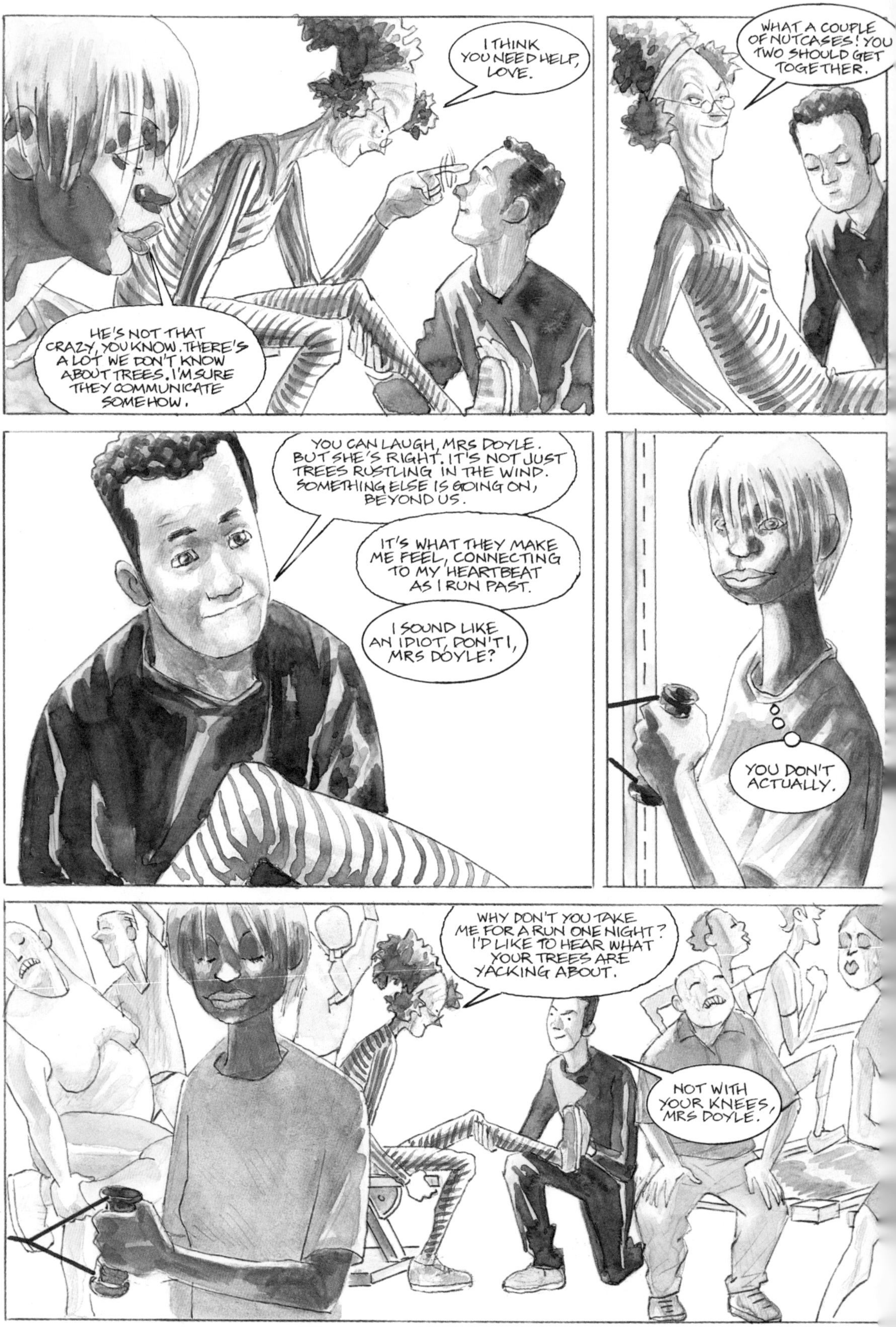
I THINK YOU NEED HELP, LOVE.
HE'S NOT THAT CRAZY, YOU KNOW. THERE'S A LOT WE DON'T KNOW ABOUT TREES. I'M SURE THEY COMMUNICATE SOMEHOW.
WHAT A COUPLE OF NUTCASES! YOU TWO SHOULD GET TOGETHER.
YOU CAN LAUGH, MRS DOYLE. BUT SHE'S RIGHT. IT'S NOT JUST TREES RUSTLING IN THE WIND. SOMETHING ELSE IS GOING ON, BEYOND US.
IT'S WHAT THEY MAKE ME FEEL, CONNECTING TO MY HEARTBEAT AS I RUN PAST.
I SOUND LIKE AN IDIOT, DON'T I, MRS DOYLE?
YOU DON'T ACTUALLY.
WHY DON'T YOU TAKE ME FOR A RUN ONE NIGHT? I'D LIKE TO HEAR WHAT YOUR TREES ARE YACKING ABOUT.
NOT WITH YOUR KNEES, MRS DOYLE.

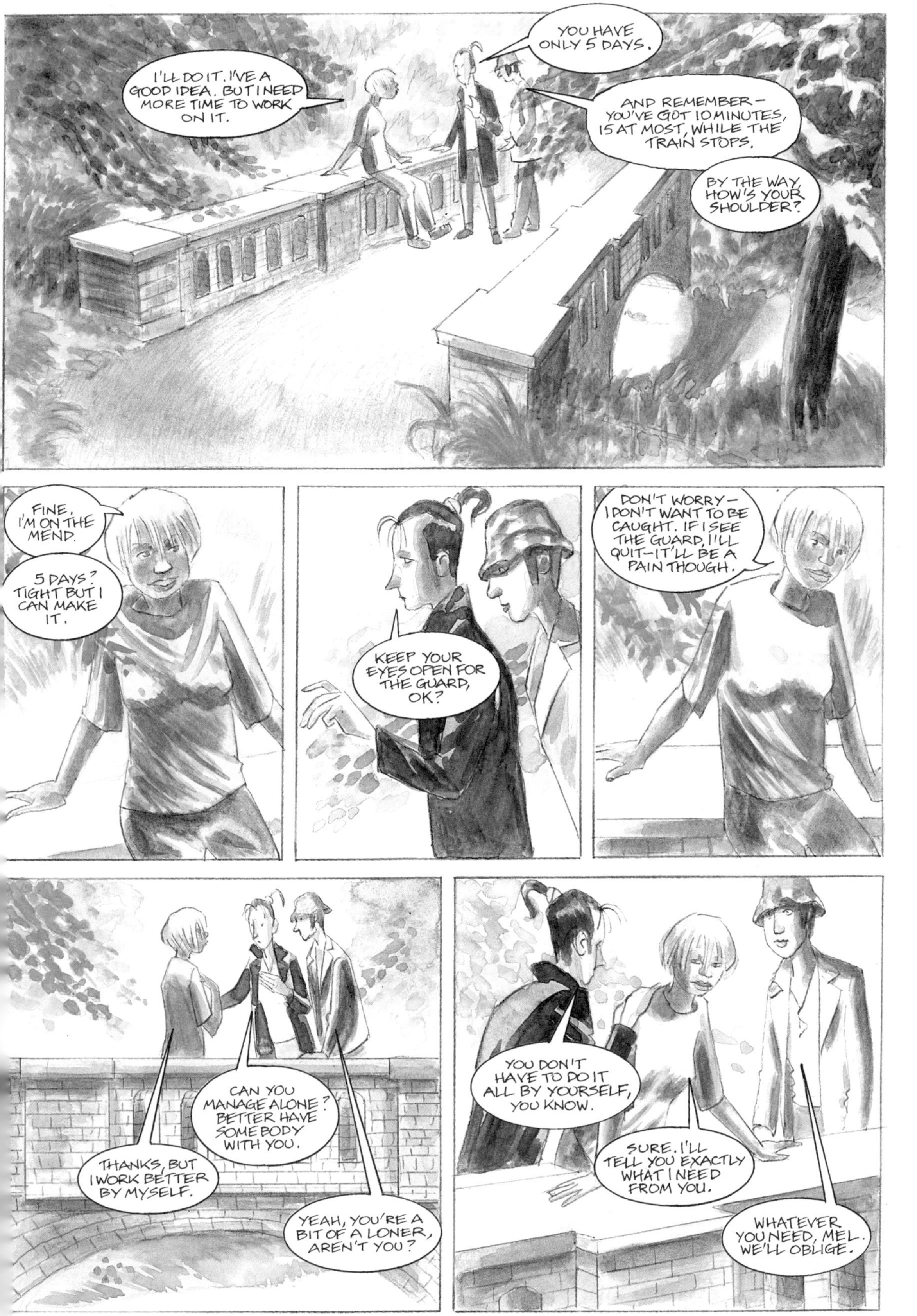
YOU HAVE ONLY 5 DAYS.
I'LL DO IT. I'VE A GOOD IDEA. BUT I NEED MORE TIME TO WORK ON IT.
AND REMEMBER – YOU'VE GOT 10 MINUTES, 15 AT MOST, WHILE THE TRAIN STOPS.
BY THE WAY, HOW'S YOUR SHOULDER?
FINE, I'M ON THE MEND.
5 DAYS? TIGHT BUT I CAN MAKE IT.
KEEP YOUR EYES OPEN FOR THE GUARD, OK?
DON'T WORRY – I DON'T WANT TO BE CAUGHT. IF I SEE THE GUARD, I'LL QUIT – IT'LL BE A PAIN THOUGH.
CAN YOU MANAGE ALONE? BETTER HAVE SOMEBODY WITH YOU.
THANKS, BUT I WORK BETTER BY MYSELF.
YEAH, YOU'RE A BIT OF A LONER, AREN'T YOU?
YOU DON'T HAVE TO DO IT ALL BY YOURSELF, YOU KNOW.
SURE. I'LL TELL YOU EXACTLY WHAT I NEED FROM YOU.
WHATEVER YOU NEED, MEL. WE'LL OBLIGE.

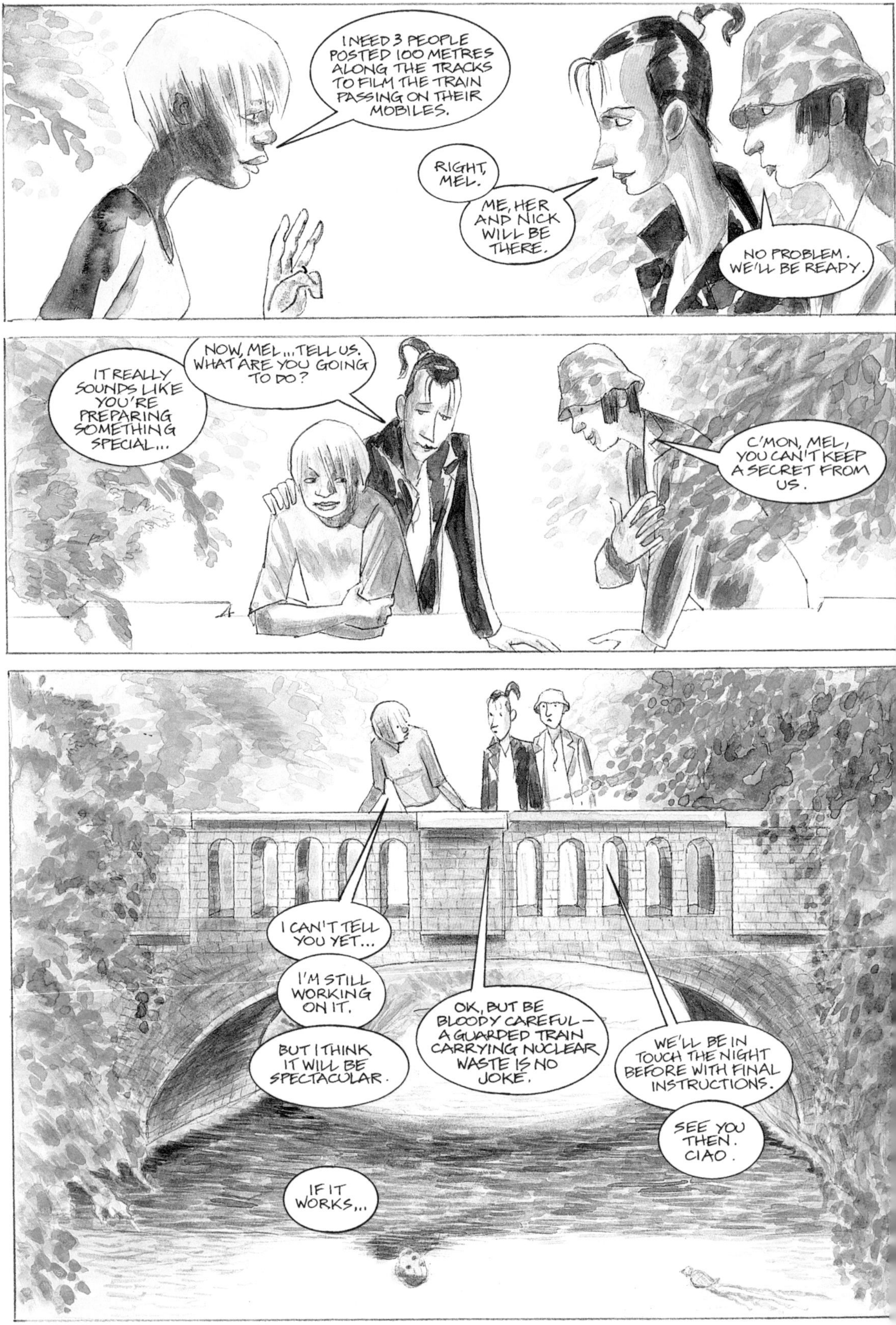
I NEED 3 PEOPLE POSTED 100 METRES ALONG THE TRACKS TO FILM THE TRAIN PASSING ON THEIR MOBILES.
RIGHT, MEL.
ME, HER AND NICK WILL BE THERE.
NO PROBLEM. WE'LL BE READY.
IT REALLY SOUNDS LIKE YOU'RE PREPARING SOMETHING SPECIAL...
NOW, MEL... TELL US. WHAT ARE YOU GOING TO DO?
C'MON, MEL, YOU CAN'T KEEP A SECRET FROM US.
I CAN'T TELL YOU YET...
I'M STILL WORKING ON IT.
BUT I THINK IT WILL BE SPECTACULAR.
OK, BUT BE BLOODY CAREFUL — A GUARDED TRAIN CARRYING NUCLEAR WASTE IS NO JOKE.
WE'LL BE IN TOUCH THE NIGHT BEFORE WITH FINAL INSTRUCTIONS.
SEE YOU THEN. CIAO.
IF IT WORKS,...

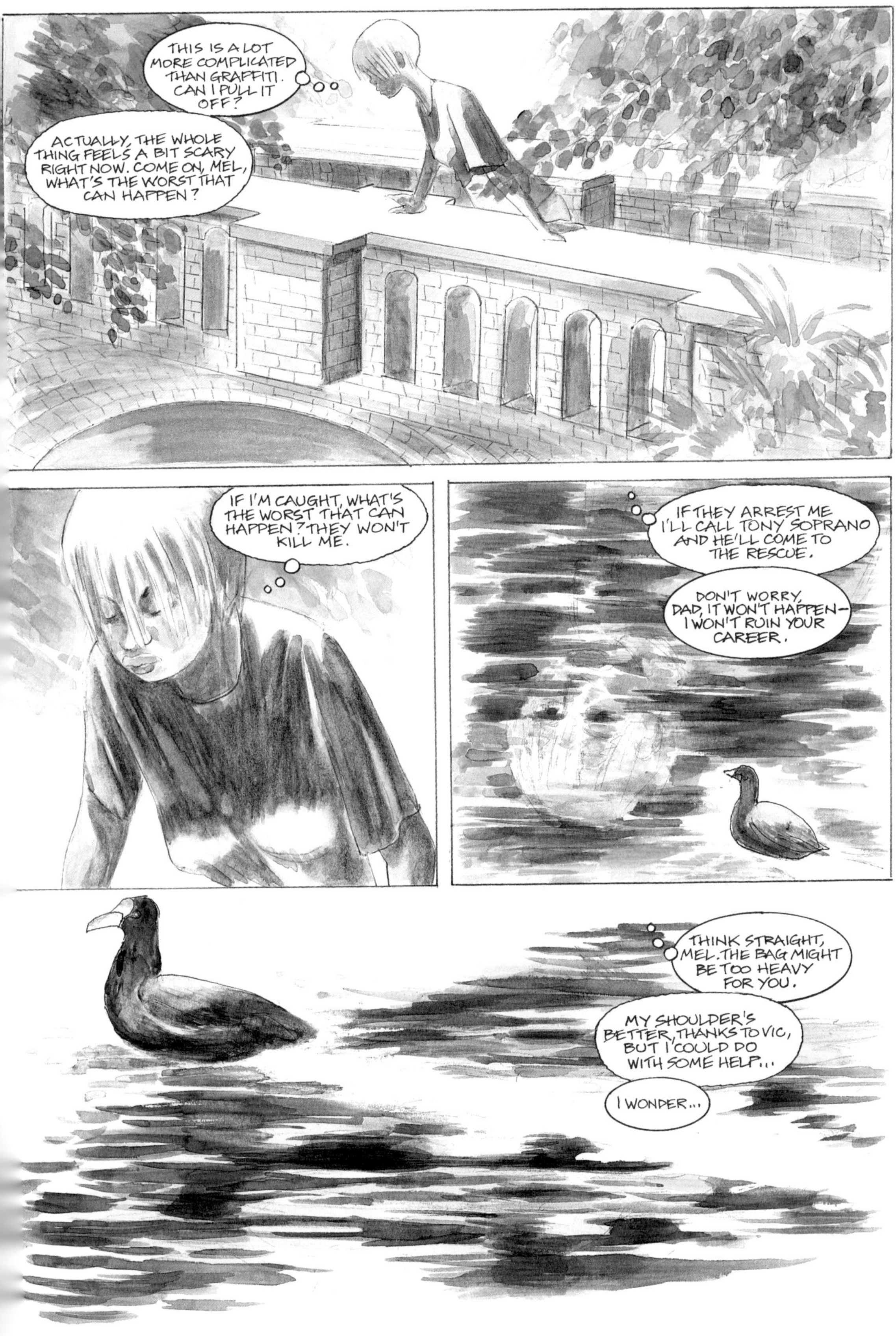
THIS IS A LOT MORE COMPLICATED THAN GRAFFITI. CAN I PULL IT OFF?
ACTUALLY, THE WHOLE THING FEELS A BIT SCARY RIGHT NOW. COME ON, MEL, WHAT'S THE WORST THAT CAN HAPPEN?
IF I'M CAUGHT, WHAT'S THE WORST THAT CAN HAPPEN? THEY WON'T KILL ME.
IF THEY ARREST ME I'LL CALL TONY SOPRANO AND HE'LL COME TO THE RESCUE.
DON'T WORRY, DAD, IT WON'T HAPPEN- I WON'T RUIN YOUR CAREER.
THINK STRAIGHT, MEL. THE BAG MIGHT BE TOO HEAVY FOR YOU.
MY SHOULDER'S BETTER, THANKS TO VIC, BUT I COULD DO WITH SOME HELP...
I WONDER...

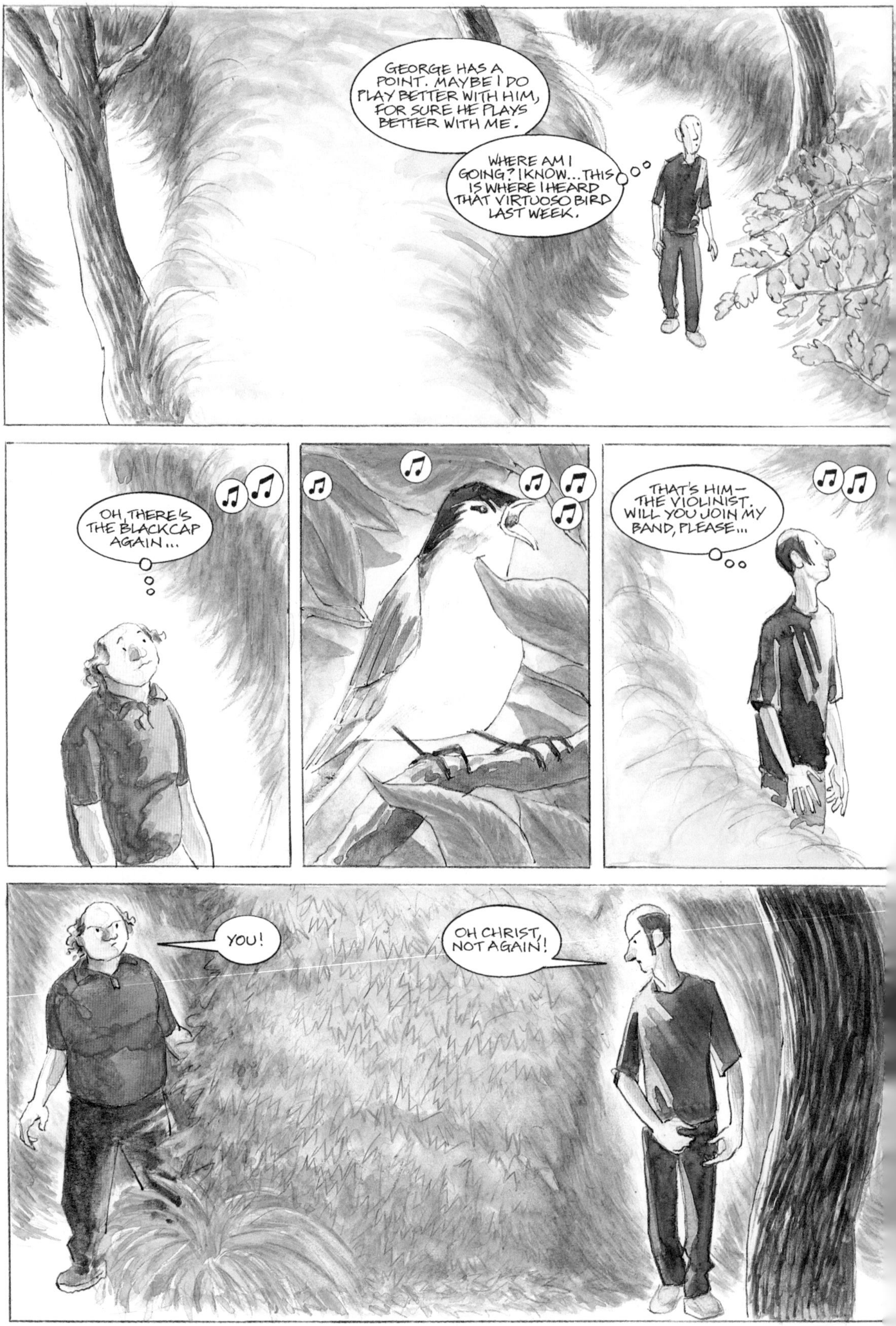
GEORGE HAS A POINT. MAYBE I DO PLAY BETTER WITH HIM, FOR SURE HE PLAYS BETTER WITH ME.
WHERE AM I GOING? I KNOW... THIS IS WHERE I HEARD THAT VIRTUOSO BIRD LAST WEEK.
OH, THERE'S THE BLACKCAP AGAIN...
THAT'S HIM— THE VIOLINIST. WILL YOU JOIN MY BAND, PLEASE...
YOU!
OH CHRIST, NOT AGAIN!

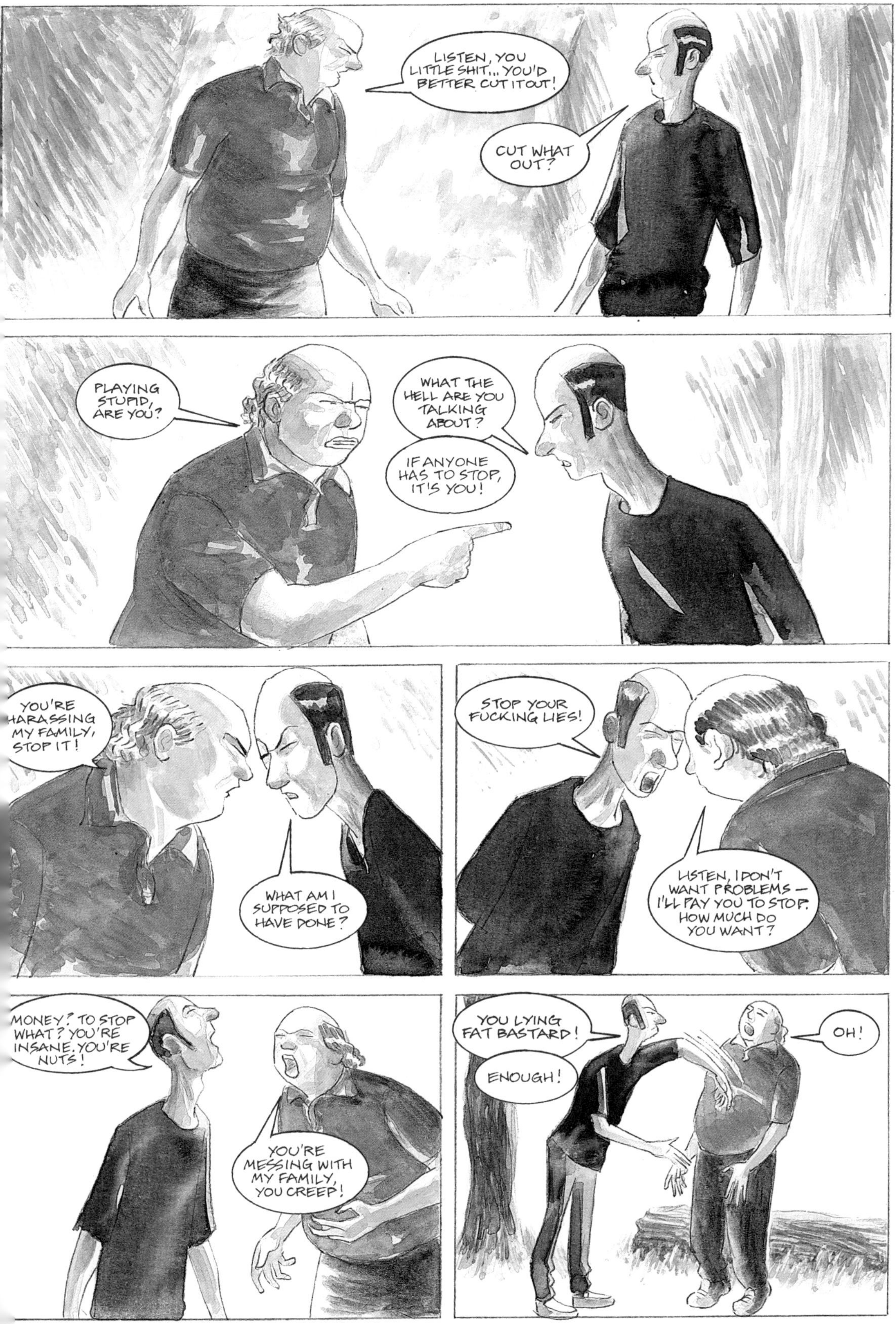
LISTEN, YOU LITTLE SHIT... YOU'D BETTER CUT IT OUT!
CUT WHAT OUT?
PLAYING STUPID, ARE YOU?
WHAT THE HELL ARE YOU TALKING ABOUT?
IF ANYONE HAS TO STOP, IT'S YOU!
YOU'RE HARASSING MY FAMILY, STOP IT!
WHAT AM I SUPPOSED TO HAVE DONE?
STOP YOUR FUCKING LIES!
LISTEN, I DON'T WANT PROBLEMS — I'LL PAY YOU TO STOP. HOW MUCH DO YOU WANT?
MONEY? TO STOP WHAT? YOU'RE INSANE. YOU'RE NUTS!
YOU'RE MESSING WITH MY FAMILY, YOU CREEP!
YOU LYING FAT BASTARD!
ENOUGH!
OH!

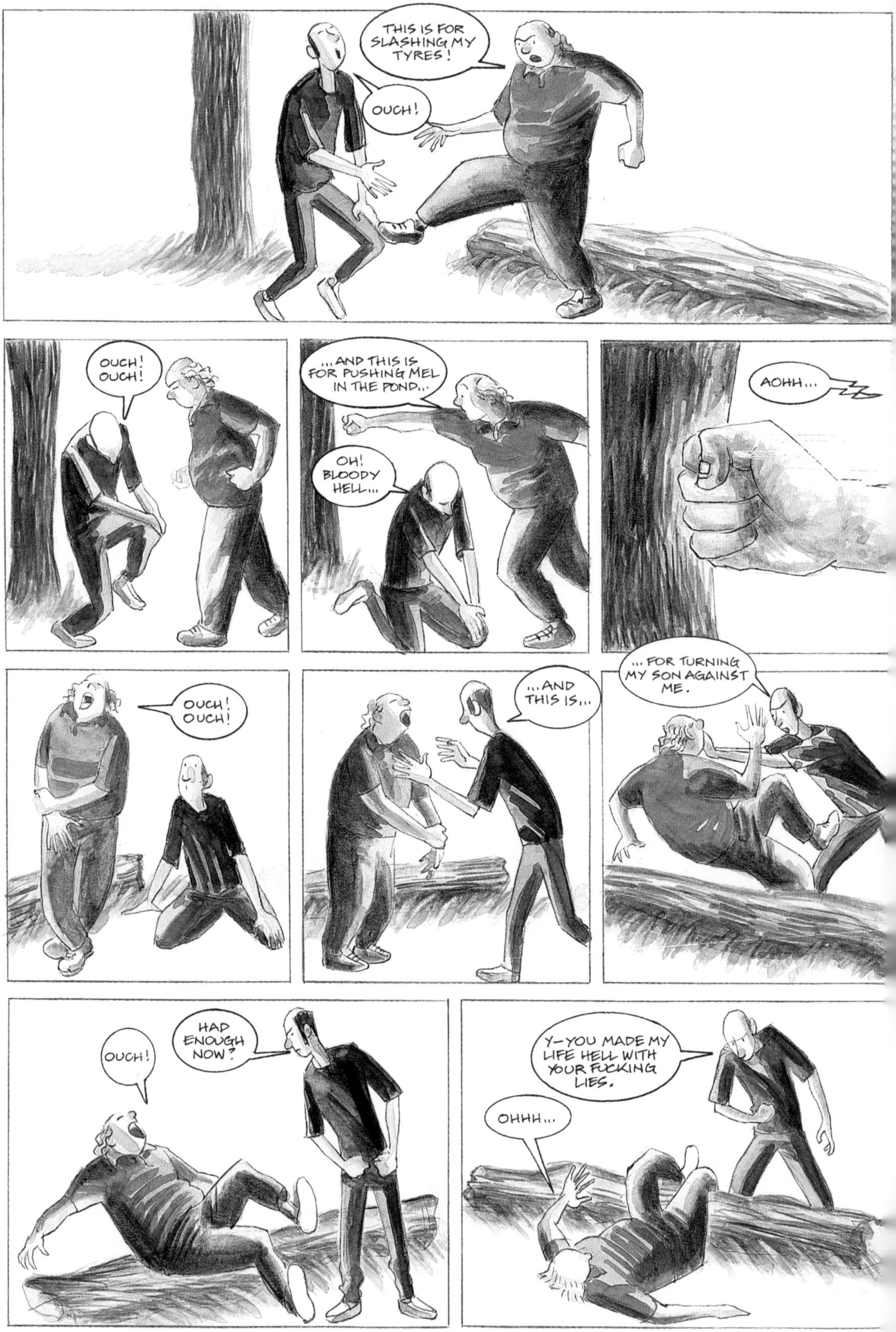
THIS IS FOR SLASHING MY TYRES!
OUCH!
OUCH! OUCH!
...AND THIS IS FOR PUSHING MEL IN THE POND...
OH! BLOODY HELL...
AOHH...
OUCH! OUCH!
...AND THIS IS...
...FOR TURNING MY SON AGAINST ME.
OUCH!
HAD ENOUGH NOW?
Y-YOU MADE MY LIFE HELL WITH YOUR FUCKING LIES.
OHHH...

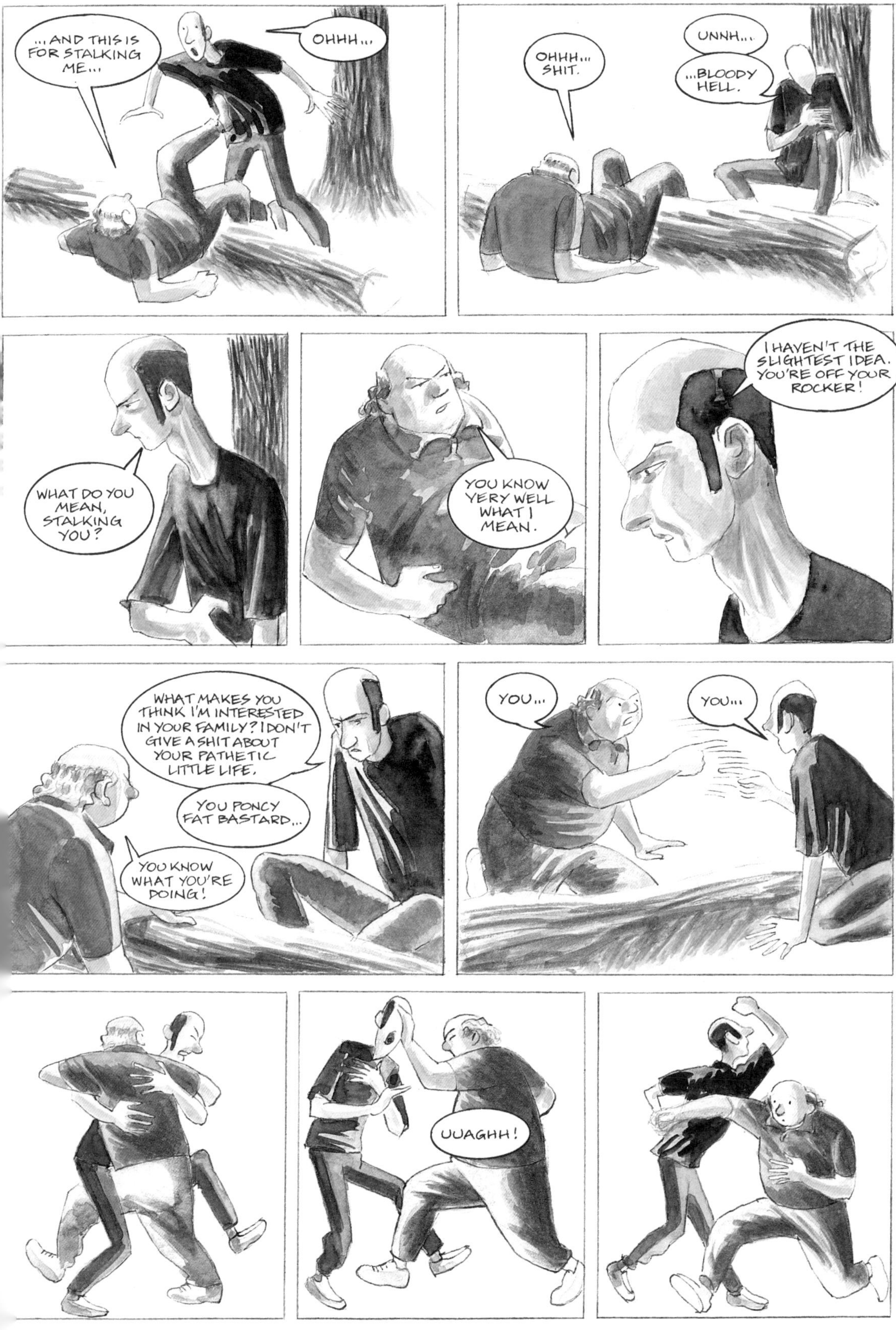
...AND THIS IS FOR STALKING ME...
OHHH...
OHHH... SHIT.
UNNH...
...BLOODY HELL.
WHAT DO YOU MEAN, STALKING YOU?
YOU KNOW VERY WELL WHAT I MEAN.
I HAVEN'T THE SLIGHTEST IDEA. YOU'RE OFF YOUR ROCKER!
WHAT MAKES YOU THINK I'M INTERESTED IN YOUR FAMILY? I DON'T GIVE A SHIT ABOUT YOUR PATHETIC LITTLE LIFE.
YOU PONCY FAT BASTARD...
YOU KNOW WHAT YOU'RE DOING!
YOU...
YOU...
UUAGHH!

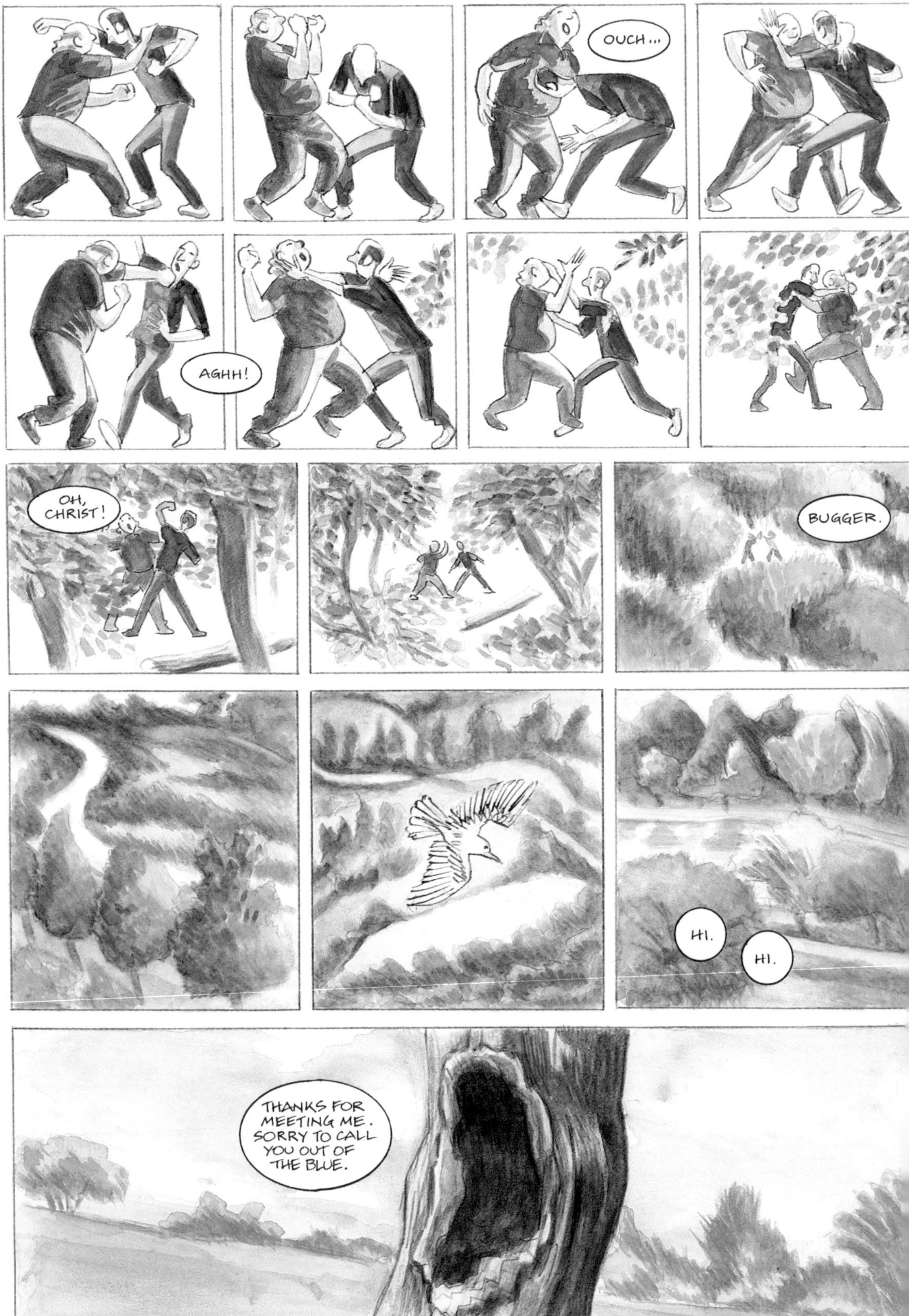

OUCH...
AGHH!
OH, CHRIST!
BUGGER.
HI.
HI.
THANKS FOR MEETING ME. SORRY TO CALL YOU OUT OF THE BLUE.

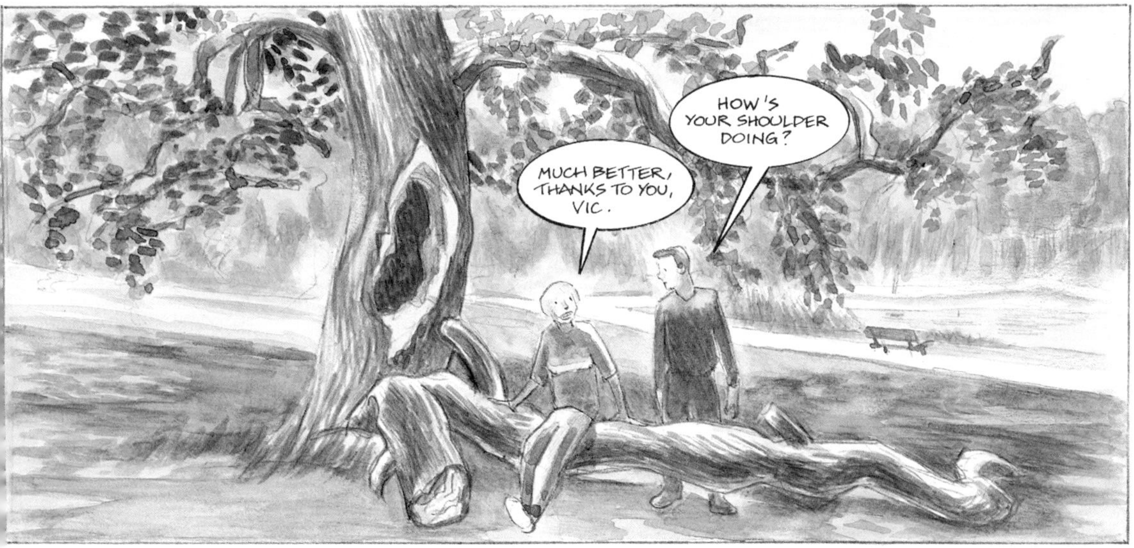
HOW'S YOUR SHOULDER DOING?
MUCH BETTER, THANKS TO YOU, VIC.

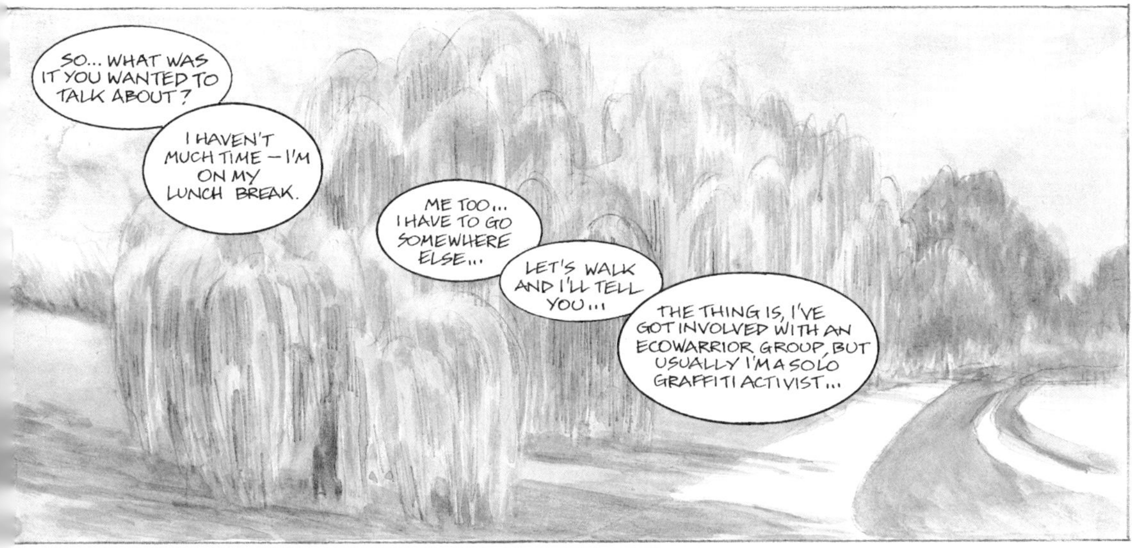
SO... WHAT WAS IT YOU WANTED TO TALK ABOUT?
I HAVEN'T MUCH TIME — I'M ON MY LUNCH BREAK.
ME TOO... I HAVE TO GO SOMEWHERE ELSE...
LET'S WALK AND I'LL TELL YOU...
THE THING IS, I'VE GOT INVOLVED WITH AN ECOWARRIOR GROUP, BUT USUALLY I'M A SOLO GRAFFITI ACTIVIST...

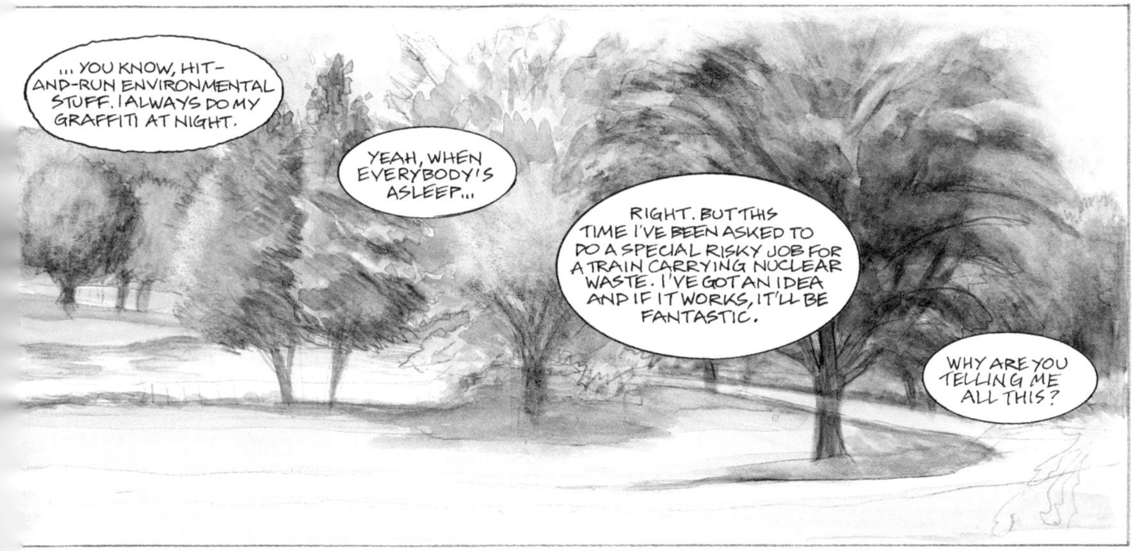
... YOU KNOW, HIT-AND-RUN ENVIRONMENTAL STUFF. I ALWAYS DO MY GRAFFITI AT NIGHT.
YEAH, WHEN EVERYBODY'S ASLEEP...
RIGHT. BUT THIS TIME I'VE BEEN ASKED TO DO A SPECIAL RISKY JOB FOR A TRAIN CARRYING NUCLEAR WASTE. I'VE GOT AN IDEA AND IF IT WORKS, IT'LL BE FANTASTIC.
WHY ARE YOU TELLING ME ALL THIS?

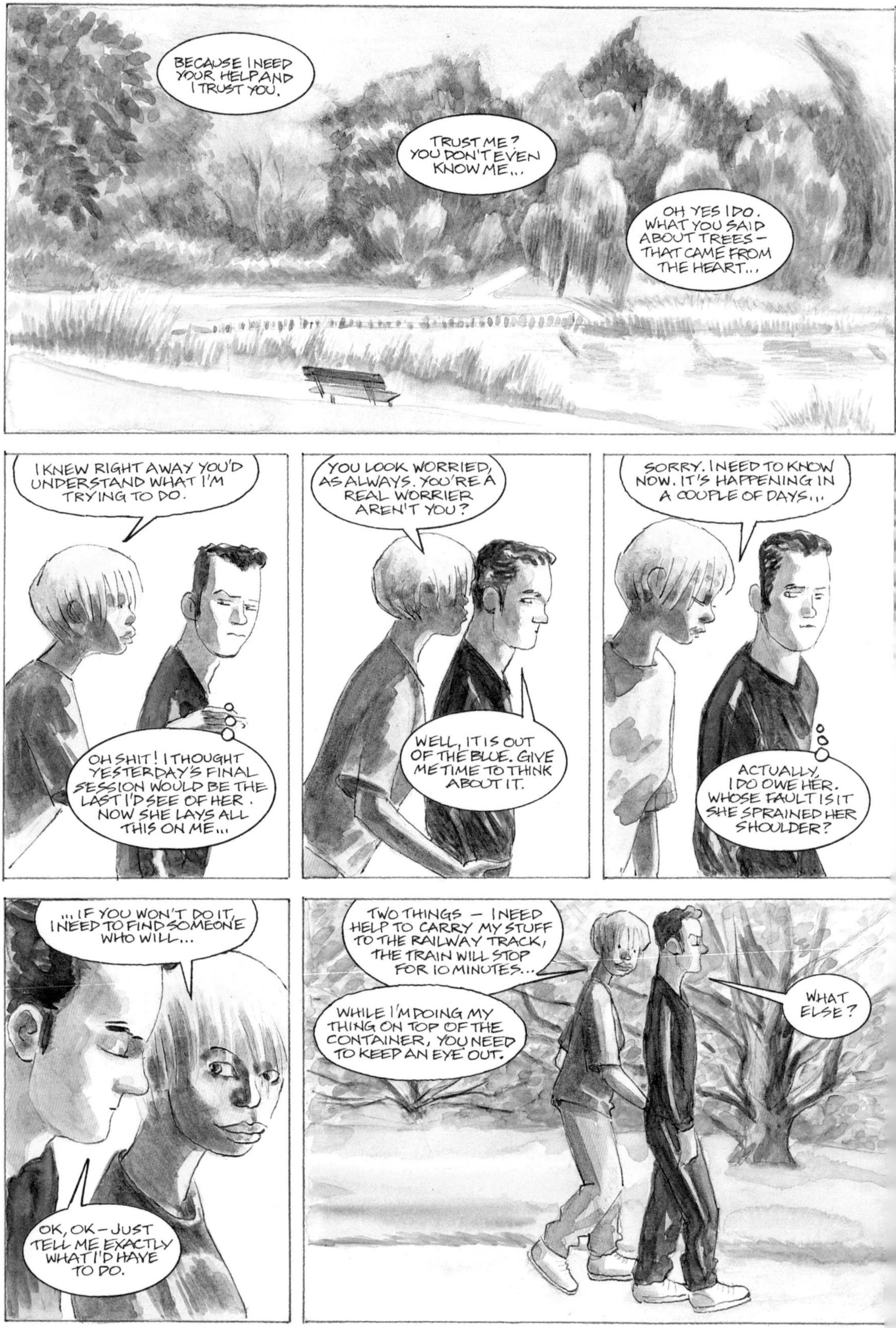
BECAUSE I NEED YOUR HELP AND I TRUST YOU.
TRUST ME? YOU DON'T EVEN KNOW ME...
OH YES I DO. WHAT YOU SAID ABOUT TREES – THAT CAME FROM THE HEART...
I KNEW RIGHT AWAY YOU'D UNDERSTAND WHAT I'M TRYING TO DO.
OH SHIT! I THOUGHT YESTERDAY'S FINAL SESSION WOULD BE THE LAST I'D SEE OF HER. NOW SHE LAYS ALL THIS ON ME...
YOU LOOK WORRIED, AS ALWAYS. YOU'RE A REAL WORRIER AREN'T YOU?
WELL, IT IS OUT OF THE BLUE. GIVE ME TIME TO THINK ABOUT IT.
SORRY. I NEED TO KNOW NOW. IT'S HAPPENING IN A COUPLE OF DAYS...
ACTUALLY, I DO OWE HER. WHOSE FAULT IS IT SHE SPRAINED HER SHOULDER?
... IF YOU WON'T DO IT, I NEED TO FIND SOMEONE WHO WILL...
OK, OK – JUST TELL ME EXACTLY WHAT I'D HAVE TO DO.
TWO THINGS – I NEED HELP TO CARRY MY STUFF TO THE RAILWAY TRACK, THE TRAIN WILL STOP FOR 10 MINUTES...
WHAT ELSE?
WHILE I'M DOING MY THING ON TOP OF THE CONTAINER, YOU NEED TO KEEP AN EYE OUT.

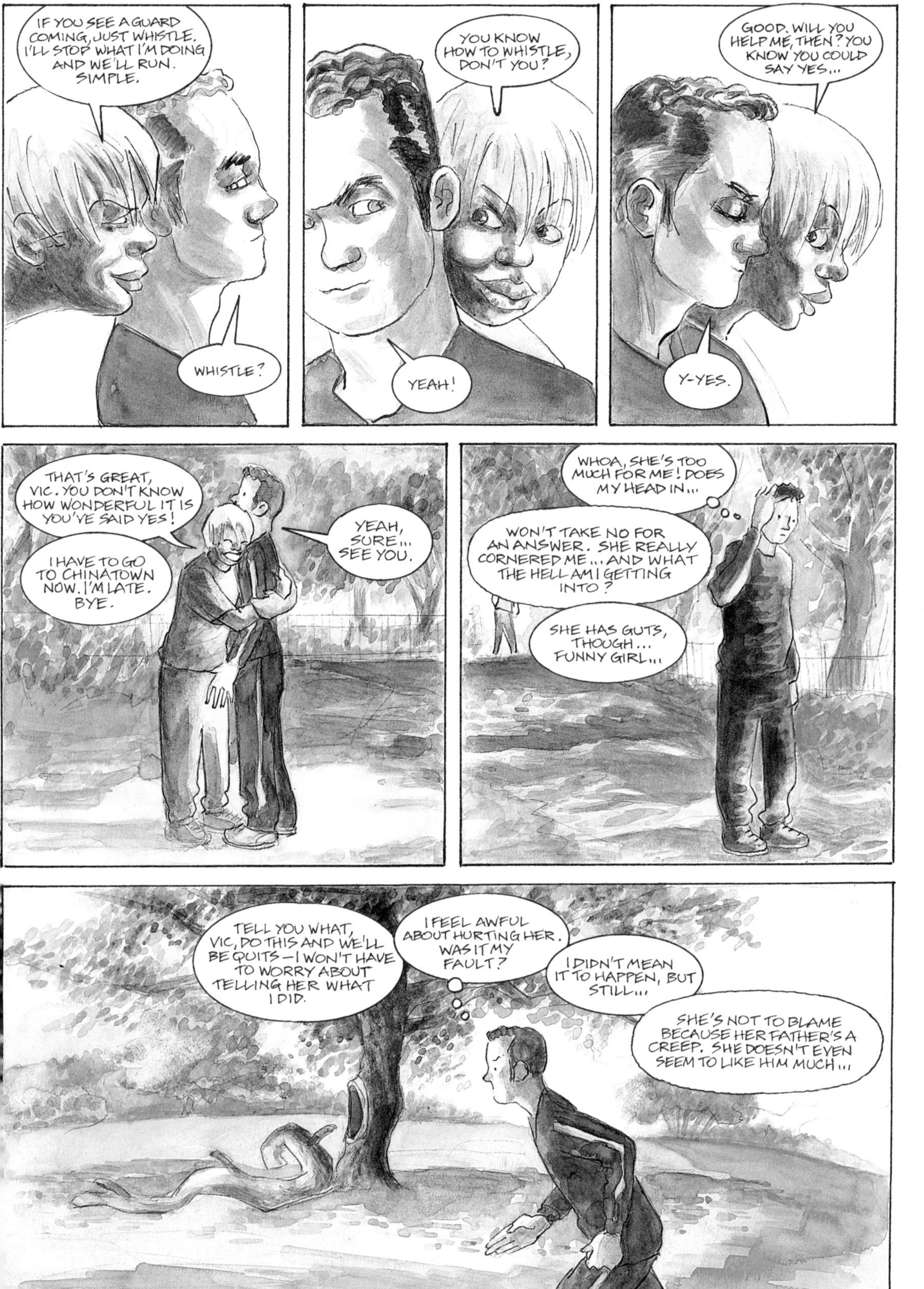
IF YOU SEE A GUARD COMING, JUST WHISTLE. I'LL STOP WHAT I'M DOING AND WE'LL RUN. SIMPLE.
WHISTLE?
YOU KNOW HOW TO WHISTLE, DON'T YOU?
YEAH!
GOOD. WILL YOU HELP ME, THEN? YOU KNOW YOU COULD SAY YES...
Y-YES.
THAT'S GREAT, VIC. YOU DON'T KNOW HOW WONDERFUL IT IS YOU'VE SAID YES!
I HAVE TO GO TO CHINATOWN NOW. I'M LATE. BYE.
YEAH, SURE... SEE YOU.
WHOA, SHE'S TOO MUCH FOR ME! DOES MY HEAD IN...
WON'T TAKE NO FOR AN ANSWER. SHE REALLY CORNERED ME... AND WHAT THE HELL AM I GETTING INTO?
SHE HAS GUTS, THOUGH... FUNNY GIRL...
TELL YOU WHAT, VIC, DO THIS AND WE'LL BE QUITS — I WON'T HAVE TO WORRY ABOUT TELLING HER WHAT I DID.
I FEEL AWFUL ABOUT HURTING HER. WAS IT MY FAULT?
I DIDN'T MEAN IT TO HAPPEN, BUT STILL...
SHE'S NOT TO BLAME BECAUSE HER FATHER'S A CREEP. SHE DOESN'T EVEN SEEM TO LIKE HIM MUCH...

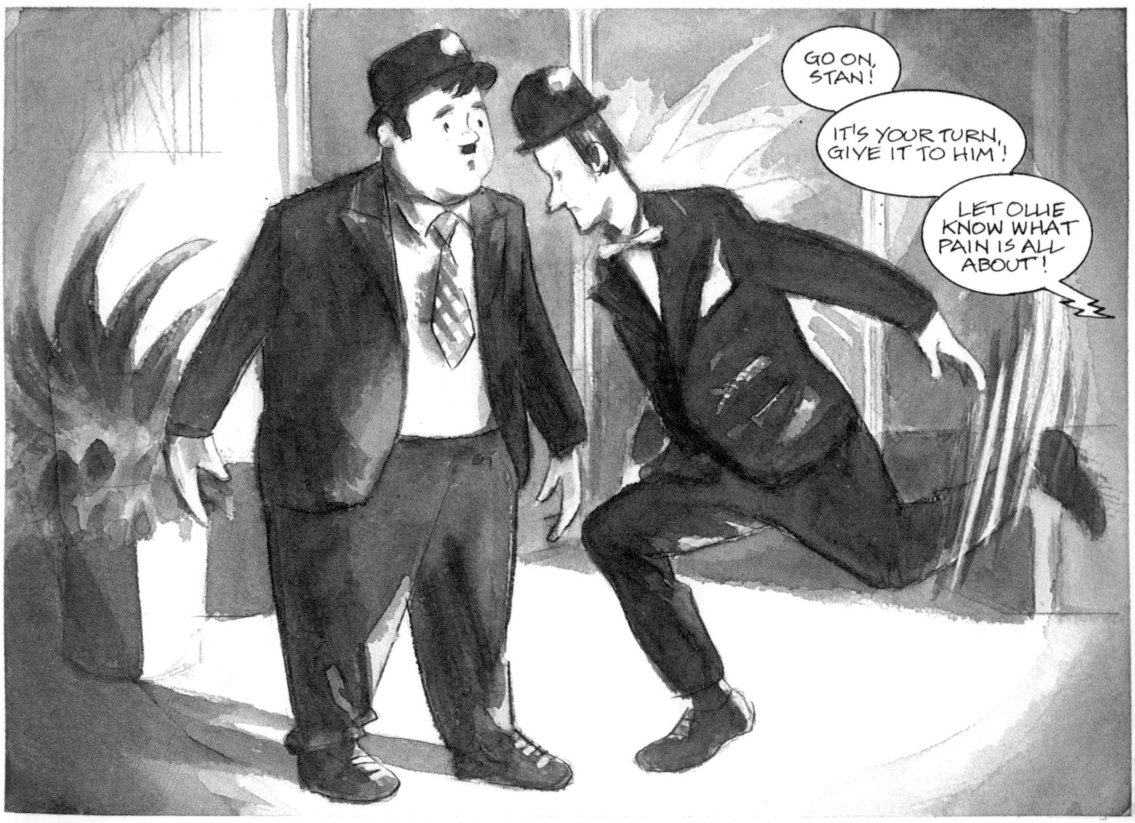
GO ON, STAN!
IT'S YOUR TURN, GIVE IT TO HIM!
LET OLLIE KNOW WHAT PAIN IS ALL ABOUT!

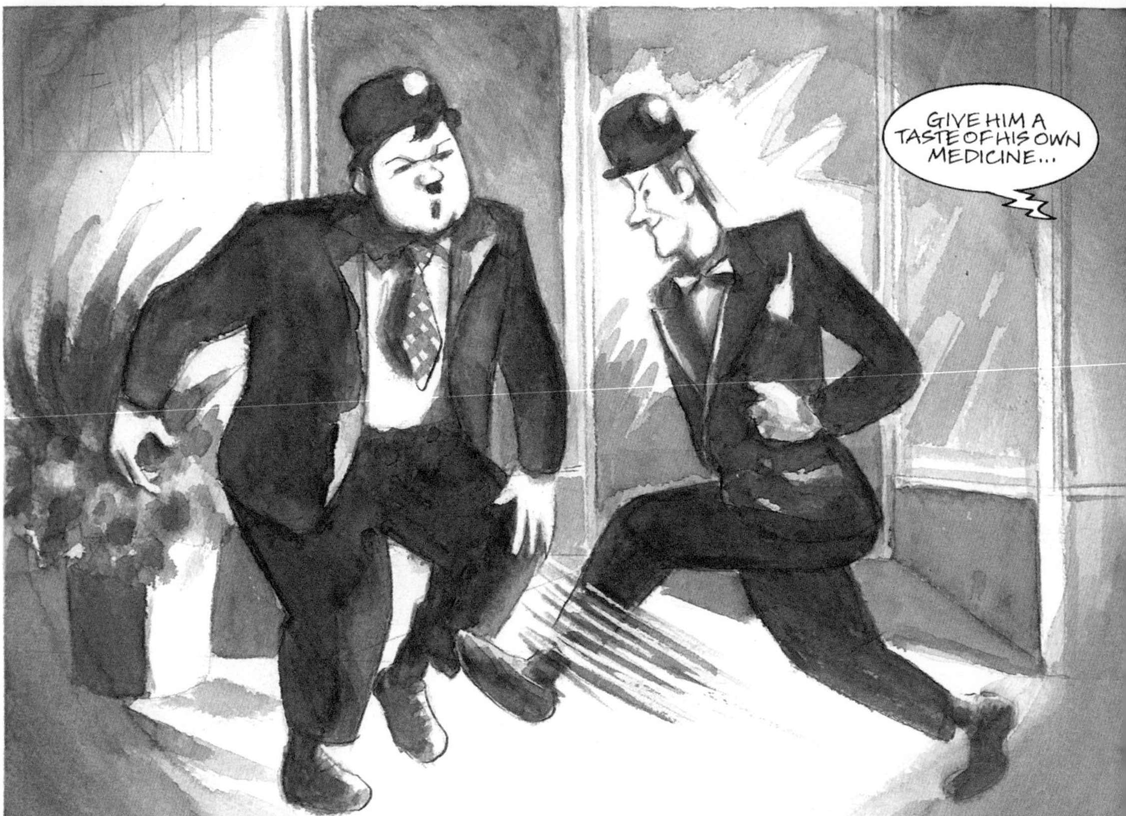
GIVE HIM A TASTE OF HIS OWN MEDICINE...

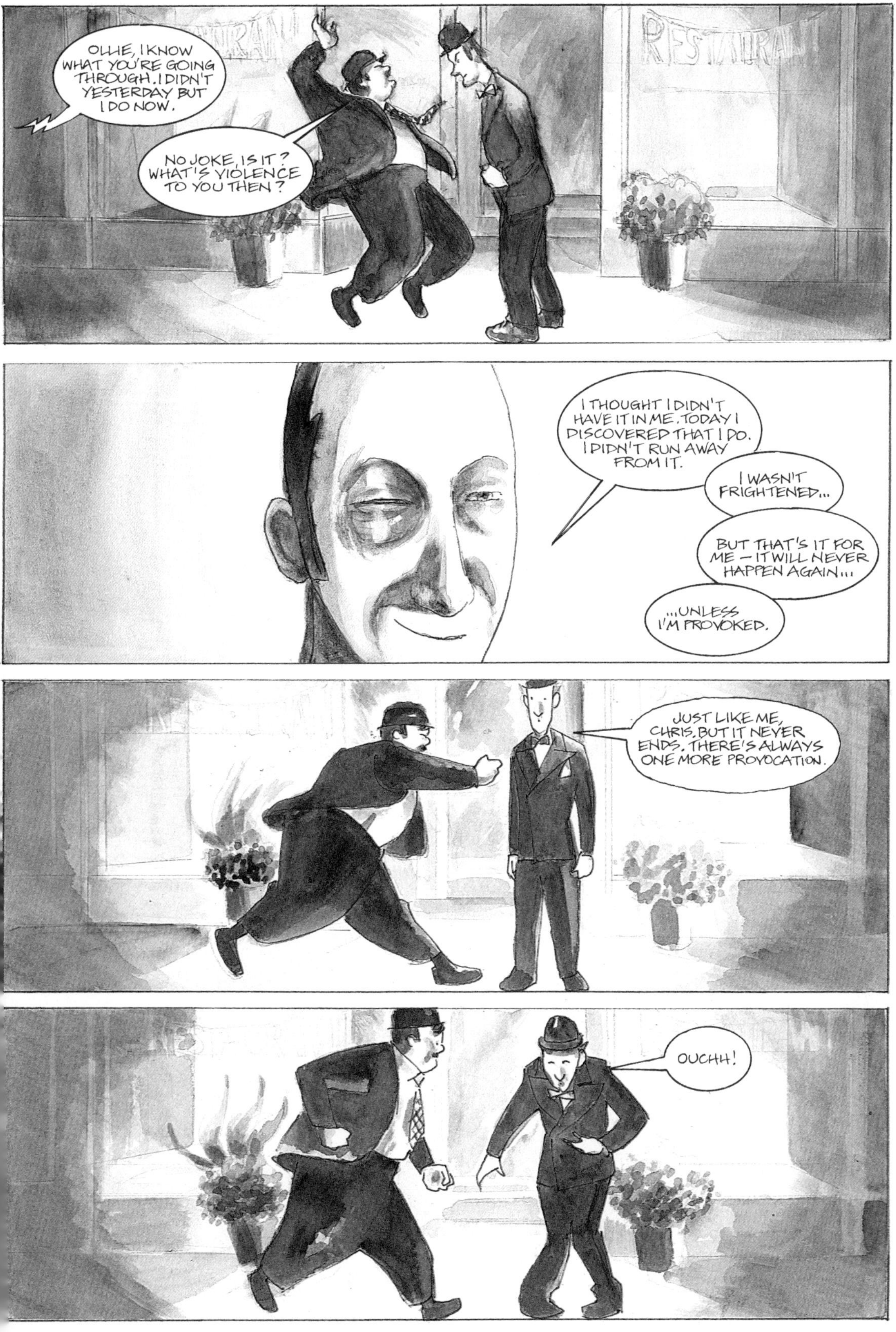
RESTAURANT
OLLIE, I KNOW WHAT YOU'RE GOING THROUGH. I DIDN'T YESTERDAY BUT I DO NOW.
NO JOKE, IS IT? WHAT'S VIOLENCE TO YOU THEN?
I THOUGHT I DIDN'T HAVE IT IN ME. TODAY I DISCOVERED THAT I DO. I DIDN'T RUN AWAY FROM IT.
I WASN'T FRIGHTENED...
BUT THAT'S IT FOR ME — IT WILL NEVER HAPPEN AGAIN...
...UNLESS I'M PROVOKED.
JUST LIKE ME, CHRIS. BUT IT NEVER ENDS. THERE'S ALWAYS ONE MORE PROVOCATION.
OUCHH!

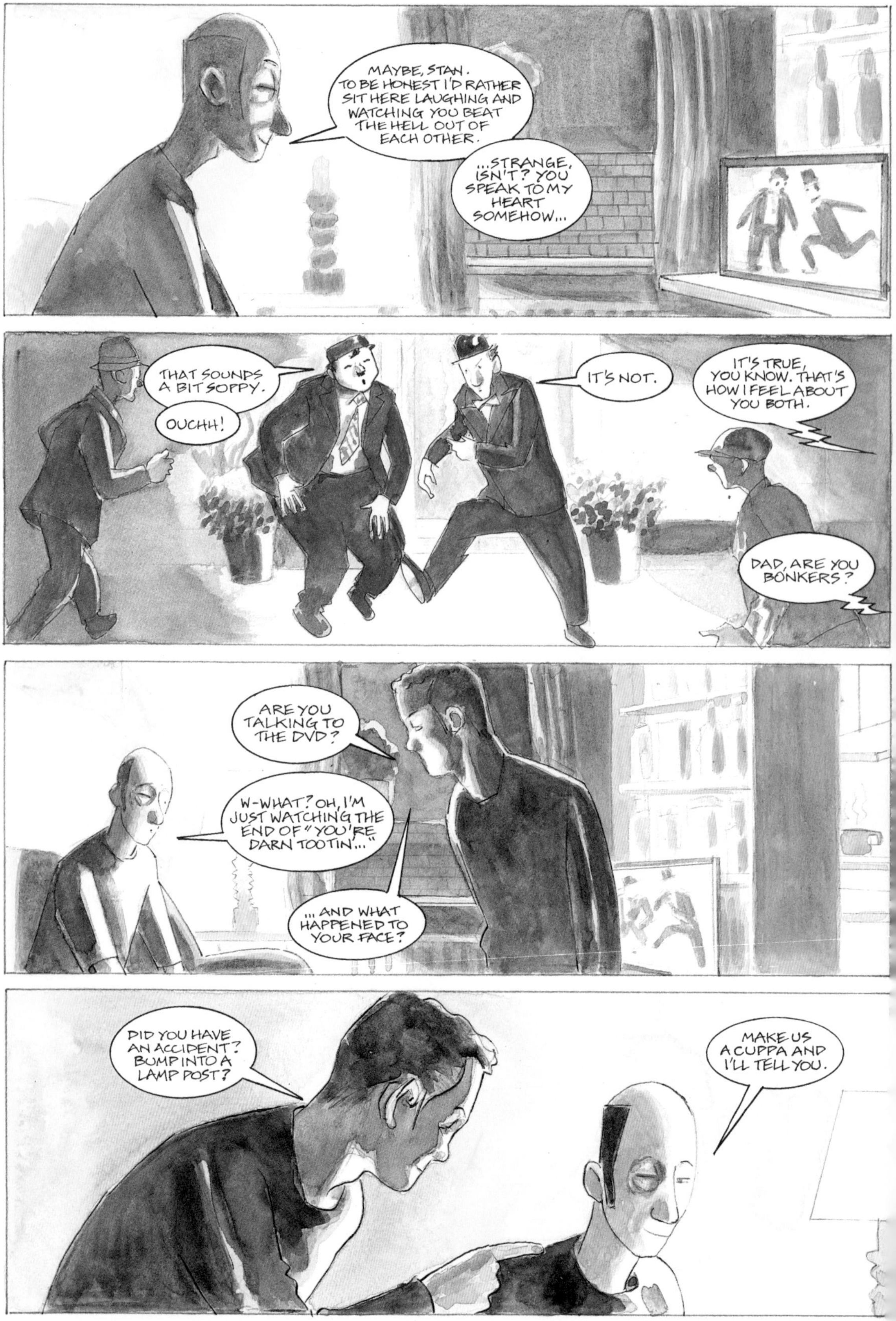
MAYBE, STAN. TO BE HONEST I'D RATHER SIT HERE LAUGHING AND WATCHING YOU BEAT THE HELL OUT OF EACH OTHER.
...STRANGE, ISN'T? YOU SPEAK TO MY HEART SOMEHOW...
THAT SOUNDS A BIT SOPPY.
OUCHH!
IT'S NOT.
IT'S TRUE, YOU KNOW. THAT'S HOW I FEEL ABOUT YOU BOTH.
DAD, ARE YOU BONKERS?
ARE YOU TALKING TO THE DVD?
W-WHAT? OH, I'M JUST WATCHING THE END OF "YOU'RE DARN TOOTIN'..."
...AND WHAT HAPPENED TO YOUR FACE?
DID YOU HAVE AN ACCIDENT? BUMP INTO A LAMP POST?
MAKE US A CUPPA AND I'LL TELL YOU.

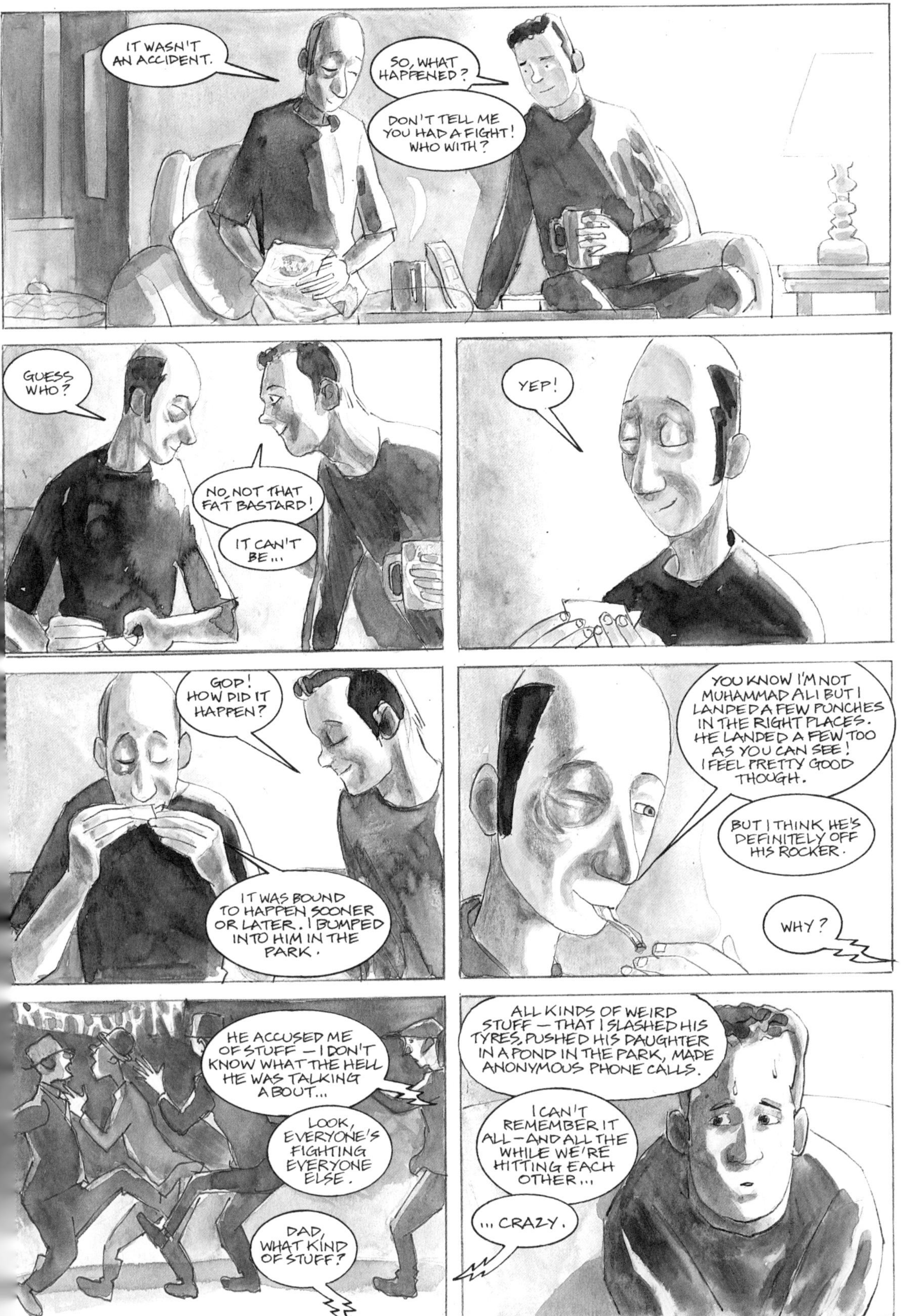
IT WASN'T AN ACCIDENT.
SO, WHAT HAPPENED?
DON'T TELL ME YOU HAD A FIGHT! WHO WITH?
GUESS WHO?
NO, NOT THAT FAT BASTARD!
IT CAN'T BE...
YEP!
GOD! HOW DID IT HAPPEN?
IT WAS BOUND TO HAPPEN SOONER OR LATER. I BUMPED INTO HIM IN THE PARK.
YOU KNOW I'M NOT MUHAMMAD ALI BUT I LANDED A FEW PUNCHES IN THE RIGHT PLACES. HE LANDED A FEW TOO AS YOU CAN SEE! I FEEL PRETTY GOOD THOUGH.
BUT I THINK HE'S DEFINITELY OFF HIS ROCKER.
WHY?
HE ACCUSED ME OF STUFF — I DON'T KNOW WHAT THE HELL HE WAS TALKING ABOUT...
LOOK, EVERYONE'S FIGHTING EVERYONE ELSE.
DAD, WHAT KIND OF STUFF?
ALL KINDS OF WEIRD STUFF — THAT I SLASHED HIS TYRES, PUSHED HIS DAUGHTER IN A POND IN THE PARK, MADE ANONYMOUS PHONE CALLS.
I CAN'T REMEMBER IT ALL — AND ALL THE WHILE WE'RE HITTING EACH OTHER...
... CRAZY.

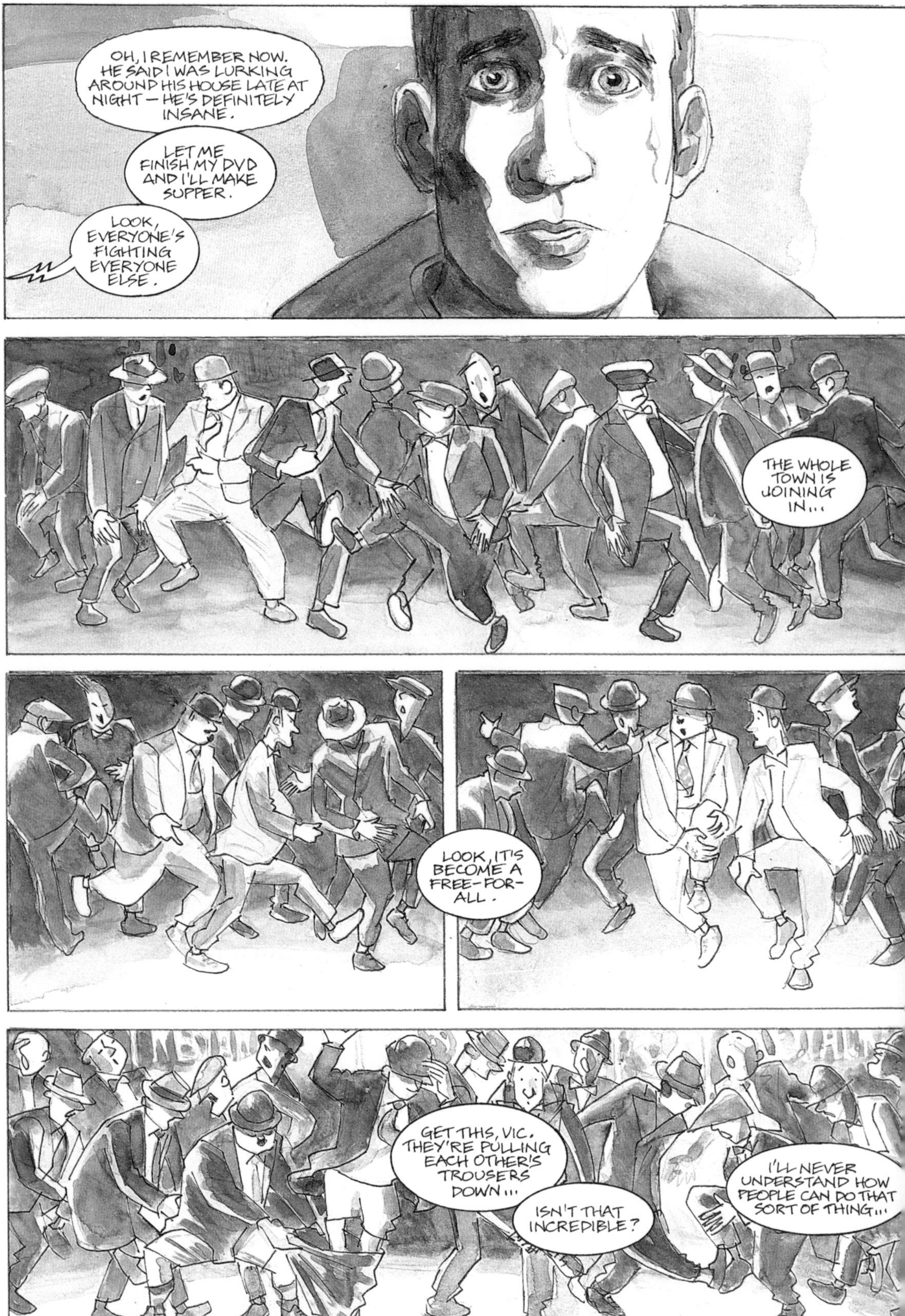
OH, I REMEMBER NOW. HE SAID I WAS LURKING AROUND HIS HOUSE LATE AT NIGHT — HE'S DEFINITELY INSANE.
LET ME FINISH MY DVD AND I'LL MAKE SUPPER.
LOOK, EVERYONE'S FIGHTING EVERYONE ELSE.
THE WHOLE TOWN IS JOINING IN...
LOOK, IT'S BECOME A FREE-FOR-ALL.
GET THIS, VIC. THEY'RE PULLING EACH OTHER'S TROUSERS DOWN...
ISN'T THAT INCREDIBLE?
I'LL NEVER UNDERSTAND HOW PEOPLE CAN DO THAT SORT OF THING...

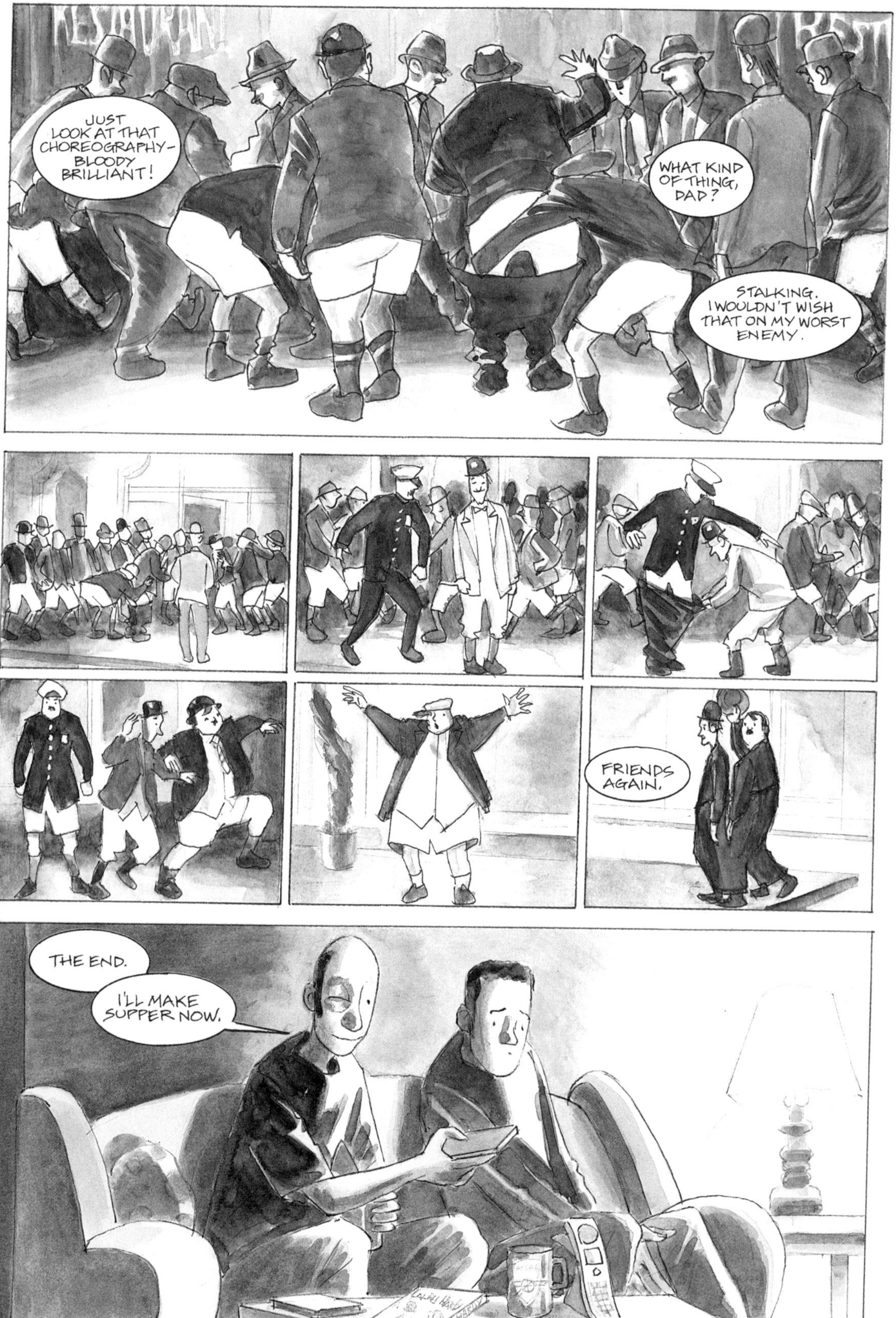

JUST LOOK AT THAT CHOREOGRAPHY - BLOODY BRILLIANT!
WHAT KIND OF THING, DAD?
STALKING. I WOULDN'T WISH THAT ON MY WORST ENEMY.
FRIENDS AGAIN.
THE END.
I'LL MAKE SUPPER NOW.

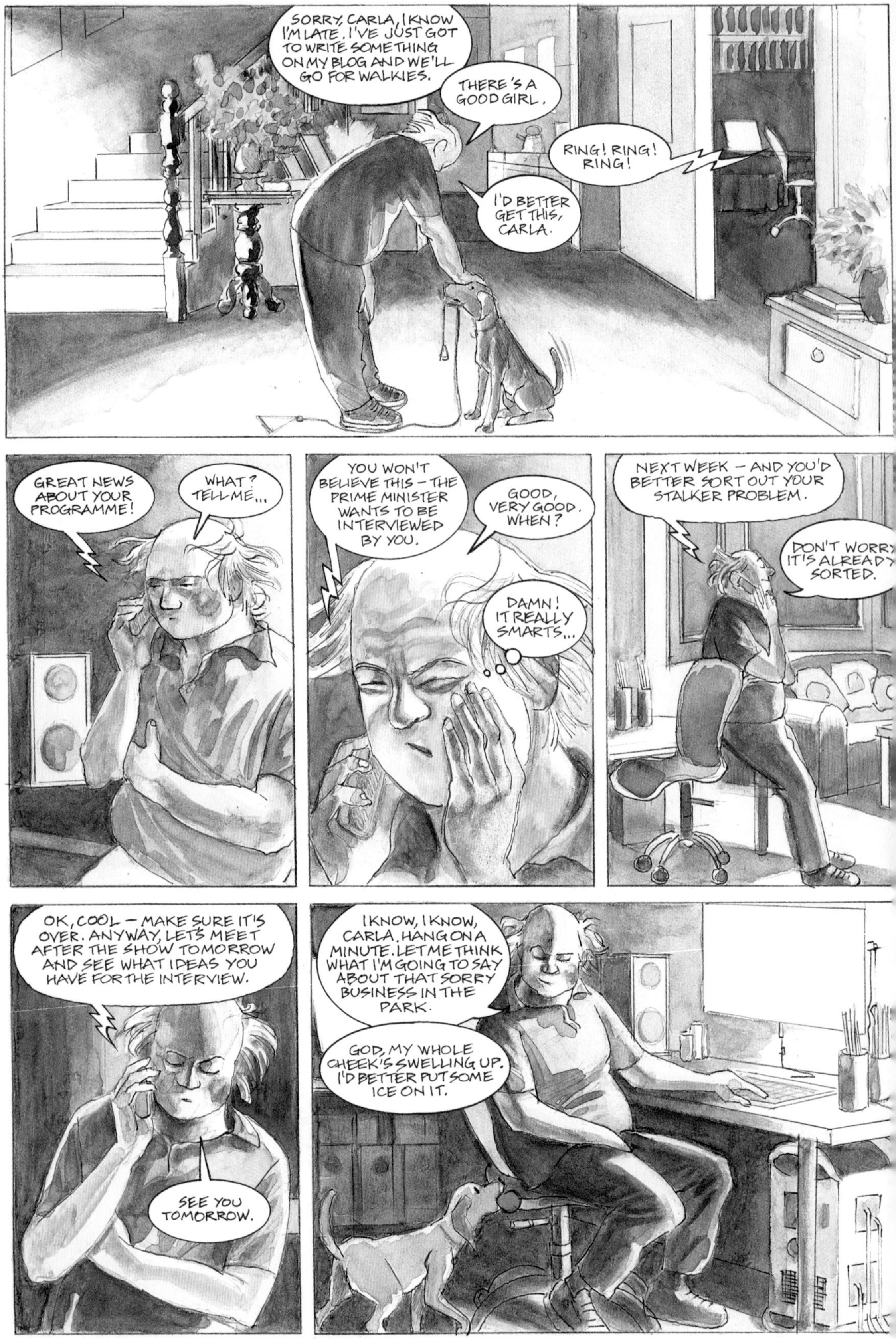
SORRY, CARLA, I KNOW I'M LATE. I'VE JUST GOT TO WRITE SOMETHING ON MY BLOG AND WE'LL GO FOR WALKIES.
THERE'S A GOOD GIRL.
RING! RING! RING!
I'D BETTER GET THIS, CARLA.
GREAT NEWS ABOUT YOUR PROGRAMME!
WHAT? TELL ME...
YOU WON'T BELIEVE THIS – THE PRIME MINISTER WANTS TO BE INTERVIEWED BY YOU.
GOOD, VERY GOOD. WHEN?
DAMN! IT REALLY SMARTS...
NEXT WEEK – AND YOU'D BETTER SORT OUT YOUR STALKER PROBLEM.
DON'T WORRY IT'S ALREADY SORTED.
OK, COOL – MAKE SURE IT'S OVER. ANYWAY, LET'S MEET AFTER THE SHOW TOMORROW AND SEE WHAT IDEAS YOU HAVE FOR THE INTERVIEW.
SEE YOU TOMORROW.
I KNOW, I KNOW, CARLA. HANG ON A MINUTE. LET ME THINK WHAT I'M GOING TO SAY ABOUT THAT SORRY BUSINESS IN THE PARK.
GOD, MY WHOLE CHEEK'S SWELLING UP. I'D BETTER PUT SOME ICE ON IT.

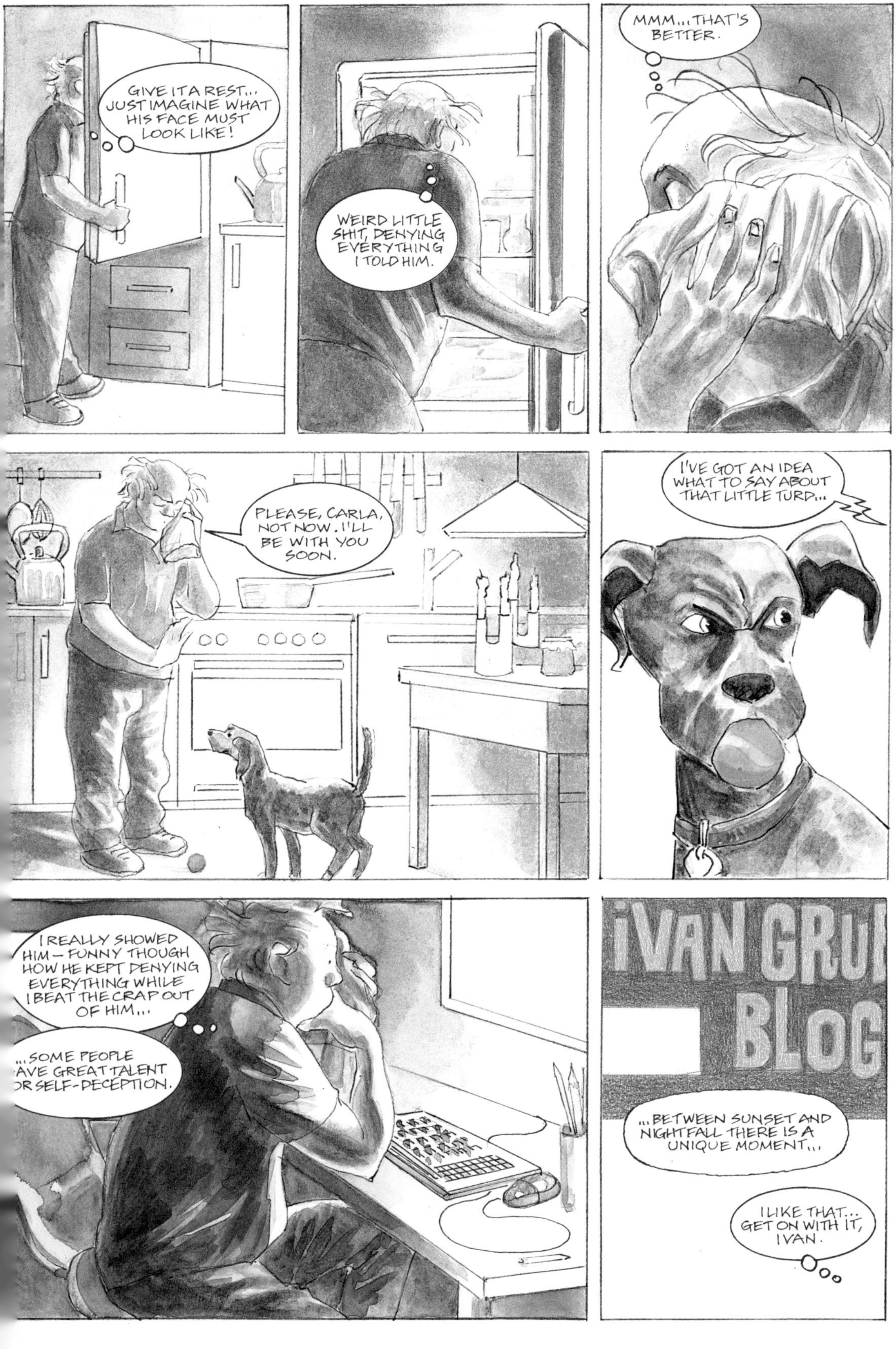
GIVE IT A REST... JUST IMAGINE WHAT HIS FACE MUST LOOK LIKE!
WEIRD LITTLE SHIT, DENYING EVERYTHING I TOLD HIM.
MMM... THAT'S BETTER.
PLEASE, CARLA, NOT NOW. I'LL BE WITH YOU SOON.
I'VE GOT AN IDEA WHAT TO SAY ABOUT THAT LITTLE TURD...
I REALLY SHOWED HIM – FUNNY THOUGH HOW HE KEPT DENYING EVERYTHING WHILE I BEAT THE CRAP OUT OF HIM...
...SOME PEOPLE AVE GREAT TALENT OR SELF-DECEPTION.
IVAN GRU
BLOG
...BETWEEN SUNSET AND NIGHTFALL THERE IS A UNIQUE MOMENT...
I LIKE THAT... GET ON WITH IT, IVAN.

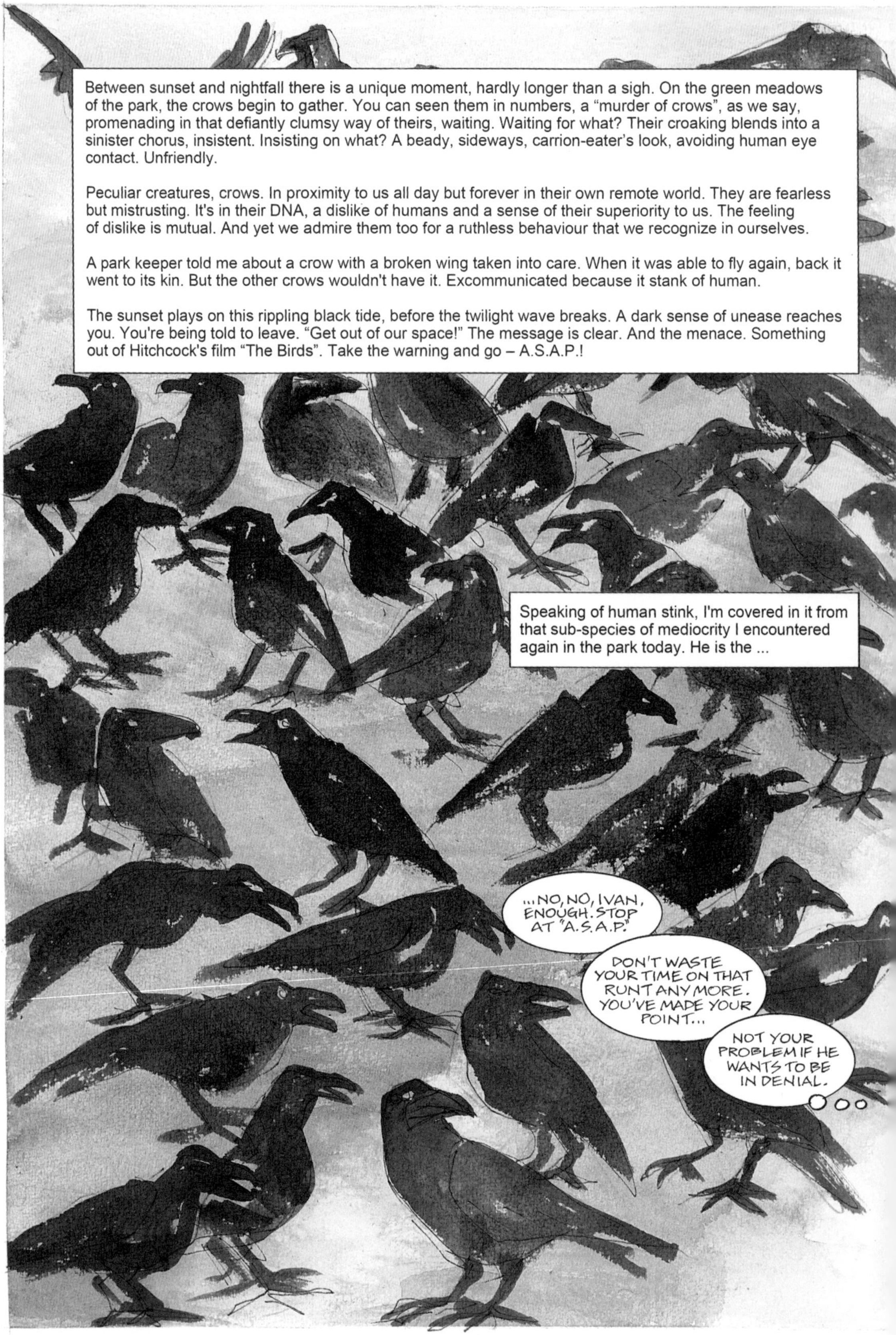
Between sunset and nightfall there is a unique moment, hardly longer than a sigh. On the green meadows of the park, the crows begin to gather. You can seen them in numbers, a "murder of crows", as we say, promenading in that defiantly clumsy way of theirs, waiting. Waiting for what? Their croaking blends into a sinister chorus, insistent. Insisting on what? A beady, sideways, carrion-eater's look, avoiding human eye contact. Unfriendly.
Peculiar creatures, crows. In proximity to us all day but forever in their own remote world. They are fearless but mistrusting. It's in their DNA, a dislike of humans and a sense of their superiority to us. The feeling of dislike is mutual. And yet we admire them too for a ruthless behaviour that we recognize in ourselves.
A park keeper told me about a crow with a broken wing taken into care. When it was able to fly again, back it went to its kin. But the other crows wouldn't have it. Excommunicated because it stank of human.
The sunset plays on this rippling black tide, before the twilight wave breaks. A dark sense of unease reaches you. You're being told to leave. "Get out of our space!" The message is clear. And the menace. Something out of Hitchcock's film "The Birds". Take the warning and go – A.S.A.P.!
Speaking of human stink, I'm covered in it from that sub-species of mediocrity I encountered again in the park today. He is the ...
...NO, NO, IVAN, ENOUGH. STOP AT "A.S.A.P."
DON'T WASTE YOUR TIME ON THAT RUNT ANY MORE. YOU'VE MADE YOUR POINT...
NOT YOUR PROBLEM IF HE WANTS TO BE IN DENIAL.

THE POINT IS, CARLA, WE DON'T HAVE TO WORRY ABOUT HIM ANY MORE.

HE DEFINITELY GOT THE MESSAGE.

DENIAL... HMM... INTERESTING CONCEPT. MAYBE I CAN USE IT FOR THE INTERVIEW WITH THE PM.

"...PRIME MINISTER, THE COUNTRY SAYS YOU'RE IN DENIAL ABOUT THE NATIONAL HEALTH SERVICE..."

"...PM, THE COUNTRY SAYS YOU'RE IN DENIAL ABOUT THE LEVEL OF INFLATION..."

"...PM, THE COUNTRY..."

I'M ENJOYING THIS SHIT...

WHAT'S THE MATTER WITH YOU TODAY, CARLA?

MY FACE IS KILLING ME, I'M GOING TO BED. WE'LL PLAY TOMORROW.

GOOD NIGHT, CARLA.

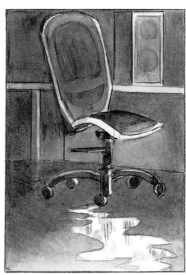

131

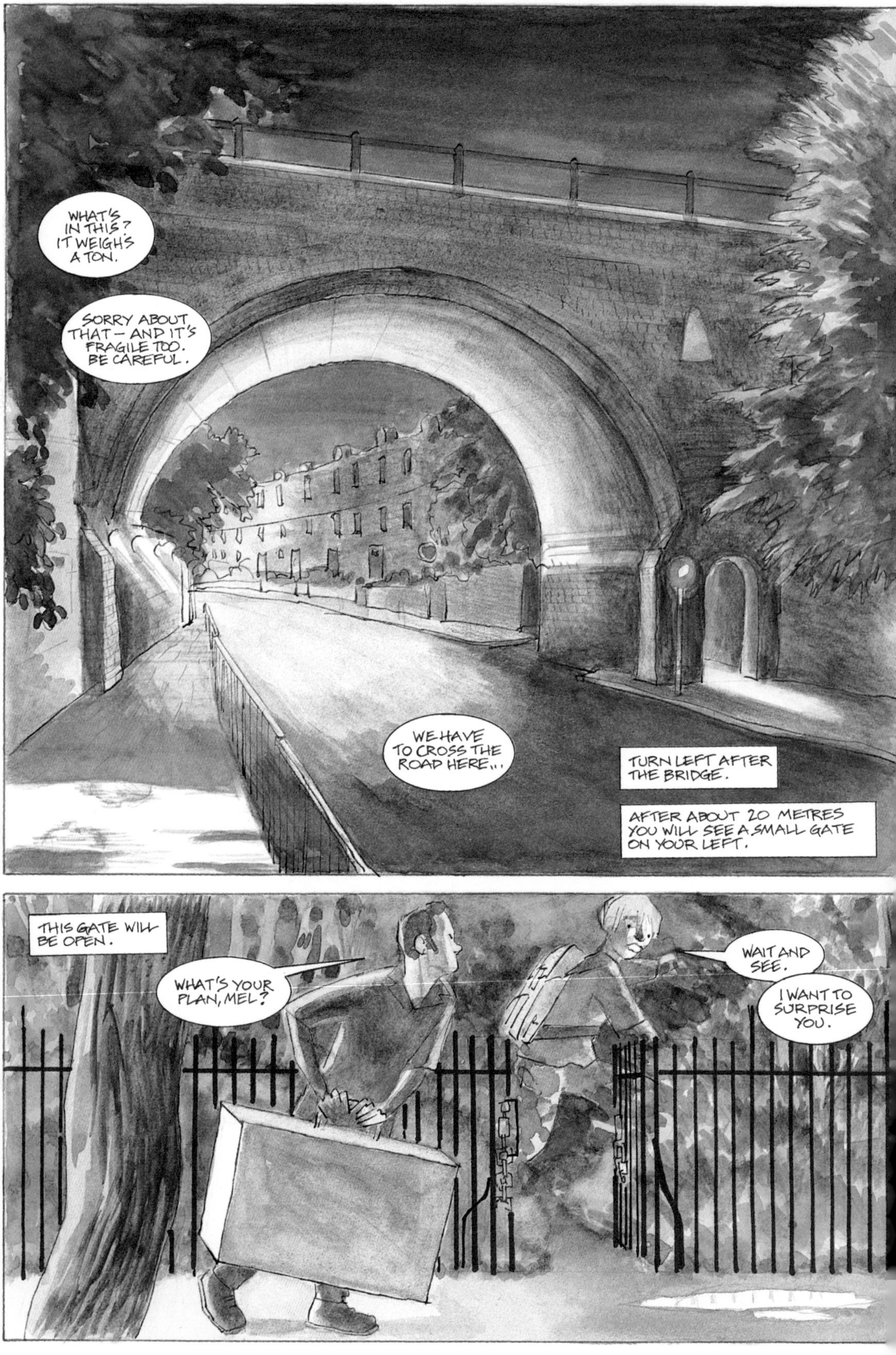
WHAT'S IN THIS? IT WEIGHS A TON.
SORRY ABOUT THAT — AND IT'S FRAGILE TOO. BE CAREFUL.
WE HAVE TO CROSS THE ROAD HERE...
TURN LEFT AFTER THE BRIDGE.
AFTER ABOUT 20 METRES YOU WILL SEE A SMALL GATE ON YOUR LEFT.
THIS GATE WILL BE OPEN.
WHAT'S YOUR PLAN, MEL?
WAIT AND SEE.
I WANT TO SURPRISE YOU.

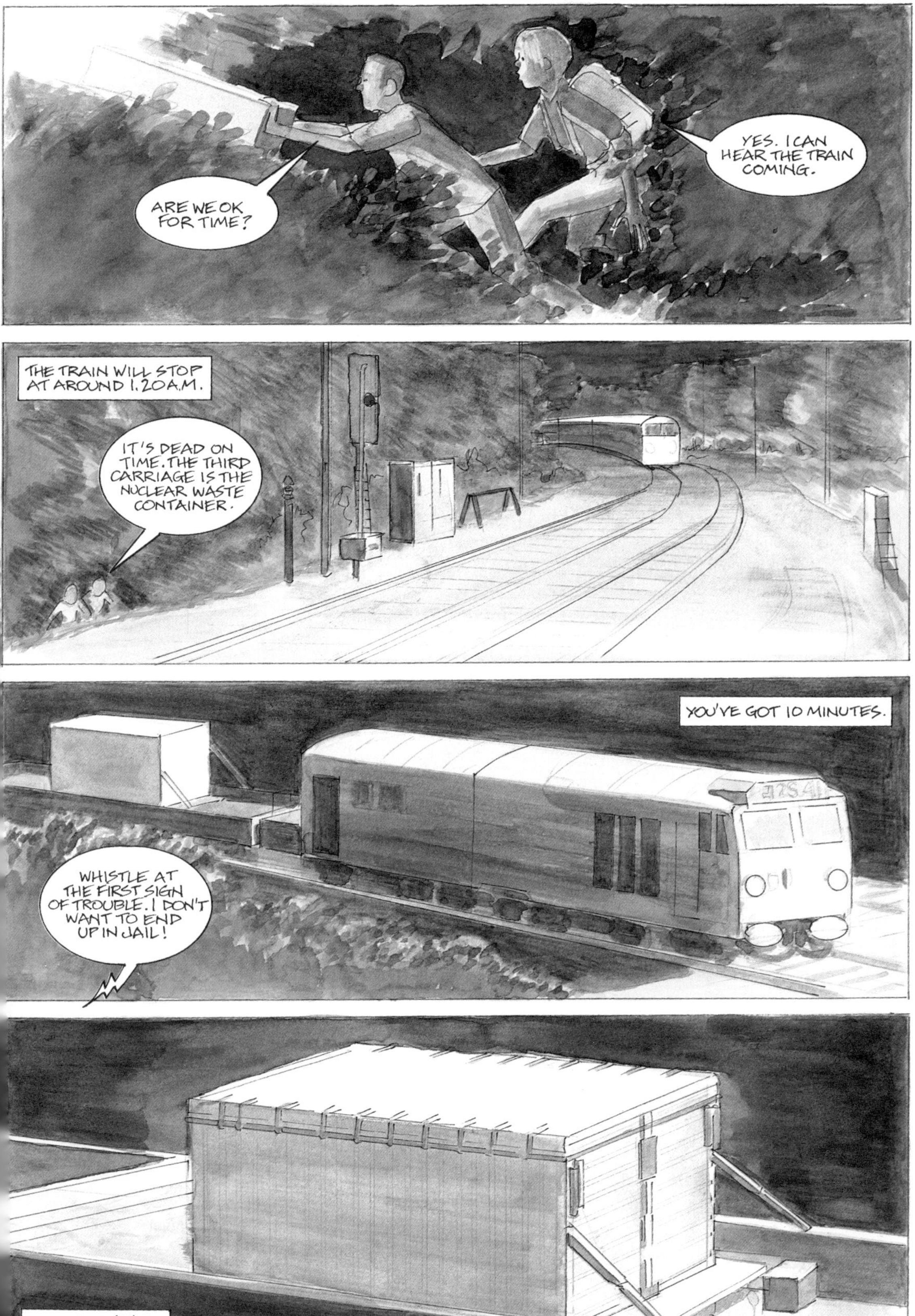

ARE WE OK FOR TIME?
YES. I CAN HEAR THE TRAIN COMING.
THE TRAIN WILL STOP AT AROUND 1.20A.M.
IT'S DEAD ON TIME. THE THIRD CARRIAGE IS THE NUCLEAR WASTE CONTAINER.
YOU'VE GOT 10 MINUTES.
WHISTLE AT THE FIRST SIGN OF TROUBLE. I DON'T WANT TO END UP IN JAIL!
GOOD LUCK, MEL.

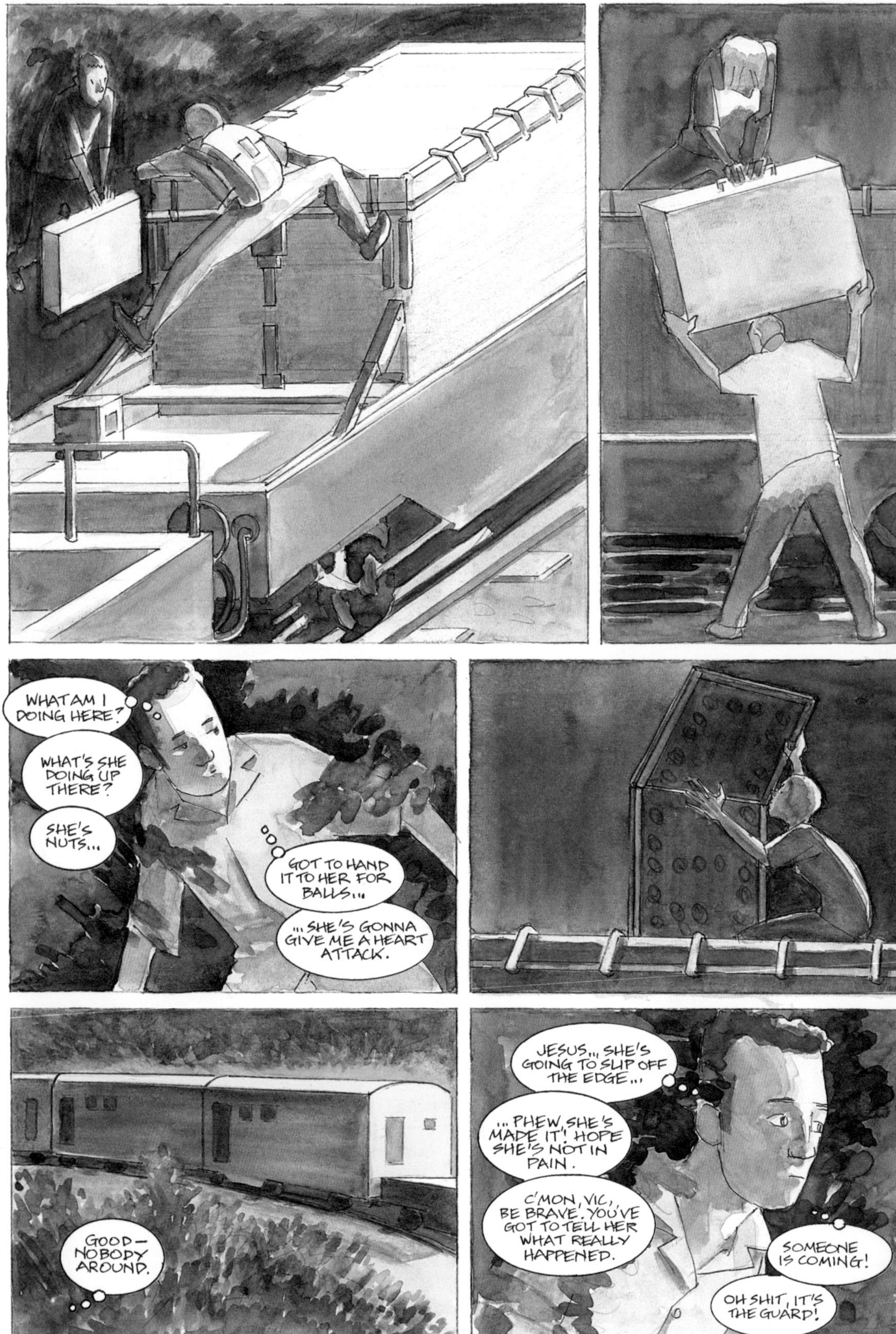
WHAT AM I DOING HERE?
WHAT'S SHE DOING UP THERE?
SHE'S NUTS...
GOT TO HAND IT TO HER FOR BALLS...
...SHE'S GONNA GIVE ME A HEART ATTACK.
GOOD— NOBODY AROUND.
JESUS... SHE'S GOING TO SLIP OFF THE EDGE...
...PHEW, SHE'S MADE IT! HOPE SHE'S NOT IN PAIN.
C'MON, VIC, BE BRAVE. YOU'VE GOT TO TELL HER WHAT REALLY HAPPENED.
SOMEONE IS COMING!
OH SHIT, IT'S THE GUARD!

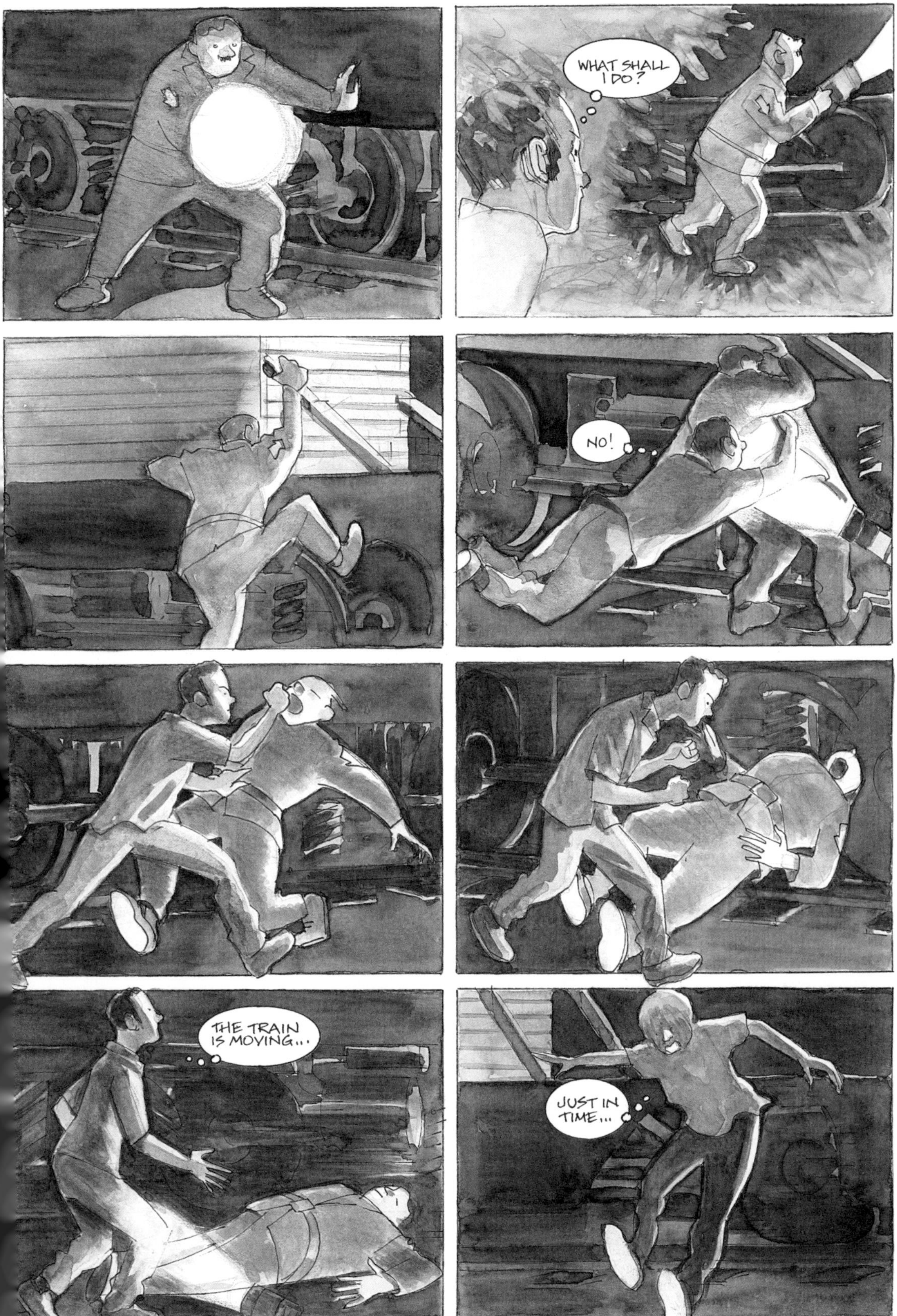
WHAT SHALL I DO?
NO!
THE TRAIN IS MOVING...
JUST IN TIME...

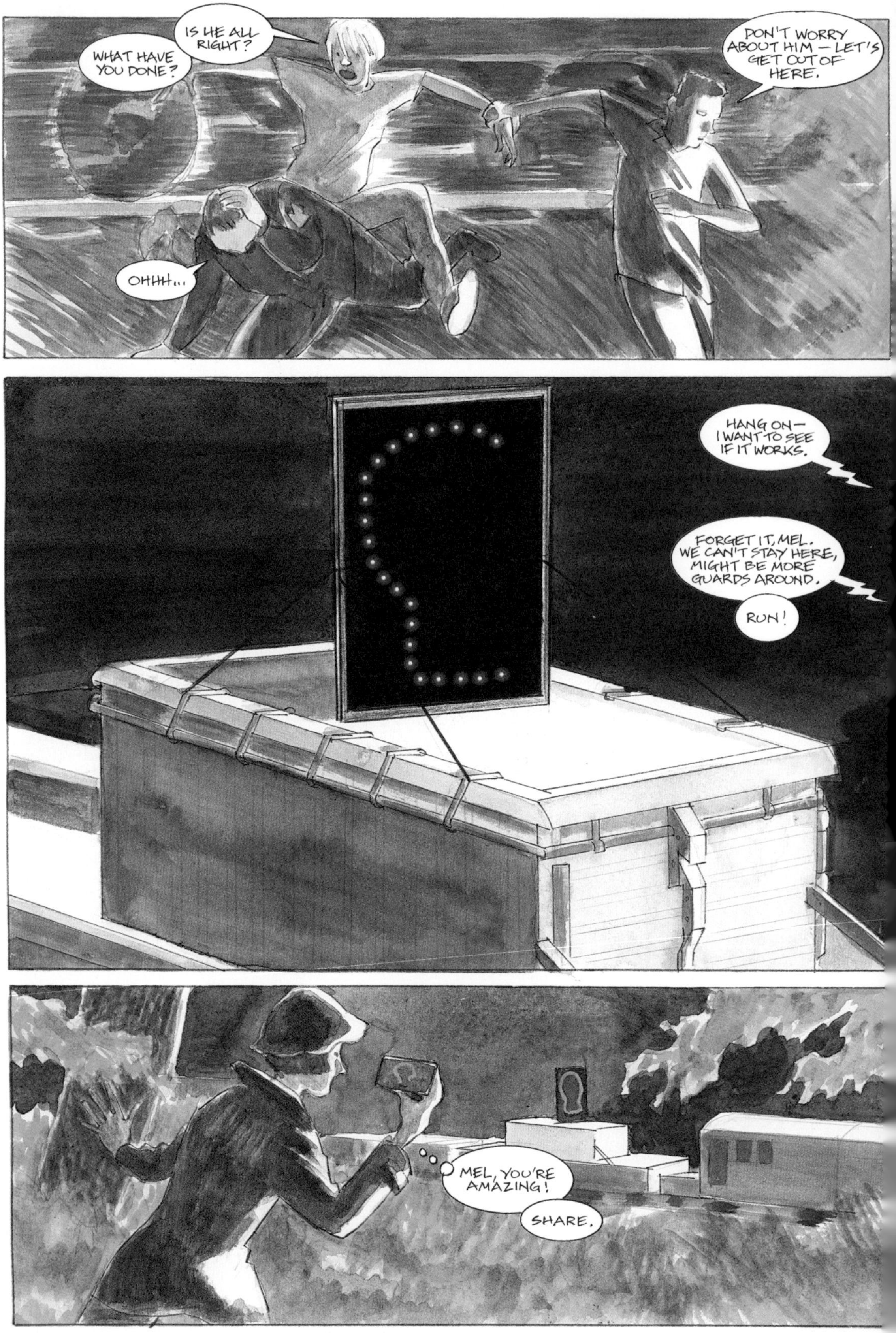
WHAT HAVE YOU DONE?
IS HE ALL RIGHT?
DON'T WORRY ABOUT HIM — LET'S GET OUT OF HERE.
OHHH...
HANG ON— I WANT TO SEE IF IT WORKS.
FORGET IT, MEL. WE CAN'T STAY HERE, MIGHT BE MORE GUARDS AROUND.
RUN!
MEL, YOU'RE AMAZING!
SHARE.

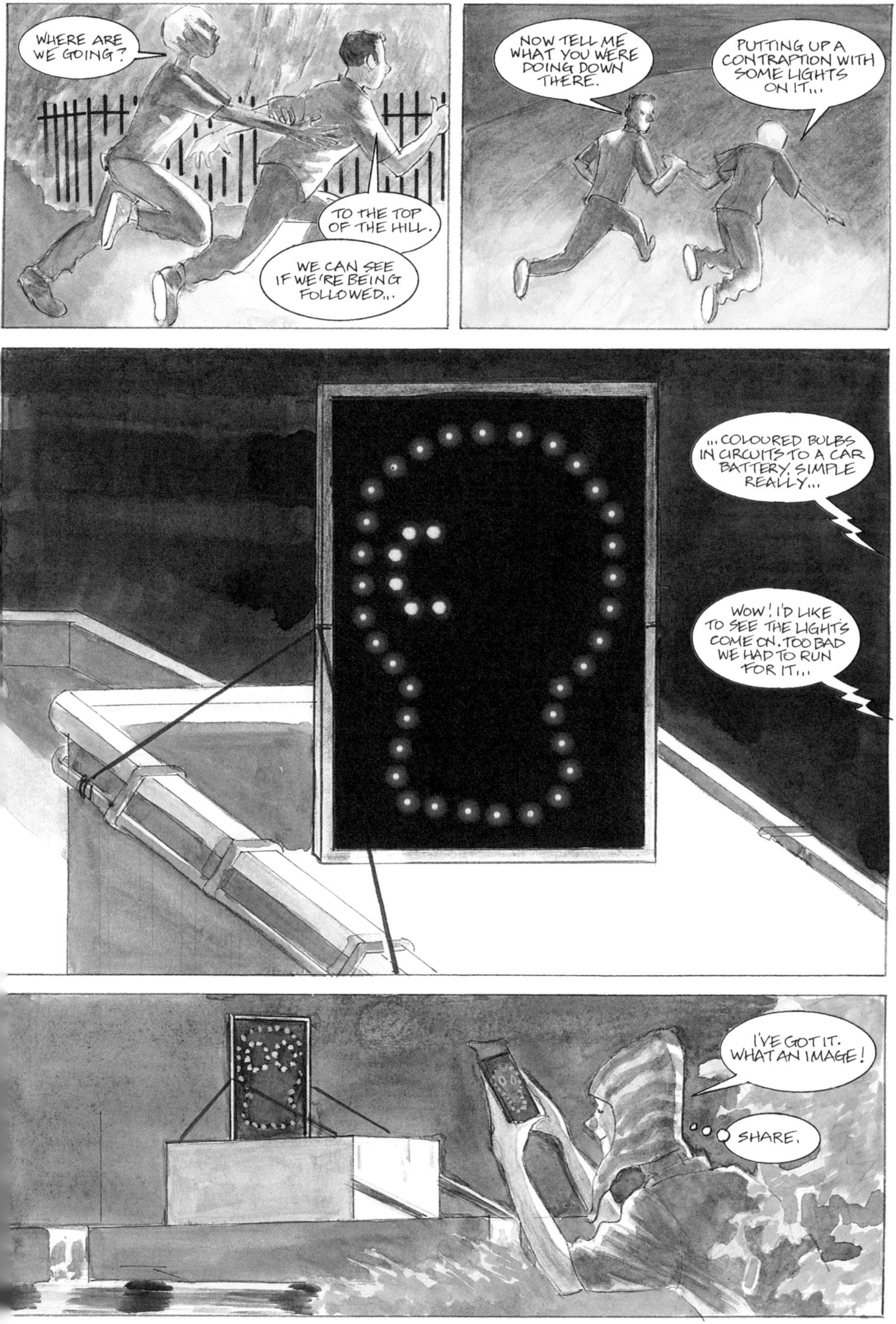
WHERE ARE WE GOING?
TO THE TOP OF THE HILL.
WE CAN SEE IF WE'RE BEING FOLLOWED...
NOW TELL ME WHAT YOU WERE DOING DOWN THERE.
PUTTING UP A CONTRAPTION WITH SOME LIGHTS ON IT...
...COLOURED BULBS IN CIRCUITS TO A CAR BATTERY, SIMPLE REALLY...
WOW! I'D LIKE TO SEE THE LIGHTS COME ON. TOO BAD WE HAD TO RUN FOR IT...
I'VE GOT IT. WHAT AN IMAGE!
SHARE.

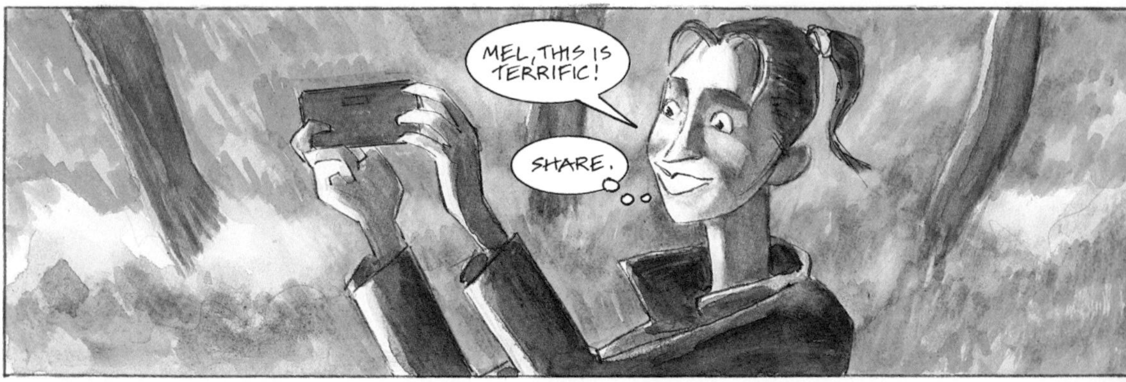
MEL, THIS IS TERRIFIC!
SHARE.

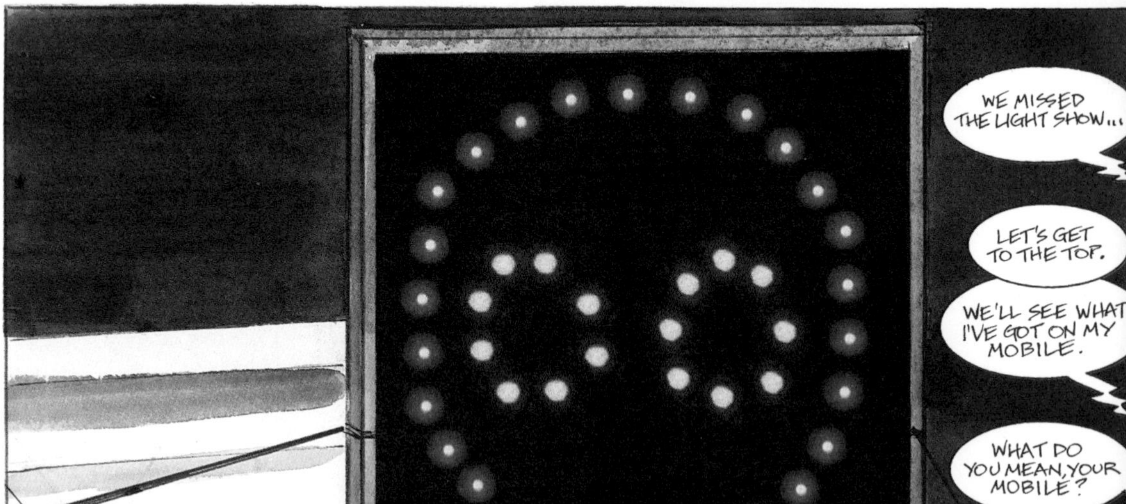
WE MISSED THE LIGHT SHOW...
LET'S GET TO THE TOP.
WE'LL SEE WHAT I'VE GOT ON MY MOBILE.
WHAT DO YOU MEAN, YOUR MOBILE?
WAIT AND SEE.
PUFF... PUFF...

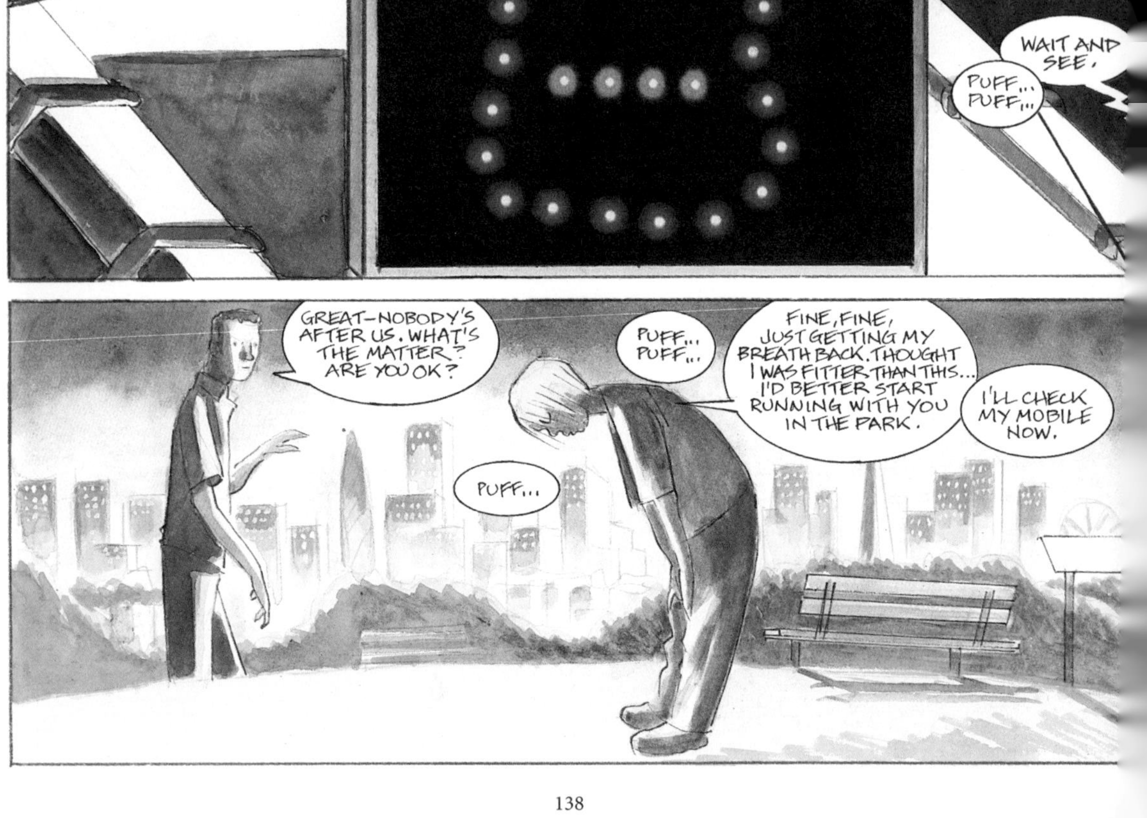
GREAT—NOBODY'S AFTER US. WHAT'S THE MATTER? ARE YOU OK?
PUFF... PUFF...
FINE, FINE, JUST GETTING MY BREATH BACK. THOUGHT I WAS FITTER THAN THIS... I'D BETTER START RUNNING WITH YOU IN THE PARK.
I'LL CHECK MY MOBILE NOW.
PUFF...

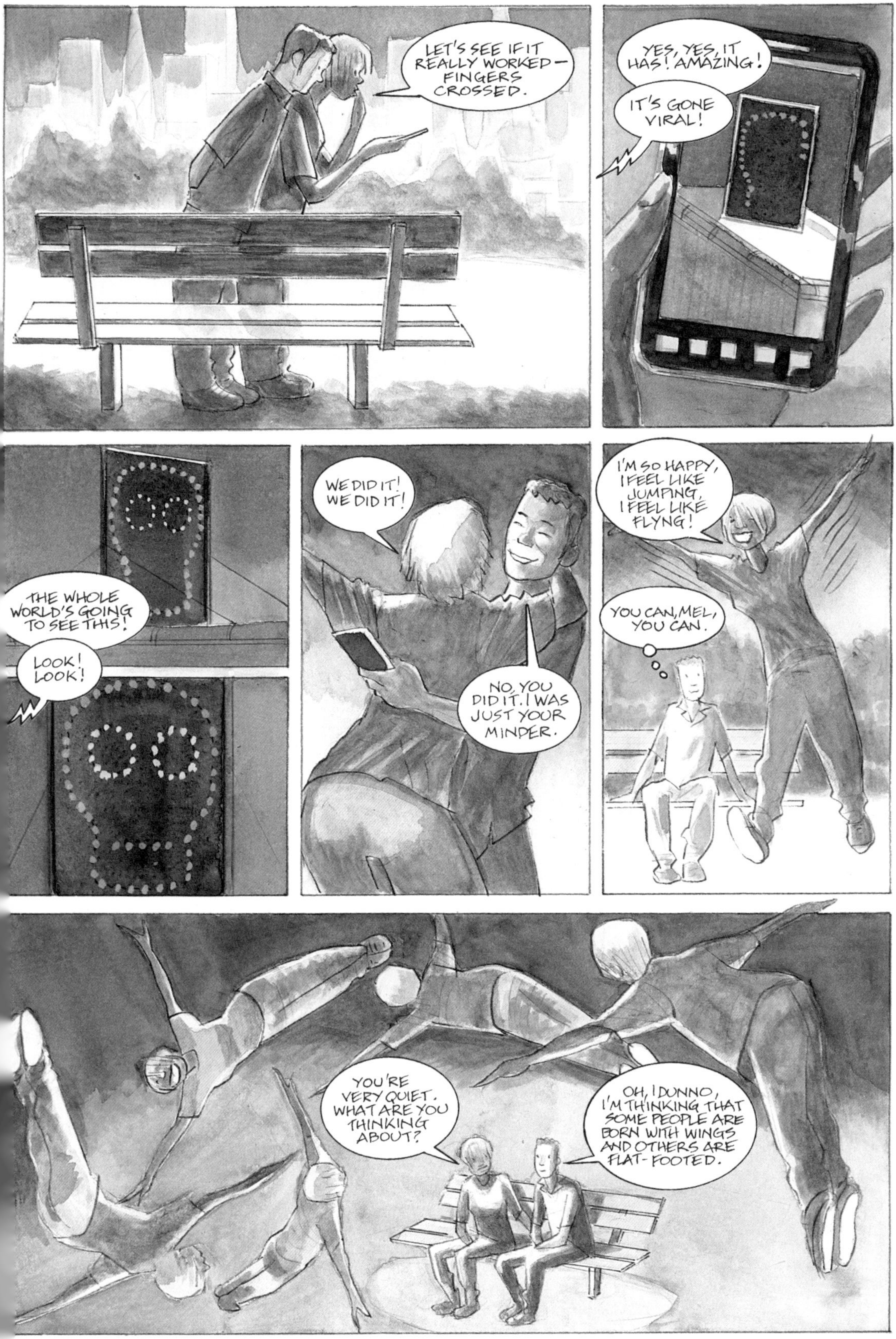
LET'S SEE IF IT REALLY WORKED — FINGERS CROSSED.
YES, YES, IT HAS! AMAZING!
IT'S GONE VIRAL!
THE WHOLE WORLD'S GOING TO SEE THIS!
LOOK! LOOK!
WE DID IT! WE DID IT!
NO, YOU DID IT. I WAS JUST YOUR MINDER.
I'M SO HAPPY, I FEEL LIKE JUMPING, I FEEL LIKE FLYNG!
YOU CAN, MEL, YOU CAN.
YOU'RE VERY QUIET. WHAT ARE YOU THINKING ABOUT?
OH, I DUNNO, I'M THINKING THAT SOME PEOPLE ARE BORN WITH WINGS AND OTHERS ARE FLAT-FOOTED.

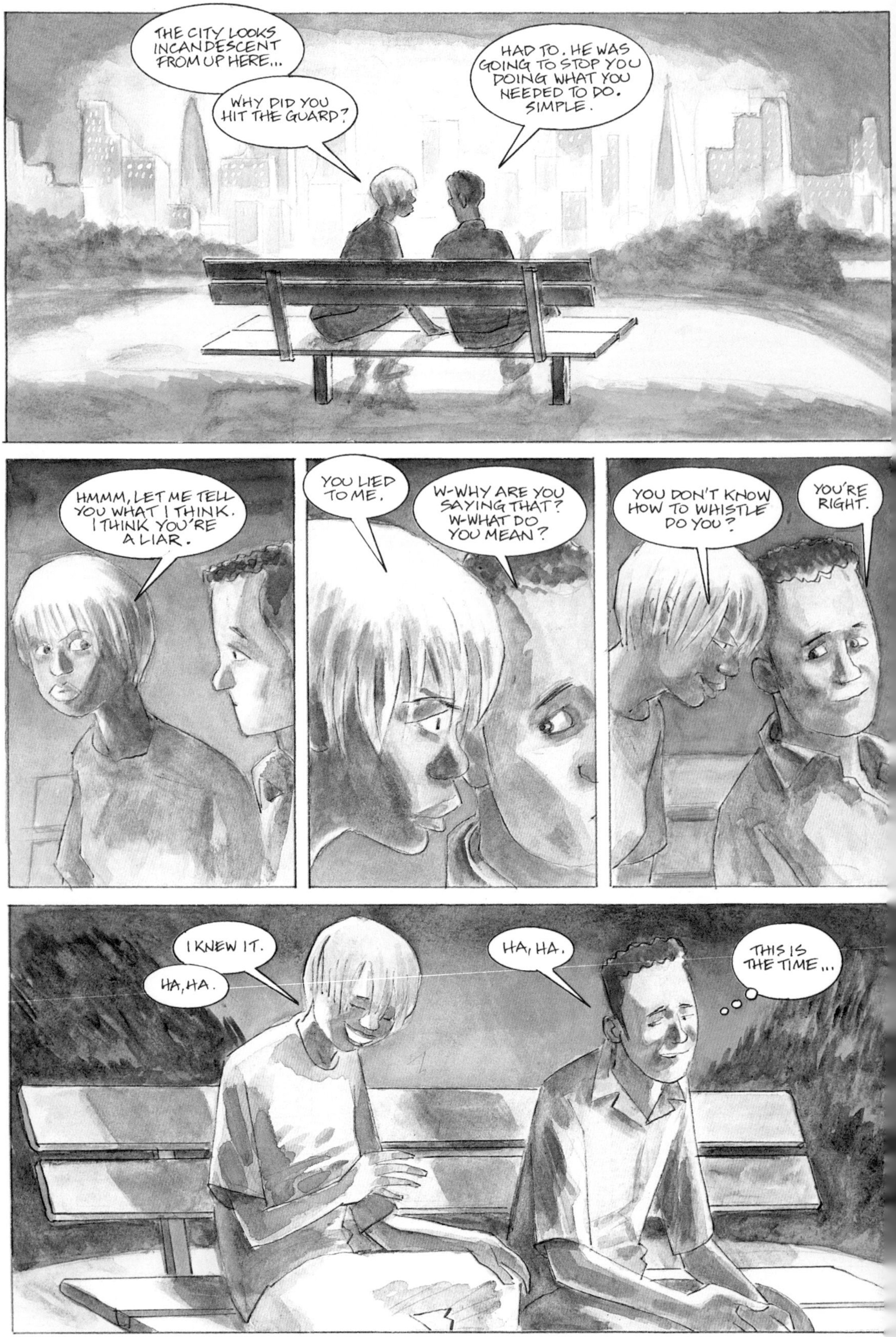
THE CITY LOOKS INCANDESCENT FROM UP HERE...
WHY DID YOU HIT THE GUARD?
HAD TO. HE WAS GOING TO STOP YOU DOING WHAT YOU NEEDED TO DO. SIMPLE.
HMMM, LET ME TELL YOU WHAT I THINK. I THINK YOU'RE A LIAR.
YOU LIED TO ME.
W-WHY ARE YOU SAYING THAT? W-WHAT DO YOU MEAN?
YOU DON'T KNOW HOW TO WHISTLE DO YOU?
YOU'RE RIGHT.
I KNEW IT.
HA, HA.
HA, HA.
THIS IS THE TIME...

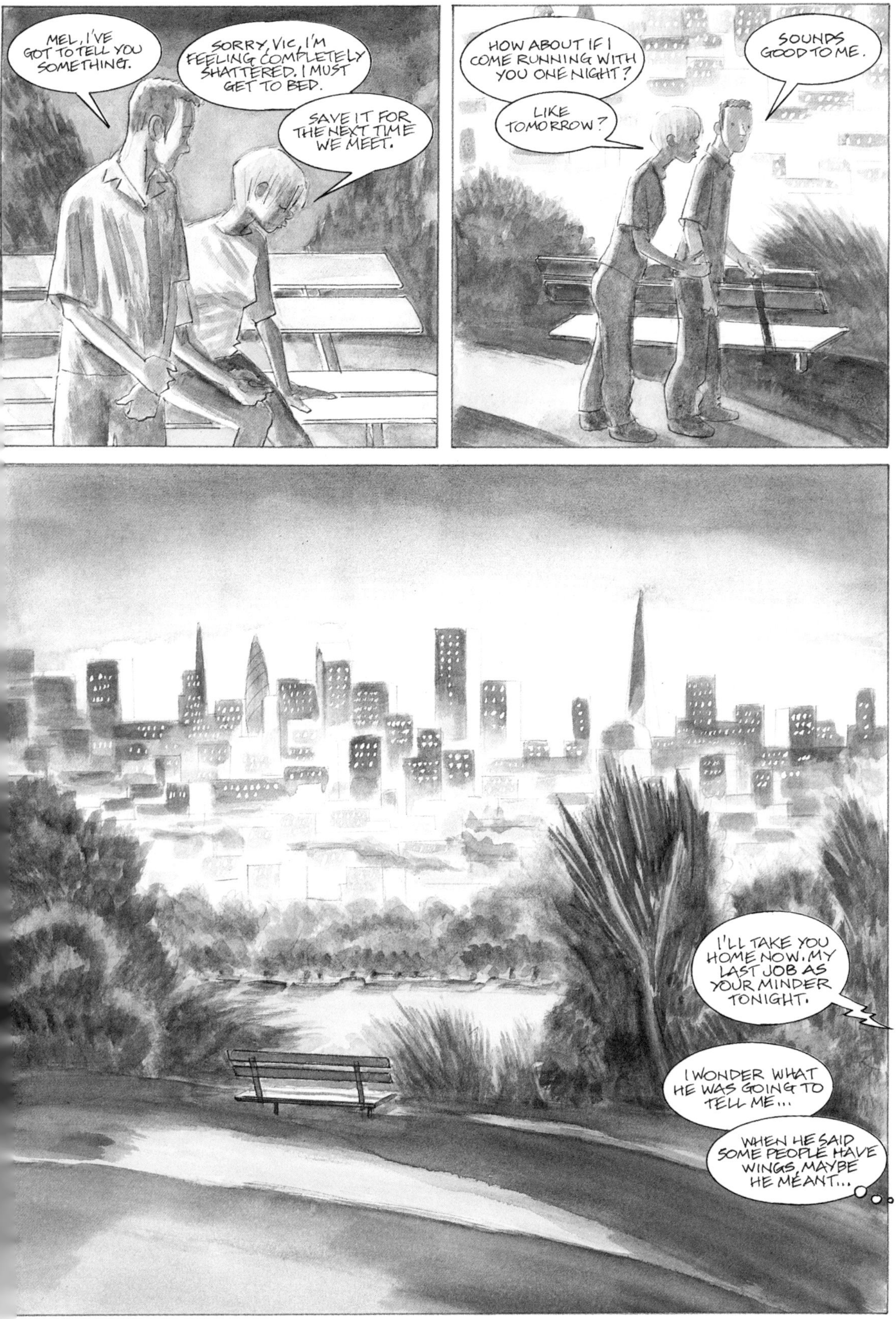
MEL, I'VE GOT TO TELL YOU SOMETHING.
SORRY, VIC, I'M FEELING COMPLETELY SHATTERED. I MUST GET TO BED.
SAVE IT FOR THE NEXT TIME WE MEET.
HOW ABOUT IF I COME RUNNING WITH YOU ONE NIGHT?
LIKE TOMORROW?
SOUNDS GOOD TO ME.
I'LL TAKE YOU HOME NOW. MY LAST JOB AS YOUR MINDER TONIGHT.
I WONDER WHAT HE WAS GOING TO TELL ME...
WHEN HE SAID SOME PEOPLE HAVE WINGS, MAYBE HE MEANT...

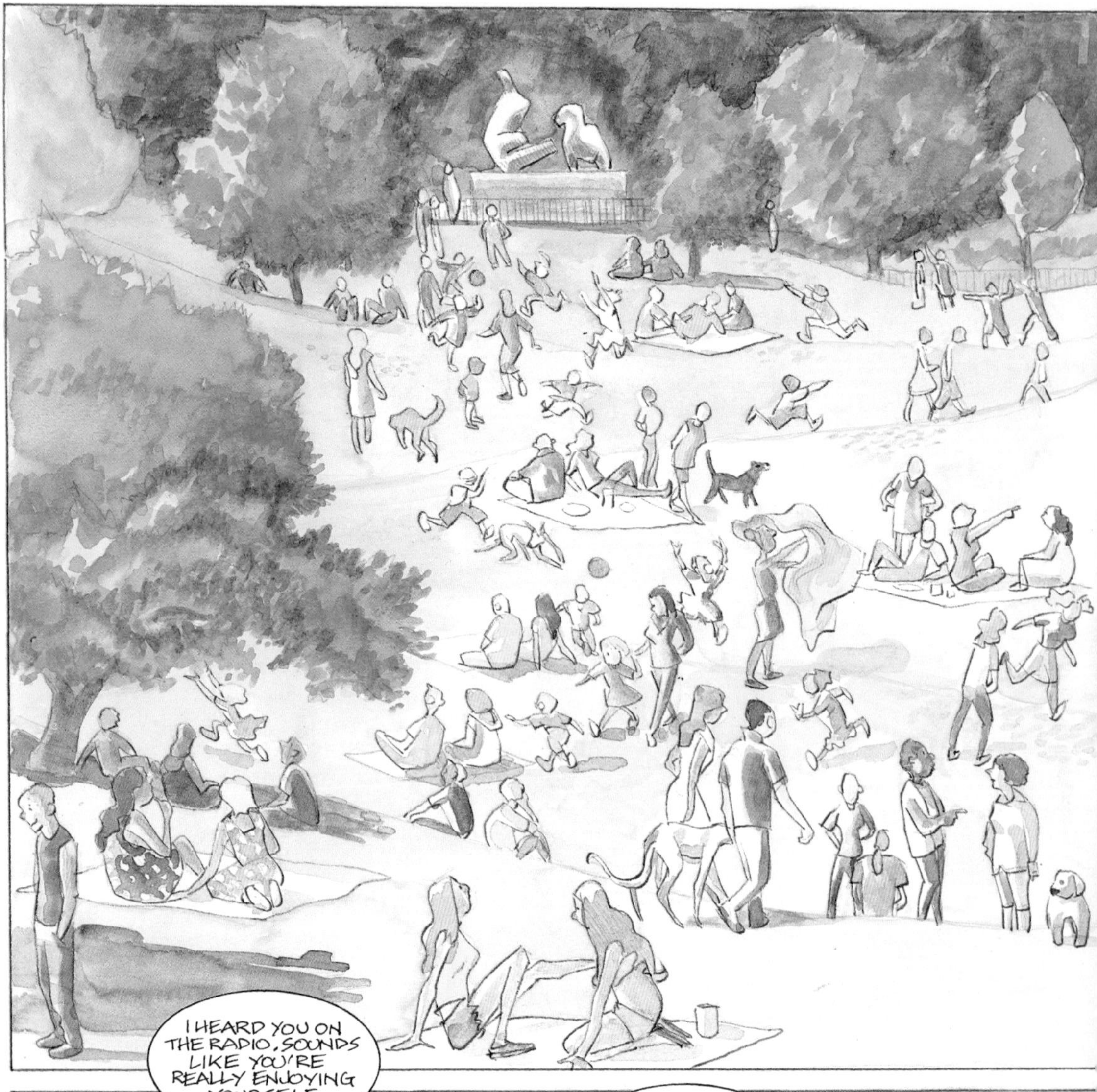

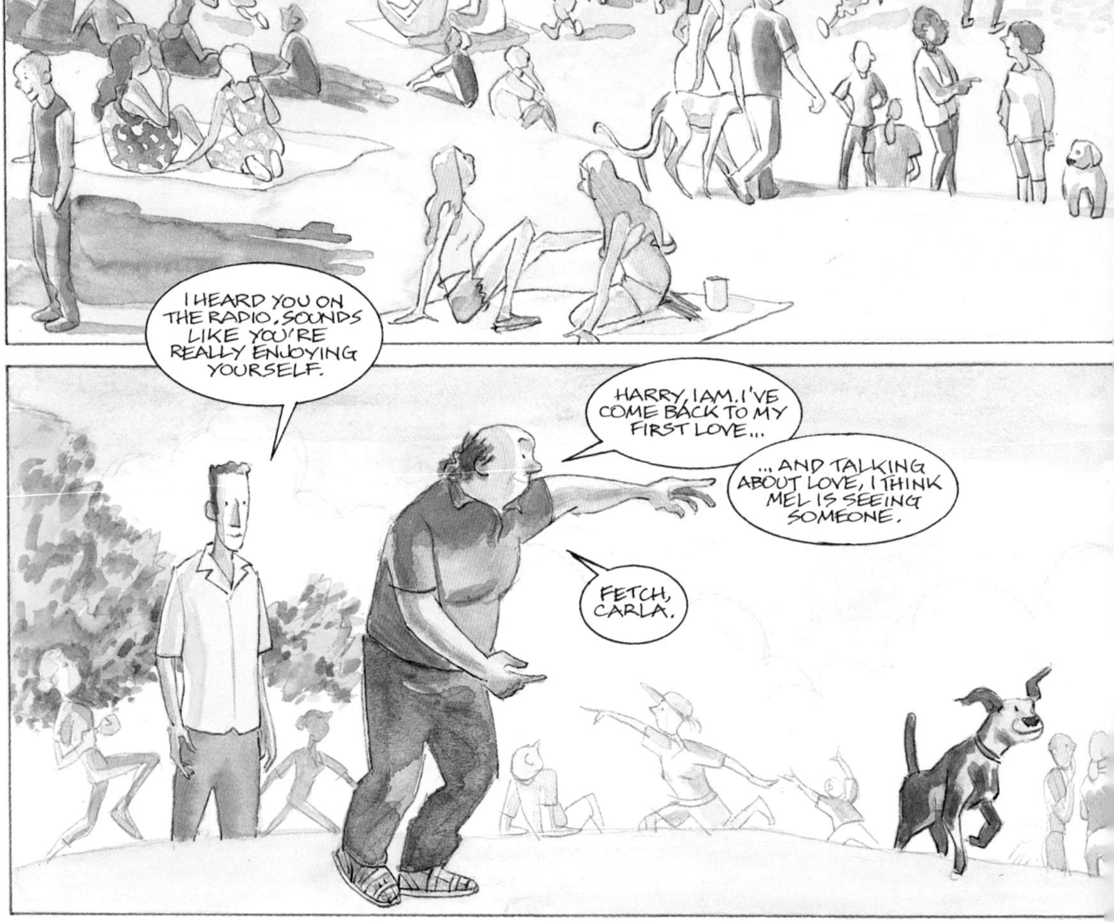
I HEARD YOU ON THE RADIO. SOUNDS LIKE YOU'RE REALLY ENJOYING YOURSELF.
HARRY, I AM. I'VE COME BACK TO MY FIRST LOVE...
...AND TALKING ABOUT LOVE, I THINK MEL IS SEEING SOMEONE.
FETCH, CARLA.

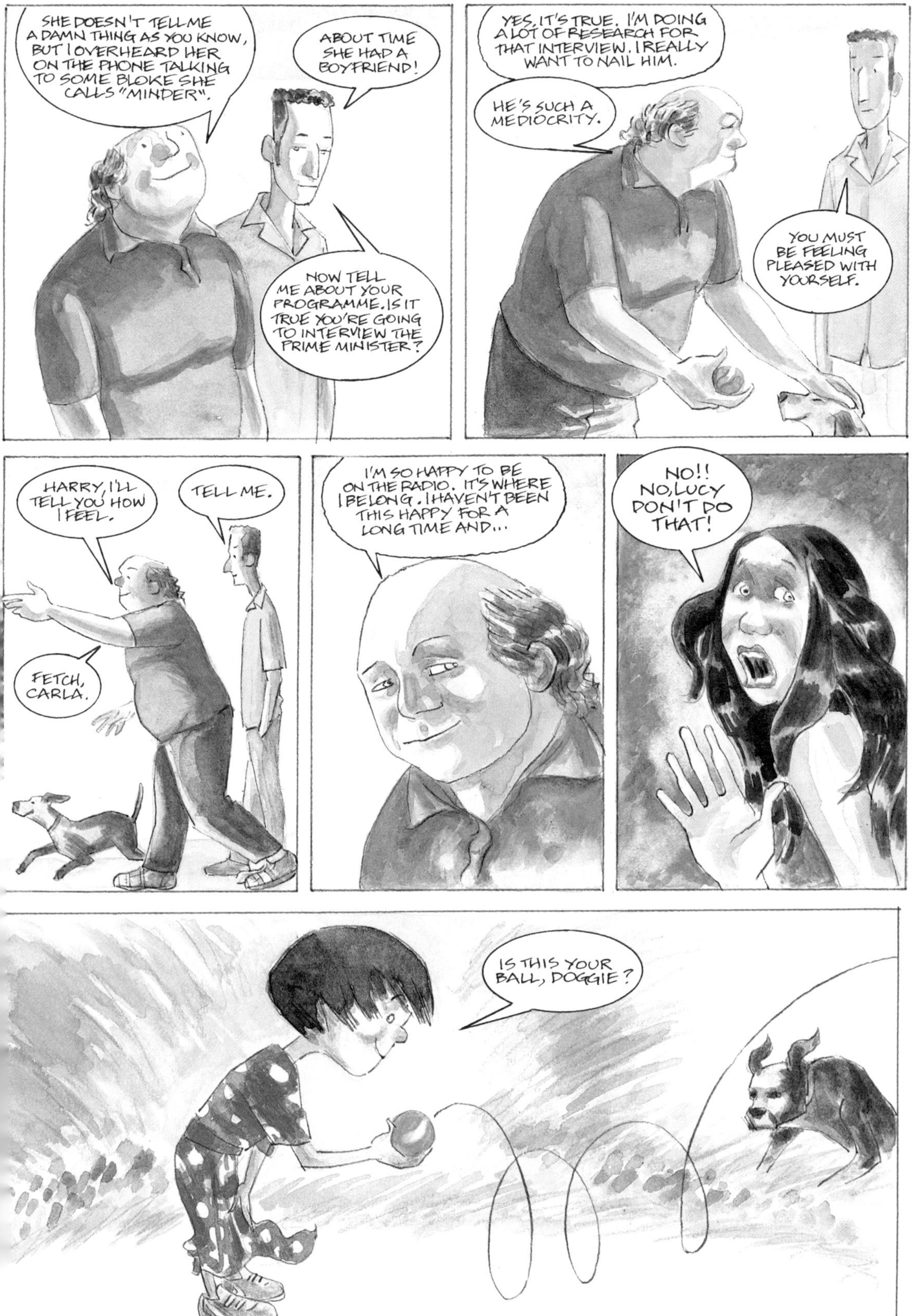
SHE DOESN'T TELL ME A DAMN THING AS YOU KNOW, BUT I OVERHEARD HER ON THE PHONE TALKING TO SOME BLOKE SHE CALLS "MINDER".
ABOUT TIME SHE HAD A BOYFRIEND!
NOW TELL ME ABOUT YOUR PROGRAMME. IS IT TRUE YOU'RE GOING TO INTERVIEW THE PRIME MINISTER?
YES, IT'S TRUE. I'M DOING A LOT OF RESEARCH FOR THAT INTERVIEW. I REALLY WANT TO NAIL HIM.
HE'S SUCH A MEDIOCRITY.
YOU MUST BE FEELING PLEASED WITH YOURSELF.
HARRY, I'LL TELL YOU HOW I FEEL.
TELL ME.
FETCH, CARLA.
I'M SO HAPPY TO BE ON THE RADIO. IT'S WHERE I BELONG. I HAVEN'T BEEN THIS HAPPY FOR A LONG TIME AND...
NO!! NO, LUCY DON'T DO THAT!
IS THIS YOUR BALL, DOGGIE?

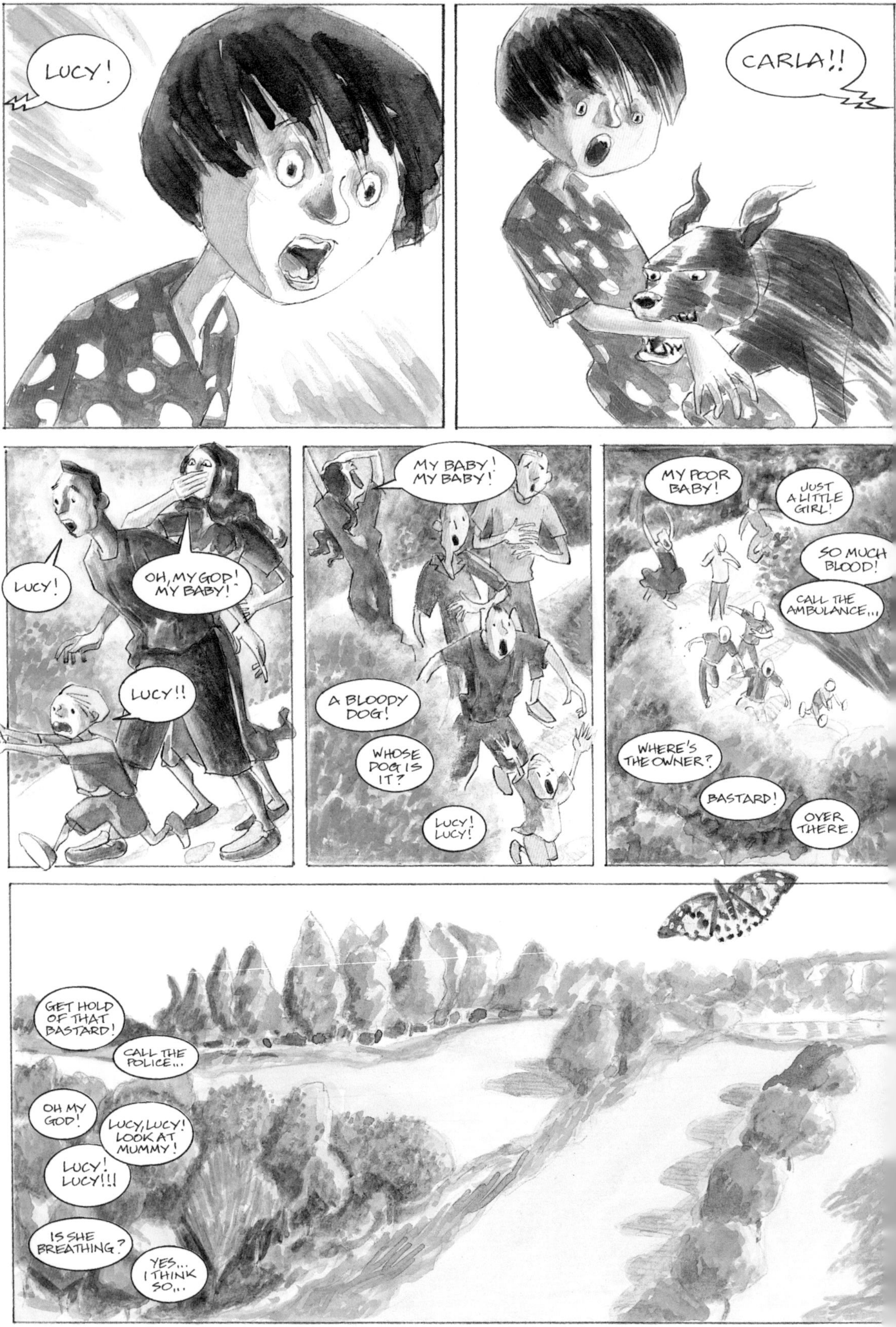
LUCY!
CARLA!!
LUCY!
OH, MY GOD! MY BABY!
LUCY!!
MY BABY! MY BABY!
A BLOODY DOG!
WHOSE DOG IS IT?
LUCY! LUCY!
MY POOR BABY!
JUST A LITTLE GIRL!
SO MUCH BLOOD!
CALL THE AMBULANCE...
WHERE'S THE OWNER?
BASTARD!
OVER THERE.
GET HOLD OF THAT BASTARD!
CALL THE POLICE...
OH MY GOD!
LUCY, LUCY! LOOK AT MUMMY!
LUCY! LUCY!!!
IS SHE BREATHING?
YES... I THINK SO...

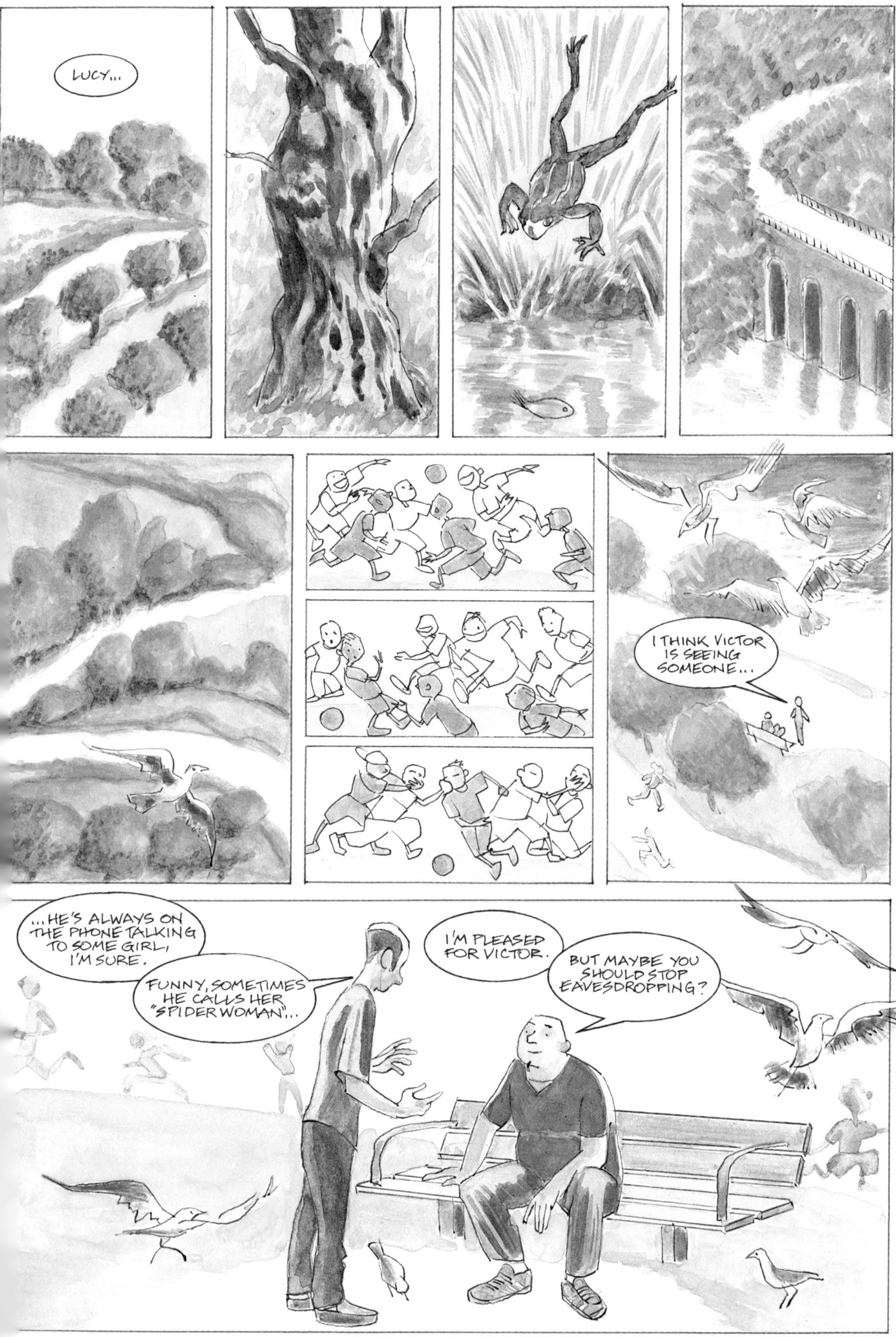
LUCY...
I THINK VICTOR IS SEEING SOMEONE...
...HE'S ALWAYS ON THE PHONE TALKING TO SOME GIRL, I'M SURE.
FUNNY, SOMETIMES HE CALLS HER "SPIDER WOMAN"...
I'M PLEASED FOR VICTOR.
BUT MAYBE YOU SHOULD STOP EAVESDROPPING?

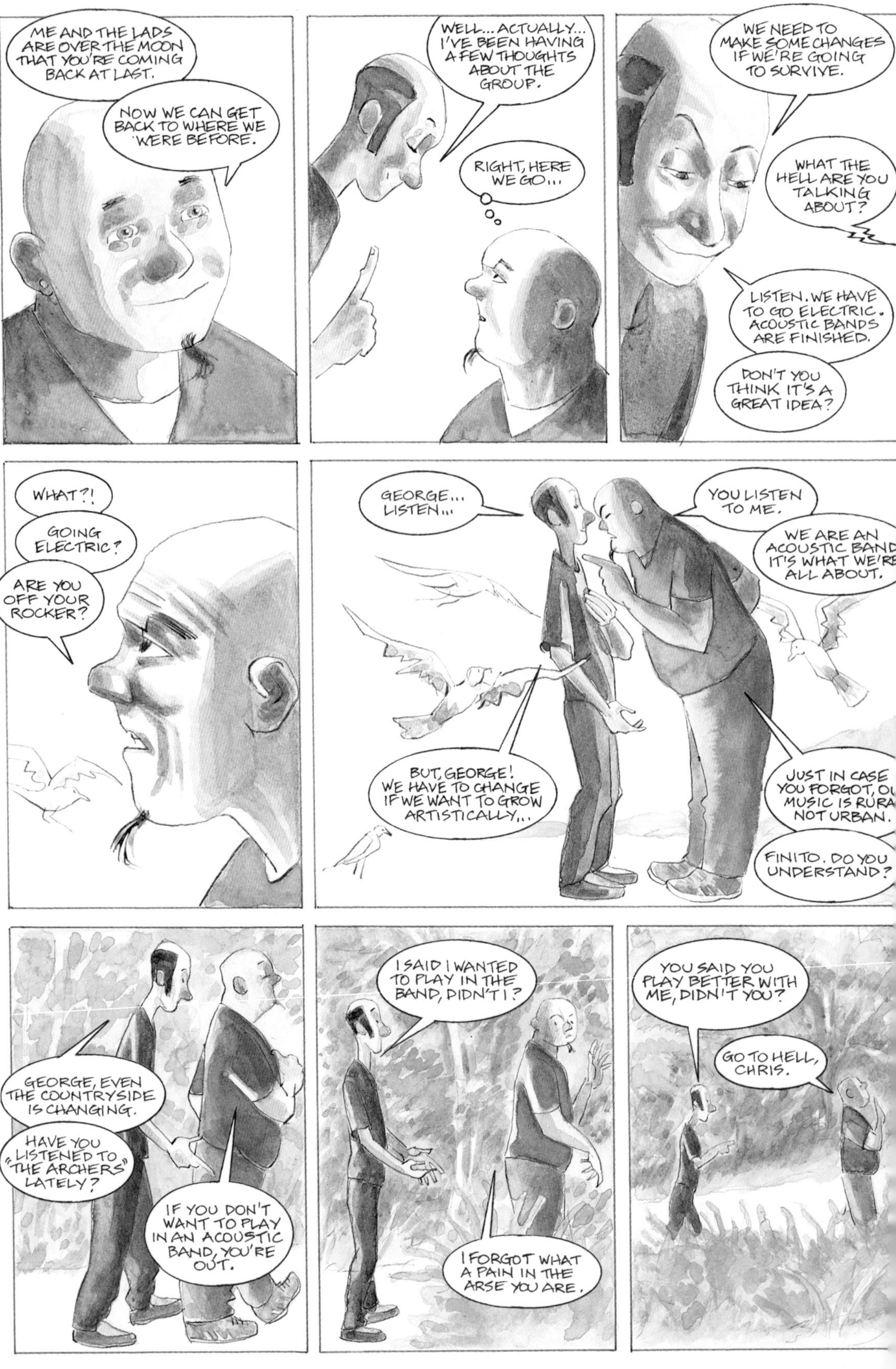
ME AND THE LADS ARE OVER THE MOON THAT YOU'RE COMING BACK AT LAST.
NOW WE CAN GET BACK TO WHERE WE WERE BEFORE.
WELL... ACTUALLY... I'VE BEEN HAVING A FEW THOUGHTS ABOUT THE GROUP.
RIGHT, HERE WE GO...
WE NEED TO MAKE SOME CHANGES IF WE'RE GOING TO SURVIVE.
WHAT THE HELL ARE YOU TALKING ABOUT?
LISTEN. WE HAVE TO GO ELECTRIC. ACOUSTIC BANDS ARE FINISHED.
DON'T YOU THINK IT'S A GREAT IDEA?
WHAT?!
GOING ELECTRIC?
ARE YOU OFF YOUR ROCKER?
GEORGE... LISTEN...
YOU LISTEN TO ME.
WE ARE AN ACOUSTIC BAND IT'S WHAT WE'RE ALL ABOUT.
BUT, GEORGE! WE HAVE TO CHANGE IF WE WANT TO GROW ARTISTICALLY...
JUST IN CASE YOU FORGOT, OUR MUSIC IS RURAL NOT URBAN.
FINITO. DO YOU UNDERSTAND?
GEORGE, EVEN THE COUNTRYSIDE IS CHANGING.
HAVE YOU LISTENED TO "THE ARCHERS" LATELY?
IF YOU DON'T WANT TO PLAY IN AN ACOUSTIC BAND, YOU'RE OUT.
I SAID I WANTED TO PLAY IN THE BAND, DIDN'T I?
I FORGOT WHAT A PAIN IN THE ARSE YOU ARE.
YOU SAID YOU PLAY BETTER WITH ME, DIDN'T YOU?
GO TO HELL, CHRIS.

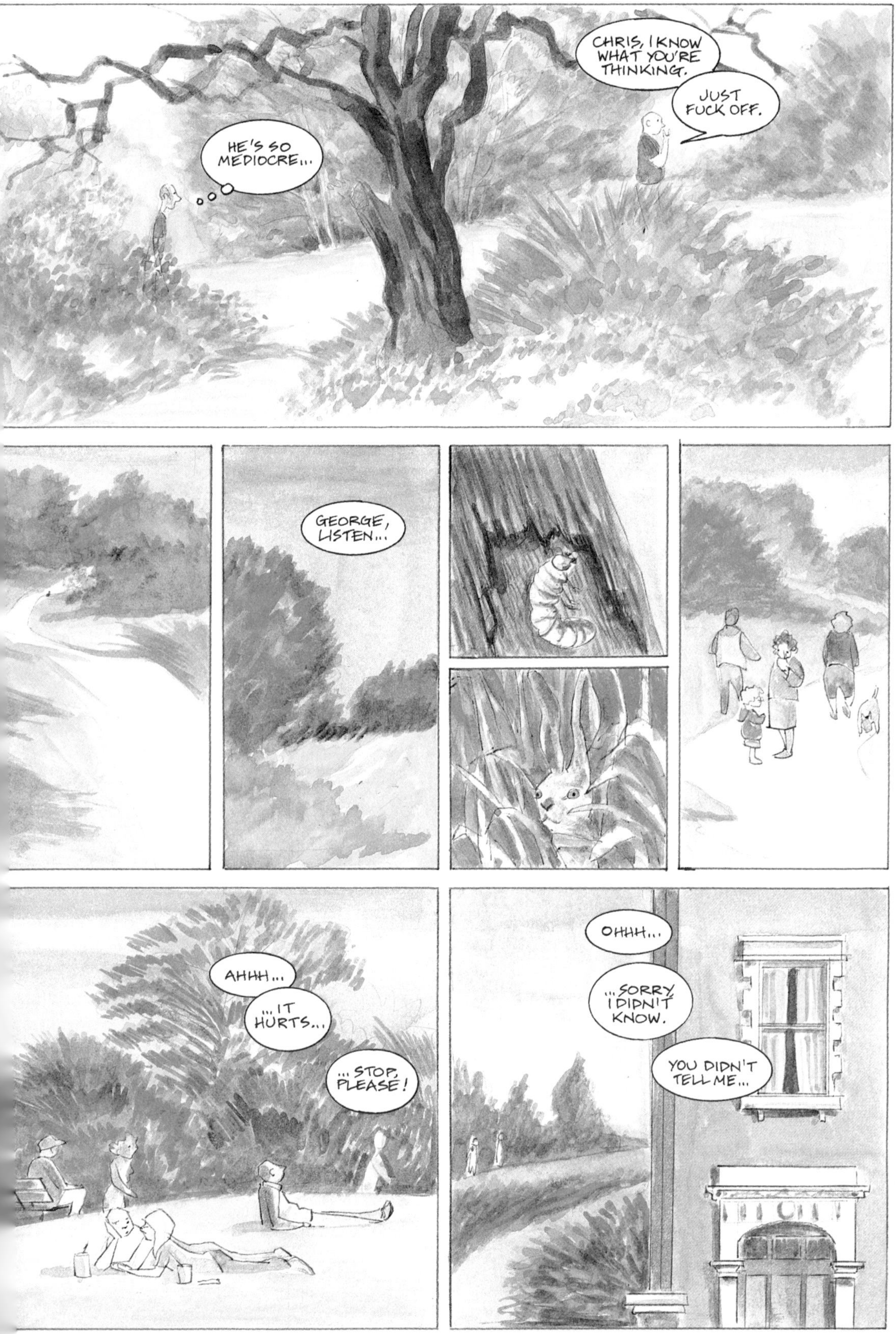
HE'S SO MEDIOCRE...
CHRIS, I KNOW WHAT YOU'RE THINKING.
JUST FUCK OFF.
GEORGE, LISTEN...
AHHH...
...IT HURTS...
...STOP, PLEASE!
OHHH...
...SORRY, I DIDN'T KNOW.
YOU DIDN'T TELL ME...

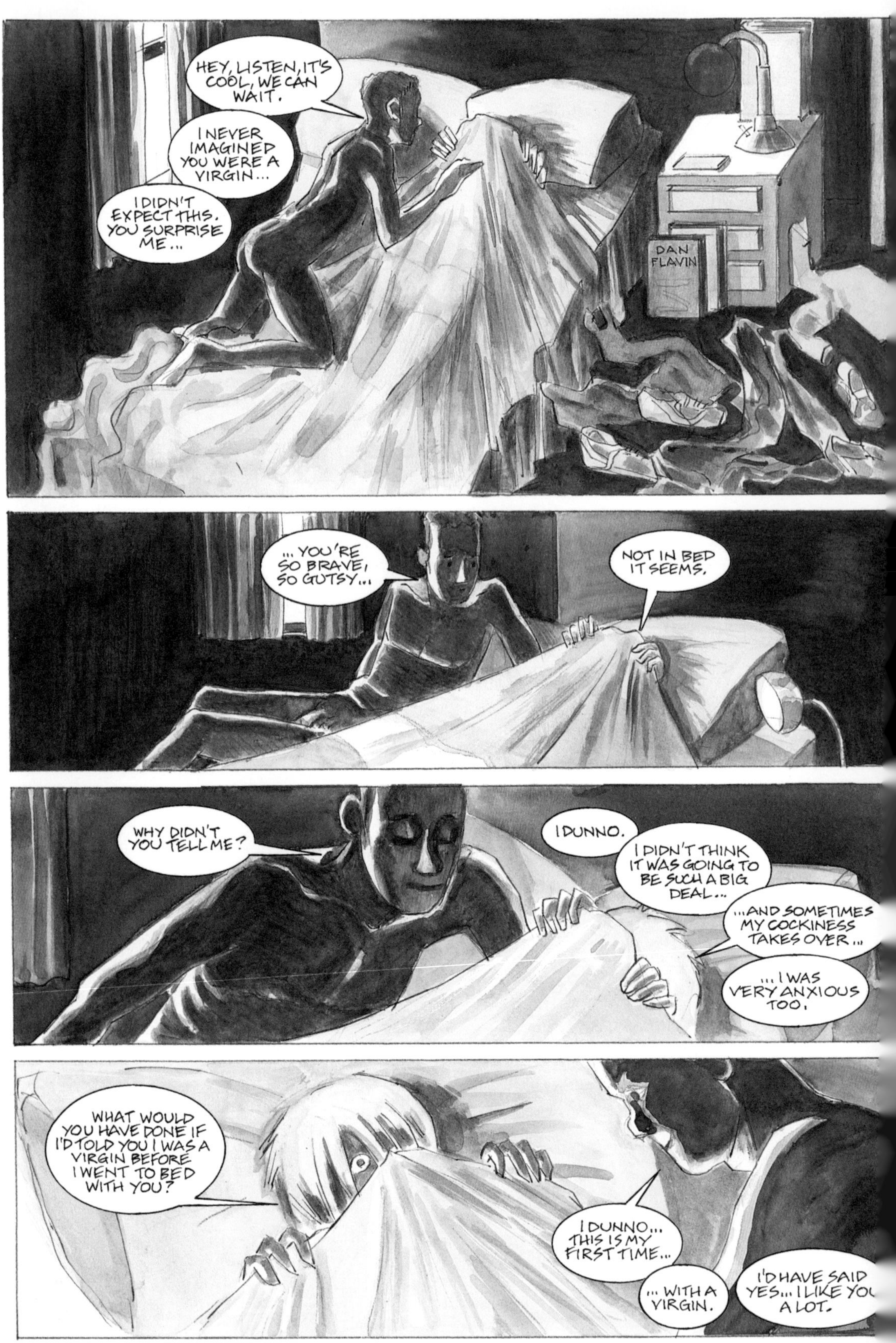
HEY, LISTEN, IT'S COOL, WE CAN WAIT.
I NEVER IMAGINED YOU WERE A VIRGIN...
I DIDN'T EXPECT THIS. YOU SURPRISE ME...
DAN FLAVIN
...YOU'RE SO BRAVE, SO GUTSY...
NOT IN BED IT SEEMS.
WHY DIDN'T YOU TELL ME?
I DUNNO.
I DIDN'T THINK IT WAS GOING TO BE SUCH A BIG DEAL...
...AND SOMETIMES MY COCKINESS TAKES OVER...
...I WAS VERY ANXIOUS TOO.
WHAT WOULD YOU HAVE DONE IF I'D TOLD YOU I WAS A VIRGIN BEFORE I WENT TO BED WITH YOU?
I DUNNO... THIS IS MY FIRST TIME...
...WITH A VIRGIN.
I'D HAVE SAID YES... I LIKE YOU A LOT.

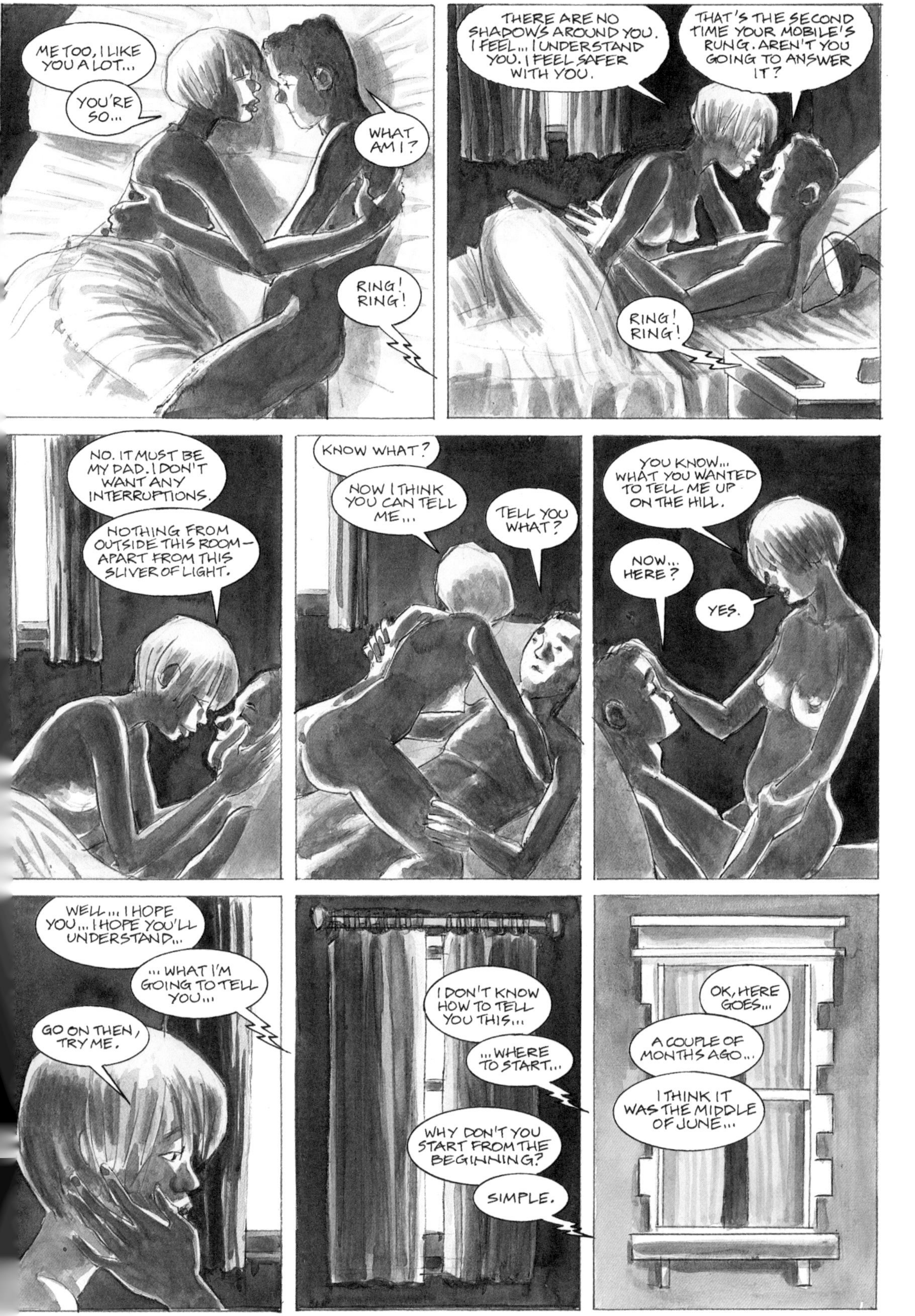
ME TOO, I LIKE YOU A LOT...
YOU'RE SO...
WHAT AM I?
RING! RING!
THERE ARE NO SHADOWS AROUND YOU. I FEEL... I UNDERSTAND YOU. I FEEL SAFER WITH YOU.
THAT'S THE SECOND TIME YOUR MOBILE'S RUNG. AREN'T YOU GOING TO ANSWER IT?
RING! RING!
NO. IT MUST BE MY DAD. I DON'T WANT ANY INTERRUPTIONS.
NOTHING FROM OUTSIDE THIS ROOM– APART FROM THIS SLIVER OF LIGHT.
KNOW WHAT?
NOW I THINK YOU CAN TELL ME...
TELL YOU WHAT?
YOU KNOW... WHAT YOU WANTED TO TELL ME UP ON THE HILL.
NOW... HERE?
YES.
WELL... I HOPE YOU... I HOPE YOU'LL UNDERSTAND...
... WHAT I'M GOING TO TELL YOU...
GO ON THEN, TRY ME.
I DON'T KNOW HOW TO TELL YOU THIS...
...WHERE TO START...
WHY DON'T YOU START FROM THE BEGINNING?
SIMPLE.
OK, HERE GOES...
A COUPLE OF MONTHS AGO...
I THINK IT WAS THE MIDDLE OF JUNE...

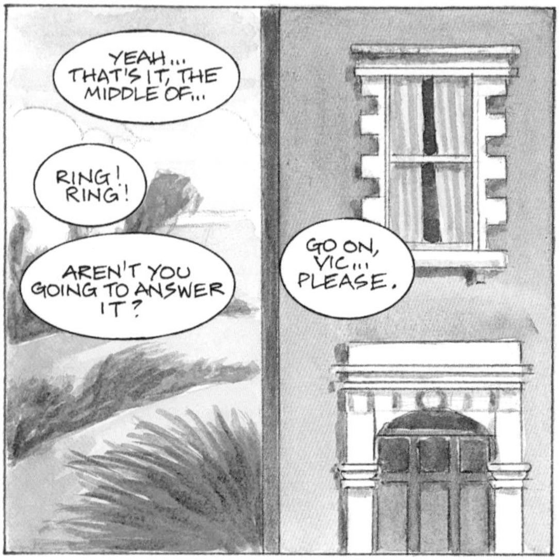
YEAH... THAT'S IT, THE MIDDLE OF...
RING! RING!
AREN'T YOU GOING TO ANSWER IT?
GO ON, VIC... PLEASE.

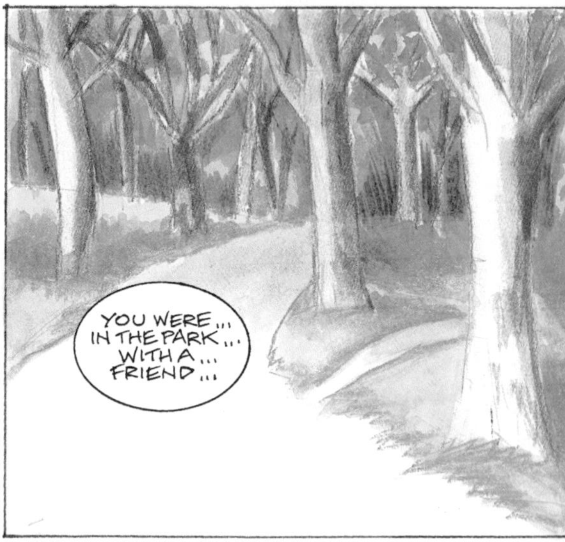
YOU WERE... IN THE PARK... WITH A... FRIEND...

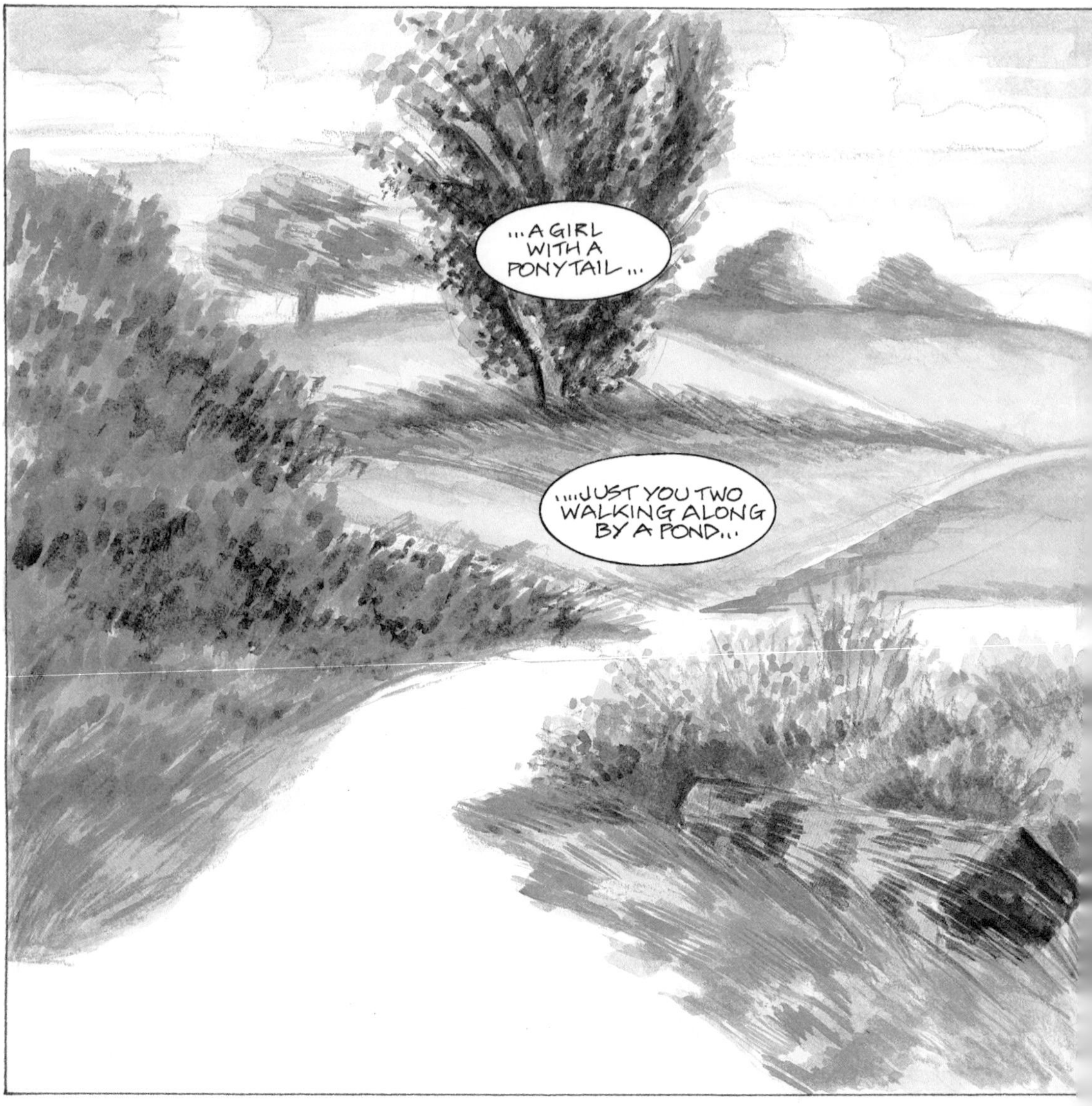
...A GIRL WITH A PONYTAIL...
...JUST YOU TWO WALKING ALONG BY A POND...

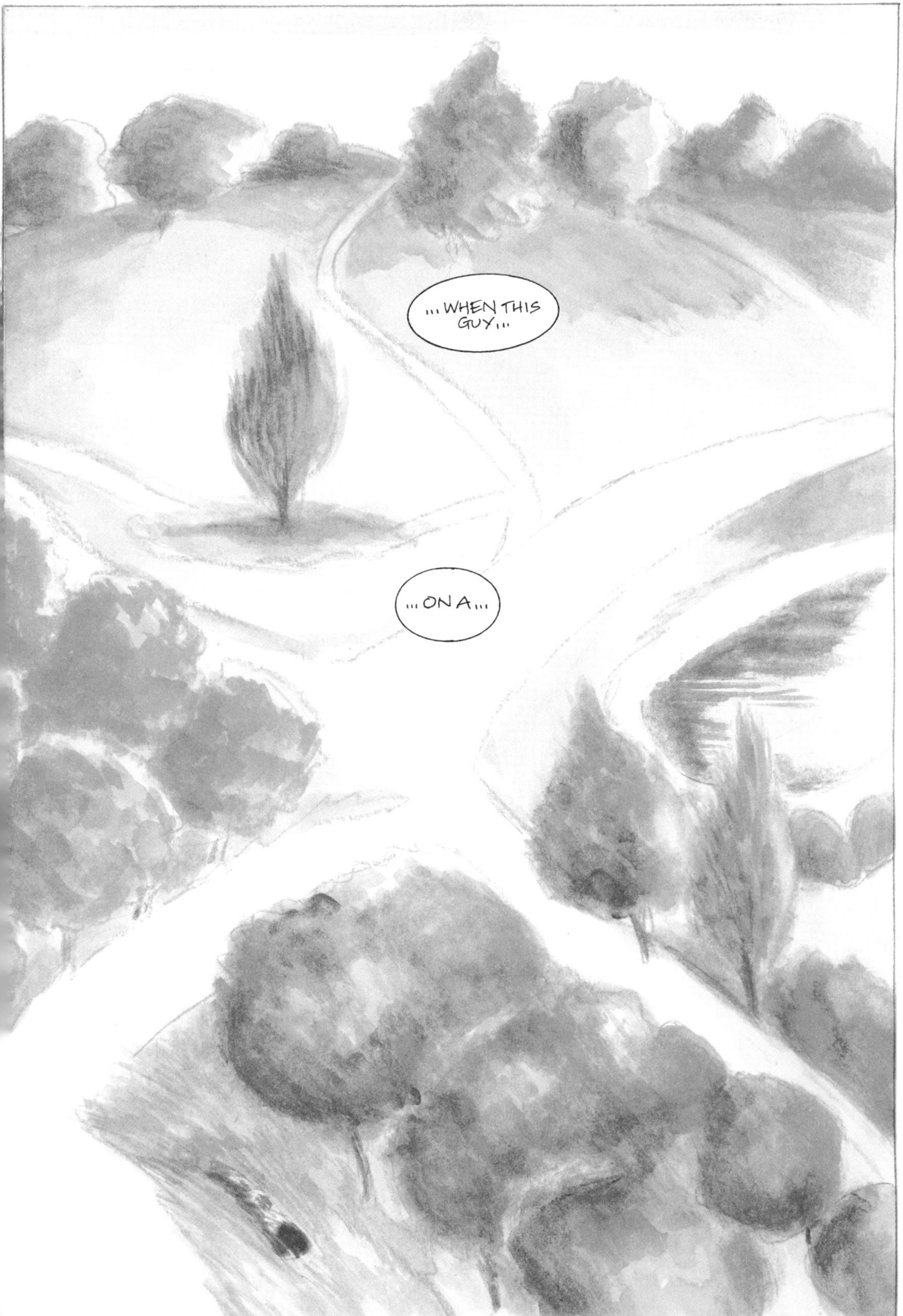
...WHEN THIS GUY...
...ON A...

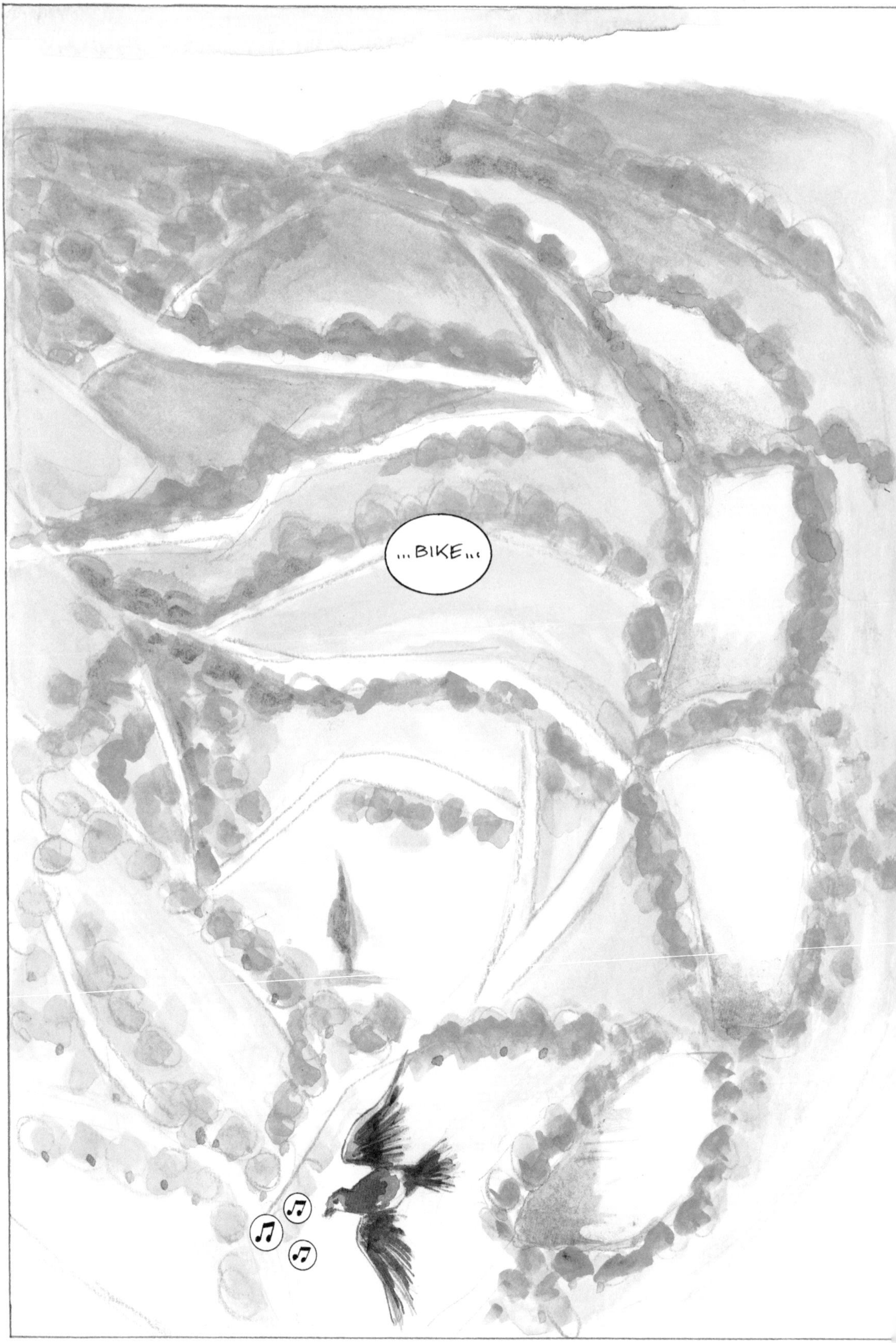
...BIKE...

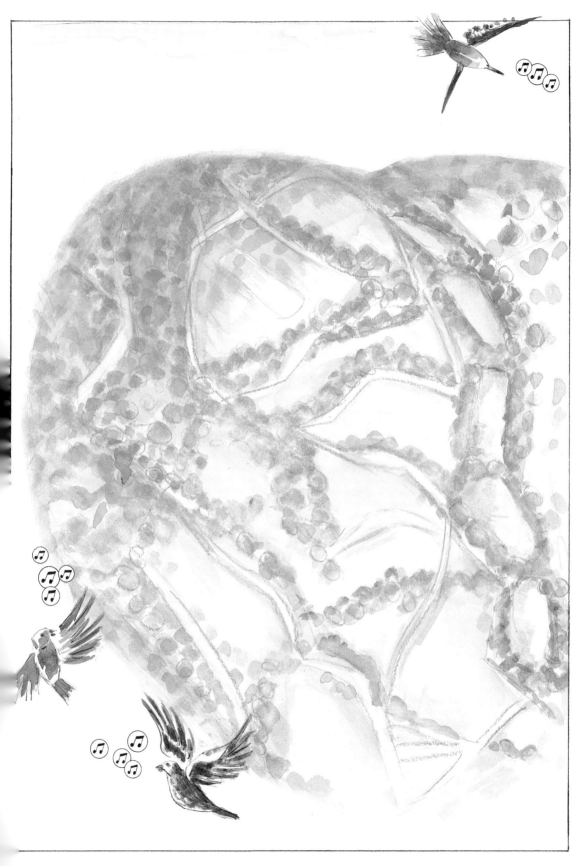

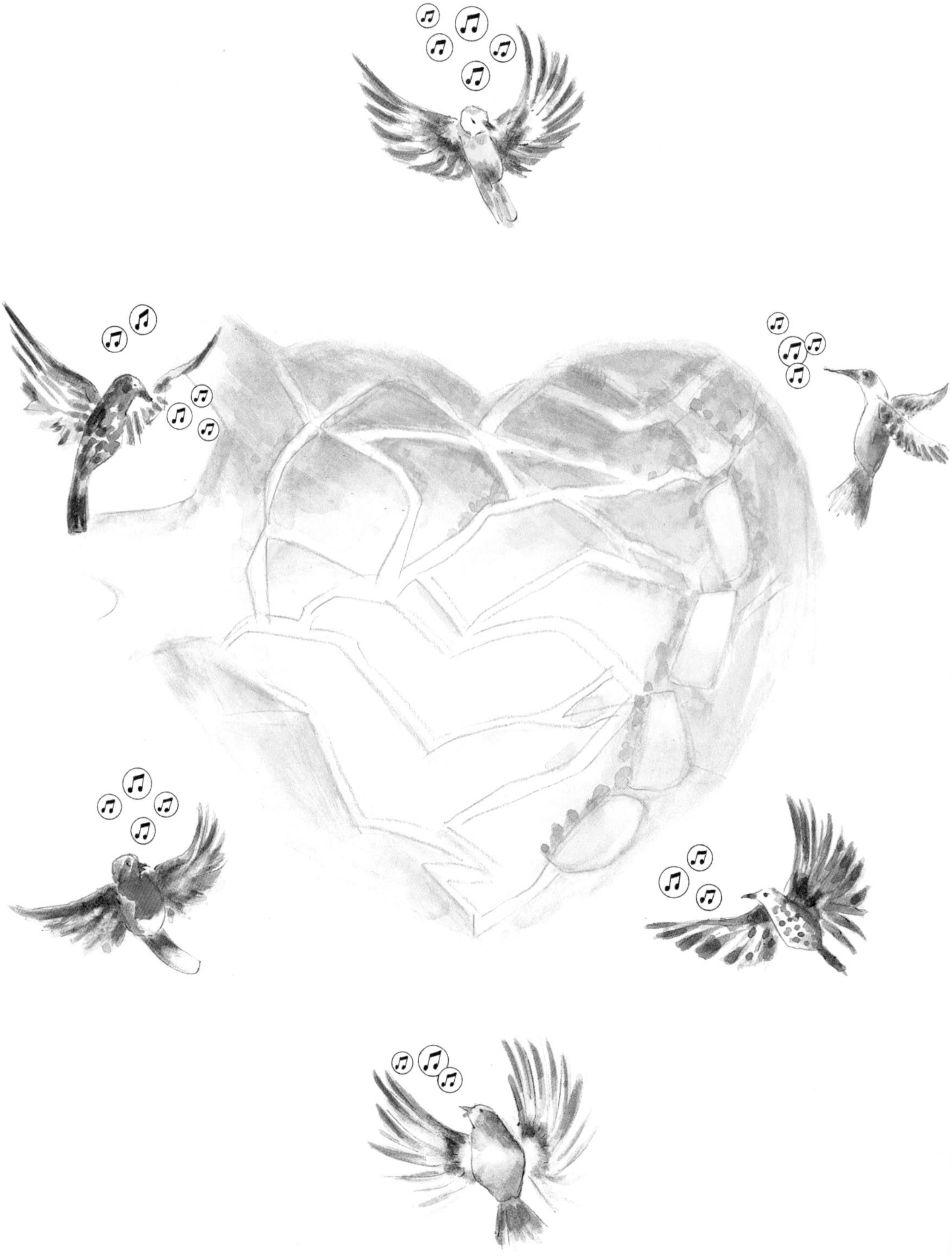

Acknowledgements

For the talking, listening, reading, looking, walking,
encouragement and support I'd like to thank:

Raphael Appignanesi - Bahue Aranovich - Pete Ayrton - Judy Cooper
- Ben Harding - Txabi Jones - Alan Moore - Mavis Pilbeam -
Absolute Print - Alexei Sayle - Bryan Talbot - Morgan Zarate

My special thanks to:

Emma Hayley - Lizzie Kaye - Sam Humphrey - Paul Smith

Mis maestros

Hugo Pratt - Roy Crane - Hector G. Oesterheld

To Hazel Hirshorn, for all her encouragement and creative input
throughout this book, my endless thanks.